"Though he was never a member of the academic cast, William Stringfellow was the most significant biblical theologian of his generation. Bill Wylie Kellermann has put together an extraordinary volume that will introduce Stringfellow to a new generation. For all of us whom Stringfellow mentored and for anyone committed to a radical biblical witness, the publication of this book is a great event."

— **JIM WALLIS**
Editor of *Sojourners*

"Aggravatingly deliberate of speech, searingly incisive about how the institutional church had missed the mark of the New Creation, ruthlessly clear about the biblical message and passionately committed to it, William Stringfellow stands in the line of Amos, Micah, Isaiah, Jeremiah, and Jesus of Nazareth."

— **VERNA J. DOZIER**
Author of *The Dream of God*

"Reading William Stringfellow in the 1990s is not an exercise in nostalgia. We need to hear him now on vocation, conscience, death-dealing, principalities and powers, the resurrection, and the Spirit active in history. His words — like the Word they serve — cut both ways, through ecclesiastical as well as political cant. The clarity of his vision is as bracing as a stiff breeze off Block Island."

— **JOSEPH CUNNEEN**
Coeditor of *Cross Currents*

CW00952018

"Bill Wylie Kellermann has made an important contribution to the law and the legal profession with this compilation of William Stringfellow's writing. The developments in the profession during the last decade have been, to say the least, troubling. At a time when the legal profession is struggling to recover a sense of vocation, there is no voice more poignant than that of Stringfellow writing from his storefront office in East Harlem more than thirty years ago to remind those of us who are lawyers that we are, first of all, a servant profession."

— **ANDREW W. McTHENIA**
Washington and Lee University
School of Law

"Here is the best of William Stringfellow's thought and writing in one extraordinary volume. For aficionados, the book affords a marvelous revisitation of Stringfellow's witness, reinvigorating us with a cold shower of truth page after page. For those who did not know him, it provides a unique entrée into his work and words, engagement with this rare man who embodied fidelity to the Word of God whatever the cost and consequence. This book is a generous gift from Bill Wylie Kellermann, whose comprehensive research and clarifying organization make Stringfellow's ideas more readily accessible than ever before. Dipping into the various sections of the book, one finds Stringfellow as teacher, companion, and witness. . . . This is a book to be treasured."

— **ROBERT RAINES**
Director, Kirkridge Center

"*A Keeper of the Word* will help us all be faithful, biblically literate disciples of Christ and, like Stringfellow, sons and daughters of God — peacemakers."

— **JOHN DEAR, S.J.**
Author of *Seeds of Nonviolence*

A Keeper of the Word

Selected Writings of William Stringfellow

Edited with an Introduction by

Bill Wylie Kellermann

WILLIAM B. EERDMANS PUBLISHING COMPANY
GRAND RAPIDS, MICHIGAN

Copyright © 1994 by Wm. B. Eerdmans Publishing Co.
255 Jefferson Ave. S.E., Grand Rapids, Michigan 49503
All rights reserved

Printed in the United States of America

00 99 98 97 96 95 94   8 7 6 5 4 3 2 1

Library of Congress Cataloging-in-Publication Data

Stringfellow, William.
[Selections. 1994]
A keeper of the Word: selected writings of William Stringfellow /
edited with an introduction by Bill Wylie Kellermann.
p.   cm.
Includes bibliographical references and index.
ISBN 0-8028-0726-7 (pbk.)
1. Stringfellow, William. 2. Theologians — United States — Biography.
3. Lawyers — United States — Biography. 4. Radicals — United States — Biography.
5. Mission of the church. 6. Church and the world. 7. Christianity and politics.
8. Powers (Christian theology). 9. Church and social problems — United States.
I. Kellermann, Bill Wylie.
BX4827.S7954A3   1994
230'.044 — dc20   94-19501
                                                    CIP

For Daniel Berrigan

Contents

II. THE VOCATION OF THE CHURCH

CONGREGATIONS AND COMMUNIONS

Contents

BAPTISM, ORDERS, MINISTRY

THE BIBLE

III. PRINCIPALITIES AND POWERS

A THEOLOGY OF THE POWERS

PARTICULAR POWERS

IV. LIVING HUMANLY

Contents

Acknowledgments

The thanks of my heart:

To William Stringfellow for being William Stringfellow, nothing more and nothing less, and for offering these words in the humanity of his vocation;

To Gary Lueck, then a seminary intern, for putting *Instead of Death* into my hands as high school student;

To Dan Berrigan for introducing me to Bill, and for first uttering the title to this volume in his Block Island eulogy;

To Jim Wallis, Scott Kennedy, and Ned Hastings — friends of Stringfellow and trustees of his estate — for encouraging this project by a number of means;

To Uncas McThenia, my compatriot in assorted projects Stringfellonian, for his wisdom and insight;

To Bill Eerdmans, Stringfellow's first publisher, for honoring yet again that vocation;

To students at the Whitaker School of Theology, the Seminary Consortium on Urban Pastoral Education, and Ecumenical Theological Seminary for delighting in and commenting on certain of these writings;

To Jim Tyler and his archival cohorts at the Cornell library for care and efficient assistance;

To Jim West for plugging away in solitude on the bibliography herein appended;

To Mary Carter for taking seriously and so enjoying Stringfellow's words as she transcribed them;

To a number of additional people who read or made suggestions or otherwise contributed to this anthology: Joe Agne, Gene Davenport, John Dear, Mary Miller, Walter Wink;

To Bob Raines and Cynthia Hirni for plotting a Stringfellow festival at Kirkridge and joining all the aforementioned in conspiring his theological revival;

To Jeanie Wylie-Kellermann, for thinking often as not like Stringfellow, for suffering my editorial insomnia, for enduring and enjoying a Block Island honeymoon, but above all for working out our salvation within the vocation of marriage (a marriage blessed once upon a time by Bill with a reading from the Book of Common Prayer — Service for the Burial of the Dead, to this effect: "The One that raised up Jesus from the dead will also quicken our mortal bodies.").

Alleluia. That blessing be upon you all.

Further thanks are due the following publishers and copyright holders for permission to reprint:

The Witness (1249 Washington Blvd., Suite 3115, Detroit, MI 48226-1868) for "Advent as a Penitential Season," December 1981; "Christmas as a Parody of the Gospel," December 1982; "On Being Haunted by the Angel of the Church at Sardis," September 1975; "An Open Letter to the Presiding Bishop," January 1980; "The Politics of Pastoral Care: An Ecumenical Meditation concerning the Incumbent Pope," February 1984.

Sojourners (2401 15th Street NW, Washington, DC 20009) for "Exemplary Disbelief," March 1980; "High Crimes and Misdemeanors: The Macabre Era of Kissinger and Nixon," January 1984; "Kindred Mind and Brother," June 1977; "Myths, Endless Genealogies, the Promotion of Speculations and the Vain Discussion Thereof," August 1977; "Nuclear Principalities: A Biblical View of the Arms Race," in *Waging Peace,* ed. Jim Wallis, Harper & Row, 1982.

Christianity and Crisis (537 W. 121st Street, New York, NY 10027) for "Does America Need a Barmen Declaration?" vol. 33, no. 22, December 24, 1973.

The Christian Century for "Harlem, Rebellion, and Resurrection," November 11, 1970. Copyright 1970 The Christian Century Foundation.

The Christian Scholar (now owned by *Soundings: An Interdisciplinary Journal*) for material from "The Christian Lawyer as Churchman," vol. 4, 1957.

Commonweal (232 Madison Ave., New York, NY 10016) for "Impeach Nixon Now," vol. 96, May 26, 1972.

Criterion (The University of Chicago Divinity School, Chicago, IL 60637) for material from "Introduction to Theology: Conversations with Karl Barth," vol. 2, Winter 1963.

Abingdon Press for material from *Simplicity of Faith: My Experience in Mourning.* Copyright 1982 by Abingdon. Used by permission.

Sheed and Ward for material from "Reparations: Repentance as a Necessity to Reconciliation," from *Black Manifesto: Religion, Racism, and Reparations,* Robert S. Lecky and H. Elliot Wright, eds. (1969).

Word, Inc. (Dallas, TX) for material from *Conscience and Obedience* (1977) and *An Ethic for Christians and Other Aliens in a Strange Land* (1973). Used with permission.

Mel Schoonover for the foreword to *Making All Things Human* (New York: Holt, Rinehart and Winston, 1969).

Paul West (110 W. Cooper, St. Athens, PA 18810) for the bibliography. His annotated version is available directly from him.

The Rare Book and Manuscript Collections, Cornell University Library, for permission to use the following unpublished manuscripts: "Authority in Baptism," "Advent Bible Study Guide," and Introduction to *Grieve Not the Holy Spirit.*

The Trustees of the William Stringfellow Estate for: "Authority in Baptism"; "Advent Bible Study Guide"; "Introduction to *Grieve Not the Holy Spirit*"; Unpublished Address to the National Convention of Integrity, Denver, CO, September 7, 1979. Also for material from: *The Death and Life of Bishop Pike* (Doubleday and Company, Inc., 1976); *Dissenter in a Great Society* (Holt, Rinehart and Winston, 1966); *Free in Obedience* (Seabury Press, 1964); *My People Is the Enemy* (Doubleday & Company, Inc., 1964); *The Politics of Spirituality* (The Westminster Press, 1984); *A Second Birthday* (Doubleday & Company, Inc., 1977); *Suspect Tenderness* (Holt, Rinehart and Winston, 1971); Introduction to Daniel Berrigan, *They Call Us Dead Men* (The Macmillan Company, 1966).

Introduction

IN THE spring of 1962 William Stringfellow was one of eight theologians on the panel that questioned Karl Barth during his visit to the United States. Stringfellow's participation was remarkable in several respects. Apart from being the youngest and the only "non-academic" theologian in the group, his exchanges with Barth were the most lively, conversational, and political (circumventing Barth's reticence on the latter score).[1] At one point before answering another panel member's query, Barth deferred unexpectedly to Stringfellow who dutifully held forth. (He answered, in fact, by all but reciting a passage on preaching and prophetism from *A Private and Public Faith* [1962], his first book just then published, which critiqued the state of American Protestantism.) At another point, in the midst of their exchange, Barth turned to the audience and said, "You should listen to this man!" If the great theologian had so remarked about any of the other panelists, then employed in eminent universities, it would have been money, quite literally, in the bank. For Stringfellow it was a blessing and an admonition to become notorious.

The University of Chicago exchange was remarkable in a further respect. The care of Stringfellow's lengthy questions as well as the thoughtfulness of Barth's response presaged what was to become one of his theological and political passions: the principalities and powers. The crises of recent decades have virtually required a revival of this

1. See pp. 187-91.

1

New Testament understanding, and no one has been more influential in articulating a theology of the powers, in a concrete, practical, and engaged sense, than Stringfellow. The stunning series on the powers recently accomplished by Walter Wink,[2] for example, is a direct fruit of Stringfellow's ground-breaking work.

His comprehension of the powers originated in experience. As a lawyer in East Harlem beginning in 1956 he had met them on the street in authorities, agencies, and bureaucracies:

> Slowly I learned something that folk indigenous to the ghetto know: namely, that the power and purpose of death are incarnated in institutions and structures, procedures and regimes — Consolidated Edison or the Department of Welfare, the Mafia or the police, the Housing Authority or the social work bureaucracy, the hospital system or the banks, liberal philanthropy or corporate real estate speculation. In the wisdom of the people of the East Harlem neighborhood, such principalities are identified as demonic powers because of the relentless and ruthless dehumanization that they cause.[3]

Subsequently, in the late sixties Stringfellow received a Guggenheim Fellowship and took a sabbatical from the Harlem legal practice to work on "an American moral theology." Apart from the dominating contribution of Reinhold Niebuhr through the Depression and World War II, he discerned a void in American theological ethics, especially since the rise of nuclear empire or since technology and race had become so distinctively juxtaposed in social crisis.[4] His seminal treatment of the principalities and the ethics of freedom was already published in *Free in Obedience* (1964). He would go further. Then, almost as if the powers sensed their imminent exposure, Bill was struck down with debilitating illness. Hospitalized and in severe pain, all he could manage was a concise little (and little known) study guide on the reigning American idols of religion, work, money, race, and patriotism, called *Impostors of God* (1969).

2. Walter Wink, *Naming the Powers* (Philadelphia: Fortress Press, 1984); *Unmasking the Powers* (Philadelphia: Fortress Press, 1986); *Engaging the Powers* (Philadelphia: Fortress Press, 1992).

3. *Instead of Death*, 1967 ed., p. 5.

4. *A Second Birthday*, p. 39. See pp. 59-60.

At the time it may have seemed his illness was preempting and postponing further theological consideration of ethics and the powers. In truth, not so. Stringfellow was simply experiencing and engaging the principalities at a more personal depth, on the one hand in the commercial powers of technocratic medicine, but more so in the incursion of death that illness always represents.

In good time the "American moral theology" took shape as a trilogy comprising *An Ethic for Christians and Other Aliens in a Strange Land* (1973), *Conscience and Obedience* (1977), and a book only begun (and published herein for the first time) on the charismatic and the demonic. In brief, the ethic these books urge is sacramental or incarnational, eschatological, and charismatic.

The first of them (one pauses and hesitates before making such pronouncements) is really his finest. In *Ethic* Stringfellow articulates most completely his theology of the powers, but more than that he does so by looking the American beast in the face, without either flinching or failing. Here he reads America biblically. He unmasks the rule of death we suffer. He names it Babylon.

The book was enormously influential in identifying and nourishing a "community of resistance" at the heart of American empire. It was circulated there, in prisons cells, action planning retreats, and communities taking shape. It was passed hand to hand, almost mimicking the underground circulation of the book of Revelation, from which it took inspiration. It spoke to the conscience. It had the power to circulate, once again hand to hand, such resources as courage and hope. It named and it freed. To that I can add my own testimony: no other single book has been more important in shaping my own ministry.

Stringfellow wrote in small company. The coincident sympathy of Stringfellow and the French theologian Jacques Ellul is often noted (occasionally by Stringfellow himself).[5] That harmony is most prominent in *Ethic*. Unless it is truly attributable to the Holy Spirit, I believe he wrote in conversation with Ellul's *The Meaning of the City*.[6] That book, by the way, though it kept scrupulously to the biblical narrative and

5. "Kindred Mind and Brother," *Sojourners,* June 1977, vol. 6, no. 6, p. 12. See pp. 360-61.

6. *The Meaning of the City* (Grand Rapids: Eerdmans Publishing Company, 1970).

idiom, was Ellul's theological companion volume to his own scathing sociological work, *The Technological Society.*[7] *Ethic* combines biblical theology with social analysis, but, like *The Meaning of the City,* it turns upon recognizing, here and now, the presence of Babylon and Jerusalem.

In a related way, *Conscience and Obedience* examines political authority through a juxtaposed reading of Romans 13 and Revelation 13. Written during the U.S. Bicentennial, it considers political legitimacy in the era of Watergate, unconstitutional war, and ubiquitous surveillance and harassment (which Stringfellow himself endured). In the end, Stringfellow concludes the judgment of legitimacy inadequate, opting instead for a Christian ethic that anticipates imminently the impending devastation of *all* political authority in the Second Coming of Christ. Reinhold Neibuhr might not have agreed.

Lastly the unfinished charismatic book would have developed themes first touched upon in *Ethic,* in particular the suggestion that the charismatic gifts (which he took to include all human capabilities vocationally renewed in the Spirit) remain the primary resources for sustaining sanity, conscience, and human community against the aggressions of the principalities. To see that book lie incomplete is a great sorrow. We are bereft to that degree. Nonetheless, similar themes were taken up in his last completed book, *The Politics of Spirituality* (1984), which concerns the political meaning of justification and sanctification.

On Being out of Print

Although he sometimes smarted under his recurrent designation as a "lay theologian," and even though he wrote some fifteen books and scores of theological articles (no small volume given his fragile and often perilous health, his work as a lawyer, or his political and pastoral involvements), Stringfellow never considered himself to have a vocation as a theologian. Even less did he envision a theological "career." Writing theology was something he did. It was part of his work. He suffered it. He enjoyed it. He spent himself offering it as a gift, sometimes unwelcome, to the church. Likewise, though he was trained at Harvard Law School, and practiced first in Harlem and then on

---

7. *The Technological Society* (New York: Vintage Books, 1964).

Block Island, much the same may be said of his work as a lawyer. He did not count it his vocation, nor did he brook *any* career. Careers, as a matter of fact, he counted among the principalities. As he put it succinctly, in his conversion he "died to career."

His vocation, he thought, was to be William Stringfellow, nothing more and nothing less. And he understood all human beings to enjoy a comparable vocation: to be who they were called in the Word of God to be, to live in the fullness of their humanity, to offer their gifts renewed. Those who knew or heard or read Stringfellow will largely concur: he was faithful to his calling.

Stringfellow would be pleased, not surprised, that his work should be compiled into an edition such as this. By the time of his death in 1985, all but his last book were out of print. Now everything is. That may be attributable, on the one hand, to the principalities and, on the other, to his practice of theology.

I do not suggest that his books were systematically suppressed (though neither would I preclude it), but merely note that publishing houses are corporate powers, many rapidly being devoured by media conglomerates and even larger commercial fish. In such an environment, publishing institutions distort or even forget entirely their original vocation to serve the church, say, or human society at large, by bringing the truth to light and sustaining it even at some risk or cost. Their ethic comes to be one of "survival," as Stringfellow notes, and their service is in bondage to the idols of profit and efficiency. On one occasion, when *Instead of Death* (1963, 1976) was republished somewhat later in an expanded second edition (the only instance of that), the publisher submitted the title to computerized scrutiny and declared that the word *death* must be removed or replaced if it were to sell adequately in the market then current. Stringfellow resisted the technocratic muscling, and death went by its proper name. In any event, market logic is in general unlikely to serve good theology. We may be gladdened that a handful of publishers honor the vocation and refuse the spirit of conglomeratization.

The other cause may be the nature of his theology. Stringfellow's writing was not systematic in the academic spirit of abstraction that renders such work, even the faddish varieties, "timelessly" above history. His was engaged, as they say. Or empirical, as he was inclined to put it, or even incarnational, to use the orthodox terminology.

When he wrote theology it was full of examples from the moment; more precisely it grew out of those events, personal and historical, which were his examples. So a conversation with an addict, a civil rights case, local political dealings on Block Island, the state of the war in Southeast Asia, the actions of the incumbent regime, or a public liturgy of the resistance movement: such things as these are woven into his theological observation. They give the appearance, falsely, of being time-bound and dated. And books are too soon remaindered.

This is, however, the necessary nature of theology in biblical practice. I suppose that the chronicles of Israel, or the prophetic utterances, or the letters of Paul, or the Gospels themselves are equally "dated." They are engaged and concrete; they discern and tell the Word in lives and history.

Perhaps the best example of this is *Dissenter in a Great Society* (1966). As the title intimates, it is a social critique of Johnson era events and mythology. So it includes treatment of the 1964 Republican Convention or reflections on the civil rights movement or the failures of the "War on Poverty." Yet read against the resilience of resurgent racism, against events like the Simi Valley verdict and the 1992 Los Angeles uprising, its reading of racial crisis is remarkably prescient and prophetic. Its theology, above all, endures and abides.

Or again, for several years now I have been using *Ethic* in a course on urban principalities. Written in the early 1970s, it is rife with examples from the era of the Nixon regime. Yet whether we read it during the Gulf War or a Chicago election, these seminary interns are almost startled. "Who is this guy?" they say. "And how can we have gotten through seminary without ever hearing of him?" Indeed.

Biography, Theology, and the Matter of Time

Normally an introduction of this sort would include a brief biographical sketch of the writer. Because so much of his theology was autobiographical or laced with personal examples, that turns out to be unnecessary here. Reflecting on his years as a street lawyer in East Harlem, Stringfellow wrote *My People Is the Enemy: An Autobiographical Polemic* (1964). The subtitle suggests almost a new literary genre. By it I believe that he meant not only a life actively contending with churchly and political powers, but a self-accounting that carries the public engagement further yet. Combined with *A Second Birthday* (1970), which tells of that near fatal bout with illness, and *A Simplicity of Faith* (1982), a remembrance and reflection on the death of his friend and companion Anthony Towne, Stringfellow regarded the three as composing an autobiographical trilogy.

Incidentally, it demonstrates the eclectic genre of his biographical theology that these same books also might serve well as texts in courses on ministry. *My People* certainly addresses and illustrates the worldly service of advocacy and intercession, which is the calling of every lay person in baptism. *Second Birthday* is so rich in pastoral insights about pain and healing, it might fruitfully be tucked in the drawer of any hospital bedside stand. And *Simplicity* is the most lucid pastoral tract on grief and mourning that I have ever read.

Be that as it may, the opening section of this anthology provides a brief outline of Stringfellow's life by drawing from the trilogy and supplementing with additional sources. The decision to organize it chronologically was not as straightforward as one might imagine. Stringfellow's autobiographical works and illustrations were *not* necessarily ordered that way but structured according to other logics. So, in fact, there has been a certain violence in usurping and excerpting them from larger theological contexts and resituating things in linear fashion. His non-chronological style reflected a theological conviction. In vocational crises (like those brought on by the move to Harlem, or life-threatening surgery, or the death of his closest friend) all sorts of past personal (and political) events came to bear in an intensely present way for him. His conversion, which is to say his encounter with the Word of God vocationally, would be implicated and his whole life thereby recalled. So surgery evokes the adolescent decision not to be a priest, the move to Harlem his father's social and financial standing, and Anthony's death their travels together with a circus. For Stringfellow the coherence of events had nothing to do with time.

When Stringfellow and Towne collaborated on a biography, *The Death and Life of Bishop Pike* (1976),[8] they rejected the chronological

---

8. Stringfellow had previously served as Pike's canonical lawyer in defending him against the heresy charges in 1966 and with Towne had written about that in *The Bishop Pike Affair* (New York: Harper & Row, 1967).

principle and began (as the title underscores) with the account of Pike's death in the Judean wilderness. They did this not simply because it was so infamous but "to show that the story of his life was simultaneously the story of his dying; but then, furthermore, to affirm in the construction of the title that resurrection succeeds death."[9]

Once at a forum in Battle Creek, Michigan, a questioner was utterly taken back when in answer to his question about the marks of Christian discipleship, Stringfellow replied that the first was "freedom from bondage to time." He regarded time as an aspect of the Fall, an aspect of the rule of death.

> The Fall is not, as the biblical literalists have supposed, an event in time; the Fall is the era of time as such — the Fall is the time of time, as it were. Human knowledge is temporal, fallen, and, as St. Paul emphasizes, in bondage to death. Time is the realm of death.[10]

Resurrection, for Stringfellow, meant living in freedom from both. To pray, he would aver, everywhere and always invokes the Communion of Saints, because it is an act of spiritual solidarity with everyone who has, at any time, prayed and who will, at any time pray.[11] Paradoxically, his diabetes and other medical complications entailed a strict daily timetable of multiple mealtimes and insulin injections. The clock's heavy hand. And yet the monastic freedom of *Eschaton,* his home on Block Island, was always, as his guests will attest, an easy respite from the mainland's time-driven realm.

I trust, by mentioning all this, none will esteem me foolish for resorting to a flatly chronological framework in the biographical section. It seemed simplest and most helpful. The alternative is not really another form of anthology but reading the actual corpus beginning to end, or end to beginning. And either procedure may be commended.

---

9. *A Simplicity of Faith,* p. 31.
10. *Second Birthday,* pp. 122–23.
11. *A Simplicity of Faith,* p. 69.

Word and Time

The remaining sections of this reader are organized thematically. Unless some principle of logic or clarity overrides, the selections within are generally arranged in the order they were written. So in each grouping one may notice some development or refocusing of his thought.

Stringfellow himself, however, took little personal interest in such "development:"

> The ideas I nurture and the views I assert are responses to human beings and happenings; my thoughts issue from involvement. As such, to compare my thinking now to what it has been at any other point yields only that apparent coherence that hindsight affords — after the ambiguities of making a decision and the stress of action have receded — and is probably not very accurate. This means, simply, that I am not hung up on the ethic of consistency (consistency, conceived as a necessity or even as a value is a contrivance of the Greek mentality, as it were, to escape confronting life as it is in this world). How my mind has changed in ten years is, thus, something of which I am not self-conscious and am more or less incompetent to say, though, at the same time, I feel assured that the way my mind works has not changed. It is the latter that is more significant, as I see it, rather than either consistency or change in belief or opinion.[12]

Who I am, he said, is what I think (not the other way around.)

It hardly needs saying that the constant of Stringfellow's identity and language was its biblical character. As he wrote in *Count It All Joy* (1967):

> When a person becomes that mature as a human being, one is freed to listen and at last to welcome the Word in the Bible, and one is enlightened to discern the same Word of God at work now in the world, in (of all places!) one's own existence as well as in

---

12. From "Harlem, Rebellion and Resurrection," *Christian Century,* December 11, 1970, vol. 87, pp. 1345–48. See pp. 79-82.

(thank God!) all other life. Thus is established a rhythm in the Christians' life encompassing one's intimacy with the Word of God in the Bible and one's involvement with the same Word active in the world.[13]

I hope you will find that rhythm in this anthology. It is in all of his writing. Virtually every book is focused and rubricked with Scripture. None could properly be called commentaries as such, though any number of them illuminate the issues of a specific book: Hebrews, say, or James, or Corinthians, or Revelation. It will not be noticeable in this anthology, but it should also be known that those books that were written in the deepest pain and distress find their roots and schema in the psalms, which he discovered to be his consolation and prayer. Stringfellow prayed as he wrote: from within the Scriptures.

One change of language may be apparent over time: for the last decade of his life, in books and articles and talks, he tended to employ the *Word of God* as the *name* of God, in preference to the mere term *God*. (He took note of this, almost offhandedly, in *The Politics of Spirituality*.)[14] So, to take an example straight from the Trinity, he understood the Holy Spirit to name the faithfulness of the Word of God to creation, indeed the militant presence of the Word of God inhering in the life of the whole creation.

This bears on a change of language that will not be manifest from this volume alone, namely the influence of feminism on Stringfellow in the elimination of sexist language. (His involvement with the first women ordained to the priesthood in Anglicanism had put him in touch with some of the most rigorous of feminist theologians.) In editing this volume I have made those changes (the idol of consistency notwithstanding) based on the alterations that he himself made in the text of *Instead of Death* when it was reissued in 1976. Although he went further in the ensuing decade, I took that effort as authorization and sanction for these simple modifications.[15] On

13. *Count It All Joy* (Grand Rapids: Eerdmans Publishing Company, 1967), p. 20.

14. *The Politics of Spirituality* (Philadelphia: Westminster Press, 1984), p. 33.

15. I have, for example, rendered *mankind* as *humanity*. *Man* (singular) becomes *person* generally; and *man* (inclusive) may become *all human life*, or *human beings*, or

the other hand, though a similar case might be made, I have not changed "Negro" or "black" or racial-ethnic designations on the premise that these are representative idioms of particular periods.

One shift in language that I notice in his later writing is a tendency to substitute "the whole of creation" for "the world." I believe that usage stemmed in part from his conviction that the principalities needed to be seen within the created order as *creatures* accountable to the judgment of the Word of God. Moreover, he saw their assault as going deeper and further than upon human life only; theirs is an attack on all realms of creation. His experience on Block Island was the immediate local verification. Meanwhile, the global environmental crisis finally overtakes his language. Creation is a big theological topic. It is a spirituality. A consciousness. Stringfellow's language lights up differently in our moment. And I believe it may represent an important theological juncture.

Creation spiritualists will not like his redundant emphasis on the Fall. Like others in a broader theological stream, they have credited the doctrine with justifying domination and have emphasized instead the "original blessing" of creation. While theological witchhunters confront them with "biblical orthodoxy," Stringfellow's quarrel would be more with a consequential blindness to the powers. If fallenness is obviated and a shift in paradigm or consciousness is all that's advocated as necessary in social struggle, then there will be an utter indifference to the demonic agency of the principalities, which actively undertake the assault on creation. The powers, in fact, give living embodiment to the very system and method of domination. Yet they may be the more unseen, unintentionally written off the theological map. If this anthology fuels renewed interest in Stringfellow's theology of the powers, I hope it may find readership within the community of those interceding on behalf of the created order. Baptism for him, by the way, authorizes nothing less: it is

———————

again *humanity.* Sometimes I have shifted to a plural rendering so that pronouns become generic. With reference God, I have eliminated pronouns generally by substituting *God* for *He* throughout. I assume that these and similar transpositions will be familiar to readers and that they employ similar remedies in their conversation or writing. I do not believe they are intrusive or even, as a rule, noticeable.

the sacrament of the extraordinary unity among humanity wrought by God in overcoming the power of and reign of death; in overcoming all that alienates, segregates, divides, and destroys human beings in their relationship with each other, within their own persons, and in their relationship with the rest of creation.[16]

There are friends of mine, all thoughtful, intelligent, biblically literate, and politically alert, who find Stringfellow's writing virtually unreadable. I know it demands an effort. They would not deny that he is invariably precise in his language. Nor do they complain of his exercise of vocabulary. They only object that his construction is, perhaps unduly, elaborate, dense, and digressionary. They may be right, though I wish they would persevere.

After reading Walter Wink's observation that in the New Testament, "expressions for power tend to . . . attract each other into series or strings, as if power were so diffuse and impalpable a phenomenon that words must be heaped up in clusters in order to catch a sense of its complexity,"[17] I wondered if Stringfellow hadn't unconsciously emulated that biblical style. Look, when you read, for those exhausting lists and interminable world-class sentences packed with thought.

When he first put together *Instead of Death* it was under a commission to write a study guide for high school students. While he addressed the topics of their inevitable concern (sex, loneliness, work, identity), he nonetheless wrote precisely in his accustomed style. Asked about it once, he replied that many young people had thanked him for it. They much appreciated not being talked down to. They had persevered together or alone.

Providence is a mystery in time: under the tutelage of a young seminary intern at our church, that little volume was *my* introduction to William Stringfellow — as a high school student in Detroit. It was for me a light going on. Although I'd been raised in the church, indeed in a parsonage family, and had a firm foundation in the faith, it was the first time I recall "thinking theologically." It effected my conversion. I can name a host of others for whom reading this or that of Stringfellow's altered the course of their lives. I suppose that should

16. *Instead of Death* (New York: Seabury Press, 1976), pp. 111–12.
17. *Naming the Powers*, p. 8.

sound as a suitable caution to all who might persevere through these pages. It may prove more than an interesting or even edifying exploit.

The other person who figured in my conversion, though somewhat later, in seminary, was Daniel Berrigan. He changed forever the way I read the Bible; he hyphenated word and deed in the living; and he brought me, in the providence of time, face to face with Stringfellow. I feel free to mention that here because Dan comes up repeatedly in these pages. That may be attributable to an editor's bias, but I think not. Over a period of two decades, Stringfellow would point to the "Berrigan witness," a phrase intended to include his brother Philip and also Liz McAlister (and their community), as exemplars of the biblical testimony. There was, of course, the book *Suspect Tenderness: The Ethics of the Berrigan Witness* (1971). It stemmed from the Catonsville draftboard action in 1968, Berrigan's underground resistance to the prison sentence, his arrest by the authorities at Stringfellow and Towne's Block Island home, and their subsequent federal indictment for "harboring a fugitive." But more than that Berrigan is invoked to illustrate the nature of conscience, the freedom of resurrection, the improvisational character of living humanly, the practice of politically informed exorcism or liturgical renewal, the ordinariness of sanctification, the "foolishness" of resistance, the sacramental dimension of ethics, or the reality of an American confessing movement. Really. Read on. The two of them had once conceived of doing a book together, an extended conversation on friendship to be transcribed and edited, but Stringfellow's death put off for the moment that exchange. So yes, friendship is expressed in these pages, but finally more: it is testimony joining testimony in the witness of the Word.

That is the reason, beyond my own gratitude, why these selected writings of the one are dedicated to the other.

Books by William Stringfellow

1962   *A Private and Public Faith* (Grand Rapids: Eerdmans Publishing Company, 1962)

1963   *Instead of Death* (New York: Seabury Press, 1963)

1964   *My People Is the Enemy* (New York: Holt, Rinehart and Winston, 1964)

1964   *Free in Obedience* (New York: Seabury Press, 1964)

1966   *Dissenter in a Great Society* (New York: Holt, Rinehart and Winston, 1966)

1967   (With Anthony Towne) *The Bishop Pike Affair* (New York: Harper & Row, 1967)

1967   *Count It All Joy* (Grand Rapids: Eerdmans Publishing Company, 1967)

1969   *Impostors of God: Inquiries into Favorite Idols* (Washington, DC: Witness Books, 1969)

1970   *A Second Birthday* (Garden City, NY: Doubleday, 1970)

1971   (With Anthony Towne) *Suspect Tenderness: The Ethics of the Berrigan Witness* (New York: Holt, Rinehart and Winston, 1971)

1973   *An Ethic for Christians and Other Aliens in a Strange Land* (Waco, TX: Word, 1973)

1976   (With Anthony Towne) *The Death and Life of Bishop Pike* (Garden City, NY: Doubleday, 1976)

1976   *Instead of Death,* 2nd edition (New York: Seabury Press, 1976)

Books by William Stringfellow

1977   *Conscience and Obedience* (Waco, TX: Word, 1977)
1982   *A Simplicity of Faith: My Experience in Mourning* (Nashville: Abingdon, 1982)
1984   *The Politics of Spirituality* (Philadelphia: Westminster Press, 1984)

I. AUTOBIOGRAPHICAL POLEMIC

Biography as Theology

Keep me, O God, for in thee have I found refuge.
I have said to the Lord,
"Thou, Lord, art my felicity."
The gods whom earth holds sacred are all worthless,
and cursed are all who make them their delight;
those who run after them find trouble without end.
I will not offer them libations of blood
nor take their names upon my lips.

PSALM 16:1–4

I consider the theological treatment of biography — and, more broadly, history — to be biblically apropos; after all, the Old Testament is, to a large extent, Israel's story, just as the Gospel accounts tell the story of Jesus and his disciples, while the Book of the Acts is biography of the apostles and the other pioneer Christians who became the Apostolic Church. Similar affirmations can be made of the Epistles, and, for that matter, the prisoner's diary, which is the Book of Revelation.

The theological exploration of biography or the theological reconnaissance of history are apt, and even normative, styles because each is congruent with the definitive New Testament insight and

From *A Simplicity of Faith,* 1982, pp. 19–21

instruction: *the Incarnation*. Biblical faith is distinguished from all religions, all philosophies, and all ideologies by its redundant insistence upon the presence and vitality of the Word of God in common history; and Christians particularly confess that the involvement of the Word of God in the life of this world becomes most conscientious, comprehensible, and intentional in the event of Jesus Christ. This historic, incarnate activity of the Word of God signifies the militancy of the Word of God, both in cosmic dimensions of space and time, and in each and every item of created life, including *your* personhood and *your* biography or mine. It is this same basis of the Christian faith that is so often diminished, dismissed, omitted, or ignored when theology is rendered in abstract, hypothesized, propositional, or academic models. There is, then, with the latter something incongruent about the mode of theological discourse — something inherently inappropriate about the method being employed to present the gospel. So, I believe, biography (and history), *any* biography and *every* biography, is inherently theological, in the sense that it contains already — literally by virtue of the Incarnation — the news of the gospel whether or not anyone discerns that. *We* are each one of us parables.

What I am referring to here amounts, of course, to a doctrine of revelation. What I am discussing is how the living Word of God is implicated in the actual life of this world, in all its tumult and excitement, ambiguity and change, in the existence of the nations and principalities, human beings and other creatures, in every happening in every place in every moment (cf. Rev. 19:11–16). This world is the scene where the Word of God is; fallen creation — in all of its scope, detail, and diversity — is the milieu in which the Word of God is disclosed and apprehended; Jesus Christ verifies how the Word of God may be beheld by those who have sight and hearing to notice and give heed to the Word of God (cf. John 1:1–14).

Biography, thus, is rudimentary data for theology, and every biography is significant for the knowledge it yields of the Word of God incarnate in common life, whether or not the subject of the biography is aware of that significance of his or her own story. *Vocation* is the name of the awareness of *that* significance of one's own biography. To have a vocation or to be called in Christ means to discern the coincidence of the Word of God with one's own selfhood, in one's own being, in its most specific, thorough, unique, and conscientious sense.

Free of Money

I WAS born during the Depression and remember that my father, a knitter in the hosiery industry, was often out of work for long periods of time. After the depression waned, the hosiery industry was radically changed by the introduction of nylon, and, in the consolidation of the industry that ensued, many firms, including the one for which my father worked, moved South to take advantage of tax concessions and cheaper labor. Poverty for white working-class Americans is not nearly as profound economically, socially, or psychologically as it is for urban Negroes. As a child I was not really aware that we were poor. It was only when I was in high school and first talked with my parents about going to college that I realized that my family could not afford a college education for me and that if I wanted one I would somehow have to pay for it pretty much by myself. So I did. It was, I think, far easier for me to do it than it would be for a Negro boy. I had no difficulty getting jobs, after school and in the summers. In fact, during my senior year in high school I managed three jobs simultaneously — one picking asparagus before dawn, another as a stock clerk in a store in the afternoons, and then, at night, as a soda jerk in the ice cream parlor where most of the kids hung out. Moreover, the school I attended was an excellent one academically and had teachers who took great interest in their students. Scholarship

My People Is the Enemy, 1964 ed., pp. 36–37

opportunities were available. Before I graduated from high school, I had the choice of three scholarships. The fact that my family was relatively poor did not affect, in any way that I can see, our social relationships in the community while I was growing up. A good many of my friends and playmates were from families of some wealth and social prominence, though I do not recollect that any of us even thought about such matters. In short, the poverty familiar to the families of white industrial workers in America in times of depression and high unemployment is not nearly so confining and dehumanizing as the poverty of the black ghettos. We were poor, but I was not deprived. We were poor, but I was readily accepted in the homes of the rich. We were poor, but I could "pass" in white bourgeois society. We were poor, but I had a chance. That is not the way it has been for most Negroes in America.

Confirmation

THIS whole matter of the elusive significance of so-called spirituality comes into acute focus, for me, in the cursory and profane
regard that the name of the Word of God as the Holy Spirit suffers,
more often than not, within the churches. I remember, for instance,
that I was very impatient to be confirmed in the Episcopal Church.
In my rearing as a child in that church I had come to think that
confirmation was the occasion when the secrets were told. Confirmation, I supposed, was the event in which all the answers that had
been previously withheld from me, because I was a child, would
be forthcoming. In particular, I recall, I was eager to be confirmed
because I expected in confirmation to learn the secret of the Holy
Spirit. At last, I anticipated, my curiosity concerning this mysterious
name would be satisfied.

In my experience as a child in the church, when adults named
the Holy Spirit in the presence of children, it was always an utterly
obscure, unspecified, literally spooky allusion.

It did not specifically occur to me as a child to suspect that
adults in the church did not, in fact, know what they were talking
about when they used the name of the Holy Spirit. The reference,
anyway, was always intimidating. The mere invocation of the name,
without any definition, connection, or elaboration, would be effective

Politics of Spirituality, 1984, pp. 16–18

in aborting any issues raised by a child. "The Holy Spirit" was the great, available, handy estoppel.

Needless to say, confirmation turned out to be a great disappointment to me. I waited through catechism, but no secrets were confided. If anything, the name of the Holy Spirit was put to use in confirmation instruction with even deeper vagueness. On the day of confirmation I learned no secret except the secret that adults in the church had no secrets, at least so far as the Holy Spirit is concerned.

It was only later on, after I had begun to read the Bible seriously, on my own initiative, that the cloture about the Holy Spirit was disrupted and the ridiculous mystification attending *this* name of the Word of God began to be dispelled. In contrast to my childish impressions from experiences in church, I found the Bible to be definitive and lucid as to the identity, character, style, and habitat of the Holy Spirit. In the Bible, the Holy Spirit is no term summoned simply to fill a void, or to enthrall rather than instruct the laity, or to achieve some verbal sleight of hand because comprehension is lacking. Biblically, the Holy Spirit names the faithfulness of God to his own creation. Biblically, the Holy Spirit means the militant presence of the Word of God inhering in the life of the whole of creation. Biblically, the Holy Spirit is the Word of God at work both historically and existentially, acting incessantly and pervasively to renew the integrity of life in this world. By virtue of this redundant affirmation of the biblical witness, the false notion — nourished in my childhood in the Episcopal Church — that the Holy Spirit is, somehow, possessed by and enshrined within the sanctuary of the church was at last refuted, and I was freed from it. Coincidentally, as one would expect, the celebration in the sanctuary became, for me, authentic — a eucharist for the redemption of the life of the whole of creation in the Word of God — instead of vain ritual or hocus-pocus.

It was the biblical insight into the truth of the Holy Spirit that signaled my own emancipation from religiosity. It was the biblical news of the Holy Spirit that began, then, to prompt the expectancy of encounter with the Word of God in any and all events in the common life of the world and in my own life as a part of that. It was — it is — the biblical saga of the Word of God as Agitator, as the Holy Spirit, that assures me that wheresoever human conscience is alive and active, *that* is a sign of the saving vitality of the Word of God in history, here and now.

Not to Be a Priest

FROM adolescence I had been at once fascinated and bothered by the means through which a person decides. While in my early teens I rejected, albeit with very great effort and with a certain passion that has never departed from me, the simplistic notion of decisions being mere choices between self-evident good and evil. That conception of both personal and social decisions had very great prominence in the white Anglo-Saxon Protestant America of my upbringing. It was part of the indoctrination of schoolchildren. It was the cornerstone (instead of the Bible) in the instruction of the young in church. It was part of the prevalent family ethic among whites, although, mercifully, within my own family it had been challenged by the Depression experience and my own parents had a better sense of the moral ambiguity of human circumstances than did many others.

My own realization of ambiguity and my emphatic repudiation of moral simplistics came, as might have been anticipated, in the making of an actual decision: I decided, at fourteen, not to become a priest.

The parish church had been a more than routine part of my childhood; it was at least as central as school in terms of its claims upon time, interest, and loyalty. There were not only the conventional programs of the parish in which to participate — the services, church

---

Second Birthday, 1970, pp. 79–83

school, a young people's fellowship, the acolytes' guild — but the parish premises and the rectory were places where I spent other hours — playing, doing errands and odd jobs, loitering, watching. I was religiously precocious, read much about religion, and pursued long and sometimes esoteric religious discussions with the clergy. This religiosity, as I now see it, became focused and personified in my relationship with one of the priests of the parish and, after a time, I found myself being much urged by him to decide upon the priesthood as a vocation. I do not know — and, fortunately, I am not the judge in the matter — how that minister regarded our relationship. I do not know his motives, and I no longer care what they may have been, whatever they may have been. I do not think he had a serious appreciation of what was happening to me in my side of our encounter. What was happening was a gradual intensification of pressures upon me to decide to be a priest and thereby to emulate him. Somehow, from him, the impression came to me that it was only by being ordained that it would be vouchsafed that I was a Christian, indeed, only in that way that it was sure that anyone was a Christian.

I was, for a long time, assailed by the multiple ambiguities attending this decision. I had an almost overwhelming sense of being possessed and, thus, coerced, and I harbored the premonition that to choose to be a priest, or even to undertake the steps in collegiate and seminary education that would make me a postulant under coercion of any sort would be intolerable. Another pressure was economic; my family, never well-to-do, had been impoverished in the Depression years, during which I had been born, and, like other working-class families, had little economic security, much less resources for my education beyond secondary school. I understood that if I made a commitment to the priesthood, the financial barriers to college and graduate study could be overcome without burden to my parents. Religion beguiled me, but I was also beginning to comprehend that the gospel was, somehow, not about religion but reached beyond religion. That caused a strong resistance intellectually and emotionally within me to this idea that this influential priest had managed, whether inadvertently or by design, to communicate to me — that to be a priest was the seal of the Christian life and that the priesthood embodied a higher or better or more conscientious or more certain disposition of one's life as a Christian.

That a priest was in any sense more exalted than any other person, in the life of the gospel in the world, could not be true. And if a priest were that in the life of the church, then it could only betray something profoundly false in the church. That was my decision. It was made fiercely — more than likely because I was only in my early teens at the time. *I would be damned if I would be a priest.* That was what I decided. I would not be a priest and, moreover, I would spend my life refuting any who suppose that to be serious about the Christian faith required ordination. I would be a Christian in spite of the priesthood, in spite of all the priests, in spite of this priest who had, as I saw it at the time, importuned me.

Spite is the right word; it was a good many years before my hostility toward the priesthood as an institution and an occupation and my sensitivity against the particular priest I have mentioned abated. They were years in which I excelled in the politics of the churches and of their youth and student movements. Within one of those years, at the height of my career as a student Christian, I presided at the first national ecumenical student conference, was prominent in the United Christian Youth Movement, served as vice-chairman of the National Student YMCA, headed the New England Student Christian Movement, was chairman of the National Student Christian Federation, represented Episcopalian youth at the World Conference of Christian Youth, and represented American students at the World's Student Christian Federation. I was proving, I suppose, that one could be recognized as a Christian without being a priest or a candidate for the priesthood. I was becoming a professional Christian without the conventional and supposedly necessary credential of professional Christians — ordination. I was becoming a pharisee. That my situation was pathetic and incongruous, in the context of the gospel, had not yet dawned on me. That, in truth, I was no Christian as such at the time, or that I can only be said to have become a Christian later in my life, in radically different circumstances, and yet was known as a super-Christian is evidence of the ferocity of my adolescent decision. That was as well a measure of the ambiguity of the whole of the event of the decision not to be a priest.

An Early Sit-in

I MYSELF was involved in what must have been one of the original sit-ins — back in 1948* — when I was in college in Maine. Some of us had observed that Negroes were not served at a certain hotel and that discrimination existed and was practiced in some other public accommodations, although it must be said that the issue was hardly noticed publicly in Maine because there were comparatively few Negroes in the state. There was, however, discrimination in some places against French Canadians who had migrated to Maine. A bill was introduced into the legislature that condemned racial or ethnic discrimination and that sought to establish a commission against discrimination. Several of us were working for the bill's enactment. One day the legislator who had sponsored the measure, a man of French extraction, came to see us to report that the legislation had almost no chance to pass, since there was so little public interest in the issue. After long discussion, it was decided that three of us would go with a Negro to the hotel that barred Negroes and ask to be served. It was arranged in advance that the legislator would be dining in the same hotel that evening and would have with him a news-paperman. The expectation was that we would ask to be served and, as had been the custom in the hotel, be refused. We would protest,

* Both editions cite this date as 1943, but that clearly is a typographical error.

My People Is the Enemy, 1964 ed., pp. 103–5

and the legislator, having noticed the incident, would intervene in our behalf while the newspaperman took photographs and got a story. The publicity of the incident was supposed to enhance the prospects for the passage of the bill. At the appointed hour, our party arrived at the hotel and went into the dining room. The senator and the reporter were halfway through their entrées. After we had been sitting at the table for several minutes, we noticed that the waiter had gone to speak to the manager. We could not hear their conversation, but soon the waiter came and asked to take our order. We had to order something of course. Ironically, we had already eaten at the college, so sure we were that the hotel would not serve us. Among the four of us we had only about five dollars, so the unfortunate senator ended up paying the check — for our second dinner of the evening! That was the result achieved in this pioneer sit-in.

It is against the background not only of Harlem, but of a bit broader involvement than that, that I conclude that the decisive front in the racial crisis in America is the urban North, and not the South. I have immense admiration for the restraint, dignity, and resourcefulness of the civil rights movement in the South, but the case remains that the immediate and stated objectives of that movement in the Southern jurisdictions are goals that have already been substantially achieved in the Northern cities, at least so far as court decisions and legislation are concerned, and also, to a significant degree, so far as integration in public transportation, hotels, restaurants, and the like is concerned. These things were attained in the North for the most part in the years after the Second World War, and what is to be seen, when one looks now at the Northern city, is what happens after these legal rights and remedies, which the Southern demonstrations seek to win, have been won. The Northern city, in other words, is setting the precedent for what is in store for the Southern cities, once the legal struggle to vindicate the civil rights of Negroes has been concluded. And if, in the days that lie immediately ahead, the relations between the races are not somehow resolved peacefully, then the whole nation is in for an ominous and dreadful holocaust.

Let no one take comfort in the racial troubles of the Northern cities, least of all any white person from the South, any more than any white Northerner can appease his conscience or rationalize her indifference by the racial strife in the South. No one is made innocent by the mere culpability of another human being.

A Lawyer's Work

IF POLITICS, from time to time, has spawned for me prosaic temptation to mistake career for vocation, being a lawyer has not bothered me in any comparable way. I was spared that before I even entered Harvard Law School because of my disposition of the substantive issue of career versus vocation while I was a graduate fellow at the London School of Economics and Political Science. As I have remarked heretofore, I had elected then to pursue *no* career. To put it theologically, I died to the idea of career and to the whole typical array of mundane calculations, grandiose goals, and appropriate schemes to reach them. I renounced, simultaneously, the embellishments — like money, power, success — associated with careers in American culture, along with the ethics requisite to obtaining such condiments. I do not say this haughtily; this was an aspect of my conversion to the gospel, so, in fact, I say it humbly.

In the time that intervened between London and Harvard (part of which I spent traveling extensively in Europe and in Asia — often at the behest of the World Student Christian Federation — and the remainder of which I served in the Second Armored Division — *Hell-on-Wheels* was its watchword — assigned to the North Atlantic Treaty Organization forces) my renunciation of ambition in favor of vocation became resolute; I suppose some would think, eccentric.

Simplicity of Faith, 1982, pp. 125–31

When I began law studies, I consider that I had few, if any, romantic illusions about becoming a lawyer, and I most certainly did not indulge any fantasies that God had called me, by some specific instruction, to be an attorney or, for that matter, to be a member of any profession or any occupation. I had come to understand the meaning of vocation more simply and quite differently.

I believed then, as I do now, that I am called in the Word of God — as is *everyone* else — to the vocation of being human, nothing more and nothing less. I confessed then, as I do now, that to be a Christian means to be called to be an exemplary human being. And, to be a Christian *categorically* does not mean being religious. Indeed, all religious versions of the gospel are profanities. Within the scope of the calling to be merely, but truly, human, any work, including that of any profession, can be rendered a sacrament of that vocation. On the other hand, no profession, discipline, or employment, as such, is a vocation.

Law students, along with those in medicine, engineering, architecture, the military, among others, are subjected to indoctrinations, the effort of such being to make the students conform quickly and thoroughly to that prevailing stereotype deemed most beneficial to the profession and to its survival as an institution, its influence in society, and its general prosperity. At the Harvard Law School, this process is heavy, intensive, and unrelenting, though I imagine that such indoctrinations are all the more so in pseudo-professional institutions, like those training insurance agents, stockbrokers, or realtors. Over and over again, while I was in the law school, I was astonished at how eagerly many of my peers surrendered to this regimen of professionalistic conditioning, often squelching their own most intelligent opinions or creative impulses in order to conform or to appear to be conforming.

Initiation into the legal profession, as it is played out at a place like the Harvard Law School, is, as one would expect, elaborately mythologized, asserts an aura of tradition, and retains a reputation for civility. All of these insinuate that this process is benign, though, both empirically and in principle, it is demonic. One notices that the medical establishment has gone much further than has the legal profession in indulging this sort of mythologizing, with the conspicuous collaboration of commercial television and, before that, the movies. (After all, the mythological forerunner of *Marcus Welby* was *Dr. Christian.*) I think none of the other professions has countenanced such pretentious and gratuitous self-images as the medical profession has, but the same issue of mythologizing is associated with all the professions and with most other occupations as well. There is radical discrepancy between myth and truth in internal indoctrinations focused on conforming practitioners and external publicity propagated about the various professions.

I understand in hindsight that the vocational attitude I had formed in London and, later, the experience I had as law student apprehended the legal profession specifically, and the professions, disciplines, and occupations in general, in their status among the fallen principalities and powers engaged (regardless of apparently benign guises and pretenses) in coercing, stifling, captivating, intimidating, and otherwise victimizing human beings. The demand for conformity in a profession commonly signifies a threat of death.

In that connection, my commitment to vocation instead of career began, while I was still in the law school, to sponsor far-reaching implications for how I could spend the rest of my life. Anyway, I suffered the overkill ethos of the Harvard Law School — I think — with enough poise as a human being to quietly, patiently, vigilantly resist becoming conformed to this world.

The upshot of that resistance was that I emerged from the law school as someone virtually opposite of what a Harvard Law School graduate is projected by the prevailing system to be. I do say *that* proudly and gladly.

Do not misunderstand me: I enjoyed the law school, but I did not take it with the literally dead earnestness of those of my peers who had great careers at stake. I respected the intellectual vigor of its environment, but I was appalled by the overwhelming subservience of legal education to the commercial powers and the principalities of property. I thought that a law school should devote at least as much attention in its curriculum to the rights and causes of people as it does to vested property interests of one kind or another. I also thought, while I was in law school, that *justice* is a suitable topic for consideration in practically every course or specialization. Alas, it was seldom mentioned, and the term itself evoked ridicule, as if justice were a subject beneath the sophistication of lawyers.

Since 1956, when I was graduated, I have been enabled to remain in touch with legal education in a more than perfunctory manner because I am often invited as a visiting lecturer in various law schools around the country. Thus I am aware that there have been some significant, if modest, curricular reforms in many law schools lately, including work in urban law, poverty law, consumer law, and some cross-disciplinary efforts between law and other graduate disciplines.

Be that as it may, when I went to the East Harlem ghetto directly upon finishing at the law school and began to practice law there on my own, it was regarded by most of my peers as a curious venture, idiosyncratic and controversial. *My People Is the Enemy* tells of that experience. That book had some impact in exposing the neglect of people, especially the dispossessed of the inner city regions, by the legal profession, in part attributable to the co-option of lawyers and legal education by commercial or similar principalities and powers. For instance, while Robert Kennedy was Attorney General of the United States, an emissary of Kennedy's came to me one day in New York City. He announced that the Attorney General had determined to convene a conference of lawyers from areas throughout the nation to examine issues of the law and the poor, and to consider how the legal profession might more responsibly serve the needs and interests of the poor in society. The attorney general, my informant declared, had read *My People Is the Enemy* and had been moved by it and had dispatched him, he stated, "to pick your brain" about these matters in the hope that this would yield ideas for the conference that was contemplated. "I had better tell you first, however," my visitor confided, "that you will not be invited to speak to the conference. . . . You're too radical." I found such candor appealing, and the interview commenced.

Robert Kennedy was, however, mistaken in an assessment that, as a lawyer, I am "radical." I do not think such labels — "radical," "liberal," "conservative," "reactionary" — edifying because they are so ambivalent in meaning, and I infrequently use them myself. But, if such classifications are invoked, in my opinion I could scarcely be counted as "radical" within the context of the legal tradition that has been inherited in America. My practice of law for a quarter of a century amply verifies this. I have been an advocate for the poor, for the urban underclass, for freedom riders and war resisters, for people deprived of elementary rights: children, women, blacks, Hispanics, native Americans, political prisoners, homosexuals, the elderly, the handicapped, clergy accused of heresy, women aspiring to priesthood. The consistent concerns of my practice have been the values of the constitutional system, due process of law, and the rule of law. What is radical about that? Perhaps these represent views of the law and society that could have been said to be radical in the thirteenth century, at the time the Magna Charta was ratified, but if they seem radical nowadays it is because so few lawyers care about them.

In East Harlem, on Block Island, in ecclesiastical courts as well as secular venues, as in the law school, I simply do not share in that feigned professional sophistication that sponsors and inculcates the indifference of lawyers to the constitutional priorities, particularly the Bill of Rights, or that rationalizes a preference for the laissez-faire interests of commerce as opposed to the freedom, safety, and welfare of human beings, or that asserts a so-called sanctity of property that devalues and demeans human life.

Despite the notoriety that has been attached to the witness of civil disobedience, notably in the era of Martin Luther King, Jr., and then in the antiwar movement of the sixties, there has been little threat to the rule of law in these protests. In fact, the major burden of them has been to act to redeem the constitutional system. The substantive danger to this society, so far as law is concerned, comes from the operation of lawless authority and the substitution of the power of coercion for the rule of law. For more than two decades now, the nation has suffered one outrageous spasm of official lawlessness after another. If this came into climactic focus in Watergate, in the aborted impeachment of President Nixon, and in the nominal punishment of a handful of culprits in high places, that comes nowhere near exhausting the scandal of illegal, unconstitutional, and often criminal offenses accomplished by military, police, security, and intelligence officials within the federal regime, not to mention their counterparts in state and some local agencies. Reread the Kerner Commission findings. Recall the literally fantastic machinations of successive CIA administrations and then notice as well that the CIA and the rest of the so-called intelligence complex still operates without presidential restraint, without parliamentary control, without any effectual accountability under the American constitutional system.

Meanwhile, the FBI is extolled by the incumbent president for its past flagrant infractions of constitutional limitations, and an immense and intricate scheme to rehabilitate its public image, following upon the most constitutionally obnoxious disclosures of official lawlessness under the auspices of J. Edgar Hoover, has been mounted, which involves the official procurement of crime. At the same time, the police power in most state and urban jurisdictions has been transmuted — partly under the patronage of the Pentagon — from a civilian to a paramilitary force in society, reflecting a contempt for constitutional safeguards and an overkill reliance upon violence. And all of this, and much, much more of the same, has been accompanied by the unrelenting barrage on commercial television of propaganda glorifying official violence as heroic, requisite, and efficient, even though it usurps constitutional rule.

On Being Oneself
in Harlem or Anywhere Else

IT IS a very dehumanizing and threatening experience to live in the slums. I remember, as vividly as I remember anything, that first day when I went to East 100th Street in Harlem. I had been there one or two times before, to visit some of the clergy who lived and worked in the East Harlem Protestant Parish, and I initially moved to the neighborhood at the suggestion of George Todd, a young Presbyterian minister with the parish, a friend of mine since the days when we had been colleagues in the student Christian movement. Todd had said that often they dealt with situations in which a lawyer was needed, but they had difficulty securing legal help, although there were two or three attorneys in the city who gave all the help they could to the parish. So I agreed to come to Harlem and to be associated with the parish as a lawyer, serving people from the neighborhood in need of legal assistance. The parish had arranged for me to move into the tenement on 100th Street, which, as one of the clergy put it as he handed me the keys to the place, was typical of the housing of the neighborhood. It was Labor Day 1956 when I came to the city, and I had checked my luggage at Grand Central Station before going uptown to see my new home. I had taken one precaution for my first

---

My People Is the Enemy, 1964 ed., pp. 22–27

inspection of the premises — I had a DDT bomb (of the sort that was used in the Army), which I had picked up at a military surplus store. I entered the apartment and looked around. I found a dead mouse in the toilet, which I disposed of. I opened a window, so as not to DDT myself, and then I released the bomb. I sat down on something for a moment to see what would happen. From everywhere — from every crack and corner, from the ceiling and walls and from underneath the linoleum, from out of the refrigerator and the stove, from in back of the sink and under the bathtub, from every place — came swarms of creeping, crawling vermin. I shuddered. I remember saying out loud to myself, "Stringfellow, you will never know here whether you have become an alcoholic." Who could tell, in such a place, whether or not he is having delirium tremens?

I left the place, went downtown, had a drink, checked into a hotel, and spent the night there.

The next day, as it happened, I was to have lunch with Bishop James Pike, who was at that time still the Dean of the Cathedral of St. John the Divine in New York. I told him, though it was perhaps not the most suitable subject for mealtime conversation, about the episode I have just related here. And he replied, "Oh, cheer up! We have cockroaches at the high altar in the Cathedral!"

With that comfort, I returned to East 100th Street and began to sweep up the vermin that had been killed by the DDT. That night I slept in my new home.

In the days that immediately followed, I spent a lot of time just trying to make my new household habitable. I remember using over thirty pounds of putty just to seal the spaces between the floor and the walls, and making innumerable other repairs in the apartment. My first few months in East Harlem made me a household handyman, with experience in wiring, plastering, elementary carpentry, and other such skills. It was during those days, when I was trying to make a place to live in, against the odds that prevail in such a building, that I began to realize and appreciate the extremity of the attrition that they suffer whose daily life is in such apartments, in such tenements, in such neighborhoods — they who, what with families and all, had every day much more to contend with than I did. I remember my exhaustion from trying to maintain my own one life there. How much more exacting and costly it must be for a parent of a family of five or six children, and particularly one who did not have the option, as I did, to return to the outer city.

Finally, a place to live was wrought, though I was promptly and aptly reminded that for me to make a place to live in, in the midst of the Harlem slums, still meant something quite different from what it would be for someone — a Negro or a Puerto Rican — indigenous to these same slums. One symbol of that, in my own experience, is contained in a conversation I had with a Negro from the neighborhood whom I had come to know and whom I bumped into on the street one morning. He stopped me and suggested that we have a cup of coffee, which we did. During the conversation he mentioned that he had noticed that I shined my shoes every day — a custom in which I had been indoctrinated five years before while serving with the Second Armored Division of Germany. He said he knew that this represented the continuation, in my new life in Harlem, of the life that I had formerly lived, and he added that he was glad of it, because it meant that I had remained myself and had not contrived to change, just because I had moved into a different environment. In order, in other words, as I heard him, to be a person in Harlem, in order that my life and work there should have integrity, I had to be and to remain whoever I had become as a person before coming there. To be accepted by others, I must first of all know myself and accept myself and be myself wherever I happen to be. In that way, others are also freed to be themselves.

To come to Harlem involved, thus, no renunciation of my own past or of any part of it. There was no occasion in Harlem to repudiate anything in my own history and heritage as a white Anglo-Saxon Protestant nor to seek to identify with the people of Harlem, either by attempting to imitate any of them or by urging any of them to imitate me. What was necessary was just to be myself. I had learned something about that long before moving to Harlem. I learned it, as I suppose others have, in the military service. I recall feeling somewhat resentful about military service when I first entered the army after college. It seemed an interruption in my education and career, not wholly a waste of time, given the conditions in the world then, but a sort of void that would not further me personally in any significant way. Most other guys felt about the same, I think. I soon discovered that I was dead wrong. I found that I could be, and was, fulfilled as a person just as much in the service as in school or work — that where I happen to be and what I happen to be doing does not determine the issue of who I am as a human being or how my own person may be expressed and fulfilled. I learned the meaning of vocation in the army. It was an emancipating discovery, for then it became possible to go anywhere and to do any sort of work — in full knowledge of my own identity and integrity.

So, moving to Harlem, for all its differences in empirical ways from other places where I had lived, was really an easy thing to do. And as my friend pointed out, when he noticed that my shoes were shined, coming to Harlem did not mean desertion of my past; it meant bringing it with me into a new situation. There was no need for any psychological dissociation, nor was there any practical dissociation, either. I am a lawyer, and I continued, all the years I was in Harlem, to remain in contact with colleagues in the downtown law firms and in the law schools in New York and elsewhere. I found my own practice of the law in Harlem intellectually provocative, and therefore I continued to write and speak about some of the issues of the law and the philosophy of the law with faculty and students from the law schools and with fellow lawyers. I am an Episcopalian, and I had long been active in the affairs of the Episcopal Church. This continued during the time in Harlem, in participation in the congregation to which I belonged and in many other ways as well. I am a white man, and to live in Harlem did not mean that I needed be separated from white society. In fact, as I reflect upon it, there was the marvelous luxury, in living and working in Harlem, of somehow being free and able to transcend a lot of barriers that otherwise separate men from each other. In the course of a day I crossed a good many boundaries: perhaps I would be in court in the morning with an addict or a kid from one of the gangs, then have lunch with a law professor at Columbia or N.Y.U., interview clients back at 100th Street during the afternoon, have a drink with some of Harlem's community leaders at Frank's Chop House on 125th Street, have dinner with clergy friends or with fellow parishioners at a midtown restaurant, stop for a bull session with some of the law students or seminarians, or spend the evening talking with friends from the Harlem neighborhood. Or I might return to the tenement to read or write; or, more often than not, do a little more work in rehabilitating the place, go out late to get the *Times,* and visit with people on the streets. I crossed a lot of boundaries in the course of a day. That in itself is not so important. What is *very* important is that in crossing boundaries of class and race and education and all the rest, I remain myself.

Street Law

THE prospect of practicing law in Harlem had, of course, to be considered in relation to other opportunities that presented themselves during my last year in law school. One possibility was to return home — to Northampton — where it would have been possible either to join an established firm or open my own practice and where there were certain political opportunities that commended themselves. There was also the possibility of joining a large Boston firm with an excellent and interesting practice. But my experience in law school had been such as to interest me mainly in courses and cases that involved direct contact with clients — and, at that, with clients who are people, not institutions. The Boston practice would not have provided that. There was also an invitation to work for the Church Society for College Work of the Episcopal Church, in a ministry devoted to law students and faculty, focused upon the meaning of the Christian vocation for lawyers. However, it seemed to me that I would first have to practice law for a while before such an undertaking full-time would make sense, though subsequently I have engaged in such work part-time.

While I pondered these and other alternatives, [George] Todd came to see me in Cambridge and made his suggestion that I come to Harlem to practice law there in collaboration with the parish. I

My People Is the Enemy, 1964 ed., pp. 35–36, 37–38, 41–45, 47–52, 53–54

visited the Harlem neighborhood, met some of those who would be my associates, talked with the clergy of the parish, and finally decided to settle there myself.

I knew that there was little money to be made in practicing in Harlem, but I had never had much money anyway and, as the rich gratuitously complain, had never had to suffer the burden of wealth. . . . In any case, not being accustomed to much money, it was no particular sacrifice to move to Harlem. There was nothing to be given up economically in going there. I had savings of about $1,800 — and that's all. And, not being bred to wealth or class, there was nothing in my inheritance as a person to repudiate psychologically in moving to Harlem. To decide to live and work in Harlem was an essentially simple decision for me.

The main reason for the decision was that I had come to feel — I suppose that I had been indoctrinated at law school — that the health and maturity of the American legal system depend upon whether or not those who are outcasts in society — the poor, the socially discriminated against, the politically unpopular — are, as a practical matter, represented in their rights and complaints and causes before the law. Harlem seemed to be a place where a lawyer might find out something about that issue, and so I decided to go there.

To be concerned with the outcast is an echo, of course, of the gospel itself. Characteristically, the Christian is to be found in his work and witness in the world among those for whom no one else cares — the poor, the sick, the imprisoned, the misfits, the homeless, the orphans and beggars. The presence of the Christian among the outcasts is the way in which the Christian represents, concretely, the ubiquity and universality of the intercession of Christ for all. All human beings are encompassed in the ministry of the Christian to the least. I had to find out more about the meaning of that, too.

What I found out — what I found out theologically — from my stay in Harlem is, of course, that all human beings are outcasts in one sense or another. It is only more vivid that people are outcasts in a place like Harlem. No one, however, escapes this condition; no one avoids alienation from others; no one evades the Fall. . . .

Given the widespread neglect by established society, including the legal profession, of the outcasts, and particularly the outcasts of the urban slums, how does one begin, as a person and as a lawyer, to reach and serve these people?

My own recollection is of having no particular rules or strategy about how to be accepted, trusted, and thus used as a lawyer in Harlem. If I had any rules or deliberate tactics, they were very simple. I decided in advance that I would speak to no one, take no initiative in making a relationship with anyone, but just live there as long as I had to until I was noticed and until someone sought me out. It is true that I had both the advantage and disadvantage of coming to the neighborhood, initially, under the patronage of the East Harlem Protestant Parish. That meant that through the parish and its staff I met a certain number of people fairly quickly and easily. But, mainly, I was on my own. And I decided that I would make no independent overture to anyone, for after all *I* was the outsider, entering, probably intruding, upon the lives of these people, and if they would welcome me and accept me, that was up to them. There was nothing I could or should do, apart from just being myself and being present among them day after day.

For quite a long time — for two or three months — I did not speak to anyone, nor did anyone speak to me, though I saw many people from the block and the neighborhood and though they recognized and watched me.

Then, one night a boy called Monk came to see me. I had seen him before around the block and knew that he was the war counselor of one of the gangs. He said he had heard that I was living in the neighborhood and that I was a lawyer, and he said that a friend of his was in trouble with the law and he wanted to ask me a few questions. I welcomed him. We had some beer and talked. It quickly became apparent that his friend with the legal problem did not exist. This was just a story, an excuse by which the boy could come to see me and talk with me and, I suppose, size me up. He stayed about three hours and we talked about many things. We got along fine. The next morning I walked over to Hell Gate post office, about twelve blocks away, and as I went back to 100th Street, I was stopped and greeted by ten or twelve of the boys who were on the street. They were friendly and knew my name and told me theirs. After our meeting the previous night, Monk evidently had vouched for me.

Thereafter I felt welcome on the street, spent more time there, and many of the people — not only the boys, but some of the older people — would wait around until I came along to discuss legal matters of all sorts, as well as gossip about the news and happenings of the neighborhood. The street became as much of an office as I ever had in Harlem.

The street is perhaps an unorthodox place to counsel clients, but whatever the inconveniences of such a practice, there were advantages as well. For one thing the overhead was very low. Moreover, I admit enjoying the freedom of wearing chinos and sneakers while practicing law. I remember one afternoon going to the northern part of East Harlem to visit an old woman who was having difficulties with the welfare authorities. The matter took several hours to settle, and by the time I was returning to East 100th Street, it had turned rather cold. I had gone out in the afternoon, when it was warmer, dressed only in a shirt, chinos, and sneakers, but now that the weather had changed, I was shivering from the cold. About two blocks from my tenement, a boy I knew, who had been loafing on the corner, called out that he wanted to ask me something. As we talked he saw that I was freezing to death and so he took off his jacket and gave it to me to wear. The boy is an addict and I happened to know that the clothes on his back were virtually the only ones he had — he had pawned everything else. Sometimes, when his clothes were being laundered, he would have to stay in the house because he had nothing else to wear, unless he could borrow something from someone. But he saw that I was cold and gave me his jacket. That is what is known as a sacrament.

Practicing law in Harlem has some similarities to small-town practice. The differences between the inner city and the outer city induce and enforce an intense localism and immobility. Many of my neighbors, especially women and younger children, seldom left the block. The localism, the attachment to one block, is sanctioned by apprehension about places that are unknown or unfamiliar, but it is also sanctioned by a sense of being unwelcome anywhere but on the block where one lives. I found, for example, that grocery prices were higher generally in the little stores in my immediate neighborhood, and so I used to go five blocks south — across the border and outside of East Harlem — to buy food at a supermarket. Several times I asked women on the block why they did not do the same and thereby save a little money, but the answer was usually that the place where I shopped was "a white man's store," though an additional factor is the relatively easy credit extended by the stores on the block.

The cases that arise in a law practice such as this are usually acutely personal: family squabbles, truancy, desertions, addiction, abandoned children, gang fights, evictions, securing repairs or heat or light from a slum landlord, intervening with the welfare investigators, legitimizing children, stopping repossession of furniture, complaining about police abuse of persons arrested. Legal counseling in such cases is as much a vehicle of pastoral care as it is of the practice of law.

To practice law in Harlem requires more than a professional identification with these kinds of cases. It involves more than knowledgeability about the neighborhood, and something different from just sympathy for the people of the ghetto. Humanitarian idealism is pretentious in Harlem and turns out to be irrelevant. It is, rather, more important to experience the vulnerability of daily life. It is necessary to enter into and live within the ambiguity and risk the attrition of human existence. In a way, it is even more simple that than: it is just essential to become and to be poor.

I do not say this in a moral sense, but exactly the contrary; I do say it in a theological sense and, therefore, in the most concrete and most practical sense (for unlike philosophic morality, theology deals with the care of God for all human beings in the common life of the world as it actually is now, while morality deals with some ideal life out of this world). As a practical matter, then, it is essential to share life just as it is in a place like Harlem. It is the only way there is to honor the Incarnation. In some other situations, I suppose that it might be possible for a lawyer simply to be a technician, but cases in Harlem almost invariably require face-to-face encounter with a client. For that communication, it is important to have known clients as persons before the case arose, to have seen or met or talked with them around the neighborhood, to have accepted them and to have been accepted by them, to have lived in the same place and similar circumstances as their own, and to expect continued relationships after the particular case, as such, is closed.

To Join the Club?

THE meeting had been called to consider whether something might be done to expose and oppose police brutality in Harlem. There had been a noticeable increase in the number of incidents reported that summer, and the people of the community were provoked, angry, and restive.

About thirty people had been asked to the meeting. Some were clergymen, others journalists, a few were businessmen, two were in politics, some represented civil rights organizations, and some were attorneys. All, as it happened, were Negroes, except for myself.

I was late arriving at the meeting, which was held in central Harlem, having been in court all morning on a case, by coincidence, involving police abuse.

Most of those present were friends — by now we had worked together in a variety of matters and we knew and trusted each other. There were two persons present whom I had not yet met.

The chairman of the meeting interrupted the discussion when I came in and introduced me to the two to whom I was a stranger.

"This is Bill Stringfellow," she said. "He's a lawyer over in East Harlem. I've known him for five years"

"It's safe for us to talk in front of him."

My People Is the Enemy, 1964, pp. 64–66

In coming to Harlem, I was as much concerned about the politics in such a community and about the ministry of the church in such a neighborhood as in living and working as a lawyer there.

It was not very long before I was contacted by an emissary from the district political club, which at that time was affiliated with Tammany Hall. It was dominated by an Italian leadership and had very few Negroes or Puerto Ricans as members. The man who made the contact told me that the club was aware I had moved into the neighborhood and had some sort of connection with the East Harlem Protestant Parish. (The parish had a reputation for active involvement in politics. One of its clergy had once run against the Tammany district leader, so the parish was not regarded very favorably by the political leadership of the club.) But, the man explained, they knew that I was a lawyer — not one of those ministers — and that, therefore, I might be more practical than the clergy and might wish to join the Tammany club instead of "making trouble" in the neighborhood, as some of the clergy had, he felt, been doing. He contended that everyone wanted to improve the neighborhood but that the only way this could be done was by supporting the incumbent leader. After all, this was *his* district and if anything was to be done to change its conditions, the leader was the only one who could do it. "Nobody at city hall will listen to anyone else from up here," he assured me. "Nobody else can get anything done."

He underscored his invitation to join the club as the "realistic" way to "get something done" for the neighborhood, with promise of some patronage. He claimed that if I joined the club, and if I sought to keep the clergy from interfering with things "they didn't know anything about," I would be put on the club's list of lawyers and thereby be in line for appointment as counsel by the courts in certain cases. For example, the state provides counsel fees in capital cases for indigent defendants, and it is a common practice for four or five lawyers to be appointed as defense counsel and then divide the fee among themselves. Whether the defendant receives a competent defense in instances where these appointments are a distribution of patronage is, perhaps, open to question.

I told him that I appreciated the invitation but was obliged to decline it. And I went on to explain that politically speaking I was not in league with the clergy nor responsible for any of their views or past actions, though I would agree with some of them and not with others. Besides, I suggested somewhat sarcastically that if he wanted to buy me with the offer of patronage, he would have to begin by making a considerably better offer than the one he had made.

He seemed to get the message. He knew, much better than I, that if I had joined the club under the proposed conditions, I would have had no voice in the policy-making of the club. There was only one man — the district leader — who had such a voice. Membership in the club meant, at most, access to the club premises to play cards and drink whiskey and run errands for the boss and, maybe, after doing this long enough to be trusted, there might be a court appointment on a case worth a few hundred dollars. He seemed to understand that if I had any interest in patronage, it would involve much more than he was authorized to discuss.

After this encounter, the Tammany emissary and I became friends — of a sort; at least there was a candidness in our relationship that I valued, and he knew that if I told him something, it was the truth. In turn, I always found him as good as his word. The fact that we disagreed radically about the political remedies appropriate to the district did not mean that we had to be enemies or to deceive each other on the occasions when we had to deal with each other.

Meeting Anthony

THE first time I saw Anthony Towne was at a party that I had been invited to in New York City in honor of W. A. Visser t' Hooft, then General Secretary of the World Council of Churches. Anthony had been engaged as bartender for the occasion — it was a crowded and rather elaborate event — by the host, a mutual friend, Marvin Halverson, the originator of the Foundation for the Arts, Religion and Culture. This happened at a period in my life when I still used alcohol and, indeed, drank enthusiastically; hence, Anthony and I became well acquainted during that evening.

One morning, a few months later, Anthony came to my law office, reporting that he was at that very hour being evicted from his apartment in Greenwich Village. I spent most of the remainder of the day on the matter, but it was by then simply too late to frustrate or forestall the eviction. We did recover Anthony's possessions — books, mostly, and an old typewriter — from the clutches of the sheriff, and in the late afternoon, I suggested to Anthony that he stay at my place pending opportunity to consider the situation. And so our acquaintance became friendship, then, eventually, community.

Sometime before Anthony and I had met, Anthony had suffered a terrifying episode — he referred to it as his "psychotic break" —

which, for awhile, had rendered him profoundly apprehensive, morbid, hysterical, dysfunctional. I never probed him about it, but he would mention it now and then, and, occasionally, the experience, or aspects of it, would reprise. . . . Although I think I did not pry, I gathered, from this and that, that the original episode had much to do with Anthony's response to the death of his father. That had happened while Anthony was young. It was an automobile accident that had killed his father, but Anthony regarded the accident as his father's suicide, and he somehow construed his mother to be morally responsible for his father's death. Anthony's exegesis of his father's death in turn spawned obvious and redundant tensions in the relationship between himself and his mother, although, on his part, those tensions were often repressed, and, usually, she seemed oblivious to the complexity and delicacy of the issues between them.

Parenthetically, I found the situation of Anthony and his parents somewhat bewildering, I suppose because my own relationship with my parents has not been similarly agitated. On the contrary, it has been, for as long as I can recall, straightforward and simple. For one thing, my father and my mother have accorded me autonomy and privacy, even in my days of childhood and adolescence. For another, I love my parents, and I have never had reason to be skeptical about their love for me; but, what is perhaps more relevant, I *like* my parents as people. Therefore (as with other peers of mine who complained of traumatic parental relationships) I encountered and observed Anthony's problems in this realm with a certain dismay and a little surprise, given the benefit of my own parents.

Anthony had been through psychoanalysis and a period of private therapy in the aftermath of his horrors experience, and, by the time that he and I had met, he was still involved in a weekly group therapy session. He was obviously fond of the group and gave high priority to his participation and relationships in it. . . . Anthony considered himself alcoholic, and his use of alcohol and its effect upon him was very ambiguous. On the one hand, his perception of reality was so sharp and so detailed, so directly felt, so aware, so remarkably intelligent that it was as much a burden as it was a gift; alcohol diminished or subdued that perception, made it seem more ordinary or more bearable, and furnished him some kind of respite from his own brilliance. On the other hand, at times, drinking apparently prompted or induced the reprise of the dread that he had known and suffered. In that experience — insofar as anyone else can speak of it — Anthony was, I think, haunted by an overwhelming apprehension of nonexistence, by the kind of fear of the ultimacy of death that is so momentous that the dread of death paradoxically becomes a dread of living, an immobilizing dread wherein there is no one, there is nothing to identify and affirm who one is or even *that* one is.

The transcendence of the power and presence of death in just such dimensions of dread as these is what the death in Christ, as it has been previously discussed, concerns. The secret of the relationship of Anthony and myself was not that we were able to identify and affirm each other in defiance of dread, but that we were each enabled to apprehend and mediate to the other the truth that the Word of God alone has the ability to identify and affirm either of us as persons or to offer the same to any other human being.

The peril in the experience of dread is in succumbing to the idolatry of death in one's own being. The extent to which this society is death-ridden and the culture motivated by the worship of death, as has been described, constitutes relentless pressure on everyone to surrender and to conform to that idolatry. Those who do conform die promptly; they die morally as human beings. Anthony did not succumb; he did not conform.

Sojourn with the Circus

ONE of the bonds between Anthony and me was that we shared, each in his own style, a sense of absurdity — an instinct for paradox — a conviction that truth is never bland but lurks in contradiction — a persuasion that a Hebraic or biblical mentality is more fully and maturely human than the logic of the Greek mind. The gospel version of the event of Jesus Christ (including those propagated under churchy auspices) verifies the significance of this incongruous tension between the Word of God and the common existence of the world (read 2 Corinthians 11, 12). The assurance of faith, in biblical terms, is that we live in that awesome incongruity until it is reconciled *as* the Kingdom of God.

In other words, eschatology impinges incessantly upon ethics. A biblical person is one who lives within the dialectic of eschatology and ethics, realizing that God's judgment has as much to do with the humor of the Word as it does with wrath.

Anthony understood this, on his own authority, and that is why he abided my attraction to the circus. My most vivid memory, that night after the requiem, was of the year when Anthony and I spent most of the summer weeks traveling with the Clyde Beatty-Cole Bros. Circus through New England and part of New York state.

It was 1966, and there were already signals that trouble with my

Simplicity of Faith, 1982, pp. 86–88

health was impending. That may have had something to do with our decision to spend the summer the way we did. In any case, we outfitted a station wagon so that it could be used for sleeping and joined the circus company en route, booked in a new city each day, traveling late each night in the circus convoy to the next day's stand. As Anthony had foreseen, the experience did not satiate my fascination with the circus as a society but only whetted it.

It is only since putting aside childish things that it has come to my mind so forcefully — and so gladly — that the circus is among the few coherent images of the eschatological realm to which people still have ready access and that the circus thereby affords some elementary insights into the idea of society as a consummate event.

This principality, this art, this veritable liturgy, this common enterprise of multifarious creatures called the circus enacts a hope, in an immediate and historic sense, and simultaneously embodies an ecumenical foresight of radical and wondrous splendor, encompassing, as it does both empirically and symbolically, the scope and diversity of creation.

I suppose some — ecclesiastics or academics or technocrats or magistrates or potentates — may deem the association of the circus and the Kingdom scandalous or facetious or bizarre, and scoff quickly at the thought that the circus is relevant to the ethics of society. Meanwhile, some of the friends of the circus whom we met that summer may consider it curious that during intervals when Anthony and I have been their guests and, on occasion, confidants, that I have had theological second thoughts about them and about what the corporate existence of the circus tells and anticipates in an ultimate sense. To either I only respond that the connection seems to me to be at once suggested when one recalls that biblical people, like circus folk, live typically as sojourners, interrupting time, with few possessions, and in tents, in this world. The church would likely be more faithful if the church were similarly nomadic.

Move to the Island

I HAD moved to Block Island, Rhode Island, from New York City in the fall of 1967, together with the poet Anthony Towne, who had been coauthor with me of *The Bishop Pike Affair,* which was published about that same time, in the midst of the so-called heresy charges that had been leveled against Bishop Pike. Our common interests in theology and social ethics had made Anthony and me colleagues in work as well as friends, and our collaboration in thought and deed extended, as it still does, far beyond the *Pike* book. The congeniality of our thinking on most issues is astonishing (unless one credits the Holy Spirit); we can truly read each other's mind. Anthony tends to be more reticent, while I am more an activist, though his thinking is more radical, both theologically and practically, than my own. For some years, he and I had been vaguely searching for a location outside the city that could be used in any season for rest and reflection and writing. Our common household in New York had become a kind of salon, to which all sorts of people came, and were welcomed, but with such abundance and frequency that it had become difficult to keep up with emptying the ashtrays, much less concentrate enough to write. Thus, we sought some circumstances in which to establish, as it were, our own monastery. There were other considerations: some are political and are intimated later on; another was my health, which

Second Birthday, 1970, pp. 17–20

I had obstinately neglected so long as I had lived in the city and which, by 1967 — my eleventh year in New York — had gradually deteriorated to such an extent that I had received an emphatic medical admonition to get rest by establishing a different pace somewhere outside the city. We had discovered Block Island the year before, made several visits there, become enchanted with its moors and cliffs, been attracted by its solitude, and decided to immigrate there.

The move from New York City seemed in the circumstances prudent and necessary, but, in my consciousness at least, it carried no intent to desert the city. In this culture it is literally impossible to flee from the city's dominance anyway — as all those white suburbanites have discovered — and, in my belief, the city is the central theological symbol of society. That is not only the contemporary reality in America, it is the biblical insight as well. Biblically, the city is the scene of *both* doomsday and salvation. There is Babylon, but there is also Jerusalem. The city is the epitome of the Fall, yet the city is the sign of the Eschaton. These connotations of death and life associated with the city empirically and theologically mean that the city cannot be escaped and that the city must not be rejected by human beings, as it seems to be by the utopian hippies and their commune movement, for example, and least of all can it be repudiated by professed Christians. (Billy Graham, if he were more attentive to the Bible, might realize this and cease his facile preaching against the city as a realm of sin and give up his proclamation of a pastoral image of salvation generally identified with the hinterland of the American South or Midwest.) Coming to Block Island was not a romanticized change, and, in terms of commitment, it was no change at all. Practically, I maintained affiliation with the law firm that I had joined in founding, following the years of practicing alone in Harlem, and continued work on some cases, while at the same time making some lecture engagements and working on publishing commitments.

. . . That first winter on Block Island was arduous. No accurate and, as it turned out, no competent diagnosis of my ailment had been accomplished, despite resort to various doctors in the city, and none was to be had until a fortnight was spent at Roosevelt Hospital, in the spring of 1968, when it was established that I suffered from a radical impairment in my body's capability to absorb, digest, and utilize food. In the meantime, during the months of winter, there had been a sudden and accelerating loss of weight — nearly sixty pounds in seven weeks — accompanied by a gradual intensification of pain assaulting me intermittently at first, but then become incessant, unremitting, and, as it seemed to me, insatiable. I was dying of malnutrition.

Therapy and Theology

THROUGH the spring and summer of 1968, following my release from Roosevelt Hospital, I remained on Block Island pursuing the regime of rest and medicine that, it was hoped, would arrest the weight loss and alleviate the pain. Massive quantities of animal enzymes, taken with small portions of food every two or three hours, were tried to remedy the former; various drugs were prescribed from time to time for the latter. It was arranged that I would return to the city periodically to be examined and for follow-up tests at the hospital, as might be indicated, and, while on the Island, remain under the general care and surveillance of the doctor there.

I was loyal to the new way of life, and within a month of leaving Roosevelt there had been a perceptible, if ever so modest, improvement: I gained a pound. For a while, too, I enjoyed spasmodic relief from pain, at least just after taking a prescription for that purpose. These evident gains soon faded. By summer's end I weighed the proverbial ninety-nine pounds; a succession of increasingly potent pain antidotes proved helpful only briefly, as my tolerance for such material matured and as the severity and continuity of the pain grew. Much reluctance on my part to confess it would not mitigate the truth of that season: the therapy was failing.

To have rest was the hard aspect of the therapy, if only because

Second Birthday, 1970, pp. 35–42

of its novelty for me. For a dozen years, since being graduated from law school, the pace of my life had been hectic and crowded. Although the time I lived and practiced law in Harlem had been lonely — and thus exacting in a psychical sense — it had also been arduous enough physically and intellectually so that I was not self-conscious about that. Subsequently, when two colleagues from Harvard Law School, Frank Patton and William S. Ellis, joined with me in founding a law firm, which both inherited the Harlem practice and diversified with other cases, I undertook the keeping of regular and more conventional office hours. At about the same period, I began to write and publish and, in turn, receive many invitations for lecture engagements and preaching assignments. These responsibilities meant that after spending a day in court or at the firm, I would devote three or four hours at night to writing and then on weekends be on the road for speaking engagements. There were, at this same time, frequent journeys overseas, sometimes as a member of the Faith and Order Commission of the World Council of Churches, on other occasions for lecture tours, or, as with a trip to Vietnam in 1966 that converted me to radical opposition to the American war there, to observe, to listen, and, hopefully, to learn. The household that Anthony and I had established in Manhattan was a hospitable one, and he and I shared there in an unpretentious — and almost unintentional — pastoral ministry to an astonishing diversity and far-flung number of persons. Besides all that, we each dabbled in city politics, tenants' strikes, assorted demonstrations and protests, and the affairs of a congregation. Occasionally, through all of this activity, there would be episodes for me of devastating fatigue, and, then, spasms of pain, like the one, mentioned earlier, by which I was misfortuned to become acquainted with a dilettante physician and was briefly hospitalized.

On the whole, however, I thrived upon the tension in which I labored — or so it seems to me — though I did recognize, vaguely, an improvidence of such an existence. If I procrastinated in the face of lucid warnings within my own body of disease at work and failed, until entering Roosevelt, to locate competent medical care, I also sought no help, such as it might have been, from psychiatry, despite now and then considering the matter. In retrospect, I have a small regret that I did not explore this possibility. I did not do so, I suppose, because of an inherited Yankee attitude that begins with a general skepticism toward the field, on a practical level, and ends with a suspicion that resort to a psychiatrist can easily if not inevitably be an exercise of extravagant vanity. On the other hand, I was not inhibited from consuming much alcohol during these busy years in legal practice and on the lecture circuit and whatnot. Consistent with my denominational identity as an Episcopalian, I had, as an adult, always had an enthusiasm for drinking, but, as my days became more feverish, I knew that I was becoming unduly dependent upon alcohol. It was no longer a condiment of living but a substitute, though scarcely a sensible one, for rest and, sometimes, for food, and, as might be expected, an insulation from the incessancy of daily demands. And, as sporadic pain visited me, I sometimes used alcohol for a superficial and transient relief it seemed to bring. I stopped drinking completely in January of 1968. It was no New Year's resolution; it involved no exertion of will power, no positive thinking, no prayer — at least in any conventional connotation — no admonitions from doctors, no inspiration from friends. I just stopped because I had lost a taste for alcohol. It was, as far as I can discern, a physiological happening: my body would no longer tolerate the stuff.

Meanwhile, I had taken some initiative to alter the pace of things. I decided to take leave of daily practice, curtail public engagements, and spend a year or more reading and thinking and writing. I had had a notion for quite a while about a work in moral theology, specifically, so to speak, in *American* moral theology — seeking to relate the American experience of society and nationhood to the biblical saga and social witness. This is a pitifully neglected realm. There has been curiously little moral theology, which has had currency and impact in this country in the present century, that can be said to have indigenous American origination. Most moral theology that has been articulated in the American context has actually been composed out of European experience and transplanted here. Aside from fugitive materials, the singular exception in this situation has been the immensely influential and useful contributions of Reinhold Niebuhr in the era between the Great Depression and the end of the Second World War. Neither the moral theology imported, as it were, from Europe nor the witness of Niebuhr is vitiated by the fact, but it does remain an odd void that a moral theology related to the distinctive American experience since the detonation of the first atomic weapon or since America became a pervasive imperial presence in the world or since technology and race became uniquely juxtaposed in social crisis in America has not yet emerged. All things considered, it seemed to me the time to pursue that. I received a Guggenheim Fellowship for this sabbatical, altered my relationship with Ellis, String-fellow, and Patton from partner to counsel to the firm, and prepared to embark on the project, living on Block Island but planning one excursion to Eastern Europe and to Cambridge University, as well as some domestic travels along the way. I made a modest headway on this agenda, despite increasingly frequent interruptions of pain, until, in the spring of 1968, the illness had become virtually immobilizing and I entered upon the therapy determined by the diagnosis accomplished at Roosevelt Hospital.

I have not had an explicit conviction about where my interest about what I call an American moral theology might lead. Conceivably, the void I sense has not been filled because it cannot be. Perhaps the void is in itself *the* significant insight into the American national experience of the last quarter century, so far as moral theology is concerned. Whatever the case, this represents an issue to which I mean to return and a work I want, somehow, to finish. In fact I feel little frustration about it, since I have never abandoned or even postponed it in my mind and since the experience of my disease appears to me, ironically, relevant to the subject. It could hardly be otherwise for me because, insofar as I may be said to be a theologian, I am not a theological scholar (I have not the temperament for that) but an empirical theologian (which the scholar is also, if in a less obvious manner, whether it is admitted or not). Meager jokes had passed between Anthony and me during these months of sickness and convalescence as to whether the pain would affect my theology; obviously it has both in ways that I can discern and in ways of which I can never be completely aware. That is exactly as it should be. Or, to put it a bit differently, Christians are Hebrews in their mentality, not Greeks. Biblical theology, especially the moral theology of the Bible, is itself empirical, a testimony wrought in experience, not academic, in the sense of abstraction. There is nothing whatever in the experience in history of human beings or nations that is not essentially theological, and the discipline of academics is not to speculate or innovate from some (supposed) stance on the outside of common experience but to expound and enlighten empirical reality, relating inheritance, memory, and the happenings of the past to the contemporary scene, alert for portents of that which is to come in this world. In the biblical witness, the Incarnation is the illustrious instance in point: the event of God acting in history in Jesus Christ addresses the experience of human life contemporaneously. That is the case, according to St. Paul, *even* where and when human beings have never heard explicitly of Jesus Christ. There is no "once upon a time," much less hypothetical, connotation attaching to the Incarnation, and, thus, to affirm the Incarnation is not a matter of having a blessed memory, much less of earnest persuasion, but to suffer this action of God empirically, here and now.

The Ambiguity of Pain

THE therapy failed and I become possessed by pain.

There is an ambiguity in pain that is truly exquisite. It is no wonder that medical science is so ignorant about what pain is, beyond knowing what any victim of pain realizes without asking a doctor: pain involves a delicate joinder of the physiological and the psychosomatic and is *never* but one or the other of these. Nor, given the dignity of the mystery of pain, is it very surprising that so little has been uttered since Job himself, concerning the theology of pain. American religiosity (as distinguished from biblical faith or theology), meanwhile, remains so hapless and absurd that, generally, it denies the reality of pain or else treats pain as a punishment for immorality. It is such religious attitudes about pain that explain the profound and primitive indifference of institutional religion in America to human suffering occasioned by social injustice. Moreover, by the way, the association of these typical views of pain with the equally entrenched notion that acquisition or control of money or credit is an evidence of virtue is what has allowed the commercialization of medicine, of which previous complaint has been made. Obviously, to the religious, if pain is either an illusion or a punishment, and if money or its equivalent signifies moral rectitude, then one must be able to purchase the absence of or relief from pain, and those who cannot do so have only themselves to blame for their plight.

Second Birthday, 1970, pp. 45–54

Part of the ambiguity attending pain is attributable to ignorance and some of it to prejudice, but much of that ambiguity has to do with the sentimentalization of pain in the experience of a particular person. I found that so myself. To maintain lucidity in the midst of pain requires an effort at once enormous and resourceful. In pain, as much or more than physical health, sanity itself is always at issue. The issue is present, subtly, even where pain is minimal and transient; it is there blatantly where pain is ferocious and obstinate. In the latter circumstances, the temptation of delusion and, beyond that, the danger of hallucination have no ruth. Moreover, the ambiguity of pain, specifically as related to lucidity, is accentuated by time, so let it be here recognized that I am actually writing now about my memory of pain — not only the memory of pain in my mind, but the memory of pain in my body — as distinct from my pain. In doing so, there is an element of distortion between the experience and the memory, though I can do nothing about that, except acknowledge it.

I said that the ambiguity of pain is exquisite: pain is inexhaustibly ambiguous. It is, I learned, difficult to identify pain, unless by its apparent absence. In the early days of my disease when the pain was episodic, it seemed to me that I could distinguish what pain is, but whatever facility of discrimination I then, or before then, had, I lost as the illness deepened and the pain became relentless and, paradoxically, so familiar that I ceased to think of myself as in pain. I am not talking about bearing pain with a stiff upper lip, or any kind of stoicism, I am referring to a state of the person, body and mind, that becomes so vulnerable to pain that there remains no comprehension of what freedom from pain is. I remember that.

While en route to this extremity, I had sought respite in various diversions. The aim in such exercises is to find a distraction sufficient to, temporarily, displace the pain as a fascination. It is, I suppose, a form of delusive sublimation. But as my immunity to medical painkillers, as they are somewhat euphemistically called, grew stronger, I resorted to such devices. I persevered in trying to work — to finish the much postponed *Imposters of God* manuscript, to further the Guggenheim project, to deal with the mail. The output was arduous, the yield meager and indifferent. More helpful, for a while, was work involving (for me) great, but briefer, concentration combined with manual effort: I learned how to make bread. At dawn, on many mornings, I left a sleepless bed and did that. I hesitate to mention it here, though it was a prominent, sometimes the only, event of some of those days, apart from the pain, because there is an odd romanticism in this culture associated with homemade bread, notably among urbanite snobs, hippies, and advocates of liturgical renewal. Although I have some involvement with all three of these factions in society, I think there was nothing corny, nothing grandiose, and nothing specially symbolic about my bread. The fact is my body's assimilation of food had become so harmed by this juncture that I was hungry all the time, which furnished a simple incentive for baking bread that other chores within the capabilities I then retained did not have. Television, which I suspect was invented as a distraction, proved of little avail against pain and may well have aggravated it. I had not been habituated to watching the machine, aside from state funerals, Senate hearings, and the like, and, only half-facetiously, I thought that, when a set is on, it is actually television that is watching you. So on days and nights when, it seemed, I was consigned to do no more than linger in distress, I and it watched each other. . . .

Reading proved more effective in providing diverting intervals from the pain. My span of concentration became too brief to read a book, though more than adequate for the *Providence Journal. The New York Times,* on Sunday, was just too formidable. The two things to which I most often turned to read, for my purpose, were the Psalter and the Sears, Roebuck and Company catalog. I had not previously had occasion to do more than scan either, though I had frequently been in circumstances where each would be cited as authority. Now I found comfort in both. They are remarkably similar volumes. With their marvelous diversity, a man with a little diligence can shop through their pages virtually certain of locating something to suit a desire or need or other disposition of the moment. I recalled, as one might anticipate, the famed remark of Karl Barth about a Christian being a man who has the Bible in one hand and the day's newspaper in the other, simultaneously attentive to the Word and the world. The Psalms, with their terrible esteem for the godliness of God, and Sears, with its infinite attention to the creatureliness of human beings and its nice detail of American culture, make apt companions for the Christian as a common reader.

One after another, such comforts or distractions as I knew were neutralized by pain. The issue drawn was whether to numbly await the perfection of pain in death or whether, somehow, pain would be transcended. Yet that concealed another issue: the vanity that pain instills in its victims. It is the vanity implicated in pain, more than the hurt itself, that has to be transcended if a victim is to remain a human being, whether or not the pain eventuates as death.

When I speak of the vanity engendered by pain, I intend a larger meaning than the facility of pain to attract attention to those who suffer it and something distinguishable from sentiments of self-pity, which the afflicted may indulge. These are the more superficial vanities of pain. On the other hand, I do not particularly have in mind human beings in such poignant circumstances that aberrations of the vanity implicit in pain occur, as seems to be the situation in both sadism and masochism. What I do mean is that peculiar vanity in which justification (or the moral significance of a person's existence) is attributed to the visitation and endurance of pain, whether such an attribution is made by the victim or those who are nearby witnesses or by society at large.

As befits a monasterial style of life, I suppose, my experience of pain was seldom mentioned in conversation in the Block Island household, though, now and then, in excruciation, I would utter the name of Jesus, not as a common profanity, but as a curse upon the pain and, really, as a curse upon the power of death. Beyond that, it did not need to be talked about; it was a pervasive, totalitarian presence, a foreigner to life in our midst which could not be ignored and which words would not diminish, yet which, paradoxically, words might intensify.

The putative interdependence of pain and justification harks back, of course, to the barbaric Protestant idea that pain is punishment for immorality, a penalty to be paid for displeasing the Almighty, an inverse way of obtaining justification by works where bearing pain is substituted for doing good deeds. The pursuit of justification by *any* means — moralistic conduct, dogmatic conformity, charitable enterprise, daily work, or burnt offerings — is, in the biblical perspective, the essence of human vanity in its denial of God's freedom to affirm life without contingency, dependency, or equivocation. Such notions of justification refute God's capability of love, and to view pain as a means of justification — even for the most apparently reprehensible person — is an especially pathetic ridicule of God as well as a radical demeaning of the human vocation. It ends in futility — as all practice of justification by works does — in a bizarre futility in which the victim becomes an idolater of his own pain.

Pain, manifestly, is not, however, the ultimate idol but only a demigod representing death. The same is true of other varieties of works, but with pain, as contrasted with charities or rituals or pietism or whatnot, surrogation to the power of death is the more obvious since pain is literally a symptom of the advent of death. To endure pain is to suffer anticipation of death, in both mind and body. The experience of pain is a foretaste of the event of death. Pain is an ambassador of death. Pain is one of death's disguises, though not one of the more subtle ones. It is the surrogate, really, servant relationship evident between pain and death that causes me to write of pain so much in personified terms. Death, after all, is no abstract idea, nor merely a destination in time, nor just an occasional happening, nor only a reality for human beings, but, both biblically and empirically, death names a moral power claiming sovereignty over all people and all things in history. Apart from God, death is a *living* power greater — because death survives them all — than any other moral power in this world of whatever sort: human beings, nations, corporations, cultures, wealth, knowledge, fame or memory, language, the arts, race, religion. One speaks, therefore, appropriately, and most precisely, of the power of death militant in history after the same manner in which one refers to other moral powers or, indeed, after the manner in which one makes mention of God. And, then, since pain partakes of the reality of death, it is meet as well as accurate to think of pain personified: to regard pain as an acolyte of the power of death.

A Political Trial

A NOVEL and extraordinary energy, inexplicable in terms of my emaciation, sustained me in going to Baltimore, the situs of the trial of the "Catonsville Nine" accused by the state of conspiracy to obstruct the administration of the draft. The defendants, to notarize their opposition to the slaughter in Vietnam and their apprehension about the militarization of American society, had concocted a batch of napalm, using an Army training-manual recipe, which they used to destroy selective service files at a draft board office in Catonsville, Maryland. Two of the nine on trial were and are particular friends of mine — the Berrigan brothers, Philip, a Josephite priest, and Daniel, a Jesuit. A good many other citizens — lots of whom I knew from other causes and struggles — had assembled in Baltimore in visible and vocal support of the accused and of the protest that the defendants represented against American barbarism. At the courthouse and at a church where they assembled each evening during the trial, these citizens were, literally, surrounded by hundreds of federal agents and double agents and marshals and police turned out and deployed as troops, weapons at the ready. It was, superficially, a startling sight, reminiscent of a Nazi newsreel, but that was an impression that survived only until one remembered that the federal surveillance of citizens is now as routine as it is ubiquitous, that the FBI ignores the

Second Birthday, 1970, pp. 129–33

First Amendment practically as a matter of policy, and that it was nearly a decade ago that the transmutation of the police into a military organization began and that it is now virtually complete. That the Baltimore scene during the trial of the Catonsville Nine seemed a caricature of Nazism, say, of the vintage of 1936, intrigued the mind only until one focused on the fact that this was but one of several patently political prosecutions that the state had lately used for the purpose of intimidating dissenters. Because I have fully supported such protest ever since I became enlightened about the wickedness and stupidity of this war during the visit I made to Vietnam in early 1966, I take nothing away from the dignity and necessity of the antiwar protest, in this trial as well as otherwise, if I mention that other issues besides the war are involved, profoundly, in the Berrigan trial and similar political proceedings, notably including those against the Black Panthers. In fact, the survival of due process of law — which is, of course, the hallmark distinguishing a free society from totalitarianism — is at stake. How long can the public authorities — the police, the investigative and intelligence agencies, the public prosecutors, and, alas, sometimes, the judges — abuse, circumvent, or subvert due process before it is effectually destroyed both as an idea and as an institution? And so I was brought to Baltimore, brought there by my past, by the conjunction, there, of many issues and the congregation of many persons with which I had been engaged before: the protest against the war and the very survival in this society of dissent as such; the friendship of the Berrigan brothers, and my esteem for their Christianity, and my admiration for their guts; the assault instigated by the state against the only thing in which citizens have safety from the state — due process of law — and the pathetic struggle to save due process; the embodiment in so many of the others in Baltimore that day of other involvements now, somehow, summed up in the gathering at the trial.

In the evening I went, with Anthony, who had been there with Bishop Pike since the opening of the trial, and with Rafael Martinez, a friend of many years and in many battles in New York, to the church where everyone was to congregate. The attitude of the ecclesiastical authorities toward the defendants had been made emphatic, a day or two earlier, in a statement to the press of the archbishop of Baltimore, within whose jurisdiction the protest had been made, which was reported to say that he "washed his hands" of the clergy and others who had accomplished the witness. Hearing of this, I had tried to reassure the Berrigan brothers: "Cheer up," I told them, "maybe this shows that the archbishop has been reading the Bible."

The congregation — I suppose, technically, it was a paracongregation — which that night assembled, save for the numerous and ludicrously obvious government agents who had been assigned to infiltrate and spy upon the happening, in poignant contrast to the disclaimer of the chief priest, acclaimed the accused. I suspect the spies present thought the event political and very radical at that. Radical it was: one of the more radical liturgies in which I have ever participated. And political, too, but in the elementary eschatological sense that all biblically authentic liturgy is political, not in the corny ideological simplistics in which the FBI construes politics.

I was exhausted, but this scene was exhilarating. The pain was unspeakably severe and had not been appeased by any medicine, but, amidst this congregation, it was not debilitating. I could walk only with extreme effort, but I was not enfeebled. Dan Berrigan asked if I would speak. I said that I would just greet everyone. When I stood before them and the words came out, however, they were not a salutation. The words were a benediction:

> Remember, now, that the state has only one power it can use against human beings: death. The state can persecute you, prosecute you, imprison you, exile you, execute you. All of these mean the same thing. The state can consign you to death. The grace of Jesus Christ in this life is that death fails. There is nothing the state can do to you, or to me, which we need fear.

There was some silence. Then there was an ovation, which took me by surprise, until Anthony pointed out that it was the failure of death that the people applauded. Then, spontaneously, the congregation sang.

Decision as Vocational Event

IT IS the ubiquity of God's judgment — extending to every time and place — and the universality of God's judgment — reaching every person and every principality or power — and the secrecy of God's judgment — which embraces all creation — taken together with such knowledge as there is of the character of God's judgment — namely, that judgment is a facet of God's grace — that authorizes the emphasis of St. Paul on the extraordinary freedom of the Christian, in making decisions, from anxiety about how those decisions are judged by God. Paul redundantly boasts that human beings are not the judges of one another, that the state is not the judge, that the company of the church is not the judge, that he as an apostle is not the judge, that a person is, least of all, his or her own judge. And Paul considers the presumption to judge, on the part of institutions or persons, a moral dissipation. Genesis, incidentally, affirms the same truth. A nation that usurps God's office as judge vitiates its own authority as a nation. Human beings cannot play judge, even of themselves, without suffering profound corruption in their identities as human beings.

Not to be judge and not to judge, and not to be subjected to judgment by others, or principalities, describes, as Paul well knew, the freedom to decide this or that in grace — in fear and trembling — in the audacity that takes the place of anxiety over one's moral

Second Birthday, 1970, pp. 91–92, 94–98

justification. It is the maximal freedom that a human being can experience. It is, for human beings, the definitive freedom, showing both the most mature humanity and the proper limits of the institutional powers. And if there be complaint that such a remarkable freedom, when practiced, causes perpetual revolution in all things, then let the complaint stand as a fair designation of how the gospel sets forth the vocation to be human.

That is, of course, what is really at the heart of decision. Decision is a vocational event. . . .

Biblically, vocation does not have any connotation limited to work. Vocation pertains to the whole of life, including work, of course, if and when there is work, but embracing every other use of time, every other engagement of body or mind, every other circumstance in life. In the gospel, vocation does not mean being professionally religious, it has no special reference to the ecclesiastical occupations, it does not imply "full-time Christian service" (as some preachers still put it), it does not require extemporizing prayer into business and political situations — especially at breakfast time — it has nothing to do as such with philanthropy — tax deductible or otherwise; it is not about honesty, sobriety, thrift, loyalty, or similar homely virtues on the job, it does not concern positive attitudes and is alien to the success ethic. Moreover, in the gospel, vocation always bears an implication of immediacy — there is really no such thing as preparing to undertake one's vocation when one grows up or when one graduates or when one obtains a certain position or when one gets to a certain place. Vocation is always here and now, without anxiety where one might be tomorrow, what regard there is for tomorrow and tomorrow's issues are sufficiently anticipated, so far as vocation is concerned, in today's unconditional involvement in life as it is. Vocation has to do with recognizing life as a gift and honoring the gift in living. To that, the question of whether another day will be added to one's life, and, if that comes to pass, how the gift will be spent on the morrow, is a distraction or diversion from living of the gift today. Carried, as the Letter of James cautions, too far, a concern about how to live faithfully tomorrow causes infidelity in living today. Carried to its ultimate absurdity, the anxiety for tomorrow becomes a preoccupation with a fantasy afterlife, a notion without biblical support, albeit popularized in churches, at the cost of squandering or repudiating the immediate gift of life.

In the gospel, vocation means being a human being, now, and being neither more nor less that a human being, now. And, thus, is the vocation of other people illuminated and affirmed, and so also is the vocation of the institutional powers and the principalities of this world exposed and upheld. And, thus, each and every decision, whether it seems great or small, whether obviously or subtly a moral problem, becomes and is a vocational event, secreting, as it were, the very issue of existence.

My state of mind, when it became apparent that the therapy had failed and that the practical options open to me were limited and, in each case, both disagreeable and dangerous, was informed privately chiefly by the terms with which I had come to deal with the pain — that pain is not something extraordinary or abnormal but the same reality as work, the concrete experience of fallenness — and by my understanding of the vocational character of decision. It was a state of mind freed, in this way, from potential hang-ups of all sorts. That is to say, I knew that there was nothing traumatic, nothing heroic, nothing tragic, nothing stoic, nothing dramatic in my situation. In truth, mine was a commonplace experience, not only in relation to the circumstances of other human beings, but also in relation to my own history. I realized I had to make some decision, but it was as if I had already rehearsed that decision one million times whenever I had theretofore made any decision about anything. Moreover, I knew that it did not matter what my decision would be vocationally. The decision might well affect how long I survived, it certainly would affect the physiology of my survival, but neither of these matters altered the vocational issue, which is to live as a human being while one lives. Nor did survival, for whatever time and in whatever health, change the moral significance of my decision, since that pertains to God's own judgment, about which I could only confess ignorance, together with a confidence in God's mercy.

With this outlook, the decision was made, and quite matter-of-factly, without excitement, lucidly, unanxious about any future, almost casually. I would have surgery.

I felt like a human being. I felt free.

Thorns in the Flesh

THERE had been a return from the threshold of death, which had been called "spectacular," healing had begun; with patience, common sense, and medicine my recuperative prospects were excellent. Yet death is not merely a destination or state of being, which, for want of more suitable words, human beings describe as a place. It *is* that, all right, and I could readily picture the course of the illness and what had happened in surgery as a journey to the site of death. Death, however, as I have already intimated, is a moral reality in *this* place — in the world, a domineering principle in the common existence of human beings and principalities and all things. If I had not crossed death's threshold, I was still not absent from the presence of death, immune from the wiles of death, ignorant of the work of death, or indifferent to the power of death. If anything, being so spared from death has made me more acutely aware of the manifold forms of death and the more respectful of the moral ubiquity of death.

All of this was made very concrete in the aftermath of surgery, which has left me without the physiological capabilities of naturally furnishing enough enzymes to utilize food and of producing enough insulin to control the body's sugar intake. The necessary removal of diseased and damaged portions of the pancreas, which has both these enzyme and insulin functions, has made me permanently deficient in

---

Second Birthday, 1970, pp. 185–94

enzymes and a pseudodiabetic. I had been forewarned of these likely residual liabilities by the surgeon and suffered no surprise that my prognosis was, in these respects, conditional. Both the enzyme deficiency and the diabetes are subject to medical management and while both involve restrictions in diet and activity and personal regime, which a person could happily do without, neither is nor need be disabling in a drastic way. When the time arrived for me to assume responsibility for the daily supervision of my new condition, I had already come to regard it as more of a nuisance than a hindrance.

What did impress me much, rather than the techniques of consuming animal enzymes and injecting insulin in awkwardly located regions of the anatomy, was that these consequences of the operation, which are, in one sense, an advantageous exchange for death, are tangible evidences of the continued vitality of death in the context of my own life. Death may have been, in terms of the illness, foiled or cheated or detoured or put off, but the power of death had not abandoned me. What particularly evoked attention, in adjusting to the postoperative realities, is the prominence of time, in relation to death — a matter, it will be recalled with which I had struggled during the illness and about which there had been some insight on the day previous to surgery. Such is the juxtaposition of time and death in the kind of medical control that is prescribed for a person in my health limitations, that neglect or other inability to follow routine in timely fashion could be fatal. Not only is sudden death a potentiality, but sustained unpunctuality could be so debilitating that it eventuates in death. Beyond the risks of these relatively quick or slow deaths, time and death are related, in my circumstances, in another way, that is, morally. The peril of death is concealed in the issue of whether a person with such health necessities is *so* obedient to time that he or she becomes enslaved to it, allowing one's whole existence to be regimented. If such a person is not able to master the medical requisites and is, instead, totally regulated in life by them, then he or she becomes a chronic victim and morally dies. Then, the very procedures commendable for sustaining life become radically dehumanizing and the actual state of the person is the moral equivalent of death. This is a tyranny of time that, obviously, has close parallels in many jobs and occupations where workers become so intimidated by schedules and deadlines and temporal priorities that (ironically) they have no time to live humanly and become, as it is said, "as good as dead." My musing in the hospital, as I began to be acquainted with these issues involving time with death in various ways, was refreshed by the prospect that I would be living, and, when the time came, working on Block Island. There is little idolatry of time on the island, in fact, the prevailing spirit of the community is somewhat contemptuous of time, having more of a sense of history than of destiny, and the style of life there implicitly ridicules the ethics of mainland society that makes humans slaves of time. The island would be a propitious place for my recuperation. No doubt Giselle would discern the providential in the fact that this is where I would return.

Of the two frailties — the enzyme deficiency and the diabetes — the former is the more readily managed and far less erratic. Regulation of the diabetes, as some millions of other American diabetics appreciate and as millions more undetected diabetics need to know, is a delicate and elaborate matter, partly because there is still vast scientific ignorance about it, partly because there are so many variables to cope with, both for a particular diabetic and among diabetics as a class.

The eccentricities of diabetes and the foibles attending its treatment and management have occasioned the development of a cultus around the disease that has, I fear, rendered many diabetics vulnerable to exploitations, both economic and psychological. There is a constituency of diabetics in this country who are induced to regard their affliction in pseudoreligious terms, quite similar to the ethos one beholds in havens of fantasy and aberrant religious practice like the Masons or the Eastern Star. The publications of the American Diabetic Association, for a specific example, reek with such overtones. The obscurity of the ailment itself and the idiosyncrasies of the present therapy lend themselves easily to this cultism. Diabetes and its control involve an array of attributes and practices strikingly parallel to those usually found in organized religion or the secular imitations of religion familiar in fraternal orders. At the center of it is an extraordinary secret, to which only an elect are admitted. There are rites of initiation (an insulin injection), which must, thereafter, be fastidiously repeated (the daily insulin injections), preceded by a purification ceremony (the sterilization of the syringe and swabbing the injection site), together with dietary regulations (the computation of food elements and the preparation of special recipes), times of special obligation (the regularization of medication, meals, exercise, and rest). And these ablutions and other rituals are mandatory for the initiated, sanctioned by the threat of punishment in distress, pain, or even death (the perpetual risks of insulin shock or diabetic coma). There are even established congregations or lodges in this cult (the so-called lay chapters of the American Diabetic Association).

As a diabetic, I can only speak as a novice (to use the appropriate religious terminology). I am aware that similar cults exist with respect to other diseases, but that only fortifies my uneasiness with the diabetic cult. I suppose such machinations can be rationalized as uplifting the morale of diabetics or even as affording an elementary group therapy. I just say, here and for now, that it offends me as a human being to be addressed as if my diabetes is a mark of honor or a privilege or a source of special status. I think that is morbid, infantile, and essentially unhealthy, psychogenically and physiologically. Diabetics, or those with other diseases or disabilities in comparable circumstances, who are induced to become cultists are too vulnerable to commercial exploitation by the health industry — the medical profession, the pharmaceutical business, charities' promotions, the manufacturers and merchandisers of cultus products. The cult phenomenon is offensive because it leaves adherents *so* defenseless, such inviting prey, that in American society it would be utterly astounding if diabetics are not being importuned. And the necessary further inference is that con-scientious, impartial, non–commercial research and treatment is, at the least, retarded or deprived or denied priority because of the indulgence of the cult.

The diabetes and the enzyme incapacity were not the only thorns in the flesh in surgery's wake. While in the hospital and during convalescence on the island, there were other signs of the vigor and persistence of death. In a succession that seemed to me remarkable, a number of persons, some of them close associates, all of them men who had swayed my thinking and conduct, all with whom I felt specially identified, died. Karl Barth's death was among these. So was the death of Norman Thomas, whom I had first met more than twenty years ago and with whom I had occasional conversations, particularly about the ethics of social change. Thomas, it will be recalled, occupied his first and only pulpit at the Church of the Ascension in East Harlem, and that fact had been an encouragement to me when I worked, much later, in the same neighborhood. Brooks Quimby died within days of Barth and Thomas. A professor at Bates College, where I had been an undergraduate, he had a dogged passion for ascertaining the facts and a fierce integrity in expounding his convictions (with which I, mainly, disagreed); he was, easily, the most influential teacher of my experience. Then there was the bizarre accident in Bangkok that killed Thomas Merton. He had been glad about *My People Is the Enemy* and from that a communication between us had developed. Twice arrangements had been made to meet at the monastery in Kentucky where he lived and twice my illness had thwarted our intentions. I regretted this, as Merton did, although I do not honestly think that our communication was diminished just because we did not meet. A few weeks later, news reached Block Island that Ralph McGill was dead. We had met in Atlanta. I revered him, intuiting that he was some kind of patriarch. Hoping for an untroubled convalescence, I had agreed to go on Good Friday, 1969, to Atlanta to preach the traditional three-hour meditation on the last words from the cross at the congregation of which McGill was a communicant. I wished much to be able to do this, partly because the event was to be in Atlanta and that date would be the first anniversary of Dr. King's assassination, as well as a more ancient anniversary, and also because it would mean a conversation with Ralph McGill.

"All of my heroes are dying," I remarked to Anthony, ruefully. It was not so much any one of these deaths by itself, though each man was mourned for himself, but the association of these deaths in time, the gathering of the deaths of these men together, which troubled me and challenged me. I thought about this succession of deaths, now and again, in the months of recuperation. That they represented further tokens of death's power, as if any more were needed, was plain enough, but I was vaguely conscious of there being some other connection among those who had died and between them and myself. For a while I could not quite grasp it or articulate it, but I nevertheless knew it to be a vocational connection.

The matter at last took focus because of the death of another man whose life I affirmed in the same way as the others: James Pike. No doubt the interval between the day Pike was known to be lost in the desert and the discovery of his body caused me to concentrate upon the issue of that vocational connection. Then, too, the congregation at Saint Clement's Church in New York City asked if I would preach at their requiem for Bishop Pike, and the preparation of that homily proved to be edifying. What is connective in all of these deaths and my own life has nothing, as such, to do with imitating the work of any of these men or any efforts to continue their tasks, their ideas, their concerns, but that does have everything to do with vocation, with vocation as each of them exemplified vocation, with my vocation, with the vocation to which all are called, with the vocation of living as a human being. There is the ubiquity and tenacity of death, but there is, in the midst of that reality, the continuity and continuance of life. Curiously, but also appropriately, as Anthony mentioned after the service at Saint Clement's, the preparation and utterance of the homily commending James Pike was the first work that I had been enabled to do since the surgery about which I had vocational conviction. I had recuperated.

How My Mind Has Changed

. . . When I recollect the sixties, I think immediately of persons and events, *not* of abstract notions or convictions. The ideas I nurture and the views I assert are responses to human beings and happenings; my thoughts issue from involvement. As such, to compare my thinking now to what it has been at any other point yields only that apparent coherence that hindsight affords — after the ambiguities of making a decision and the stresses of action have receded — and is probably not very accurate. This means, simply, that I am not hung up on the ethic of consistency (consistency, conceived as a necessity or even as a value is a contrivance of the Greek mentality, as it were, to escape confronting life as it is in this world). How my mind has changed in ten years is, thus, something of which I am not self-conscious and am more or less incompetent to say, though, at the same time, I feel assured that the way my mind works has not changed. It is the latter that is the more significant, as I see it, rather than either consistency or change in belief or opinion.

To put it somewhat differently and more succinctly, what I think is autobiographical. I do not wish to imply by this that my thinking is unusually introspective: I *mean* autobiographical — though if an Anglo-Catholic would prefer the name incarnational, instead, I would not fuss

---

"Harlem, Rebellion, and Resurrection," *Christian Century,* December 11, 1970, pp. 1345–48

about the substitution. What I think is authorized by common life and implicates my whole experience, momentarily and immediately, rationally, physiologically, intellectually, psychically, morally, intuitively — in a word, existentially. Who I am is what I think (not the other way around).

This style of thought, which really represents a way of living in history, has been abundantly evident during the past decade in what I have written, particularly so in *My People Is the Enemy* (which I began to write in 1962 and which was first published in 1964) and in *A Second Birthday* (which I wrote late in 1969 and which was published a few weeks ago). As books these are companions; both are autobiographical in the sense I am using that term; both are polemical in that ideas and arguments depend upon the communication of actual experiences; together they document what has occupied my attention and other energies during this period; together they tell, more fully than is appropriate to this article, the extent to which my mind has changed. Without being redundant of these books, I would sum up my experience of the sixties this way.

The decade locates me, at its outset, deeply in the midst of work as a white lawyer in Harlem, but it closes in fragile survival of prolonged, obstinate, desperate illness. It begins in social crisis; it ends in personal crisis. For me, these are equally profound *because* the aggression of death is the moral reality pervasive in both and, moreover, the grace to confront and transcend death is the same in each crisis. Indeed, I do not think the two episodes, which roughly mark personally the boundaries of the last decade, are essentially distinguishable. I doubt, in other words, that I could have had the capability to lately survive radical disease, unremitting pain, and the shadow of death had I not spent those earlier years in the Harlem ghetto, discerned there something of the moral power of death, and learned, from neighbors, clients, and Harlem inhabitants at large, something of the triumph of life that human beings can enter and celebrate despite death's ubiquity and vitality. Harlem is the scene in which I first comprehended the veracity of the resurrection — and that prepared me, more than any other single thing, for devastating illness and ruthless pain. Had I known only what I had heard about the resurrection in Sunday school or from pulpits or from within the American white Anglo-Saxon Protestant ethos, I believe that I would have surely died — most likely toward the end of 1968.

Do not read into these remarks a rejection on my part of the institutional church as such. Read only that the Holy Spirit is alive and militant and, in America, dwells in Harlem or wherever else human beings so esteem life as a gift that they become insistent upon living as human beings in society (this is the quality sometimes called "soul" — as in soul music or soul food or soul brother) instead of the way most Americans seem wont to exist as dehumanized automatons dominated by unaccountable and seemingly uncontrollable institutional powers, or as malleable victims of an environment gravely, perhaps fatally, damaged by the jealous abuses of science, war, technology, and mercantilism, or as hapless pawns cowered by official rhetoric and deception and conformed by intimidations to privacy and liberty, or, otherwise, as slaves consigned to pathetic idolatry of death elevated and enshrined as social purpose for the nation. What Harlem began to suffer nearly fifty years ago, when Harlem was made a racial — and political and educational and economic — ghetto, excluded from but exploited by the rest of society, portended a reign of death, with its attendant waste and repression, decadence and chaos, in store for the whole of America and, now, coming to pass. What neither white people nor racist institutions have been capable of comprehending, from the time when Harlem and similar black regions were separated (and, really, from the era of chattel slavery), is that black ghettoization begets white ghettoization and that such a radical polarization of society does not tolerate freedom for anyone, but requires totalitarianism of one form and degree or another. As Harlem endured the brunt of this brutalizing process long before most of the rest of America, so, too, the revolt of human beings against such an order has origins in Harlem. Now hear the previous paragraph again: *resurrection is verified where rebellion against the demonic thrives. . . .*

I am not being romantic in using Harlem as symbol, particularly when I refer to Harlem in rebellion signifying the resurrection. I do not ignore or gainsay the ambiguity of the witness to the resurrection in revolution. I am, however, affirming that in the black ghetto there is a resistance to death as social purpose, a perseverance in living as human beings, a transcendence of the demonic which is at least *an* image of resurrection which exposes and challenges the reign of death in this society and which, thus, benefits all human beings.

The ambiguity, as I see it, enters where violence against persons becomes the recourse of rebellion. Where the ethics of change practices violence and, thereby, imitates the moral power upon which the enemy of human beings solely relies, then revolution — no matter how idealistic, how necessary, how seemingly glorious — is essentially bereft of hope even if it empirically prevails.

I am not an ideological pacifist, or, for that matter, an ideological person of any species, but, as with the Berrigans, I am persuaded as a Christian that resort to violence to topple the idol of death in the state and in society invariably results in idolatry of death in some refurbished form. This is, in truth, the central, contemporary, theological issue. It is the point at which ethics and eschatology meet, for if the practice of violence, even in the name of revolution, is hopeless, the practice of non-violence, even where it seems unavailing, represents a most extraordinary hope.

In the last conversation I had with Bishop James Pike, a previous contributor to this series, reference was made to the same matters of which I have here written. I had only shortly before been removed from surgery, which had lasted eleven hours, and I was not an especially lively conversant. The bishop had just anointed me, in the ancient rite of unction, and undertook the main part of our discourse. After listening for awhile, I said to him: "My illness is a preparation for the concentration camp."

The bishop understood, I am sure, that I meant this to be a cheerful comment.

Talking Theology with the FBI

(On August 10, 1970, Daniel Berrigan was arrested at Bill and Anthony's Block Island home. Berrigan had been underground for several
months, speaking and writing, having refused to submit to the authorities for sentencing for the Catonsville action.)*

I have mentioned earlier that I became persuaded to write
[*Conscience and Obedience*] while engaged in writing *An Ethic for
Christians and Other Aliens in a Strange Land.* That was no conclusion
abstractly reached. It was mainly occasioned by the actual political
situation in which *An Ethic* was written. On the very day that Daniel
Berrigan, S.J., then a political fugitive because of his opposition to
the war in Southeast Asia and his resistance to the war regime, was
seized at the home of Anthony Towne and myself on Block Island
by the federal police, I was typing the manuscript of that book.
Subsequent to Berrigan's capture, Towne and I were subjected to
harassment, official defamation, and surveillance by the authorities,
including a remarkable incident in which a government agent, once
again intruding upon my work on *An Ethic,* sought to interrogate me
about theology and politics. He began the interview this way: "Dr.
Stringfellow, you're a theologian." (I thought his introit faintly sarcas-

---

* See "An Authority over Death," pp. 335-41.

From the Preface to *Conscience and Obedience,* 1977, pp. 15–16

tic.) "Doesn't the Bible say you must obey the Emperor?" His query startled me, I admit, not so much for its thrust as for the evidence it gave of how minutely the ruling powers scrutinize citizens. I could not concede the simplistic premise about the Bible that his question assumed, and I rebuked him about this, taking perhaps forty-five minutes to do so. During the discourse, he wilted visibly, and, when I paused momentarily, he abruptly excused himself and departed. This was some disappointment to me, for I had only just begun to respond to the multifarious implications of the issue he had raised. The episode contributed to my conviction to write this book.

A Statement by the Accused[*]

A STATEMENT BY ANTHONY TOWNE AND WILLIAM STRINGFELLOW OF BLOCK ISLAND, R.D., CONCERNING INDICTMENT NUMBER 7709 IN THE UNITED STATES DISTRICT COURT FOR RHODE ISLAND.

Grave charges have been made against us by the public authorities and we have pleaded innocent to those charges because we *are* innocent. In due course, a jury of our fellow citizens will have an opportunity to uphold our innocence and we await their verdict with cheerful expectations.

Daniel Berrigan is our friend. We rejoice in that fact and strive to be worthy of it. Our hospitality to Daniel Berrigan is no crime. At a certain time and in a certain place we did "relieve, receive, comfort, and assist" him and we did "offer and give sustenance and lodging" to him. We did not "harbor" or "conceal" him. We did not "hinder" the authorities.

Father Berrigan has and had no need to be concealed. By his

---

[*] Stringfellow and Towne were indicted by federal authorities on December 17, 1970, for "harboring a fugitive." They were subsequently acquitted.

From *Suspect Tenderness,* 1971, pp. 120–22

own extraordinary vocation, and by the grace of God, he has become one of the conspicuous Christians of these wretched times. We have done what we could do to affirm him in this regard. We categorically deny that we have done anything to conceal him.

We are not disposed to hide what light there is under a bushel.

Our indictment has not happened in a void. We cannot ignore the scene in which such a remarkable event takes place: the manifold and multiplying violence of this society, the alienation between races and generations, the moral fatigue of Americans, the debilitating atmosphere in which citizens become so suspicious and fearful of their own government that they suppose silence is the only safety and conformity the only way to survive.

Because we are innocent, we believe that we would not have been indicted but for the pervasiveness of the spirit of repression that has lately overtaken the nation.

In that respect, we consider that whatever happens to us will, in truth, be happening to all Americans.

And so, to our fellow citizens, we say:

The violence must end.

All violence must stop.

The vainglorious war in Asia must cease now, but, more than that, the war enterprise must be dismantled, and the military predominance in our society must be reversed.

And the violence of political terrorists must end now. Arson, kidnapping, bombing in fact sabotage the social change the nation so pathetically needs, and such tactics are just as wrong and just as futile as the violence of war and racism and repression.

The psychological violence, sometimes officially condoned, by which citizens are accused and impugned without opportunity for appropriate reply and are otherwise harassed, spied upon, frightened, or intimidated must be stopped now.

These are all works of death. Only when our country is free of them will it be a society in which persons can rejoice as human beings.

We make this statement as our Christmas greeting — especially to Daniel and Philip Berrigan, to all prisoners of conscience, and to all Americans who wish to be free.

Anthony's Death

ANTHONY'S death was a shock — a momentous shock — to me, but at the same time, in a curious way, it was no surprise.

It happened in a single day. On Monday, the 28th of January, 1980, he suddenly became desperately ill, was taken by the Block Island rescue squad to the nearest mainland hospital, in Westerly, Rhode Island, lingered for some hours, and died. The only forewarning of his death, if it be that, had come a few days earlier, on Wednesday of the previous week, when Anthony complained at breakfast that he felt tired and supposed he might have the flu. He decided to return to bed to rest. He opposed calling the town physician: he had little confidence in the medical profession anyway, regarding most doctors as parasitical. His attitude was, in part, influenced by my experiences in illness, but only partly so. There had been some other episodes, an earlier experience of his own, that he never fully related to me, which had originated his suspicious conviction. So he remained in bed for a few days nursing himself — he drank lots of juices and took a few aspirins, snoozed, and read. He had a slight fever, fatigue, a diminished appetite, but there seemed to be no cause for alarm. He assumed as I did, that he had influenza. It was epidemic in the region then, as it commonly is in January in New England.

I had for a long time been booked to go to London, Ontario,

Simplicity of Faith, 1982, pp. 25–33

to give some lectures at the University of Western Ontario and at certain of the neighboring seminaries during the week beginning January 27. On that morning Anthony arose and had a normal breakfast at table with me. His temperature had virtually returned to normal. His morale seemed good and he said he felt much improved and considered that the "flu" would pass in another day or two. I raised the question of deferring the Canadian trip, but he was insistent that I undertake it, as scheduled. I accepted his judgment on the matter but asked a neighbor to visit the house each day during my absence to see that Anthony was all right and to care for his meals and other needs. The neighbor, Nancy Greenaway, came over on that Sunday afternoon and discussed these arrangements with both Anthony and me. Later that day I departed for Ontario.

My trip to London was unremarkable — in fact, it was boring. As soon as possible after my arrival, I retired. I slept very fitfully, a rare circumstance for me, but something I attributed to the adjustments of travel. I rose at sunrise, as I do every day, prayed, worked some on the lectures to be given, injected my flank with insulin, dressed, and took a walk, found a newspaper, had breakfast, and waited for the rest of the world to wake up. Around nine o'clock I telephoned Block Island. Nancy answered the call and told me that everything at *Eschaton* (the name of our household) seemed fine and that Anthony was still sleeping. I said that I would phone again later in the day. Some minutes before I was supposed to deliver the first of the lectures, at a luncheon for faculty and chaplains at the university, I received an urgent message to telephone the island. This time Mary Donnelly, the resident nurse on the island, told me that Anthony had very suddenly become "disoriented," that she had been summoned and had found indications that he was bleeding internally, so the rescue squad had been called to take Anthony to Westerly Hospital. Mary considered that Anthony's condition was extremely grave and advised me to return quickly. . . .

My recollection of the trip to the hospital is a blur of surrealistic sights and impressions in which I cannot sharply distinguish between what was happening in my mind — flooded, as it was now, by the recall of everything that Anthony and I had ever shared in our common life — and what was otherwise happening as I went through the routines of travel — changing tickets, submitting to airport "security" screenings, being processed through customs, hustling to make connections between planes. I have traveled enough to become conditioned to endure such procedures numbly, though I resent them as indignities, and that experience sustained me, in a practical way, on this somber journey.

I managed to make calls to the hospital three times while en route and learned that Anthony was in intensive care. Each report of his condition was more ominous than the one before. I tried, also, to reach Anthony's mother, Margaret Towne, at her home in Haverhill, Massachusetts, but none of my phone calls were completed to her. Between planes in Toronto I bought some candy and some orange juice in order deliberately to increase my blood-sugar count and thereby spare myself an insulin shock occasioned by the stress of the trip. Meanwhile, most of the time, my attention was elsewhere, preoccupied in the recall of our friendship. At times, I used the *Book of Common Prayer* to ratify my endeavor in Anthony's behalf.

The air taxi from the island met the flight in Providence and took me to Westerly, where a cab was waiting to drive me to the hospital. I arrived at the intensive care unit shortly after ten o'clock. Somehow word had reached Anthony's mother and she had driven to the hospital and had reached Anthony's bedside only minutes before my own arrival. Nancy Greenaway was there — she, thoughtfully, provided me with some orange juice — and Father David Joslin, the rector of Christ Church, Westerly, who also served the congregation of St. Ann's mission on Block Island, to which Anthony and I had been connected. The doctor on duty told me there was no hope that Anthony would survive.

I spent some time alone with Anthony. His body had been fitted with an array of medical contraptions. He would not have wanted that, had he the choice. I remembered his vigil when I had been in similar distress and how Bishop Pike had joined him there and unction had been given to me. I touched Anthony's brow, making the sign of the cross. I let my tears anoint him. His eyes saw me and in a faint sound he greeted me. Then he sighed, exhausted.

Bruce Gillie, who is my physician for the treatment of my diabetes, came in. He, principally, had been caring for Anthony all day, and he told me what had happened since Anthony had been admitted to the hospital that morning. The internal bleeding had not been controlled, and the cause of it had not been determined. There had been a steady deterioration, punctuated by the failure of one body system after another. I asked about the contraptions, realizing that Anthony would dislike them, and about any risk that he would linger indefinitely. Anthony's conviction, like my own, opposed any contrived, mechanistic, or artificial maintenance when a person had irretrievably lost the human faculties, so I made it very clear that I would not countenance any such tort against Anthony. When I joined the others in vigil, I mentioned the same issue to Margaret, and she indicated that she respected Anthony's position in the matter.

The precaution was not needed. I again visited the room where Anthony lay. His body stirred, but I do not suppose that he could see anymore. I took a hand of his in one of mine. The only thing I said to him was, "Thank you." I looked at the clock. It was 11:28 P.M.

I have mentioned that Anthony's death was an immense shock to me but that it was, in a sense, no surprise. It was traumatic in every obvious way that the sudden and apparently premature death of a loved one is. Anthony was only fifty-one years old; he was, from all appearances, robust; there had been no forewarning in illness, apart from that touch of "flu"; he had been, I think, at the prime of his gifts as poet; he had transcended the threat of alcoholism that, earlier, had harassed him; he remained an unusually shy and private person, but he no longer was tempted to be a recluse, and, indeed, he had in the past few years assumed a significant role in the Block Island community; he was a friend to many, a pastor to some; his life had specific meaning for an astonishing diversity of people, both on the island and in America (as the mainland is called by islanders).

The shock for me at his death, for reasons such as these, was accentuated by the fact that, between ourselves, Anthony and I had contemplated that I would be the first to die. That was the common-sense expectation ever since what Anthony sometimes referred to as my "famous illness," simply because the conditions of my living were so precarious, so complicated, so delicate. Both of us had been required by the peculiar circumstances of my health to consider the prospect of my death, and so, to that extent, each of us was prepared for it. As I say, it was taken for granted between us that I would likely die before Anthony did.

Be that as it may, I was aware that Anthony would prefer, if we did not die in a common disaster, to be the first to die, and, as the *Book of Common Prayer* puts it, "depart hence in the Lord."

That is one reason that his death, albeit traumatic, was not a surprise. Death was a familiar reference in our household, and there is little, I think, that death can do that would astonish either Anthony or myself. By death, in this context, I mean something more than death deemed a destination or something different from death in its vulgar funereal connotations; by death, here, I name the (paradoxically) *living,* moral reality of death present in this history, pervasive in every aspect of the existence of this world, insinuating ultimate significance, and, therefore, claiming imminent consequence for human life and for the life of the whole of creation.

Death, so construed and so apprehended, is a redundant biblical topic, and, for that reason, it was a frequent reference in the dialogue of the community of Anthony and me. We were constantly discussing death — in its multifarious manifestations, public and personal. The same subject recurs frequently in Anthony's poetry and prose, as it does in my writing about theology and ethics.

I do not imply that death was a morbid fascination for either of us but, rather, that both of us shared the belief that all of history — and all particular experience within history — consists of the drama and the dialectic of death and resurrection. Artistically authentic poetry exposes that drama; biblically authentic theology elucidates that dialectic. Well, we each took death very seriously as death deserves, and that was evident, in many different ways, in our common life. Anthony always read all the obituaries in the *New York Times* every day. He would brief me about these reports and, when it seemed appropriate or necessary, names would be mentioned and people remembered in the intercessions we customarily shared at mealtime.

Among many other episodes that had formed our convictions and attitudes toward death was, of course, my "famous illness," but that was hardly the only one. There was as well our long and close involvement with Bishop Pike eventuating, some time after his death, in the biography, *The Death and Life of Bishop Pike.* The juxtaposition in the title of *Death* and *Life* is very deliberate in order to indicate the manner in which the death of Pike was foreshadowed in his life, or, to put the same idea differently, to show that the story of his life was simultaneously the story of his dying; but then, furthermore, to affirm in the construction of the title that resurrection succeeds death. The issues that, in Anthony's life, occasioned the threat of alcoholism had also much to do with the militancy of death, and these became part of our shared effort to comprehend death and to avail ourselves of the Word of God, which has broken the reign of death in this world.

And, as would be expected, very prominent in our common experience was that of our being the "Block Island Two" — as Eugene McCarthy had styled us — indicted by the regime of Richard Nixon and John Mitchell and J. Edgar Hoover for harboring Daniel Berrigan, the fugitive priest. That was how we learned, firsthand, of the chill of death incarnated politically in the perversion of the legal process. We realized at the same time, in 1970 and 1971, that the target of that assault was our humanity — the very *esse* of our humanness: sanity and conscience — and we struggled hard not to succumb to paranoia while we were under ubiquitous surveillance and relentless harassment. We often laughed, later on, when the truth — or some of it — about the Nixon-Mitchell-Hoover cabal began to be exposed and it turned out that their schemes far, far exceeded our worst imaginations. Realistically, our endangerment was actually much greater than our fear, and what we called our paranoia was virtually complacency, so portentous was the effort mounted during the Nixon reign to neutralize the constitutional inheritance and subvert due process of law. Whatever our naivety, in the circumstances, at the time, we were able to recognize that the Nixon administration quite literally stank of death and embodied the idolatry of death as its operative morality.

In these and in innumerable other ways, Anthony and I had become well acquainted with the power of death in the life of this world. In that sense, we were different in our routine of life from those, say, who presuppose in their lifestyle that death is somehow remote from history or merely a destination or a biological condition, or from those who, incredibly, pretend that death does not exist. In such a context, Anthony's death came as no surprise to me.

The Freedom of the Dead

ANY season of grieving is riddled with temptations to render death an idol, and though these may sometimes be bizarre, they are as often subtle. The subject is tender and attended by an etiquette that discourages candor. Other people, intending to be considerate of the bereaved, or supposing that they are easing the burden of a survivor, readily, if unwittingly, abet delusion.

I have already alluded to the common temptation to follow the dead into death either by deliberately and directly committing suicide or, perhaps more often, by resigning from living and, instead of making the effort to continue to live, indulging some fantasy of the past or spending the remainder of one's time literally awaiting death. In such circumstances, the death that has happened works an estoppel of the life of one who survives.

Succumbing to such resignation is, I observe, accentuated significantly in situations of mandatory retirement at a specified age, regardless of health or capability for work, which have become routine in the American economy. The connotation of retirement institutionalized in this manner is that of waiting for death. The moral implication of such retirements is that a person is no longer useful or worthwhile in society and is, withal, officially discarded. So the outcast, having been pronounced as good as dead, waits to die to ratify his or her

Simplicity of Faith, 1982, pp. 117–22

status as dead, by filling the time with passive diversions, practicing boredom, and dwelling in apprehension of death. The only thing that makes such an existence bearable, for multitudes, is the companionship of a spouse, but then it seems a further indignity should the couple not die simultaneously.

There are more temptations in grief and many variations of each.

One of the most commonplace, I think, and one with which I had to struggle following Anthony's death, was the temptation to keep everything as it had apparently been, to freeze time by ritualizing the routine of household that had prevailed before his death. I know of neighbors on the island who have been bereaved who keep the clothing and similar personal items or the personal space of the dead just so, as if in readiness for an imminent return of the dead. It is a morbid fantasy and a pagan practice, and to oppose it and eschew any hint of it I promptly removed almost all of Anthony's personal possessions from the house, giving them away or discarding them.

I realized there was a special problem in the bedroom where Anthony had slept because Pollyanna, our eldest dog, a pensive creature, as she has always seemed to me, was long accustomed to waiting there each evening for Anthony to retire. Then, when he would come, he and the dog would play awhile. Anthony would talk at length to Pollyanna — usually highly literate comments (not baby talk like some people inflict upon their pets) — as if she understood it all. I have no reason to doubt that she did.

When Anthony was taken to the hospital by the rescue squad, Pollyanna went to that room and began her solitary vigil on his bed. And, when he did not return from the hospital, she, neither bashful nor stoic, would softly cry each day when the hour came when ordinarily Anthony would have been expected. Pollyanna would soon become utterly disconsolate if this went on indefinitely, and so Anthony's bed was taken away and the room's appearance changed. Pollyanna no longer pines, but she and I both know she is still waiting.

In short, it was important *promptly* to acknowledge the fact of Anthony's death — even for the dogs and the cat — not only verbally but, so to say, liturgically by enacting the acknowledgment, for example, by altering the appearance of the household.

The manger posed a similar question. The next time I went

there, after having found Anthony's obituary on his desk, was some days later. Someone, who had stopped by to offer me her condolences, asked to see Anthony's study. I showed the visitor the manger, but, as I did so, I was conscious that if I kept it as Anthony had left it, it would soon become some sort of shrine, sentimental, vulgar, and profane. The next day I began to dismantle the place. I had collected, over the years, a considerable quantity and variety of circus memorabilia, so I decided the manger would become the circus library.

Anthony and I had shared a reciprocity in the practical regimen of the household at *Eschaton*. To a remarkable extent the division of responsibility between us coincided with our various capabilities or interests, and the efforts of each of us generally complemented those of the other. We did not expend much energy organizing *Eschaton,* that was a casual and spontaneous matter. This meant, however, that when Anthony died there was a gap in the rhythm of the household. For a time, I was tempted to try to fill that gap myself, until I faced the truth that much of what Anthony had done I was physically or otherwise incapable of doing. Besides, to try to substitute for Anthony's absence or to gainsay, somehow, that there was a void concealed the familiar temptation to pretend that nothing had changed. In fact, there had been a momentous change, and facing that reality was essential to creating a new mode of living in the household compatible with my own capabilities and congenial to my own priorities. *Eschaton* had been, while Anthony and I had lived together there, for ourselves and, I think, for many others from the island and from the mainland, a blessed and hospitable place, but that did not make it sacrosanct.

As one might expect, there were friends who, upon Anthony's death, began to suggest that the answer for the practical problems of conducting and maintaining *Eschaton* as a household would be for me to locate some surrogate for Anthony, someone to assume the role that (it was erroneously presumed) he had played in my life and incidentally furnish me with greater freedom to write and mobility to travel for lectures and similar engagements on the mainland. Their logic usually featured admonitions about how precarious and unpredictable my health was and how, living alone, I risked another stroke or diabetic coma or other jeopardy and might not be able to summon help by my own effort. This argument typically posed the prospect of my being inadvertently discovered, after some time of helplessness and futility, dead. The same basic proposal was commended to me by different friends, in several versions, variously casting as surrogate a secretary, a paramour, a houseboy, a bride.

I am not the sort to foreclose options quickly, and if I have any virtue, I suppose it to be open-mindedness. I listened attentively to such suggestions and appreciated the concern that prompted them. Perhaps someday, somewhere, I will have a wife, a houseboy, a paramour, or even a secretary (or all of them at once), but in the midst of both grief and mourning I yearned, more than anything else, to be alone, to return to myself, so to speak, to conserve myself for awhile, and to be freed of entanglements. I needed no surrogate for Anthony. That was very clear to me. And if I sought such a surrogate in another person it would be an imposition on that person as well as trivialize the good community that Anthony and I shared.

In that connection, the whole idea of a surrogate for the dead is an instance of the morbidness that seeks, in death, to cling to the past, maintain things as they were, and indulge the pretense that the dead are not quite dead.

Furthermore, speaking of my eccentric health, what my health required above all else, in the months following Anthony's death, was simply acceptance of the truth of his death. If that happened, as I have said before, I had no skepticism that an apropos style of living by myself would gradually, spontaneously emerge. After that, there would be leisure to cope with the further vulnerability of my life to other human beings.

In the autumn of 1980 there was a curious interlude in my grieving while I was in New York City for a few days to consult a physician. During the experience the temptation to retreat into the past in pretense that Anthony was not dead and the idea of locating some surrogate for Anthony merged, as it were. I had remained in the city for a couple of days after seeing the doctor, intending to shop and go to the theater, and perhaps also attend a movie and get a haircut — these amenities being unavailable on the island. Instead, I found myself wandering about the city one afternoon. I realized that I was not wandering aimlessly but very purposefully. I was expecting to see someone. In truth, I was searching for Anthony. I had returned to where we had first seen each other. I was retracing steps I had originally walked seventeen years earlier. I kept expecting to sight

Anthony among the passersby, though I had no idea what I would do if I did see him. When I understood whom I was looking for, the search was exhausted, and this awful temptation fled from me. I have been free of it ever since.

These matters I have touched upon here are not casual or insignificant; they are similar, I think, to those afflicting anyone seriously bereaved. What is involved in such issues, in the end, is learning to respect the freedom of the dead to be dead, honoring the dead in their status as dead people, and refraining from harassment of the dead by refusing to mythologize the dead or enshrine them. What is at stake is recognition by those in grief of the right of the dead to be regarded mortally, which is to say, to be treated humanly in death.

Grief and Mourning

I UNDERSTAND grief to be the total experience of loss, anger, outrage, fear, regret, melancholy, abandonment, temptation, bereftness, helplessness suffered privately, within one's self, in response to the happening of death. By distinction and contrast, I comprehend mourning as the liturgies of recollection, memorial, affection, honor, gratitude, confession, empathy, intercession, meditation, anticipation for the life of the one who is dead. Empirically, in the reality of someone's death, and in the aftermath of it, grief and mourning are, of course, jumbled. It is, I think, part of the healing of mourning to sort out and identify the one from the other. In any case, of all those I have known and loved and grieved and mourned, Anthony's life was the closest to my own and the most complementary, so his death is my most intimate experience in grief and mourning. From that experience — so far — what I have to say is: grieving is about weeping and wailing and gnashing of teeth; mourning is about rejoicing — rejoicing in the Lord. From that standpoint, I confess I have found mourning Anthony an exquisite, bittersweet experience. I *enjoy* mourning Anthony.

Simplicity of Faith, 1982, p. 22

Stroke

A FEW days following the committal of Anthony's ashes to the ground and the observance of the "minor exorcism," I flew into Providence to have one of those laser treatments that had been so confidently recommended to me by assorted physicians as the requisite remedy to arrest diabetic damage to my eyes and to spare my vision. I had submitted to this procedure reluctantly, as I have mentioned, while Anthony had been quite skeptical about the whole idea. The sessions had, despite all qualms, commenced in March, and as they continued, they occasioned in me both staggering fatigue and mounting distress. My attitude, physiologically as well as mentally, toward the treatments was that of resistance — a profound, spontaneous resistance.

The treatments I had found to be so utterly exhausting that I did not attempt, after having one, to return to the island immediately but stayed with friends instead or checked into a hotel to rest until the next day and then attempt the journey. Even at that, when I arrived home I found that I needed further time to recuperate. The distress that was compounding my exhaustion was connected, in part, to the circumstance that I could discern no empirical beneficial result from the laser. Another patient one day remarked to me, "The laser is really a miracle, isn't it?" to which I had to reply, "I don't know, but I don't think so!" There was no basis, in my experience, for any other response. Further-

Simplicity of Faith, 1982, pp. 58–59, 61–66

more, the routine of the treatments seemed to me to be radically dehumanized. That is, I think, a recurrent issue in all medical technology; the laser is a penultimate medical technology. There is no art in it. The physician is reduced to a mere technician: the patient becomes, literally, an appendage of the machine. One is strapped onto the apparatus so that one's body is virtually immobilized and the eye is bombarded, very rapidly, hundreds of times, by brilliant, stunning light flashes, each one of which is a distinct and separate barrage. Perchance the laser *is* therapy — I do not know whether it is — but I am certain that it is torture.

The treatment in question took place on a Thursday afternoon. It left me enervated and depressed. I obtained a taxicab at the hospital and went to the Biltmore Plaza Hotel, checked in, went to my room, and immediately slept. The next day I flew back to the island about midday. Still exhausted, I went to bed as soon as I arrived home and slept until early Saturday morning. It was the outset of the weekend in which Memorial Day is now observed and upon which the Block Island School annually holds a fair. Although I felt depleted and vaguely apprehensive, I decided to do a little housekeeping and then, later in the morning, to visit the fair. After breakfast, I vacuumed the rugs in what Anthony and I had called "the common room." At one point I knelt to adjust the machine: I was overcome with a sudden, strange sensation. The left side of my body had numbed. I tried to get to my feet, but I had no balance, and I rolled back on my ass. I waited for some moments, as if to collect my breath, and then managed to rise enough to seat myself in a nearby chair. I stayed there for a long time. The dogs — usually rowdy — came from elsewhere in the house and joined me in the chair. They were gentle. I realized that I had had a stroke. . . .

As it happened, despite the holiday, I was able to go over to the mainland to see Dr. Gillie on Monday. By that time there was a slight but discernible improvement in my control of my left arm, but my equilibrium was still awry. The question that most concerned Gillie was whether any permanent or indefinite damage had happened, and he booked me into the Westerly Hospital for a few days for tests. As it happened my hospital roommate there was recuperating from a toe amputation, in consequence of diabetes. He was a retired circus roustabout, having spent many years with the Ringling Brothers and Barnum & Bailey Circus. Since we had both common disabilities and common interests, he and I made good roommates, though I still wonder whether there had been any premeditation in the arrangement. The tests indicated that I could expect a full recovery, but Dr. Gillie advocated that I submit to more sophisticated tests, which the Westerly Hospital was not equipped to do, at a hospital in New London. Although by this time I felt virtually recovered from the stroke, I agreed to do this.

Afar off I could hear my name. A voice was calling out my name. The voice was not familiar. I could barely hear it; I had to concentrate very hard to make out what the voice was saying. "Bill! Bill!" The strange voice called my name.

I could see myself quite plainly, my body, that is. My whole body was stretched out, lying, down there. I could see my whole body, but I was up above, as if separated from by body, hovering over the scene, looking down at my body, watching myself.

It was not a dream. It was not at all like a dream. Something else was happening to me.

I was dying.

I realized that I was dying — slipping, slipping, slowly slipping into death.

I felt terribly exhausted. Death seemed attractive, tempting. I could just drift away. Then I could rest.

From wherever I was, somehow detached from myself, I beheld myself. I was lucid; I could perceive what was happening. I could ponder it. I did. I considered my plight for a very long time.

I decided not to die.

I made an enormous effort.

It was an effort so awful, so strenuous, so complete that it could not have been exceeded.

I will not die!

No longer was I anywhere outside myself. I could not watch myself any more.

Then the voice got louder. Very loud. Very sharp like a slap on the cheek.

My eyes opened, I was in bed. People were huddled around the bed. There was a contraption beside the bed with a bottle hanging upside down. A tube connected it to my right arm.

"What's that?" I asked.

"Glucose," someone spoke up. I did not like that answer because I knew what it meant.

"We found you on the floor, unconscious, in a coma, a diabetic coma," a voice admitted. It was a voice that I had heard somewhere before. Then I remembered what had happened.

Twice, now, since Anthony had died so enigmatically, I had experienced close encounters with the threat of death, and in both instances the specific auspices had been the medical profession and the hospital system.

The stroke, as far as I could conclude, had been occasioned by the distress agitated by the laser bombardment of my eyes and the dehumanized, high-tech mode in which the procedure had been executed. The eye surgeon (eventually) conceded the plausibility of this conclusion.

The diabetic coma was attributable, quite unambiguously, to the stupidity (to mention nothing more than that) of the hospital regimen. . . . At the hospital in New London I had repeatedly warned doctors, nurses, dietitians, the orderlies who brought meals, and everyone else I could induce to listen, that I was in danger of insulin shock — and all that can follow from it — because my diet at the hospital had been drastically reduced from my routine intake and the hospital schedule of meals varied so significantly from my accustomed mealtimes. Furthermore, I was not being allowed nourishment as frequently as I needed. At the same time, my insulin dosage, though kept the same in type and quantity, was being administered as much as two hours later than usual. . . . Complain as I did, attention was nominal, and help was withheld even when the situation became urgent, save a half glass of orange juice someone brought me that was, as the imminent coma proved, too little and too late. Predictably, the response my protests and admonitions elicited throughout that day was, "It's not on your chart."

As I regained consciousness, and recalled what had happened, and saw the glucose device pumping sugar into me, I was provoked. Having ignored my warnings before I collapsed, they were now overdosing me as a surety against further insulin reactions. That seemed to me a vulgar precaution.

Well, I did not become a homicide victim in the hospital, and

I have heard from other patients — or victims — far more horrific reports than that of what happened to me, but I fear that this sort of thing is endemic in the American hospital system and that most of this is covered up. What outrages me about this literally atrocious situation are not issues of incompetence and negligence of hospital professionals so much as that the hospital system treats the patient as an object, not as a person. It was exactly the same thing that offended me categorically about the laser treatments and how they had been administered. So I reiterate: *dehumanized medicine cannot heal.*

I decided in the middle of the night, as I slowly recovered from the coma, that I had to leave this dangerous place as soon as was practicable. I awaited the results from the various tests and then did depart, wary and angry.

The post-stroke tests showed no evidence of brain damage, but they confirmed that the arteries in both of my legs were obstructed. This was no news to me — I had had no feeling in my legs of any kind for about two years; they were atrophied. Two doctors strenuously argued that I submit to bypass surgery. They told me it was the only hope I had of restoring circulation to these limbs. I listened to what they said. In the circumstances of my experience in this hospital, they had, of course, a major credibility problem with me. One of them, leaning over me, as if confiding a secret, whispered, "If you have this operation, it will rejuvenate your sex life."

I looked him straight in the face. "All this time I thought I was celibate," I replied sarcastically.

The Political Temptation

CULTURALLY, and especially politically, the nation has descended into a genuine dark age — wrought not by faulted leaders, as plentiful as they are and have been, but in the politicalization of technology since the end of the Second World War — comparable, I believe, to those dark ages that other societies have from time to time suffered. That means, to me, that this is a time to nurture *everything* that can be remembered or conserved or transmitted that signifies civility in humanity. I count literacy, aesthetics, worship, the arts, and politics among such signs, and that is why I have taken Block Island politics so seriously. The island is still a society — despite what has been happening in so many places on the mainland — where there is an elementary connection between the act of voting and the event of government. That is something worth keeping and nourishing in the midst of a dark age.

I had been elected — to the general astonishment of everyone who noticed — second warden of Block Island in 1976, but there had been earlier overtures ventured suggesting that I become a candidate for the town council. The earliest of these came in 1970, while my health was very fragile. John Donnelly, a stalwart leader of the Democratic minority in the town, who incidentally shared with me a keen enthusiasm for the circus, approached me about this. I was

Simplicity of Faith, 1982, pp. 76–80

frank with John about the limits of my energies but told him that, within those limits, I was not closed to his idea. He was candid with me, too, declaring that he would not anticipate that I could win a council seat but that my being a nominee might prepare the way for a later candidacy with more promising prospects of election. As it happened, that was also the summer in which our hospitality to Daniel Berrigan was interrupted by his capture by the federal police. A few days after Dan had been seized, John came by to mention to me that, in spite of his own high esteem for priests in general and Jesuits in particular, he considered that my involvement with Dan had aborted my local political prospects. Neither Anthony or I disagreed with John's political acumen.

Nevertheless, two years later, John Donnelly returned to renew his suggestion that I stand as a candidate for town council. He thought that the Berrigan episode had receded enough by then, and he said he noticed some sympathy and admiration for Anthony and myself in the ordeal of harassment and frivolous indictment that we had been subjected to because of our opposition to the Vietnam war and our friendship for Berrigan. I told John I would think about the matter and we agreed to discuss it further, perhaps being joined in that discussion by other members of the Democratic Town Committee. Meanwhile, I went, before there had been an opportunity for any meeting, to Princeton to address a very large meeting convened at the university in protest of the war. In my remarks there I argued the case for the impeachment of Richard Nixon as president. It was, of course, more than two years before his resignation and, indeed, only some months before his overwhelming reelection. Watergate was still covered up. My speech received attention in the newspapers, and when I returned to the island on the ferry the next day, John Donnelly was there on the dock to greet me. "You blew it again," he said succinctly. "You can't give a speech like that," he handed me a newspaper clipping, "and run for council here."

In sequel, the following summer, the Watergate hearings chaired by Senator Sam Ervin were telecast. They evoked, as television seldom did, the rapt attention of both Anthony and myself. After the hearings had gone on for some time, one afternoon John Donnelly appeared. He accepted a beer from Anthony and sat down and joined our watch. Several minutes elapsed. John finished his beer. "You know, Bill," he rose from his chair, "that was a good speech you made down at Princeton." Then he left us.

In the hospital in Westerly, after the stroke, I remembered John Donnelly and wondered what his advice to me would be about running, on Block Island, for first warden in 1980. John (the husband of nurse Mary Donnelly) had died in 1974. Some of his ideas for strengthening and reforming the Democratic Town Committee had by now been effected, and there seemed to be an excellent prospect of electing a working majority of the town council on the Democratic ticket; many of my colleagues in the town committee argued that my candidacy for first warden would help insure a council majority, whether or not I was myself elected. At the same time, the laser experience and the stroke accentuated qualms I already had about whether my health was sufficiently stable to allow me to run and, perhaps, to serve; or, on the other hand, whether running and being elected would debilitate my health.

There were other considerations, too, in deciding whether to run. I recognized, for one, that many of the island folk who were urging me to run were not so much making any political statement, as they were, in this way, saying to me that they hoped I would remain on the island though Anthony had died. Another aspect to consider was how much the interest in my becoming a candidate was just a sympathetic response to Anthony's death or how much might it be a transference to me of respect and affection for Anthony? That election as first warden would entail substantial loss of income, just as serving as second warden had a few years before, did not weigh as heavily in my thoughts as did the preemption of other concerns — especially writing and speaking — which incumbency would predictably cause.

I am not conscious of there having been any significant issue of personal ambition involved as I deliberated about whether to be a candidate. Such vanity as I suffer from is expressed in other terms than ambition for political office. This might have turned out differently, for I was politically ambitious in my student days. But I had died to that during the time that I was a research fellow in England at the London School of Economics. It was then that I determined not to pursue politics as a career, and that determination was later ratified when I declined opportunities to run for public office in

Massachusetts, where I was raised, and in New York City, while I was working as lawyer in East Harlem. Still my resolve, originated during the London experience, not to fashion a political career for myself was not a rejection of politics or of political involvement. It was really a decision not to expend my life and such capabilities as I have been given as a person on *any* career of *any* sort, including politics, specifically because that is the direction in which I was then heading. I realized at that time, in London, that there is no option in this world of abstention from politics: everyone everywhere *is* involved, whether intentionally and intelligently or by default or some moral equivalent of it. I knew that my decision was not concerned with withdrawal or pietism but meant that my own political involvements would not be formulated in career terms. I died to political ambition in London, as I have said, and that came about because while I was there, in a quite self-conscious sense, I renounced the notion of having a career — any career — including the goal of having a political career.

Ever since, as one would expect, though I have participated actively in a diversity of ways and roles in the politics of several institutions and communities as well as that of American society in general, I have regarded politics as a temptation, particularly promptings to run for office. These sentiments were prominent in my mind as the choice about the Block Island candidacy confronted me. In the end, it was my conviction about the island's significance for America and my conviction about the importance of demonstrating a relationship between the exercise of franchise and the way society is governed that prevailed (albeit amid a sense of ambivalence and some trepidation that were only dispelled when I learned the election result). The other candidate for first warden had been elected by a modest plurality in the absentee ballots, but he would preside over a town council with a working Democratic majority.

In the Matter of the
Mortification of the Flesh

Let not those who hope in thee be put to shame through me,
  O Lord GOD of hosts;
Let not those who seek thee be brought to dishonor
    through me,
  O God of Israel.

PSALM 69

As I was saying at the outset, in the time in which I have been writing this book on what I understand to be spirituality with precedent and authority in the biblical witness, I have been much afflicted with pain.

Diagnostically, the trouble happens in my legs where, because of the toll of advanced diabetes, the arterial circulation is sorely obstructed. It is the third time in my life when amputation of these limbs has become a serious threat, and, with the help offered in chelation therapy, I struggle against that outcome. I am at once fatigued and bored with this recurring effort and I consider giving it up. But then it comes to mind how eagerly death has pursued me, in ways that have made me self-conscious, and then I become angry toward

---

Politics of Spirituality, 1984, pp. 87–90

death and defiant. I suppose there is some spite toward death involved; in any case, my outrage seems to enhance my stamina. So I resist. I resist the power of death and that which, in the somewhat pathetic state of my health, manifestly foreshadows death — like amputation of a leg or two.

So there is pain. In the present episode there is virtually no respite from pain because I have refused chemicals as "pain relievers." I have (I will not burden you with an elaborate argument here) become convinced that such medications are more harmful to me than anything else that can be said for them. I do not consider my abstinence either brave or foolish; it is simply a circumstance typical of those that occur in fallen existence.

Pain is not a stranger in my life (nor, really, in anybody else's life), and I am familiar with some of the temptations that attend pain. . . . I know, for instance, how preemptive pain can be — excluding practically everything and everyone else from its victim's intelligence or consideration. Or I realize how pain agitates vanity and, most specifically, sponsors a false sense of being justified by suffering. So from the outset of the current affliction, I have had, from past experience, some insight, beyond gritting my teeth, into coping with the reality of pain and with some of the subtleties of pain. And while there have been moments when I have cried out, I do not think that I have been brutalized by what has been taking place, and I do not consider that I have been demoralized either.

Still, in the circumstances, I am haunted by questions: *Why is this happening to me?* and *Why is it happening now?* Or, *Is this some cruel or perverse accounting for my past sins and oversights?* And, *If I forebear to blame myself for my pain, who is left to blame but God?* Again, *Is my suffering of pain consequentially related to the massive default and multiple failures of commercialized medicine? Is pain, thus, an injustice? And in its essence more an issue of politics than of medical practice?* On the other hand, *Can this endurance of pain somehow be edifying? How is it related to the gospel?*

I just begin the roster of queries, I do not exhaust the list. I also have no settled answers to any of these questions (some of which truly rank as conundrums). I just live with such issues, as I live with the pain. And I trust the Word of God until the latter day, when all of created life, myself included, gather at the throne of the judgment of this world and when the disposition of all these questions and that of all questions whatsoever shall become notorious. *Lord, have mercy upon us; Christ, have mercy upon us; Lord, have mercy upon us.*

Meanwhile we are all called to live by grace — that is, concretely — to live in a way (even in pain) that trusts the judgment of the Word of God in history. I realize that some who are reading this book, if they have persevered to this page, would have preferred a book on "spirituality" that pronounced some rules, some norms, some guidelines, some rubrics for a sacred discipline that, if pursued diligently, would establish the holiness of a person. I do not discern that such is the biblical style, as admirable as that may happen to be in a worldly sense.

All that I can affirm, apart from complaining about how awkward it is to try to write a book in the situation in which I have found myself recently, is that pain is not a punishment; neither is pain a justification. There are no grounds to be romantic about pain. Pain is a true mystery, so long as this world lasts. Yet, it is known that pain is intercessory: one is never alone in pain but is always a surrogate of everyone else who hurts — which is categorically everybody. I consider that this is enough to know if one does trust the Word of God in judgment.

A View of Afterdeath

SOME people, I suppose, would consider it virtually obligatory — in a book concerned with death, grief, and mourning — to speculate about the afterlife, so called. I will, literally, not do so here. The term itself is (at the least) a misnomer. More often than not, *afterlife* refers to a mush of vain and pagan imaginings.

The real issue is, anyway, not *afterlife* but *afterdeath*. Any bereaved person or anyone contemplating his or her own death is likely to give some thought to what, if anything, happens experientially when a person dies. One reason such brooding is commonly incoherent or merely self-serving is that it presupposes the linear reality of time and does not probe the mystery of time, especially the relation of time to the bondage to death in the present age, in the era of the Fall, or the disruption of time and the emancipation from time that is implicated in conversion, as I have previously discussed.

The most radical confusion about afterdeath, however, has to do with the transliteration of the resurrection as some idea of immortality. This is an interpolation frequently attributable to preachers, and it is categorically false. Anyone who has read some of my work will be familiar with the significance I attach to distinguishing resurrection from immortality. In my view, immortality, essentially, is no more than an elaborate synonym for remembrance of the dead, though there are

Simplicity of Faith, 1982, pp. 137–41

attached to it multifarious notions of spiritual and/or material survival of death. Resurrection, however, refers to the transcendence of the power of death and of the fear or thrall of the power of death, here and now, in this life, in this world. Resurrection, thus, has to do with life and, indeed, the fulfillment of life *before* death.

I am aware that some may cite my own experience in a coma at that hospital in New London as if it has evidentiary significance for the idea of an afterlife. I do not. I consider that the experience warrants no such inflated inference. What happened then, so far as I understand it, was an ordinary near-death episode. It may offer some insight into death as an empirical reality; it betells nothing thereafter.

For all I know there may be, in some sense, personal survival after death, but that is not what the resurrection is, *in esse,* concerned with. Where confusion reigns and the distinction between resurrection and immortality is lost or suppressed, it is common to find people, frantic in their embrace of one or another versions of survival after death, rejecting life in this world, including, typically, the gift of their own lives. That is more than an escapist doctrine, feigning to justify withdrawal, default, or cowardice so far as life in this world in concerned; it issues in idolatry of death. And its denial of the efficacy of the resurrection of Jesus Christ is tantamount to blasphemy.

These imaginations about personal survival provoke a plethora of other questions when they are associated with reputed communications between the living and the dead. I strive to remain open-minded, and I think I have great appreciation for the intuitive realm, but the fact remains that so-called paranormal (another misnomer; if this is part of reality, the appropriate word is *normal*) experience has been, at least in American culture, so preempted and promoted by quacks, cultists, charlatans, and others exploiting the guilt inherent in grief for profit or notoriety, that intelligent opinion about the subject is practically precluded. Anthony and I exhaustively researched, for instance, the alleged communications, through assorted mediums, of Bishop Pike with his son Jim, who was thought to have committed suicide. The product of those researches is included in our biography, *The Death and Life of Bishop Pike.* We concluded that our friend, the bishop, had been cruelly importuned, though that view is quite inconclusive as to the merits of the question of whether there can be credible communication betwixt the living and the dead.

Whatever the disposition of that question, it represents a trivial aspect of afterdeath. Biblical faith promises the consummation of *all* created life, in all its range and diversity, in the end and fullness of time, and it offers images, pictures, parables, and stories characterizing that consummation (e.g., Rev. 21). There is no timetable, there are no literal descriptions, the biblical witness is no horoscope of the Kingdom. The veracity of the promise, thus, is not dependent upon prooftexts, predictions, or tests of God like those conducted in seances or similar demonstrations but upon the witness of the risen life in this history in this world, as the church, where the church is faithful, and as the communion of saints.

I am so persuaded that the resurrection means the accessibility, for human beings, on behalf of all of life, of the power of the Word of God, which the whole of Creation enjoys in being made, overcoming the power of death here and now, that I expect the consummation eagerly. . . .

Once upon a time, while Anthony Towne and I were immigrating to Block Island, a friend from New York joined the two of us in moving stuff by car and ferry from the city to the island. We arrived in Old Harbor on a gray and dismal November day and disembarked. Our friend looked all around, surveying the boarded-up shops and desolate hotels and the somewhat scruffy characters loitering around the pier. "God!" he cried with anguish, "this is the end of the world!" "No," I responded, "it is the beginning of the world!"

That evening there was a long discussion at dinner among the three of us about what to name the house and premises where we were to live on the island. We disdained names such as "Sea Breeze" or "Foggy Bottom." At last Anthony recalled the exchange of words when we had arrived on the ferry and proposed that we name our place *Eschaton,* because *eschaton* means the end of the world coinciding with the beginning of the world as the Kingdom of God. Thus, in common usage, *eschaton* means hope.

At *Eschaton,* Anthony and I lived in the simplicity of that consummate hope.

II. THE VOCATION
OF THE CHURCH

The Church as Event

TOO often Christians nowadays speak carelessly of the church and thereby make a stupid witness to the world. It is not for the sake of semantic fastidiousness that Christians must speak with responsibility of the church but for the sake of the evangelistic trust that is theirs, in other words, for the sake of the world.

The church evident as the congregation is named *event* to show a difference between a definition of "the idea of church" and an affirmation of that which actually takes place whenever the church is constituted. This attempt is not to discuss an abstraction but to describe a happening; not to speak theoretically but existentially.*

The church as event is always now and new. The church comes into being in response to the summons of God in the present moment and place. The response of our ancestors is not surety for us. Our own

---

* Dr. George Florovsky points out that it was only in the late fifteenth century that the systematic doctrine of the church was composed. "This lack of formal definitions does not mean, however, a confusion of ideas or any obscurity of view. The Fathers did not care so much for the *doctrine* of the Church precisely because the glorious *reality* of the Church was open to their spiritual vision." See his paper, "The Church — Her Nature and Task," in *Man's Disorder and God's Design* (New York: Harper and Brothers, 1949), pp. 43–58.

From "The Christian Lawyer as Churchman," *Christian Scholar,* 1957, vol. 40, pp. 211–13

response yesterday is not sufficient also for today. God's people are called now, not now and then. The church is always new and continually being renewed by God in "the new light and the new power of His Word, according to the testimony of the Bible, the new outpouring of His Spirit, and His new presence in preaching and worship, in Baptism and the Lord's Supper."* When the church is not new, when the church "degenerates into religiosity," when worship ceases, then in fact the church has "fallen into the abyss of non-existence."**

To consider the church as an event illuminates the utter dependence of the church upon God. It is God who maintains all humanity in history, in fallen creation; it is God who calls the church into being, it is God who elects the church, it is God who preserves and renews the church.

---

* Karl Barth, "The Church — The Living Congregation of the Living Lord Jesus Christ," in *Man's Disorder and God's Design,* pp. 67–77.
** Ibid.

The Folly of Religion

See to it that no one makes a prey of you by philosophy
and empty deceit, according to human tradition, according
to the elemental spirits of the universe, and not according
to Christ.

COLOSSIANS 2:8

Personally, I find no cause to be interested in mere religion. It can be
a certain diversion, I admit, to speculate and argue about religious
ideas and practices, but I am no longer in college, and my law practice
does not often permit the luxury of hypothetical and speculative
matters. It appears to me more urgent and more necessary to deal
with history, that is, with actual life as it has preceded the present
time, and with the actual life of the present time. So I do not bother,
as far as I am aware, with dabbling in religion. And if, as it may in
my own lifetime turn out, Protestantism — like Zen, or "religious
science," or the other sects — is or becomes only an institution of
religion devoted to its own maintenance and a practice of religion
for its own sake, then I am just not superstitious enough to remain a
Protestant.

But when, now and then, I turn to and listen to the Bible, or

Private and Public Faith, 1962, pp. 14–17

when, now and then, I hear the Word of God exposed in preaching, or when, now and then, I see the gospel represented in the Holy Communion and I thereupon become a participant in and witness of the real life that is given to the world, or when, now and then, I meet some Christian, or when, now and then, I discern and encounter the presence of God's Word in the ordinary affairs of everyday existence in the world — on these occasions, in these circumstances, I am reminded, if sometimes ruefully, that the gospel is no mere religion in *any* essential respect.

For in any of these circumstances, on any of these occasions, what is emphatic and lucid and — best of all — *true* is that this gospel of Jesus Christ ends all religious speculation; demolishes all merely religious ceremonies and sacrifices appeasing unknown gods; destroys every exclusiveness that religion attaches to itself in God's name; attests that the presence of God is not remote, distant, and probably out-of-reach — but here, now, and with us in this world, already. This gospel means that the very life of God is evident in this world, in this life, because Jesus Christ once participated in the common human life in the history of our world.

The Christian faith is distinguished, diametrically, from mere religion in that religion begins with the proposition that some god exists; Christianity, meanwhile, is rejoicing in God's manifest presence among us. Religion describes human beings, mind you, usually sincere and honorable and intelligent ones, searching for God or, more characteristically, searching for some substitute for God — that is, some idea of what God may be like — or would be like — and then worshiping that idea and surrounding that substitution with dogma and discipline. But the gospel tells when and how and why and where God has sought us and found us and offered to take us into God's life. Religion is the attempt to satisfy the curiosity of human beings in this world about God; Jesus Christ is the answer to the human curiosity in this world about what it means to be truly human in this world that God created. Religion is fulfilled, always, in one of two ways: either (1) in consecrating some object or power or ideology or person — or, in earlier days, some commodity or natural phenomenon or animal or any thing — as a god and as, hopefully, *the god* or (2) in projecting god beyond history, into the unknown and the unknowable, enthroned, perhaps, before this life or in some afterlife but never in *this*

120

life, out of this world, oblivious of the present existence and grandly indifferent to it, abstract, irrelevant, impotent, indifferent — a ridiculous god, in fact, no god at all.

So, just personally, religion does not particularly intrigue me, though the gospel does. Religion does not address my practical, everyday, working life, but the gospel does. I do not care — I do not mean to be impudent, but I, for one, do not care — if God lives somewhere and someplace else. But I care a lot when I hear — in the Bible, or in the church, or in the presence of a Christian, or in the ordinary happenings of my own life — that God is with us now, anyway and already, and even, thank God, before we call upon God. I care a lot, in other words, when I hear the news of Jesus Christ, because it is a different news than I receive when I encounter the various religions.

Part of the difference is, obviously, the news that God (even) cares for me (even). All those smaller gods — the gods of the various religions — are indifferent to that. What they care about, what idols are concerned with — is whether they are worshiped, is whether their own existence is verified and lauded. But Christ speaks very differently. Indeed, Christ embodies the difference between religion and the gospel. Christ bespeaks the care of God for everything to do with actual life, with life as it is lived by anybody and everybody day in and day out. Christ bespeaks *my* life: in all its detail and mistake and humor and fatigue and surprise and contradiction and freedom and ambiguity and quiet and wonder and sin and peace and vanity and variety and lust and triumph and defeat and rest and love and all the rest that it is from time to time; and, cheer up, with *your* life, just as much, in as full intimacy, touching your whole biography, abiding every secret, *with you,* whoever, wherever you are, any time, any place. Christ bespeaks the destinies of nations, and all the lesser principalities and powers, the corporations and universities and unions and utilities and the whole frighteningly complex constellation of authorities that assert themselves in the day-to-day life of the world.

In short, religion supposes that God is yet to be discovered; Christianity knows that God has already come among us. Religious speculation suspects there is God, somewhere, sometime; the gospel reports God's presence and action in this world even in those circumstances of which we are unaware. Religion suppresses the truth because the truth obviates religion.

The religious suppose that only the religious know about God or care about God, and that God cares only for the religious. Characteristically, religion is precious and possessive toward God and institutes and conducts itself as if God really needs religion, as if God's existence depends upon the recognition of religion. Religion considers that God is a secret disclosed only in the discipline and practice of religion. But all this is most offensive to the Word of God. The best news of God is that God is no secret. The news of God embodied in Jesus Christ is that God is openly and notoriously active in the world. In this news the Christian church is constituted; it is this news that the Christian church exists to spread. Where the church, however, asserts that God is hidden in or behind creed or ceremony — even those that are decent and that God gladly receives and blesses — or where God is thought to be confined to the sanctuary, then in such events the Christian church, forsaking the good news of God's presence in history, becomes a vulgar imitation of mere religion. The church, where faithful to the news, is not the place where people come to seek God; on the contrary, the church is just the place where human beings gather to declare that God takes the initiative in seeking them. The church, unlike any religion, exists to present to the world and to celebrate in the world, and on behalf of the world, God's presence and power and utterance and action in the ongoing life of the world.

Liturgy as Political Action

AT NO point in the witness of the church to the world is its integrity as a reconciled society more radical and more cogent than in the liturgy, the precedent and consummation of that service that the church of Christ and the members of this Body render to the world. Of course, there are many Protestants who regard the liturgy as peripheral to the Christian life. Some even boast that *they* have no liturgical life, but this is a betrayal of ignorance, since liturgy means nothing more than style of life. In the broadest sense, all of life is liturgical. The conventions and ceremonies of courtship are a liturgy, articulating and dramatizing the love between a man and a woman. Or, to take a less attractive example — Joe Valachi, in the Senate hearing in which the chief witness expounded at great length upon the peculiar actions and symbols and rituals which constitute the extraordinarily sophisticated liturgical fabric of the Cosa Nostra.

As for the church, all forms of its corporate life — from the Quakers sitting in silence in a circle to the exuberance and patience of a Negro congregation and the majesty and richness of the venerable Orthodox service — are liturgical. The only serious question is whether or not a given liturgical practice has integrity in the gospel. There are both laypeople and clergy who regard liturgy as an essentially religious exercise — separate, disjoined, self-contained, unrelated

Dissenter in a Great Society, 1966, pp. 150–54

— confined to the sanctuary and having nothing to do with this world. Some even regard liturgy superstitiously, as something having an intrinsic efficacy, as a means of procuring indulgences, as if God were so absurd — and so ungodly — as to be appeased by the redundant incantations of human beings.

There is, however, nothing so spooky or lucky about the liturgy and nothing magical or mechanistic about its performance. The liturgy of the gospel is, on the contrary, a dramatic form of the ethical witness of Christians in this world. In this sense, though there may be much variety in different times and cultures in regard to language, music, action, and movement, the liturgy is always characterized by certain definitive marks:

(1) *Scriptural Integrity* — The liturgy of the gospel is the theatricalization of the biblical saga of God's action in this world, thus relating the ubiquity of the Word of God in history to the consummation of the Word of God in Jesus Christ. A biblically authentic and historically relevant liturgy is always the celebration of the death and resurrection of the Lord; the most decisive event in all history is remembered and memorialized in a context in which God's every action in this world since creation is recalled and rehearsed and the hope of the world for the final reconciliation is recited and represented in the liturgical portrait.

The scriptural integrity of the liturgy requires that the laity not be spectators but participants — not as a matter of piety, not merely for their own sake, but because they gather, as a congregation, as delegates and, indeed, advocates of the world.

That is why the traditional Protestant "preaching service" — even when the preaching is an exposition of the Word of God and not some religious diatribe — is an impoverished and inadequate liturgy for the church; by the same token, that is why the Mass recited in the absence of a congregation or celebrated in a language not familiar to the people is a compromise of the scriptural integrity of the liturgy.

(2) *The Historicity of the Liturgy* — The liturgy of the Gospel is both a transcendent event and a present event. It shatters the categories of time and space and location because it both recalls and dramatizes the estate of creation in the Word of God and beseeches and foretells the end of this history. As a transcendent event, the liturgy recollects

all that has already happened in this world from the beginning of time and prophesies *all* that is to come until the end of time.

But the liturgy is also a contemporary event, involving these particular persons gathered in this specific place in this peculiar way. The reconciliation celebrated in the liturgy is not only a reconciliation remembered from creation or expected eschatologically but also in actual event the reconciliation here and now of those gathered as a congregation and society within and among themselves, and between each and all of them and the rest of the world.

That is precisely why the confessions and the intercessions of the people of the congregation within the context of the liturgy are so indispensable to its integrity. *This* is the time and *this* is the place and *this* is the way, in a most immediate sense, in which the whole, manifold, existential involvement of the members of Christ's Body in the everyday life of the world — both all that seems good and that human beings are tempted to honor or praise and all that seems evil and that they are fond of rationalizing or denying — is offered and consecrated for the discretion of Christ himself, the redeemer of all.

Thus the liturgy is the normative and conclusive ethical commitment of the Christian people to the world. The liturgy is the epitome of the service that the Christian renders the world. All authentic witness in the name of Christ, exemplifying in the world the virtue of Christ, which Christians undertake in their dispersion in the practical life of the world, is portrayed in the liturgy celebrated in the gathered congregation.

(3) *The Sacramental Authenticity of the Liturgy* — It is both this transcendence of time in time and the scriptural integrity of the liturgy of the gospel that constitute the sacramental essence of the liturgy. The actual, visible, present event retains all its own originality and contemporary significance as a particular reconciled community and at the same time is transfigured to embody to the world the cosmic enormity of the reconciling accomplishment of Jesus Christ.

Thus the liturgy as sacrament is inherently different from religious ritualism, in which the propriety of the ritual practice itself is all that matters. (Such may be sufficient for initiation or elevation in the Masons or the Knights of Columbus, but ritualistic piety is radically inappropriate to the Eucharist.) Notice, too, that the liturgy as sacrament appropriates as its ingredient symbols, among others, the ordinary things of the common existence of the world — bread, wine, water, money, cloth, color, music, words, or whatever else is readily at hand. Sacramentally, we have in the liturgy a meal that is basically a real meal and that nourishes those who partake of it as a meal. At the same time, this meal portrays for the rest of the world an image of the Last Supper, of which Christ himself was host, and is also a foretaste of the eschatological banquet in which Christ is finally recognized as the host of all humanity.

The liturgy, therefore, wherever it has substance in the gospel, is a living, political event. The very example of salvation, it is the festival of life that foretells the fulfillment and maturity of all of life for all of time in *this* time. The liturgy *is* social action because it is the characteristic style of life for human beings in this world.

The Church as Holy Nation

LET it be said that when I name the church, I do not have in mind some idealized church, or some disembodied or uninstitutionalized church, or just an aggregate of individuals. I mean the church in history, the church constituted and precedented in history at Pentecost, the church that is an organic reality: visible as a community, institutionalized as a society. I refer to the church as a new household or to the church as congregation. Most concretely, I name the church as the holy nation.

The church that is the holy nation is not metaphorical, but it is the church called into being at Pentecost: the church that is the new Israel of God in the world; the church that is both progeny of the biblical tradition of Zion and pioneer of the Kingdom of God; the church that is the exemplary nation juxtaposed to all the other nations; the church that as a principality and institution transcends the bondage to death in the midst of fallen creation; the church that presents and represents in its corporate life creation restored in celebration of the Word of God; the church in which the vocation of worship and advocacy signifies the renewed vocation of every creature; the church that anticipates the imminent and prompt redemption of all of life.

The church's calling as the holy nation has been profoundly

Conscience and Obedience, 1977, pp. 102–5

distorted since Pentecost and, manifestly, especially so under the aegis of the Constantinian détente with the rulers and regimes of the present age. Insofar as there was in the fourth century definite incentive to enter that comity in order to alleviate persecution, the purpose remains unaccomplished. If Christians have been spared the savagery of beasts or if the more notorious vulgarities of emperor worship have been abated, other forms of persecution have succeeded and the hostility of demonic principalities and powers toward the church has not diminished. By the twentieth century, the enmity of the power of death toward the church had come to be enacted in the grandiose idolatry of the destiny of British colonial imperialism, or in the brutal devastation of the church following upon the Soviet revolution, or in the ruthless Nazi usurpation of the church in the name of "Germanizing" or "purifying" Christianity so as to have this accomplice in the pursuit and in the incineration of the Jews.

Meanwhile, in America, the pluralism of religions and the multiplicity of denominations have abetted the inception of civil religion, which has assorted versions, but the major thrust of which imputes a unique moral status to the nation, a divine endorsement for America, which, in its most radical composition, disappropriates the vocation of church as the holy nation.

Thus, the church becomes confined, for the most part, to the sanctuary and is assigned to either political silence or to banal acquiescence. Political authority in America has sanctioned this accommodation principally by the economic rewards it bestows upon the church. The tax privilege, for example, to which the church has acceded, has been a practically conclusive inhibition to the church's political intervention save where it consists of applause for the nation's cause. Furthermore, the tax preference or political subsidy the church has so long received has enabled, perhaps more than anything else, the accrual of enormous, if unseemly, wealth. In the American comity, the church has gained so huge a propertied interest that its existence has become overwhelmingly committed to the management of property and the maintenance of the ecclesiastical fabric which that property affords. It is a sign certainly of the demonic in institutional life where the survival of the principality is the dominant morality. That mark is evident in very many professed churches in America. I cannot imagine any other way, at this point, to free the church to recover its vocation as the exemplary principality or holy nation than by notorious acts of disavowal of this traffic with political authority. The church in America needs to divest property, not hoard it any longer, and as part of that I urge renunciation of the tax privilege so that the church could be freed to practice tax resistance. If that portends direct collision with political authority and involves such risks as official confiscation of church properties — which it does — then my only response is that it promises a way of consolidating losses.

The suppression of the comprehension of the church as the holy nation or as the priest among the nations, whether in America or elsewhere, causes, I think, the importance of the dispersion of the church to be minimized or even overlooked. Yet, it is impossible to contemplate the nationhood of the church without retaining the sense of the eschatological imminence that has been previously discussed. The imminence is conveyed where the church lives in dispersion throughout the world, confronting every nation and tribe, tongue and culture as an embassy of the Kingdom. Such dispersion is, on one hand, incompatible with the Constantinian ethos, but, on the other, it verifies the truly ecumenical reality of the church in this world.

More than that, the dispersion inherent in the church's identity as the priest of nations and forerunner of the Kingdom is, I believe, temporal as much as spatial. The church is dispersed in space and thus indulges no dependency upon particular nations or regimes of nations but by its presence disrupts every nation and every regime. The church also remains dispersed in time, forebearing to become vested in a specific institutional mode indefinitely, or as if in perpetuity, but the event of the church constantly, repeatedly fractures time. That is to say, the church as institution or nation is, first of all, an event of the moment, gathered here or there, but that does not predetermine whether or how the church will appear again. The church is episodic in history; the church lives in imminence so that the church has no permanent locale or organization that predicates its authenticity as the church. This may seem a hectic doctrine of the church to the Constantinian mentality. It is. But it is so because it suggests the necessity of breaking away from Constantinian indoctrination in order to affirm the poise of the church awaiting the second advent of Jesus Christ.

CONGREGATIONS AND COMMUNIONS

East Harlem Protestant Parish

I HAD come initially to Harlem as a member of the group ministry of the East Harlem Protestant Parish, out of concern for the mission of the church to the poor and to those socially discriminated against in the city.

When I first moved to the neighborhood the parish was suffering from a terrific confusion as to the nature of the church and the meaning and manner of the church's task in a place such as Harlem. At the heart of these issues were some of the same matters that so divide the several churches outside of Harlem. They provoked deep divisions within the parish, particularly among the members of the group ministry, who, apart from myself and one other man, were clergymen.

Through its first years in the neighborhood the parish had become deeply conformed to the world. Conformity to the world is a temptation that assails the church no less in the slums than in the suburbs. Conformity to the world exists whenever and wherever the church regards its message and mission to be determined primarily by, or dominated essentially by, the ethos of secular life and the society that surrounds the church.

My People Is the Enemy, 1964 ed., pp. 85–97. Much of this material is elaborated from a lengthy letter of resignation that Stringfellow proffered to the ministry.

The young ministers who had come out of Union Theological Seminary to found the East Harlem Protestant Parish were much tempted to such conformity. They had seen the Protestant churches abandon the inner city, both physically and psychologically, and were aroused by this attachment and conformity of Protestantism to middle-class, American society. They would bring the ministry of Protestantism back into the inner city and work there among the poor and the dispossessed. In doing so they were confronted with how the ministry could be exercised in the midst of the long-festering, complex, and, to them — since they were white middle- and upper-class people — unfamiliar social problems that characterize urban slum society. To these problems they brought two things — a hostility toward the conventional churches outside the slums, which caused them to think they had little or nothing to learn from the life of the church outside East Harlem, and a sincere passion for social change and revolution, even, in East Harlem. These two emotions joined to underscore the view that before the gospel could be preached and received by the people of the slums, the way for the Word had to be prepared by improving the education of the people, renovating their housing, finding jobs for them, clearing the streets of garbage and debris, challenging the political status quo, alleviating the narcotics problem, and by social action of all sort. When some of these issues had been resolved, when the lives of the people were less burdened with poverty, discrimination, illiteracy, and ignorance, then the time would come to preach the gospel and then the people, no longer so preoccupied with their afflictions, would be able to hear and embrace the gospel. One of the earlier parish documents declares that the parish "is a group ministry of twelve men and women working at the neighborhood level to help people face and work on their problems." Ironically, in spite of their rejection of middle-class Protestantism, the group ministry initially seems to have seen its task as making the East Harlem neighborhood more nearly middle-class! Such a prejudgment is marred by the same sort of confusion that beset many missionaries who, in the early days of American foreign missions, went to Africa, Latin America, and the Far East, and who thought that before the people indigenous to those places could understand and receive the Word of God in Christ, they first had to be westernized.

One of the paradoxes is that, unlike the people to whom the

western missionaries venture, American Negroes are not foreign to the traditions, culture, class, ethos, and social mores of American society. All these are their own inheritance. American Negroes, in other words, are *Americans* — and have been such for as long or longer than any other ethnic group in the United States. What they remember is American, not African. What they remember is, however, an American ethos from which they have been deliberately excluded. What they remember is that they have been forcibly separated from those things that are as much their own as any other American's. What they remember are the very promises of the American Revolution — human dignity and equal treatment, fair representation and the opportunity to be politically free, the right to education and employment, and a decent place to live and raise children. No one has to instill these ideas and aspirations into American Negroes. They have inherited and remember them, despite three hundred years of slavery and segregation. They honor them by enduring their breach. They honor them more than most other Americans.

In any event, the preaching and service of the gospel do not depend upon any special social change, ideationally or in any other way. The gospel does not even depend upon the American way of life, either in its integrity or its breach.

I am as much in favor of social change in the urban ghettos as the next person, perhaps more (though I am by no means persuaded that the standard of social improvement should be that of the great American bourgeoisie), but the message and mission of the church in the world *never* depend upon the specific physical, political, cultural, social, economic, or even psychological situations in which the church, or the people of the church as missionaries, find themselves. If the gospel is so contingent as that, it is no universal gospel. If the gospel is so fragile that it may not be welcomed by those, say, who are hungry, unless they first be fed, then this is no gospel with any saving power, this is no Word of God that has authority over the power of death. The gospel, if it represents the power of God unto salvation, is a Word that is exactly addressed to human beings in this world in their destitution and hunger and sickness and travail and captivity and perishing, in a way that may be heard and embraced in any of these, or in any other, afflictions. That is, by the way, the original portrait and report of Christian witness in the world, in the days of the Acts of the Apostles.

The church is much tempted by conformity to the world, by accommodating the message and mission to the particular society in which the church happens to be, in the slums and in the suburbs, instead of honoring the integrity of the gospel for all societies and for all sorts and conditions of human life in all times and places. This temptation beguiled the group ministry of the East Harlem Protestant Parish. They plunged into all sorts of social work and social action — narcotics, politics, neighborhood improvement, education, housing, and the rest. They instituted therapy and counseling for addicts, engaged in voter registration, lobbied for new playgrounds, organized PTAs, complained about slum landlords, and, generally, made themselves a nuisance to those in power in the neighborhood. It was, in many ways, an admirable, if idealistic, and, in Christian terms, naive effort. But they neglected and postponed the proclamation and celebration of the gospel in East Harlem. In the congregations of the parish, the Bible was closed; in the group ministry there was even scorn for the Bible as a means through which the Word of God is communicated in contemporary society. The liturgical life of the congregations grew erratic and fortuitous, depending upon the personality and whim, even, of the minister presiding at the time. There was no concord or confession of the faith among either the group ministry or the lay people; there was a radical substitution of conventional charity for the mission of the church. The parish — and especially the group ministry — was becoming dependent, in its raison d'être, upon its "good works," rather than upon the gospel, as such, for its justification.

In such circumstances, the hostility of the group ministry toward the church outside East Harlem and, indeed, toward other churches within East Harlem unaffiliated with the parish — such as the Chambers Memorial Baptist Church or St. Edward the Martyr or the Church of the Good Neighbor or the Roman Catholic churches thereabouts — became more arrogant and proud. Not long after I had come to East Harlem, one of the clergy in the group ministry blandly explained that the church outside East Harlem was dead and that the East Harlem Protestant Parish represented the "New Jerusalem" — to quote his exact words — of American Protestantism, the example through which American Protestantism would be purified and renewed. The calling of the parish, he assured me, was to be the norm, in all essential realms of the church's life, for the whole church in American society. I recall replying, in more strenuous language than I will use here, that he was mistaken and that part of the reason he was mistaken in this ambition for the parish was contained in his manifest ignorance, along with others (though not all in the group ministry), about the life of the church outside East Harlem. For the fact was that very few of the clergy of the parish at this time had had any experience in the church, apart from their special experience in East Harlem itself. Of the twenty or so members of the group ministry on the scene when I first came to the neighborhood and to the parish, only five of us — George Todd, Melvin Schoonover, Geoffrey Ainger, Donald De Young, and myself — had had any significant involvement in the life of the church outside East Harlem, especially in any ecumenical sense.

The dangerous aspects of the parish's attitude were not just its wholesale reflection of the church outside East Harlem, not even its conviction that mission is dependent upon and follows charity. More important, the group ministry was intent on conformity to the world and too easily disposed to think of itself as the model of the church in American society. Members of the group ministry were filled with stereotyped opinions about the condition of the church outside the inner city, but, except for a few of us, none of them had ever lived in the church outside or had any firsthand knowledge of any church other than the parish.

At this stage in the parish's struggle to survive and to become a responsible member of the church, the parish — and specifically the group ministry — was in danger of becoming sectarian, in danger of becoming so conformed to their environment and so dominated by it that the understanding of the church that was asserted had become essentially joined to the sort of place in the world in which the parish was established. The church could be the church, to put it plainly, only in the slums. That is sectarianism, no less than it is where a church is established on grounds of class or race or language or any other secular criteria.

But this is not only sectarianism, it is romanticism. East Harlem is a frontier of the church, but it is no more a frontier of the church than the university or suburbia or anywhere else. Fanfare and special pleading and self-serving propaganda about the inner city ministry are both misleading and obscene. East Harlem, the earlier emphasis of the parish there notwithstanding, is in itself no more a frontier than any other place in this world. A frontier is wherever the church trusts the gospel in the gospel's inherent relevance to the whole of life in this world. A frontier is wherever the church exercises the freedom that God gives the church to share the burden of any one, in order to make known how Christ bears all burdens of everyone everywhere and in all times.

The sectarianism of the parish at this period was perhaps particularly sensitive to my own presence in the group ministry because I am an Episcopalian, and before coming to the parish I had had a certain experience not only within the Anglican communion but in the ecumenical movement, especially the World's Student Christian Federation and in the World Council of Churches. From that background and experience I knew something of the ministry of the church outside East Harlem and, frankly, I was not impressed with the ready assurances that the East Harlem Protestant Parish represented the prototype of the renewal of the church in the world, as much as I instinctively admired the social concern of the members of the group ministry. Even before affiliating with the parish, I had not hesitated to be critical of my own denomination or of the churches at large. Indeed, on the basis of my own involvement in the church outside of East Harlem, and in view of the lack of significant involvement in or commitment to the church outside by most, save a few, members of the group ministry, I felt authorized to say within the group ministry that not only were they not the image of the "new Jerusalem" and more than likely were building a new sect, based upon their location in and concern for the inner city, but they were guilty of the same conformity to the world that characterizes the churches and sects that take their identity and task from their place and status in the suburbs or elsewhere.

As time went on, the controversy about the nature of the church and about the mission of the church became gravely intensified within the group ministry, and, over a period of months, it focused upon two principal issues, although there were many ancillary matters that were also involved from time to time.

The first was centered upon the significance of the Bible for Christian people and for the life of the church. Some of the members

135

of the group ministry were appallingly diffident toward the Bible; and those who were the most self-serious about the analysis of culture and society were most often the dilettantes in Bible study. Those professing condolence for people showed mostly indolence for the Bible. Apparently, some of the clergy felt that Bible study was unnecessary, since they had already learned all they needed to of the Bible in seminary.

To some others in the group ministry — and to myself — this seemed astonishing in the extreme, especially among Protestants who might be expected to recall that, historically, Protestants have been a people of the Word of God in the Bible. Surely, intimacy with the Word of God in the Bible, reliance upon the Word of God in the Bible, is a characteristic of the ordinary practice of the Christian life, it seemed to those of us who urged that the group ministry and the people of the congregations engage in some corporate Bible study each week. After much controversy about the matter, it was decided that the group would spend an hour or so in Bible study just before the regular weekly staff meetings. It was often an erratic, sparsely attended — or attended to — exercise, but it exposed the fundamental disunity within the group ministry as to the content of the Christian faith and the nature of the church's life and work. In this Bible study, the minds of some were filled with notions of truth, ideas of good, with interesting hypotheses, strong sentiments, and current events — and these things were actually asserted to test the Word of God. But few seemed ready just to *listen* to the Word of God in the Bible, to ask: What *is* the Word of God? Now, later, much later, after many struggles and both indifference and resistance, with the counsel and nurture of such visitors to the parish as Suzanne de Dietrich, Hendrik Kraemer, and others, the Bible has been acknowledged as central in the life of the church and, hence, of this parish — but only after much agony.

At the heart of the conflict and disunity regarding the place of the Bible in the church — as in many other churches outside Harlem — was a fundamental misapprehension about what the Bible is. I have no inclination toward biblical literalism, but neither do I think that the Bible can be neglected, as the liberal Protestants fondly do, save for the teachings of Jesus. I am no biblical scholar, either, but I affirm the necessity for the most rigorous work of textual criticism and the like. I do not become greatly distressed by "demythologizing" the Bible unless it is used as an excuse for banishing the Bible from contemporary life. None of these approaches to the Bible essentially affects the reliance upon the Bible of the ordinary Christian as a particular means through which the Word of God is uttered and may be heard no less today than in the earlier days of the Christian people. In other words, and without denigrating an appropriate place for biblical scholarship and criticism, the characteristic approach to the Bible of the Christian is confessional. Christians confront the Bible in the expectancy that it is in and through the testimony of the Bible of God's presence and action in the common life of the world that they will behold the Word of God as such, that they will hear the Word of God in the objectivity, integrity, and serenity of God's self-witness in this history, that they will confront the *living* Word. The Word of God, in this sense, mediated through the narrative, history, praise, testimony, and exhortation of the Bible, lives by God's own initiative and generosity in this world, apart from whether or not human beings listen to God's Word, apart from human wisdom and scholarship, apart from tampering with or manipulation of the Bible, apart from the interesting and even sometimes true views and opinions of people, apart from any hardness of heart. The Word of God, in this sense, which is mediated in and through the Bible, is the very same Word of God in which all life in the whole of creation originates, the same Word embodied and exposed in Jesus Christ, the same Word by which the world is judged and in which the world is fulfilled, the same Word of God present and active in the world in the present day and in each and every event and transaction of everyday life in the world. Thus, when Christians turn to the Bible in a confessional sense, they do so in the expectancy of discerning the same Word of God with which they are confronted in their involvement each day in the common life of the world. And in their experience of the Word of God in the Bible, on one hand, and in common life, on the other hand, each is confirmed by the other. This is the case, not because someone is especially learned or wise or even diligent, but because the Word of God is indeed a living Word whose vitality is no less to be beheld and enjoyed in ordinary life today than in the saga of the Word of God in the history of the people Israel, in the gospels of Christ's ministry, in the birth and beginnings of the church, in the acts and testimonies of the first apostles and evangelists known to us through the Bible.

I count the diffidence toward the Bible in the group ministry, accompanied as it was by the neglect of reliance upon the Bible in preaching in the parish's congregations and in the liturgical practices of these congregations, as the reason for the gross misapprehension about theology in the group ministry in the days of which I speak. Somehow the parish clergy had come to think that theology is the theory of the Christian faith that, once comprehended and accepted, is to be applied and executed in practical action in the world. That is why, I suppose, that the honor given by some of us to the Bible as mediator of the living Word of God still at work in this world was unwelcome and received with such vigorous hostility by our colleagues in the group ministry. The role of human beings would be so much more important if they did not always have to watch for the presence and initiative of the Word of God in history. If this Word was not still active, God would be remote — if not, in fact, dead. Then, people could choose to justify themselves by their own words, and one could take or leave the Bible, as well as the inherited testimony of earlier Christians, according to one's own individual ethics or speculations. Carried to its logical extreme, such a position implies atheism. Although there are many sincere and honorable people who are atheists, there is no excuse for such to masquerade as Christians.

The neglect and, in some instances, outright suppression of the Bible as a mediator of the Word of God gravely influenced the ministry of the parish in its day-to-day relations to the neighborhood around it. It meant, for one thing, a failure to respect the office of the laity in the parish congregations. For all practical purposes, they were excluded from the government of the parish — they had no authority in the calling of their own ministers, in determining the service of the parish to the community, in supporting the parish's ministry in a significant way; they were, in short, appendices of the group ministry, dependent upon the leadership and resources of the ecclesiastical authorities, objects of the ministry rather than participants in the total ministry of the church in East Harlem. As has happened before, in the Church of Rome as well as in the churches of Protestantism, the group ministry at this time was becoming so overinstitutionalized, so large, so aggressive, and so self-contained that it took upon itself the prerogatives of a congregation. The group ministry not only met with great frequency — apart from the congregations — to make policy, raise and spend funds, plan tactics and the like, but it also met often, including Sunday mornings, to worship separately from the congregations. In practice, the esoteric life of the group ministry had become one that really claimed that the group ministry constituted the community of the faithful in this neighborhood and that the people who were baptized and had been made members of the several congregations of the parish were consigned to some derivative and peripheral status in the ministry of the church in East Harlem. The paradox of the group ministry, as it actually operated then, was that the group ministry itself was the chief and constant threat to the emergence of vital congregations among the people of East Harlem, while, at the same time, the emergence of some congregations in East Harlem was the most substantial threat to the group ministry as a congregation and as a paternalistic, ecclesiastical institution.

The slothfulness of the group ministry in confronting such issues as these — the place of the Bible in the church and the adjacent issues of preaching and liturgy and action in society, plus the office of the laity and its relationship to the ecclesiastical ministry — provoked some of us to leave the group ministry after a while. I resigned about fifteen months after first coming to the neighborhood but decided to stay in East Harlem, living and working as a lawyer on my own thereafter, and so remained until 1962. My resignation, let it be said, by no means terminated communication or collaboration with the people — both lay and clergy — of the parish on specific issues concerning both the church and society, but, I trust, the decision permitted both the group ministry and myself to persevere in the work that each felt called to do in East Harlem, in society at large, and in the ministry of the church.

Since that time it appears that there have been significant changes in the parish, among others the admission of the laity to a significant voice in the affairs of the parish and also a serious renewal in the parish in the recognition of the uniqueness of the Bible as an evidence and honoring of the Word of God in the world.

As I reflect upon these controversies, what they amounted to were reflections of the differences within American Protantism at large as to the meaning of God's concern for and presence in this world. From my own vantage point and experience on that issue, the Christian faith is not about some god who is an abstract presence somewhere else but about the living presence of God here and now, in this world, in *exactly* this world, as we know it and touch it and smell it and live and work in it. That is why, incidentally, all the well-meant talk of "making the gospel relevant" to the life of the world is false and vulgar. It secretly assumes that God is a stranger among us, who has to be introduced to us and to our anxieties and triumphs and issues and efforts. The meaning of Jesus Christ is that the Word of God is addressed to people, to *all* people, in the very events and relationships, any and every one of them, that constitute our existence in this world. That is the theology of the Incarnation.

Chambers Memorial

WHITE Christendom in America survives pathetically.

The traditions and ethics of the inherited, white denominations — as their adherents sense privately, and everyone else acknowledges openly — are moribund, nostalgic for a legendary past, extravagantly irrelevant to virtually anything to which one might attempt to relate them. White Christendom's institutions are truly secular, that is, utterly preoccupied with their own survival, and hence dissipated in anxiety. Their human constituency is being visibly depleted by dropouts, deaths, and other departures. The people of these churches have been stunned by the renunciation voiced by their own offspring, bewildered by the long overdue rejection of their paternalism by the blacks, and so traumatized by their guilt that their conscience has been both perverted and paralyzed. They have feted a doctrine of achievement in work and in charity that is bereft of biblical authority and that now turns out not even to have the illusion of efficacy. After seeking a justification that proved futile, they grow frantic and afraid, increasingly tempted to an anger that only a false righteousness can spawn.

The condition of white Christendom is pathological; it is, I suggest, the state designated in the Bible as "hardness of heart."

The reason for this bitter ailment is that the white churches in

---

Foreword to Melvin E. Schoonover, *Making All Things Human,* 1969, pp. vii–ix

America have long doubted the very existence, much less the vitality, of the Holy Spirit. In these denominations, on the whole, it has never been seriously granted that God has freedom and discretion in being present and active in this world; it has never been conceded that God is not dependent upon human beings and, specifically, upon the white, American bourgeois. It has been presumed instead that God needs these churches, that God's integrity requires their effort, that God's existence in history is verified by their prosperity, popularity, and power. Today, with the legitimacy of their wealth under challenge, their reputation the butt of ridicule, and their power ineffectual, it becomes clear that their god is indeed dead and, even more threatening, that their god is not and never was God.

This book brings news that the Holy Spirit thrives and that if God has been too free and too godly to be possessed and imprisoned in the shrines and sanctuaries of white Christendom, God's existence has not been thereby limited or, so to speak, lessened. If this presence has been too discreet to be much noticed among the prosperous, it is practically ostentatious among the poor. If in the conventional churches God has gone ignored or profaned, God is known in joy and honor in a small congregation of blacks and some whites, of poor and a handful of not-so-poor in the midst of the Harlem scene. And if God's presence, genius, and militancy may be beheld in the life of Chambers Church on 123rd Street, there is reason for confidence that this can also be affirmed of other congregations scattered throughout the land however strange they may appear when compared to our traditional churches.

This book is the story of the Chambers congregation, or of some years of its witness, related by a man who has been one of its pastors. It evidences the vitality of the Holy Spirit in the only way in which God's reality is ever discerned in history, that is, incarnated in humanity in community, which is, sad to say, not the way in which white Christendom has ever expected or desired to encounter God.

But there God is, at Chambers in Harlem, in the midst of this people who persevere in embracing human life as the gift that it is, and insist, both in adversity and triumph, upon living humanly together. If the triumphs seem few or subtle or mysterious while the adversities are frequent and blunt and redundant, it is the transcendence of life over death here and now — in other words, the power

142

of the resurrection — that is, in any case, the singular humanizing fact.

Because of what I have elsewhere affirmed about the actuality of the church of Jesus Christ in the world, especially in present time, white, middle-class churchpeople often ask me where there might be a model or example of the viable church. I have known the Chambers congregation for thirteen years and it seems to be possessed with empirical integrity. Chambers *is* the church as the body of Christ. I am grateful for this book because it can be edifying to multitudes of those conformed in white Christendom who remain haunted by the question of where the living church is and what it is like.

There is a temptation, however, that those who are as yet strangers to the Christian life as it is being practiced in a place like Chambers will regard the congregation as novel or exceptional. To glamorize its work would be to isolate it and ultimately to dismiss it. I hope, on the contrary, that through this book others may behold a style of life that is not remarkable, but normative, and may become acquainted with the people of Christ at Chambers, who are not heroes or super-Christians, but an ordinary folk to whom life is a matter of God's generosity, not an issue of their virtue.

St. James' Day, 1969,
Block Island, Rhode Island

An Ecclesiastical Event

I WENT to Kansas City, Missouri, to address the national convention of the Disciples of Christ denomination. I recall introspecting some about it at the time, and in retrospect, too, I see it as a token of my own ecclesiastical involvement. That had been, as I have noted, precocious and extensive. Having renounced the priesthood and any other sort of churchly occupation, I gradually found myself in extraordinary demand as a preacher and speaker and consultant and teacher and leader in blatantly churchy circles. This was already an issue for me while I was a student, but it intensified as the years passed, greatly so by my decision to work in East Harlem and later on when I began to write. It would, perhaps, not have been a problem if, in the interim between adolescence and adulthood, I had not become a confessing Christian. It would have been all right, I think, if I had managed to remain steadfast as a nominal Christian or a churchman. Instead I had been converted, if that word can here be used without its corny and profane connotations. I forbear describing *that* ordeal, for now, except to say that, along the way, I had entered into reading the Bible — a bizarre thing for an Episcopalian to do, I know, and a traumatic exploit for anybody. There is, simply, this danger in reading the Bible that one may be emancipated from the jargon, stereotypes, fables, and similar encumbrances of church tradition and hear the

Second Birthday, 1970, pp. 143–48

Word of God. Well, I was being (I am being) regularly devastated in the privacy of my encounter with the biblical Word and that kept challenging the propriety of my ecclesiastical activities.

Too much of the immense resources of American Christendom, in the National Council of Churches and in the established denominations, were engaged in playing church in endless and revolving conferences and training sessions and consultations. The whole verbose, redundant enterprise was becoming so dissipated in talking about the Christian witness in society that few energies were left over to *do* the witness, assuming — something that conscience generally precluded — that the talk was responsible or even sensible. On this scene, as I saw it, I had become something of a curiosity — a layman who was a Christian, a non-professional who could be theologically articulate. In the confidence of our friendship, Anthony and I used to joke about "William Stringfellow, the boy theologian." Others bestowed different titles, probably the most frequent reference, publicly, to my "role" was as that of "gadfly." What was meant, I guess, was that, having no vested interest in the ecclesiastical establishment (a ha! except, perchance, the gadfly role!), I was free, and otherwise competent, enough to complain and criticize, prod and plead about the churches in contemporary America. Too often the difficulty with that task, I found, was that the ecclesiastical authorities, bureaucrats, and flunkies whom I addressed actually relished criticism as a means of further avoiding reformation or renewal. They were flagellants, morbidly enjoying punishment for misbehavior in which they fully intended to persevere. My involvement as "gadfly" or whatever-you-call-it was becoming a charade.

I would drop out of it. And I did, although, in the case of my own denomination, it would be more accurate to say that, before I had a chance to drop out, I was rejected by the ecclesiastical establishment of the Episcopal Church. There were intimations of that in several situations where invitations for my participation in this or that churchly event were issued and then withdrawn. There had been a proposal to censure me at a General Convention of the church. I was informed that some Episcopal seminaries had found me to be "too controversial" to have as a visiting lecturer. The bishops of some dioceses specifically asked me not to appear in parishes within their jurisdictions; one wrote that my coming to his diocese would be "premature." These things came to some sort of culmination, of course, when Bishop Pike asked that I be his legal counsel in the heresy proceedings that had been instituted against him and when Anthony and I wrote and published the book about that conflict, *The Bishop Pike Affair.* It is, I most earnestly affirm, a responsible, scrupulously truthful book. Anthony and I had felt somewhat flattered when we learned that a Madison Avenue–type public relations man had been engaged to try to prevent the book from being reviewed on certain television programs and the like. With such enemies, we were sure, for once, we had done something right. Months later, while I was preoccupied in illness, news came of another reprisal because of that book: I had been removed from the Faith and Order Commission of the World Council of Churches, where, for six years, I had represented the Episcopal Church and where I had been the only layman and one of but a handful of persons under forty years of age. To this day I have never been informed officially about this by the elders of the church; the word first reached me from an English newspaper that lamented the deed; later letters from many colleagues on the commission filled in the details. There is a comity in the World Council of Churches, not dissimilar to senatorial courtesy, that dictates that an appointee to a council body be acceptable to the authorities of his own church. In effect, and despite protests from representatives of other churches in Africa, Asia, and both Western and Eastern Europe, I was removed because I was (I suppose I still am) personally obnoxious to the Episcopalian authorities. Ironically, of all of my churchly involvements, Faith and Order had been the one that was, though the commission be cumbersome and slow and conservative, worthwhile. Faith and Order is ponderous and, perhaps, too self-serious, but it is not a dishonest enterprise, and it is not a facetious effort, and it was these latter regions in Christendom that I had determined to quit.

I lay for a long time on a hotel bed in Kansas City attended by such reminiscences. In another hour or two I was to address this church convention. *What the hell am I doing here?* I thought. *This is not the church: this is some American aberration of the church.* I either cursed or prayed, the two being hard to distinguish. I read Ephesians. Unlike some friends of my own generation — like Harvey Cox or Malcolm Boyd — I do not denigrate institutionalism as such in the church. I

146

see, specifically in account of Pentecost, that the church's peculiar vocation is as an institution — as the exemplary principality — as the holy nation. So ideas of a non-institutional church or a deinstitution-alized church or underinstitutionalized church seem to me to be as nebulous as the Greek philosophy from which such ideas come and contrary to the biblical precedent. That does not temper my critique of the inherited churchly institutions; in fact it sharpens it and makes it more urgent. Now that mark that verifies the integrity of the church as institution and sets the church apart from the other institutions — the state, the university, the Pentagon, General Electric, et al. — as the exemplary or pioneer or holy institution is the freedom of the church from primary and controlling concern about her own survival. Survival of the institution is the operative ethic of all institutions, *in their fallenness.* The church is called into being in freedom from that ethic of survival and where renewal or reformation in the church happens for real, that very freedom is being exercised and the church is viable and faithful. *It's all there, in Ephesians,* I smiled. *My speech is in Ephesians.* And so it was.

147

On Being Haunted by the Angel
of the Church at Sardis

> To the angel of the church at Sardis write: "These are the words of the One who holds the seven spirits of God, the seven stars: I know all your ways; that though you have a name for being alive, you are dead. Wake up, and put some strength into what is left, which must otherwise die! For I have not found any work of yours completed in the eyes of my God. So remember the teaching you received; observe it, and repent."
>
> REVELATION 3:1–3a

This is a moment of remarkable uncertainty for the destiny of the Episcopal Church.

I do not suppose that the public existence of this church is threatened: there is sufficient accrued wealth to maintain the ecclesiastical façade of the Episcopal Church in the United States indefinitely. The issue, instead, concerns the viability of this church as an institution. What is urgently and poignantly in question is whether this church is capable, in the foreseeable future, of being worthy of the

---

The Witness, September 1975, pp. 4–6

commitment and participation of human beings. Having "a name for being alive," is the Episcopal Church consigned to death? The angel of the church at Sardis now haunts the Episcopal Church.

What has lately brought this situation into sharp focus is the contention about the ordination of women to the priesthood and, most specifically, the actual ordination of eleven women to the priesthood.

There might readily have been some other precipitating issue and event — it could have been anything directly implicating the recognition and acceptance of persons in full dignity. Thus, I think this church would be approximately where it today is even if the ordination matter had not become timely. That view is verified by the fact that other churches in America, of comparable vintage and status, simultaneously suffer profound crises.

Indeed, to place it in comprehensive reference, the Episcopal Church's tribulation is but an instance of the disintegration in the present day of the Constantinian Accommodation, which has shaped Christendom in the West since the fourth century, by which the church, refuting apostolic precedent, acquired a radical, vested interest in the established order and became culpably identified with the institutional status quo in culture and society, in economics and politics, in warfare and imperialism, in racism and sexism. At last, as Kierkegaard anticipated more than a century ago, the comity of Constantine is collapsing, coincident with the disruption and retraction of Western domination of the world, and the churches privy to the Constantinian arrangement have been plunged into turmoil.

The trouble in the Episcopal Church is an episode in this far greater drama. If anyone feels compelled to fix blame for the precarious position of the Episcopal Church now, I beg them to spare both the women priests and the incumbent bishops. I suggest they blame Constantine.

In any case, the outcome for the new priests ordained on July 29, 1974, in Philadelphia is apt to determine whether the Episcopal Church is any longer capable of significant change for the sake of reclaiming an authentic life as a church of Jesus Christ, as a church having "a name of being alive." In this connection, I hope it will be recognized that the cause of the women who are priests and of those associated with them is not militant, not aggressive, not iconoclastic, not revolutionary. The cause is one of renewal, of recovery, of restoration, of reformation.

The controversy has reached a juncture that preaches degeneracy. The Episcopal Church is in a state of dysfunction, or, if it can be said to be working as an institution, it is so only in a grossly inappropriate manner. Recall what has happened:

At the so-called emergency meeting of the House of Bishops at O'Hare Airport last August, the presiding bishop stated, and it was then widely disseminated by the official, national press agency of the church, that the bishops had "ruled" the Philadelphia ordinations "invalid" despite the truth that the House of Bishops lacks juridical or legislative competence to utter any such ruling.

That misrepresentation — and defamation — left the new priests little alternative except to affirm their ordinations straightforwardly by exercising their priesthood respectively where invited by parishes or missions to do so.

No canonical charges have been prosecuted against any of the Philadelphia priests and, in fact, there has been an elaborate strategy to avoid ecclesiastical trials of these women.

Similarly, the Board of Inquiry convened to investigate charges against the ordaining bishops resorted to fantastic and convoluted exegesis of the heresy canon in order to evade their trials.

Meanwhile, two rectors — William Wendt and Peter Beebe — who, with the support of their vestries and parishioners, invited women priests to preside at celebrations of the Eucharist have been tried and convicted in diocesan courts.

None of these events need have happened. There is no canonical impediment to the ordination of women in the Episcopal Church. The various dioceses are free and able to ordain women as priests now. It is custom only that is challenged; the canon law or the church constitution requires no alteration, addition, or amendment. The General Convention may legislate, but such is not a mandatory prerequisite for the ordination of women by dioceses disposed to ordain women to the priesthood.

By this same token, as well as according to ample and venerable precedent in the Anglican Communion, including the recognition accorded the irregular consecration of the first American bishop, what has been needed, in the aftermath of the ordinations in Philadelphia, is the recognition of the bishops and the standing committees directly concerned with each of the women ordained in Philadelphia as priests.

This has not occurred yet. The bishops with jurisdiction over the women priests have been reluctant to act "unilaterally." It is said to be preferable to await action of the General Convention for the plenary ordination of women and thereafter — perhaps — somehow — to deal with those already ordained. The argument sounds appealing, but it has been overwhelmed by history. The church could await the leisure of General Convention only so long as the ordination of women remained a hypothetical issue. Since July 29, 1974, the matter has not been hypothetical. There are, now, those women priests. The pretense cannot be maintained that they do not exist. It is pastorally elementary that they be confronted as persons. It is precisely on that point that the great reluctance to put any of the Philadelphia priests on trial has significance. Whatever their fate in any such proceedings — from recognition to deposition — at least they would be treated as persons and rendered accountable as such for their actions. As it has developed, however, they have had to endure the absurd humiliation of witnessing others, in the position of accessories after the fact of the Philadelphia ordinations, brought to trial, so that the quashing of proceedings against the principals represents a penultimate condescension.

Whatever else may be said to have transpired that famous day in Philadelphia, the indulgence in a protracted, general policy debate on the ordination of women was obviated. After that, the matter ceased to be hypothetical; it became embodied in human beings; then the issue could no longer be dealt with, responsibly, politically, legally, theologically, or pastorally, except by confronting those women who have been ordained.

That this has yet to be done has explanation in (pardon the expression) the gentleman's agreement wrought in the House of Bishops — embellished though it be in a pseudo-theological rhetoric of "collegiality" — to restrain diocesan recognition of women already ordained and to stop new ordinations of women pending the uncertain result of the byzantine politics of the General Convention. I fear this means an appalling pastoral failure in the House of Bishops.

Can there be any reconciliation? Does the Episcopal Church retain a capacity for reconciliation? Reconciliation has no sentimental character. Reconciliation involves facing the truth and saying the truth, as hard as that may seem. Reconciliation does not mean political trading. The Book of Common Prayer cautions that reconciliation has preface in repentance and in restitution.

A sign of reconciliation, now, for the Episcopal Church would be the recognition of those ordained in Philadelphia in their various dioceses forthwith. A similar sign would be the ordination of women to the priesthood by those dioceses disposed to do so forthwith.

Perchance such signs would prompt the angel of the church at Sardis to haunt some other place.

St. Ann's-in-the-Sea

I RECOGNIZE that one way to construe my affirmations of the communities of East Harlem and Block Island, and of their similar virtues, is as *church*. The life of these communities — as I have known them — resembles the society that the church is called to be in the world. At the least, this is true of East Harlem and true of Block Island at some times. The same rubric explains my seriousness about the circus; the circus often seems to me to bear more characteristics of the church than the professed church can claim. Indeed, much the same can be affirmed concerning *any* society. Every society aspires, no matter how tawdry or ambiguous it is, to be the church. This is just another version, put backwards, of the confession that the church is called to be the exemplary principality in the midst of fallen creation.

A few years ago, some parents asked me to give confirmation instruction to their children, in the absence of an Episcopal priest on the island. I agreed, with the bishop's authorization, to do so. I almost immediately lamented that decision when I examined the materials currently being published by the established churches, like the Episcopal Church, for these purposes. The stuff was theologically untrustworthy. The day of the first class I informed the children that we would not be using any curriculum, but in its place we would do

Simplicity of Faith, 1982, pp. 100–103

some Bible study in the book of the Acts of the Apostles, because it reports the precedent of the church historically, and because the purpose in the class was to find out what it meant to be a consenting and witnessing member of the church. We would also review the catechism, as it is set forth in the *Book of Common Prayer,* to see if we could make any sense of it. (Oddly, I had once had a somewhat similar occasion to become involved in Bible study with some East Harlem adolescents; that experience is related in detail in *Count It All Joy.*) Toward the conclusion of the class, which had ten sessions during which we managed to read the first four chapters of Acts, I asked each of the students — they were all either eleven or twelve years of age — whether or not there was any reason for the church to be on Block Island, in view of what the class had discovered the church to be from reading in Acts. They were unanimous, some rather strenuous, in the opinion that, because the community as a whole acted so much like the church, there was no special cause to have a separate institution on the island that professed the name *church* (and certainly not four churches). Now Providence, and other places on the mainland, of which they had knowledge almost exclusively via television, was different, they volunteered: Providence really needs the presence of the church.

Later I shared their insights with Anthony. He readily agreed with them, both about Block Island and Providence. I did, too.

Nevertheless, in due course, they were each confirmed in the Episcopal Church. Some have remained on the island and become involved in the curious little congregation, or paracongregation, that professes to be the Episcopal Church on Block Island. When it was organized it took the name St. Ann's-by-the-Sea and in due course a small church building, featuring a sanctuary, was constructed. The congregation is said to have flourished modestly for many years until the great hurricane of 1938, which was devastating for Block Island. In that storm, St. Ann's Church literally blew away. Ever since, island wags have referred to it as St. Ann's-*in*-the-Sea. The congregation remained moribund in the aftermath of this hurricane, which, after all, was officially designated "an act of God."

Then, about a dozen years ago, St. Ann's began to revive. Initially, people — including recent immigrants to the island like Anthony and myself — gathered as a house church, reciting the daily offices or, occasionally, antecommunion, doing some Bible study, and discussing the news of the island and of the world. Once in a while a priest would visit and there would be Holy Communion. Free of the usual parish encumbrances of organization and property, the house church gradually attracted more and more people, and in the summer weeks it seemed appropriate to begin to have weekly services with a visiting priest at the site of the ruins of the building that had been demolished by act of God in 1938.

That may have been a fatal decision. Since then, the congregation has been canonically recognized as a mission of the Diocese of Rhode Island, the traditional polity for missions has been instituted, and, predictably, the sentiment for rebuilding has steadily increased. We do not do Bible study any more; we do not seriously consider the mission of the church in the world, including Block Island; we seldom ask any ecumenical questions. We are into raising money, which we will likely spend to embellish the social life of Episcopalians and their kindred in the summer colony. Has anyone ever heard this story about the church before?

Anthony and I and some few others became dissenters from the prevailing attitude in St. Ann's-in-the-Sea, with its ecumenical indifference and preoccupation with property and pretense. We have understood all this to signal the process of radical secularization that the Episcopal Church — in common with the other "established" churches in America — suffers. There has been a basic surrender to the culture in which the preservation of the ecclesiastical institution and fabric *for its own sake* has acquired a priority that trivializes the gospel of Jesus Christ and scandalizes the apostolic precedent of the church.

Authority in Baptism:
The Vocation of Jesus and
the Ministry of the Laity

Preface

Much has happened since this book was first proposed to me.

I had been invited to give some lectures by way of Bible study at a conference convened in the summer of 1982 by the Board of National Ministries of the American Baptist Convention at Denison University in Ohio. The topic of the conference was styled "Jesus' Ministry and Our Vocation." This was translated in the correspondence with me about the event to mean it was to be a conference about the ministry of the laity. My particular assignment was to comment each morning at the conference on segments of a text — Luke 4:16–21. Simultaneously Judson Press asked me to augment the Denison presentations for publication as a book suitable for study and discussion uses in congregations.

Preface to incomplete book, 1983?, unpublished manuscript. The manuscript indicates that this book would have been dedicated to Daniel Whetmore, the young seminarian who stayed with Stringfellow for several years in the early eighties.

I had acceded to both invitations even though I felt somewhat disquieted by the conference arrangements. There was, I thought, so heavy an emphasis on a theme that the whole effort risked being contrived and, as for my part of it, it tended to be prejudicial toward the open access to the Bible that I had espoused for a long, long time. The topic — reduced, as it, of course, had been to a cliché or slogan, "Jesus' Ministry and Our Vocation" — seemed to presuppose theologically the exegesis of the text to be studied. I did not then know whether or not it appropriate to speak of Jesus as having a "ministry." For one thing, ministry is, usually, an ecclesial term. That in itself may render it inapt as a reference to Jesus. Jesus Christ was not a church person (there is much New Testament evidence that he would have been an anti-church person, had he the chance and the choice). Moreover, Jesus Christ was not a Christian — a straightforward truth too often ignored. It certainly, in short, should not be presumed that he had "a ministry" in any sense comparable to the ways in which that word is now invoked. By the same token, linking "our vocation" (whatever that means!) to Jesus' putative, erstwhile ministry, so-called, is not a connection that can be taken for granted, as the theme, as stated, seems to do.

Besides, from the viewpoint of Bible study, this thematic approach more or less precluded the aspects of humor, paradox, adventure, and surprise that, in my own experience, I had come to expect in the biblical material and found most characteristic, intrinsically, of the biblical witness.

At the same time, however clumsily the conference had been entitled, it seemed clear enough that consideration of the ministry of the laity was what was intended as the subject. That, together with the passage from Luke and its' context in the gospels, necessarily raised the issue of baptism and the significance of baptism. If — at last — the American Baptists turn attention to the meaning of baptism (I thought to myself as I pondered these invitations) it could be truly momentous and certainly ought not to be greeted apathetically.

So it came to pass, despite misgivings about the advance programming of the conference, that I agreed to go to Denison and then to accomplish a book for Judson Press.

If anyone finds it gratuitous or audacious for me, an Episcopalian nominally, to address Baptists about baptism, there is ample precedent for such candor and boldness in my previous books. The diligent reader of earlier books of mine will have noticed that *theologically* I could fairly be described as a closet Anabaptist. There is nowadays (as there most certainly was in the days of Obadiah Holmes) a great distance between the assorted Baptists and the Anabaptists. Yet, remember, one and all, that the distinctions between these traditions has practically to do with comprehending the authority bestowed and distributed among the laity in baptism! The distance may seem much, but it is circular.

The extraordinary distortions of language and syntax that, in the technocratic society, victimize us all, inhibiting our listening to one another as human beings, render it the more difficult to approach the Bible in an attitude of listening, inhibit or otherwise hinder us from becoming open and vulnerable to the Word.

Introduction

> And as he was walking in the temple, the chief priests and the scribes and the elders came to him and they said to him, "By what authority are you doing these things, who gave you this authority to do them?" Jesus said to them, "I will ask you a question; answer me and I will tell you by what authority I do these things. Was the baptism of John from heaven or from men? Answer me." And they argued with one another, "If we say, 'From heaven,' he will say, 'Why then did you not believe him?' But shall we say, 'From men?'" — they were afraid of the people, for all held that John was a real prophet. So they answered Jesus, "We do not know." And Jesus said to them, "Neither will I tell you by what authority I do these things."
>
> MARK 11:27–33

In circumstances in which the churches become profoundly secularized — such as *now*, in the Episcopal Church in the prevailing culture in America — attempted comparisons, recalling the biblical precedent and experience of the church yields only anomalies.

There is, for instance, much emphasis within American Christendom upon the ministry of the laity. Yet, oddly, for the most part, such discussion does not treat baptism at all, even though baptism is the sacrament of the laity: the initiation into the historic community of the people of God and the differentiation of those baptized from worldly identification and status. One might expect that, where the ministry of the laity is both the subject and concern, attention would focus upon the significance of baptism, particularly as to any of its biblical connections.

One reason for this curious neglect of baptism as the elementary topic in reconnaissance of the ministry of the laity is the endemic privatizing of the practice of baptism in the churches. More often than not, even though baptism is done in the presence of a gathered congregation, it has come to be regarded as a primarily personal, family, or religious observance rather than as the notorious, public, and political action baptism is reported to be in the New Testament.

In the apostolic community, thus, baptism signified the new citizenship in Christ that supersedes the old citizenship under Caesar. With that context, baptism, nowadays no less than in the biblical era, not only solemnizes characteristic tensions between the church and a regime but reaches beyond that to confess and uphold the sovereignty of the Word of God now militant in history over against the pretensions of any regime.

One consequence of this common disregard for baptism and for the meaning of baptism while ostensibly pondering the ministry of the laity is the belittlement of the authority that baptism vests in the laity within the polity of the American church and, simultaneously, the authority of the laity in the witness to the gospel in the world.

Considerations such as these provoke me to conclude that the starting point apropos for any exploration of the ministry of the laity is baptism and, furthermore, that the way to begin to understand baptism is in terms of the *two* baptisms cited biblically, that is, the baptism by water, epitomized in the ministry of John the Baptizer, and the baptism of the Holy Spirit, promised, redundantly, by Jesus Christ to his disciples.

In the present century at least, the churches within American Christendom have mainly allowed these two baptisms and the issue of the significance of each for the other to be usurped and vulgarized by sectarian (and, coincidentally, commercial) exploitations. Sectarian ranting has been so preemptive and just so loud that it has induced or coerced quietism in the established churches concerning the baptism of the Holy Spirit. Moreover, there has been widespread acquiescence in the churches to the fake and false idea, so much extolled by the sectarian hucksters, that the baptism of the Spirit is a uniquely private, radically pietistic, traumatic high generated by a unilateral and exclusive attention of the Holy Spirit to someone in isolation, existing in a void, disconnected from the incarnate vitality of the Word of God in the rest of humanity and, indeed, in the life of the rest of creation. Such hysterical views of the Holy Spirit at once defame the living God of history and induce hallucinations or similar fantasies, and thereby victimize and dehumanize those who espouse them. Meanwhile, these are notions that have little or no standing in the biblical message.

As a matter of history for the disciples and, for all of that, as a matter of theology for contemporary Christians, the biblical happening most pertinent to the baptism of the Spirit, is, manifestly, Pentecost. The scene, as we learn of it from the book of the Acts of the Apostles, is not private but quite public; it is not individualistic but notorious, not idiosyncratic but scandalous; and onlookers are said to behold Pentecost as provocative and controversial; it appears to have been an offense to the ruling authorities. Central in the experience of the power of the Holy Spirit among the disciples, both commonly and severally, is a transcendence of worldly distinction (as race, age, sex, class, occupation, nationality, language, tongue) that anticipates the eschatological consummation of the whole of fallen creation in the Kingdom of God. Simultaneously, in Pentecost each person receives the renewal of human gifts and capabilities, the restoration, as it were, of one's original personhood, a reconciliation with and within self in utterly intimate detail happening within the environment of each person's reconciliation with the rest of humanity and the whole of created life throughout time. These same aspects of Pentecost — the most intensely personal and the cosmic and ultimate — become, ever after, the marks of authentic and credible conversion of the baptism of the Spirit. When a person nowadays can be said to be baptized of the Spirit, it means that the person is, verily, incorporated into the experience of Pentecost.

The sectarian co-option of the baptism of the Spirit has caused some of the churches to construe the two baptisms as alternatives, as if one might *either* be baptized by water *or* baptized of the Spirit, but venerable liturgical tradition recognizes and recites the association of the two. In ancient practice baptism by water was customarily coupled with entreaties for the action of the Holy Spirit, while baptism of the Spirit was confessed and sacramentally attested by baptism and by water. The complimentary and edifying interplay of the two baptisms has been characteristic of the faithful churchly life despite the sectarian interpolations that have ridiculed baptism by water as perfunctory or as sentimental or as, somehow, mockery. A lesson to be learned from such ridicule is that the name of God is never invoked in vain — that is, without consequence or effect — even when that name is called upon vainly — that is, for some cause or purpose unworthy of the name.

Therefore, there is no reason to attribute credibility to the sectarian definitions of either baptism. As to the beneficial relationship between baptism by water and that of the Spirit in the biblical context, it is enough to recall the baptism of Jesus by John the Baptist as that was so promptly verified — and transfigured — by the initiative of the Holy Spirit.

In the same context, the passage set forth hereabove as an introit, concerning the interrogation of Jesus by the chief priests and scribes as to his authority, is equally relevant because of the thrust of the response of Jesus: *Was the baptism of John from heaven or from men?* (Mark 11:30; see Mark 11:27–33; cf. Matt. 21:23–27, Luke 20:1–8). Those I have called, here, sectarians who make presumptuous claims about baptism of the Spirit do not like the baptism by water or see its significance, because that threatens what they habitually assert about a uniquely private character of the relation between God and the person baptized. No one, however, need feel ashamed or deprived in baptism by water. It is, in truth, the confession of the church, in a gathered congregation, that the grace of the Word of God, which has been sufficient to reconcile them, within themselves, with one another, and with the whole of creation, is ample for the renewal of the life of the one presented to be baptized. Such a confession by a congregation is a most audacious political statement expounding the sovereignty of the Word of God, in its imminence as much as its ultimacy, and an open affront to all principalities or persons who feign rule in this world. That in some churchly traditions infants are baptized

161

by water only magnifies the audacity of the congregation's confession and solemnizes its undertaking to nurture the child baptized in resistance to the worldly powers that pretend to rule.

In short, neither baptism by water nor that of the Spirit authorizes or abets conformity to this world.

I believe that the two baptisms are, in truth, indivisible. The one cannot be comprehended without reference to the other — it was even so when Jesus was baptized — and if there is not that correlation, that which remains is distorted and ambivalent. Or, to put it another way, in baptism both an act of the church and an action of the Holy Spirit simultaneously are essential.

In terms of authority, both baptisms signify a self-knowledge, vouchsafed for the one baptized, that truly discerns the way the world is and that frees the baptized to live in the world and that enables the baptized to serve the evident needs of the world's common existence. In baptism, authority means the authority of a servant.

Within the polity of the church it is a facet of fidelity to the gospel to remember that everyone remains baptized, everyone participates in the ministry of the laity, everyone has the status of servant. Those who are ecclesiastically ordered, as deacons or priests or bishops or those who enter upon the monastic life, do not thereby surrender or alter or diminish their disposition as laity, as baptized people, as members of the body of Christ called to the world's service.

OUTLINE
chapter one: Creation and Baptism
    the ministry of John the Baptist
    the vocation of Jesus Christ
    baptism and dominion in creation
chapter two: Fallen Creation and Renewed Creation
    the restoration of Israel
    the sin of blasphemy
    the call to repentance
chapter three: The Acceptable Time
    what *is* the acceptable year?
    when is the acceptable year?
    the political significance of contemporary worship
    eschatology and ethics

No Priesthood: No Laity

IN THE churches of Protestantism in America, much of the popularized discussion of the ministry of the laity has overlooked the radical
interdependence and reciprocity between the functions of the priesthood and the laity in the total ministry of the Body of Christ in the
world. There is no priesthood without a laity serving the world; there
is no laity without a priesthood serving the laity. There is not one
without the other. In many Protestant churches nowadays there is
neither.

Wherever this prevails, the priesthood is abandoned or repudiated or so radically misconceived that the clergy have become a
substitute laity whose function is to represent publicly — *in place of
the laity* — the presence of the church in the world. The clergy have
become hired spokespeople for religion in human life. They have been
invited to decorate public life but restrained from intervening significantly in it. They have been relegated to the literal periphery — the
invocations and the benedictions — of secular affairs. The clergy have
become the face of the church in the world; they have become a
superficial, symbolic, ceremonial laity.

Such degrading of the ordained ministry is serious enough in
itself, but it is commonly associated in the practical life of the churches
with a laity who are mere spectators to religious exercises — paying

---

A Private and Public Faith, 1962, pp. 38, 40–41, 42–44)

their admission, as it were, to behold a pageant or cultus practice in which their critical and wholesome participation is neither expected nor welcomed.

That the clergy act as a substitute laity and the laity are just observers of religion is, of course, consistent with and probably the product of the American idea that religion has only to do with religion but not the cares of the world. . . .

In Jesus Christ there is no chasm between God and the world.

Jesus Christ means that God cares extremely, decisively, inclusively, immediately for the ordinary, transient, proud, wonderful, besetting, frivolous, hectic, lusty things of human life. The reconciliation of God and the world in Jesus Christ means that in Christ there is a radical and integral relationship of all human beings and of all things. *In Christ all things are held together* (Col. 1:17*b*).

The church as the Body of Christ in the world has, shares, manifests, and represents the same radical integrity. All who are in Christ — all members of Christ's Body in the world — know and live in the same integrity in their personal relationships with every other creature in their own, specific personal histories. Existentially and empirically, the reconciliation of the world with God in Jesus Christ establishes a person in unity with both God and the whole world. The singular life of the Christian is a sacrament — a recall, a representation, an enactment, a communication — of that given, actual unity, whether in the gathering of the congregation now and then or whether in the scattering of the members within the daily affairs of the world. To put it mildly, then, it is careless and misleading to speak of the action of God in the world in Christ in terms of "making the gospel relevant" to the secular. The Body of Christ lives in the world in the unity between God and the world wrought in Christ, and, in a sense, the Body of Christ lives in the world *as* the unity of God and the world in Christ.

The Body of Christ lives in the world on behalf of the world, in intercession for the world. In the most esoteric and even to many clergy and churchpeople, apparently remote and irrelevant image of that life, when a congregation gathers in sacramental worship, the members of the Body are offering the world to God, not for God's sake, not for their own sake, but for the sake of the world, and the members then and there celebrate God's presence in the world, and on behalf of the world, even though the world does not yet discern God's presence. . . .

For lay folk in the church this means that there is no forbidden work. There is no corner of human existence, however degraded or neglected, into which they may not venture; no person, however beleaguered or possessed, whom they may not befriend and represent; no cause, however vain or stupid, in which they may not witness; no risk, however costly or imprudent, that they may not undertake. This intimacy with the world as it is, this particular freedom, this awful innocence toward the world that Christians are given, makes them look like suckers. They look like that to others because they are engaged in the wholesale expenditure of life. They look like that because they are without caution or prudence in preserving their own lives. They look like that because they are not threatened by the power of death either over their own lives or over the rest of the world. They look like that because they are free to give their lives — to die — imminently, today, for the sake of anyone or anything at all, thereby celebrating the One who died for all though none be worthy, not even one (cf. 1 Cor. 12:19).

Christians are not distinguished by their political views, or moral decisions, or habitual conduct, or personal piety, or, least of all, by their churchly activities. Christians are distinguished by their radical esteem for the Incarnation — to use the traditional jargon — by their reverence for the life of God in the whole of creation, even and, in a sense, especially, creation in the travail of sin.

The characteristic place to find Christians is among their enemies.

The first place to look for Christ is in hell.

For those ordained by the church for the priesthood, this means that their office and ministry are located at the interstices of the Body of Christ and of the congregations that represent that Body visibly and notoriously in the world. The ministry of the priesthood is a ministry to the members of the Body in their relations to each other, relations consequent to their incredibly diversified ministry within the world. The ministry of the priesthood is one directed to the most sophisticated life of the church, the church, that is, gathered as a congregation in worship, assembled for the exposition and exhibition of the Word of God. This is the ministry addressed to the care and nurture of the members of the Body of Christ for the sake of their several, various, and common uses in the world. This is the ministry serving those people who come out of the world now and then to worship God together and encompass and include in their intercession to God the cares of the world as they know it and are involved in it. This is the ministry of confession in which the task and witness of each member of the Body is heard and related to that of all other members of the Body who are now or who have ever been or, indeed, who are yet to be. This is the ministry that cares for and conserves the tradition of the church — that is, the continuity and integrity of the Christian mission ever since Pentecost. This is the ministry devoted to the health and holiness of the Body of Christ in the world.

Protestantism's Rejection of the Bible

THE weirdest corruption of contemporary American Protestantism is its virtual abandonment of the Word of God in the Bible. That is ironic because access to the Bible and devotion to the Word of God in the Bible was that out of which authentic Protestantism came into being. It is strange, too, because though the Bible suffers such neglect in Protestantism, the Protestants continue to boast of their esteem for the Bible. In one degree or fashion or another, this condition exists in all the churches of American Protestantism: the sects as well as the established denominations, the churches with ancestries in other countries and those indigenous to America.

The Bible has been closed in preaching in American congregations, for one thing, for a very long time. It has been my fortune to circulate widely among the churches of Protestantism in all parts of the nation and in all sectors of the confessional spectrum, in churches rich and poor, rural and urban, segregated and integrated, conservative and liberal, small and large. I can barely recall having heard in them biblical preaching. Instead I have heard both dull and interesting opinions of clergy about religious etiquette, ecclesiastical politics, moral behavior and oddments, and all of this has been, where not

Count It All Joy, 1967, pp. 13–20

actually heretical, typically inane, corny, and preposterous. But very seldom is there the confident and responsible exposure of God's own Word in a manner in which the people may know and rejoice in the event of the Word of God and (to refute those who stupidly suppose that biblical preaching has no contemporary significance) be so enlightened in the biblical Word that they discern and celebrate that very Word present and militant in modern society.

Alas, it is not only in preaching that the Bible has been closed or else misused and manipulated but also in the liturgical life of much of American Protestantism, especially among the denominations and sects indigenous to this country. Remember that whether it be simple or elaborate, formal or spontaneous, any corporate public worship is liturgical. Whatever the style or dignity of a particular liturgy, the most important element is that the liturgy be biblical. It is scriptural integrity where the liturgy is a theatricalization of the Word of God in the Bible — that is indispensable to corporate worship in public, not the disposition, personal faith, or particular gifts of the clergy presiding or the sincerity, beliefs, or interest of the people gathered. . . .

Protestants, of course, have been fiercely attentive to preserving a veneer of religiosity (*not* Christianity) in secular schools. Many Protestants who become frantic, as was mentioned, about the recital of so-called prayers and whether verses of the Bible are read (inevitably out of context) in classrooms, have never even considered praying with their own children at home nor have they become upset because the Bible is virtually banned in Sunday school. Protestants in America have been so much preoccupied in maintaining the public schools nominally religious that they have defaulted in establishing either their homes or churches as places of Christian teaching and learning.

Nowadays Protestants in America are neither intimate with nor reliant upon the Word of God in the Bible, whether in preaching, in services in the sanctuaries, or in education and nurture. Yet it is the Word of God in the Bible that all Christians are particularly called to hear, witness, trust, honor, and love. It is only in that Word that Protestantism can have either vivacity or probity anymore.

I beg you not to be misled by my affirmation of the availability and centrality of the Word of God in the Bible nor by my deploration of the diffidence toward the Bible in American Protestant preaching, liturgics, and teaching. As to the latter, I know that there are, here and there, notable exceptions to the allegations made; that there are such exceptions only sharpens the indictment. As to the former, let it be said bluntly that my esteem for the Word of God in the Bible does not mean that I am a biblical literalist or a fundamentalist of any sort.

Paradoxically, the trouble with fundamentalists, as I try to listen to them, is their shocking failure to regard and use the Bible conscientiously enough. If they honored the Bible more highly they would appreciate that the Word of God will endure demythologizing, that the Word cannot be threatened by anything whatever given humanity to discover and know through any science or discipline of the world, or hindered by textual criticism or hampered by linguistic analysis, or harmed by vernacular translations. All these are welcome to Christians as enhancements of the knowledge of the fullness of the Word of God and of the grandeur of human access to the Word. More than that, if the fundamentalists actually took the Bible seriously, they would *inevitably* love the world more readily, instead of fearing the world, because the Word of God is free and active in this world and Christians can only comprehend the Word out of their involvement in this world, as the Bible so redundantly testifies.

I am no biblical scholar; I have neither competence nor temperament to be one. The ordinary Christian, lay or clergy, does not need to be a scholar to have recourse to the Bible and, indeed, to live within the Word of God in the Bible in this world. What the ordinary Christian is called to do is to open the Bible and listen to the Word.

Listening is a rare happening among human beings. You cannot listen to the word another is speaking if you are preoccupied with your appearance or impressing the other, or if you are trying to decide what you are going to say when the other stops talking, or if you are debating about whether the word being spoken is true or relevant or agreeable. Such matters may have their place, but only after listening to the word as the word is being uttered. Listening, in other words, is a primitive act of love, in which a person gives self to another's word, making self accessible and vulnerable to that word.

It is very much like that when a person comes to the Bible. One must first of all listen to the Word that the Bible speaks, putting aside, for the time being, such other issues as whether the Word is credible or congenial or consistent or significant. By all means, if you will, raise these questions, but, first, *listen to the Word*.

Let the Bible be treated, too, with at least the respect you accord a letter from a person. If you receive a letter and care to know the word of the letter, you would not open it, read a paragraph or two, then abandon it for two or three months, pick it up again to read a few more sentences on another page, leave it aside once more, and later return to it again. No. If you care about the word of the letter, you would open it and listen to it attentively as a whole. After that, you might go back to this or that part of it to ponder or dispute, but first you would read it in its own context, asking only, What is being said? What is the word? The Bible deserves that much regard. And, if one cares to discern the Word of God in the Bible, then one must listen to the Bible in the Bible's own context and not deal with the Bible in a random, perfunctory, smattering fashion.

Some will think this a naive approach to the Word of God in the Bible. I suppose it is just that. It is one that simply affirms that the Word of God has content, integrity, and life that belongs to God and that this can be received and comprehended by ordinary human beings. It is a view that regards the Bible more as a newspaper than as a systematic body of theological doctrine or as religious instruction or as moral law or, for that matter, as mere esoteric mythology. The Bible reports the news of the Word of God manifest and militant in the events of this history in a way that is accessible, lucid, and edifying for the common reader. The Word of God is for humanity, and through the Bible that Word is addressed to human beings where they are, just as they are, in this world.

Such naivety toward the Word of God does not repudiate or threaten other ways in which the Bible may be esteemed and used — as theology, mythology, poetry, literature, symbol, prophecy, ethics, or chronicle. But it does insist that anyone may listen to the Word in the Bible innocent of any special skill or learning. And it does mean that all other uses of the Bible are subject to the discipline of God's own living Word as such and *not* the other way around, when people impose their own opinions, prides, methods, and interpretations upon the Bible as if to test the Word of God by human words. God speaks for God in this world; no one speaks in God's stead, though, by God's grace, a person may hear God's Word and become a witness to it.

In the churches and outside the churches it is quite popular in the present day (though also, as the Letter to the Colossians indicates, in earlier times) to suggest that the content of the Word of God in the Bible is a matter of such indifference to God that it is only a question of interpretations and insight. The unavoidable corollary is that one person's view is as apt as another's, which is, of course, a way of denying the integrity of the Word of God and, as the "death of God" vogue illustrates, ends in a denial of the existence of God.

A similar issue arises in the relationships of persons. This introduction is, for example, being written during a visit to Australia, during which I have met a great variety of people in a diversity of situations. In another two weeks, if the world lasts that much longer, and if I live, I will be back at work in New York encountering clients and colleagues there. If, somehow, all of those with whom I have been in this time gathered together in the same room, they would each be able to speak of the one whom each has met in terms of the specific and various circumstances of each meeting. If I have integrity as a person, it will be discernible, as each one speaks of having somewhere and somehow met me, that each and every one testifies to having met the same person despite the diversity of conditions and locations of these happenings. Although the testimony of these many witnesses vary in many ways, it will nonetheless be evident that it is one person of whom they speak, who has been made known to them in different places and manifold circumstances. On the other hand, if, as a person, I have no integrity, if I am instead playing roles in these varying situations, if my own existence is a pretense and has no independence from the impressions or opinions of those whom I meet here and there, then it is as if I exist only in the interpretations of others; then it is as if I do not really exist at all.

The problem of the interpretations that people make of the Bible is similar. The Bible is a wondrously diversified testament of the Word of God disclosed to humanity in an array of events in which it is discernible that it is the same One of whom all these witnesses speak. God *is* and God possesses an existence and integrity quite free from those who witness to God or those who feign to do so. The versatility of God's self-witness in the Bible and continually in the world must not be used against God to try to prove that the Word is no more than what some interpret it to be. Rather this versatility of witness should provoke us to marvel at God's freedom and elusiveness from being captured by the intelligence, pietism, imagination, or merit of human beings. . . .

To know the Word of God in the Bible, a person must come to the Bible with a certain naivety, confessing that if God exists at all, God lives independently, though not in isolation, from anyone's intelligence, longing, emotion, insight, or interpretations, even those that divine the truth. One must be open to God's initiative, be bereft of all preconceptions, surrender all initiative. One must forego anything that would demean God to dependence upon one's own thoughts, words, entreaties, deeds, or moods. One must take the appalling risk — by giving up all hypotheses, speculations, ideas, and deductions about God — that God is not and that there is only death. When a person is so naked, so helpless, so transparent, when one so utterly ceases to try to justify oneself or anyone or anything else, one first becomes vulnerable to the Word of God, which overcomes oblivion, heals deafness, restores sight, and saves us all from manipulation, arrogance, and folly in confronting the Word of God in the Bible. When a person becomes that mature as a human being, he or she is freed to listen and at last to welcome the Word in the Bible. That person is enlightened to discern the same Word of God at work now in the world, in (of all places!) one's own existence as well as in (thank God!) all other life. Thus is established a rhythm in the Christian's life encompassing intimacy with the Word of God in the Bible and one's involvement with the same Word active in the world.

The Bible and the
Confessing Church

SHORTLY following the end of the Second World War and the ostensible defeat of the Nazi totalitarianism, I spent some time in Europe in the nations that had suffered occupation. Although still a student I visited postwar Europe as a participant in several of the early ecumenical conferences, under the aegis, generally, of the World Council of Churches and of the World Student Christian Federation. Within that ecumenical milieu I was privileged to become acquainted with many of those who had been involved deeply during the occupation and the war in the resistance to Nazism. Most of these contacts, made so soon after the war, matured into friendships renewed many times as ecumenical affairs would occasion either my own journeys to Europe or American visits of these fellow Christians and colleagues who had resisted Nazism and survived. Philippe Maury was among these, as were Madeline Barot, Bishop Bergrav of Norway, Hans Lilje of Germany, and, later on, Jacques Ellul.

Lately, as might be expected, while totalitarian tendencies have achieved so much momentum and become more obvious and more ominous in America, I have found myself recalling most vividly the

An Ethic for Christians and Other Aliens in a Strange Land, 1973, pp. 117–18, 120

conversations I attended with these resistance leaders in which I listened to them recount their anti-Nazi experiences. . . . The recollection that now visits me from listening to those resistance leaders concerns Bible study. While not a practice of the entire resistance, it strongly engaged the whole confessing movement implicated in that resistance. Most appropriately, it often included Jewish as well as Christian participants. I recall being slightly bemused at the time of which I am speaking by the strenuous emphasis placed upon Bible study. No doubt that bewilderment reflected my own biblical deprivation, a lack in my American churchly upbringing that I have since struggled gladly to overcome.

In this dimension of the resistance, the Bible became alive as a means of nurture and communication; *recourse to the Bible was in itself a primary, practical, and essential tactic of resistance.* Bible study furnished the precedent for the free, mature, ecumenical, humanizing style of life that became characteristic of those of the confessing movement. This was an exemplary way — a sacrament, really — that expounded the existential scene of the resistance. That is, it demonstrated the necessities of acting in transcendence of time within time, of living humanly in the midst of death, of seeing and foreseeing both the apocalyptic and the eschatological in contemporary events. In Bible study within the anti-Nazi resistance there was an edification of the new, or renewed, life to which human beings are incessantly called by God — or, if you wish it put differently, by the event of their own humanity in this world — and there was, thus, a witness that is veritably incorporated into the original biblical witness.

Biblical Politics

My CONCERN is to understand America biblically. This book — which is, simultaneously, a theological statement and a political argument — implements that concern.

The effort is to comprehend the nation, to grasp what is happening right now to the nation, and to consider the destiny of the nation within the scope and style of the ethics and the ethical metaphors distinctive to the biblical witness in history.

The task is to treat the nation within the tradition of biblical politics — to understand America biblically — *not* the other way around, *not* (to put it in an appropriately awkward way) to construe the Bible Americanly. There has been much too much of the latter in this country's public life and religious ethos. There still is. I expect such indulgences to multiply, to reach larger absurdities, to become more scandalous, to increase blasphemously as America's crisis as a nation distends. To interpret the Bible for the convenience of America, as apropos as that may seem to be to many Americans, represents a radical violence to both the character and content of the biblical message. It fosters a fatal vanity that America is a divinely favored nation and makes of it the credo of a civic religion that is directly threatened by and, hence, that is anxious and hostile toward the biblical

From the Preface to *An Ethic for Christians and Other Aliens in a Strange Land,* 1973, pp. 13–15

Word. It arrogantly misappropriates political images from the Bible and applies them to America, so that America is conceived of as Zion: as *the* righteous nation, as a people of superior political morality, as a country and society chosen and especially esteemed by God. In archetypical form in this century, material abundance, redundant productivity, technological facility, and military predominance are publicly cited to verify the alleged divine preference and prove the supposed national virtue. It is just this kind of Sadducean sophistry, distorting the biblical truth for American purposes, that, in truth, occasions the moral turmoil that the nation so manifestly suffers today and that, I believe, renders us a people as unhappy as we are hopeless. It is profane, as well as grandiose, to manipulate the Bible in order to apologize for America. To read this tract lucently requires (and, I trust, evokes) freedom from temptations to violate the Bible to justify America as a nation.

This book is necessarily at once theological and political for the good reason that the theology of the Bible concerns politics in its most rudimentary meaning and in its most auspicious connotations.

The biblical topic *is* politics. The Bible is about the politics of fallen creation and the politics of redemption; the politics of the nations, institutions, ideologies, and causes of this world and the politics of the Kingdom of God; the politics of Babylon and the politics of Jerusalem; the politics of the Antichrist and the politics of Jesus Christ; the politics of the demonic powers and principalities and the politics of the timely judgment of God as sovereign; the politics of death and the politics of life; apocalyptic politics and eschatological politics.

Throughout the diversity of the biblical saga as history and as literature, the priority of politics remains prominent. The Bible expounds with extraordinary versatility, now one way and then another, and another, the singular issue of salvation — which is to say, the preemptive *political* issue. It bespeaks the reality of human life consummated in society within time in this world, now and here, as the promise of renewal and fulfillment vouchsafed for all humans and for every nation — for the whole of creation — throughout time.

Despite the habitual malpractice of translating biblical politics as the American story, there is also the odd and contradictory custom among many Americans to denounce the truth that the Bible is political. Frequently, if incongruously, these two convictions are held concurrently by the same person, or by the same sect or church or social faction. American experience as a nation — as well as biblical scholarship — discredits any attempted Americanization of biblical politics and confounds the notion that the Bible is apolitical. What is surprising is that the latter belief persists even though so many of the biblical symbols are explicitly political — *dominion, emancipation, authority, judgment, kingdom, reconciliation* among them — and even though the most familiar biblical events are notoriously political — including the drama of Israel the holy nation, the Kingdom parables in Christ's teaching, the condemnation of Christ as King of the Jews by the imperial authorities, the persecutions of the apostolic congregations, the controversies between Christians and zealots, the propagation of the book of Revelation.

Well, I do not amplify the matter here, apart from noticing that the view that the Bible is politically neuter or innocuous — coupled, as it may be, ironically, with an American misuse of biblical politics — maintains wide currency in this nation. And this view sorely inhibits a biblical comprehension of America as a nation.

The Bible and Ideology

I HAVE chosen to deal with two biblical passages that represent the tension, internal to the New Testament, pertinent to political authority: Romans 13 and Revelation 13. These are the most famous texts posing distinguishable, perhaps contradictory, attitudes toward the nation within the Bible. They are also, probably, the two most abused citations among any that might be named. . . .

The historical circumstances in which each of these parts of the New Testament were uttered are quite different, and account is taken of that fact in my own comprehension of Romans, on one hand, and Revelation, on the other. I am not one, however, inclined toward using the conditioning of history to explain away discrepancy or incongruity in the Bible. At the same time, I harbor no compulsion to neatly harmonize Scripture, as I have elsewhere often remarked. The whole notion that the Bible must be homogenized or rendered consistent is a common academic imposition upon the biblical literature, but it ends often in an attempt to ideologize the Bible in a manner that denies the most elementary truth of the biblical witness, namely, that it bespeaks the dynamic and viable participation of the Word of God in the common events of this world. The militant character of the Word of God in history refutes any canon of mere consistency in the biblical witness. To read the Bible is to hear of and

---

From the Preface to *Conscience and Obedience,* 1977, pp. 10–14

behold events in which the Word of God is concerned, attended by the particularity and, to human beings, the ambiguity of actual happenings. Any efforts to read the Bible as a treatise abstractly constructed or conformed usurps the genius of the Bible as testament of the Word of God active in history. If the biblical witness were internally strictly consonant, after the mode of ideology or philosophy, the mystery of revelation in this world would be abolished; revelation itself would be categorically precluded.

What is to be expected, instead of simplistic consistency, in listening to the Bible, allowing for the vagaries and other limitations of human insight, is coherence: a basic integrity of the Word of God or the fidelity of the personality of God to creation.

I do not mean to extol inconsistency. I am glad enough to find one text of the Bible that seems, to my mind, in obvious harmony with another passage, but I do mean to caution against making a rubric of consistency that violates the most essential characteristic of the biblical witness and that, usually, nourishes vanity in reading and using the Bible, and that, invariably, issues in manipulation, or oversight, or suppression of certain dimensions of the Bible.

This is how I come to the texts from Romans and Revelation. If the two seem at odds — though variant historical situations are to be taken seriously, and while the partiality of a person's perception at a given moment has to be acknowledged — perchance it is because they *are* at odds. That, to me, becomes primarily significant as a clue to the vitality of the Word of God in the world. The revelation of the Word of God is, always, more manifold and more versatile than human comprehension. What I anticipate in the passages is not consistency so much as coherence. I can live and act as a biblical person without the former, but without the latter I cannot live.

So in the Bible and, here, in Romans and Revelation, I look for style not stereotype, for precedent not model, for parable not proposition, for analogue not aphorism, for paradox not syllogism, for signs not statutes. The encounter with the biblical witness is empirical, as distinguished from scholastic, and it is confessional, rather than literalistic; in either case, it, over and above any other consideration, involves the common reader in affirming the historicity of the Word of God throughout the present age, in the biblical era and imminently.

My esteem for the biblical witness and my approach to the Bible should be enough to disclose my skepticism about current efforts to construct political theology according to some ideological model. I refer, for one specific example, to attempts to articulate a pseudo-biblical rationale for classical Marxism, which have lately become prominent, oddly enough, simultaneously, in both some postindustrial societies of North America and Europe and in still preindustrialized regions of Asia, Latin America, and Africa. It is persuasive of the ideological bankruptcy of the former that anyone would imagine that Marxism sponsors a social and economic analysis relevant to the conditions of advanced technology and the technocratic state; in the Third World, at least, the prevailing society retains a semblance to those conditions that originally occasioned Marxism more that a century ago. Given the analytical naivety of the revived interest in Marxism in a country like the United States, it may be that the phenomenon is mainly rhetorical, with classical Marxism supplying a convenient and ample lexicon with which to denounce the regime. Or, in addition, this belated attention to Marxist ideas may express the profound frustrations of people wrought in the decadence and obsolescence of American capitalism. Or, this may also be an aspect of the vogue of nostalgia that accompanies the endemic apprehension of Americans concerning the failure of the system. If that be true, it is quaint and pathetic since nostalgia signifies an inverted eschatology, as such the most fictionalized and forlorn hope of all. Meanwhile, even in sectors of the Third World where Marxism may remain analytically cogent, the attempt to theologize, in biblical terms, ideology is untenable. Even that most venerable identification and advocacy of the biblical witness for the dispossessed and oppressed of this age does not render the biblical people ideologically captivated. The effort to distinguish a biblical apologetic for Marxism is no different from those that have sought to theologize capitalism, colonialism, war, and profligate consumption. Whatever the subject, ideology, or policy, attempts such as these trivialize the Bible.

In other words, biblical politics *never* implies a particular, elaborated political theology, whether it be one echoing the status quo or one that aspires to overthrow and displace the status quo. The gospel is not ideology and, categorically, the gospel cannot be ideologized. Biblical politics always has a posture in tension and opposition to the prevalent system, and to any prospective or incipient status quo, and to the ideologies of either regime or revolution. Biblical politics is alienated from the politics of this age.

Let no one read into these remarks gratuitous comfort for simplistic and unresponsive answers to political issues of enormous complexity, such as all the nations suffer, after the manner, for instance, of those who incant the name of Jesus superstitiously. It is literally pagan, unbiblical, to so recite "Jesus is the answer." The Bible is more definitive, the biblical affirmation is "Jesus is Lord!" The Bible makes a political statement of the reign of Christ preempting all the rulers and all pretenders to thrones and dominions, subjecting incumbents and revolutionaries, surpassing the doctrine and promises of the ideologies of this world.

Nor is there, here, furnished any pretext whatever for the neglect of the poor or the unliberated or for abandonment of the biblical advocacy of the oppressed and the imprisoned. On the contrary, the exemplification of redeemed humanity in the lordship of Jesus Christ in this age means a resilient and tireless witness to confound, rebuke, and undo every regime and every potential regime unto that moment when humankind is accounted over the nations and principalities in the last judgment of the Word of God.

The approach to Romans 13 and Revelation 13 here is confessional, that is to say, a living contact betwixt the Word of God exposed in the biblical texts and the same Word of God active now in the situation of the common reader so that the encounter in Bible study becomes, in itself, an event characteristically biblical. As such this book is not exegetical in a technical sense, though I do not imply that technical work on these passages is unimportant or that it is incompatible with a confessional style in Bible study, or that it can be ignored by laypersons. I am, rather, emphasizing that this book is primarily a pastoral endeavor. It literally seeks to encourage a biblical lifestyle in the politics of the age in — as the subtitle states — conscience and obedience in church and in nation while awaiting the promptness of the Lord.

Listening against Babel

THE single most significant credential needed for comprehending the Bible is an intention to *listen* to the Word.

For that, a person must not merely desire to hear the Word of God but must also be free to hear the Word of God. This means becoming vulnerable to the Word and to the utterance of the Word in much the same way as one has to become vulnerable to another human being if one truly cares to know that other person and to hear his or her word.

In contemporary American culture, whatever the situation in other cultures, though there is much sound, a clamor of noises, and a vast and complex profusion of words, there seems to be precious little listening amongst human beings. There is — literally — babel instead of communication; there is frustration instead of relationship; there is violence instead of love.

The extraordinary distortions of language that, nowadays, victimize us all, inhibiting our listening to one another as human beings, render it the more difficult to approach the Bible in an attitude of listening, inhibit or otherwise hinder us from becoming open and vulnerable to the Word. To transcend the babel, to have, as Jesus so often mentioned, the ears to hear the Word, it is essential, for the time being at least, to put aside *everything else:* distractions whether trivial

---

Introduction to an unpublished Bible study guide

182

or important, self-serving ideas, arguments, all opinions, preconceptions of every sort, defenses, temptations, mundane occupations. A person must come to the Bible quietly, eagerly, expectantly — ready to listen. One must (as nearly as one can) confront the Bible naively, that is, as if one had not encountered the Bible previously. And, at the same time, one must approach the Bible realistically — rather than superstitiously — recognizing that access to the same Word of God that the Bible bespeaks is given to us in the versatility of the presence of the Word of God active in common history: in the event of Jesus Christ, in the incessant agitations of the Holy Spirit, in the constitution of creation itself (see John 1:1–14). Insofar as we do this, listening happens. Then the Word of God in the Bible can be heard in the Word's own integrity and power and grace.

III. PRINCIPALITIES
AND POWERS

Introduction to Theology: Conversation with Karl Barth[*]

(Moderator Jaroslav) **PELIKAN**: Mr. Stringfellow, I think, presses you to speak from within your own setting in a way that we can hear by the next question he has put to you:

"In the United States, the many and divided churches live in a society that constitutionally professes the freedom of public worship and the public practice of religion in a formal sense. That is, attendance at services, public preaching, representation of the religious and ecclesiastical authorities and institutions in public life and the like. It increasingly appears, however, that the use of freedom — the only use that is socially approved at least — is confined to either the mere formalities of religious observance and the preservation of some religious causes or the use of religion to rationalize, to serve, or to sanctify the national self-interest — the use of religion and of jargon and images of religion for the preservation, perhaps aggrandizement

---

[*] Stringfellow was one of eight panel members who queried and responded to Dr. Karl Barth April 25–26, 1962, at Rockefeller Memorial Chapel, the University of Chicago. This portion of their conversation is included here because Stringfellow's questions, as well as Barth's replies, presage much of his work on the powers.

Criterion, 1963, vol. 2, no. 1, pp. 22–24

of the nation. Consequently, the churches do not commonly exercise a vitally critical attitude toward politics, public policy, or the nation's actual life and culture."

Now, with this observation as a preface, Mr. Stringfellow asks you, sir, "to comment upon how the church and the churches can maintain the freedom of the gospel to proclaim the gospel in such a society in which the churches seem to be constantly tempted to forswear the gospel in order to protect our freedom as external institutions in society. What bearing do the words of St. Paul in the thirteenth chapter of Romans have upon churches in such a position within such a society? If it seems appropriate to you, sir, would you compare the relationship of the churches and the state in the United States and in, for example, the German Democratic Republic of East Germany with respect to the freedom that the state practically, not just on paper, but in fact, affords to the churches and the freedom that churches in fact have to proclaim and to represent the gospel — that freedom that the gospel assures to the churches?" And Mr. Stringfellow adds in parenthesis, "(This question specifically arises out of your correspondence with those East German pastors who sought your counsel)."

BARTH: I am troubled. What I have read and heard are statements with which I am in sympathy. I like to hear you speak as you do, but statements rather than answers I could only whisper to you. But why only whisper? Because your concern is over this country — America — and I have, so to say, sworn not to enter criticisms of the American scene into the record — I cannot enter America in order to criticize you. Perhaps I could answer one very special point. You have asked what bearing does Romans 13 have upon churches in such a position in such a society. Romans 13 is a very important and very difficult and even disturbing chapter in the Bible. Romans 13 has played a great role in Germany till today and not only for the Lutherans. Paul speaks of the powers that be and he means the state, and he speaks of the Christian that should be subject to these powers. But if I understand this chapter rightly, the most important term in it, "being subject," must be understood in a more concrete way than it has been. Being subject in Greek does not mean only that "you have to obey — here is the power and we are under it, and let us submit to it," but the term includes the meaning "taxes," and taxation means you are subject to this order. In other places, speaking also of the political orders, the New Testament says you have to pray for those who are in power. Paul does not say it; but it is said in other places, "Pray for them." Romans 13 cannot be explained without this notion of responsibility. The Christian has to bear the task of the state, and that is what is lacking within many Christian circles; we are only spectators of political life. We look on as things happen and take them as they come, but we should feel ourselves asked to do our part. That is one question for us Christians — "Are we willing and able to take upon us our whole responsibility and not leave it to others to manage political affairs?"

PELIKAN: You say that submission as such is not really all that this chapter imposes upon us — but more, it is an active, essential responsibility?

BARTH: Yes, yes. Because it is submission to an order; and if we submit to an order, we go within the realm of this order — we take our place, and as human beings become responsible for what is done in this order.

STRINGFELLOW: Just a very concrete question in reference to your point, as I understand it, that to be subject to the civil authority does not mean merely an automatic obedience but a variety of actions.

BARTH: Yes, because even the term *obedience* reminds us that there is no true obedience where there is not free obedience. Not only an outward obedience, but an inner obedience that is a free act.

STRINGFELLOW: My question is, then, "When Pontius Pilate consigns Jesus Christ to be crucified, this is an expression on the part of Jesus Christ of his subjection to civil authority. Is that the case?"

BARTH: Yes. Certainly, certainly. He does it out of his own freedom. He subjects himself.

PELIKAN: There is no power given Pilate, except that it be from above?

STRINGFELLOW: Our freedom riders must remember this.

PELIKAN: Mr. Stringfellow's final question, "It appears to be widely believed, both within and, for that matter, outside the churches of the United States, that the history of redemption is encompassed merely by the saga of relationships in history between God and humanity. At the same time, it is in American Protestantism, at least, commonplace to distinguish as nothing more than archaic imagery the biblical identification and discussion of the angelic powers present in the world. What there is of Protestant moral theology in America almost utterly ignores the attempt to account for, explicate, and relate one's self to the principalities and powers. Yet, empirically more and more, the principalities and powers seem to have an aggressive, indeed, possessive, ascendancy in American life — including, alas, the life of the American churches. Who are these principalities and powers? What is their significance in the creation and in the Fall? What significance do they have with respect to merely human sin? What is their relation to the claim that Christ is the Lord of history? What is the relation of the power and presence of death in history to the principalities and powers, and therefore, practically speaking, what freedom does a Christian have from the dominion of all of these principalities and powers?"

BARTH: Well, that is a very large question. "Who are the principalities and powers today in our world?" I will mention only some of them. Everywhere that an ideology is ruling, there is such a power: a communist or anticommunist ideology; money is such a power. No need to give a description. Sport is such a power. Traditions of all kinds are such angelic powers. Fashion for men and women is also a power. What we call religion — in all kinds of expression — is also a world of powers. Angelic powers — the thing unconscious within us — that is a real power. But also what we call reason is such a power. And let us not forget sex. Now you ask me what is their significance in the creation and in the Fall? What significance do they have for human sin? I think that all these powers represent certain human possibilities that are given in the very nature of man, as he is — and given as a part, as an appearance of God's good creation in man. None of these things is bad, necessarily; but now we have to deal with the

190

man who has separated himself from God and from his neighbor. In doing so, he becomes and is alienated also from himself. He sees his natural possibilities, powers, become isolated over against him; and instead of being the Lord of them, man becomes their servant. Yes, he must now obey himself; and work and all his powers are kings and princes and emperors and führers of all kinds. We pray, "Thy Kingdom come," and the Kingdom is Jesus Christ, because in him, as the Lord, man as a sinning man is replaced by a new man; what binds him in these powers is driven away and in the coming of the Kingdom he becomes free over against these powers. In Christ's death, man as sinner, man as alienated from himself, man as prey to death, is done in, finished. In his resurrection man has appeared in the flesh as man, as God's new creature, as the beginning of a new heaven and a new earth that will be universally and definitely revealed and vindicated in the last *parousia* of the Lord. Now you ask me what practical freedom does the Christian have from the dominion of these powers? His freedom lies in Jesus Christ — in his death and in his resurrection. But you ask me what practical freedom we have? We have in him and through him the freedom to look back to his first and to look forward to his last coming and to look upon him as present and as he will come. That is freedom. That is life — the life of the children of God within the realm of his presence. Looking to him means to be concrete with that spirit — that one true spirit that is potent and mighty. In order to stand and fight these gods we need his power.

Christ and the Powers of Death

Now in putting everything in subjection to man, he left nothing out of his control. As it is, we do not yet see everything in subjection to him. But we see Jesus, who for a little while was made lower than the angels, crowned with glory and honor because of the suffering of death, so that by the grace of God he might taste death for everyone.

HEBREWS 2:8*b*–9

Christ defeats the temptations of worldly power with which death confronts him on Palm Sunday; in the days immediately following he is delivered to death by one of his disciples, condemned to death by the ruling authorities of the nations of Israel and Rome, and abandoned to death by the rest of his disciples.

Christ is neither delivered nor abandoned by his disciples into the hands of just some evil, envious, or frightened men: he is given over, and he surrenders, to Israel and Rome. And in the encounter of Christ with these powers there is exposed the relationship between Christ and all principalities and powers. The ecclesiastical and civil rulers who accuse, try, condemn, and execute Christ act not essentially for themselves as individuals, but as representatives — indeed, as ser-

---

Free in Obedience, 1964, pp. 49–59, 62–64, 70–73

vants — of the principalities. It is, of course, in the name of these powers that Christ is put on trial. He is accused of subverting and undermining the nation, of threatening the nation's existence, survival, and destiny.

That *this* is the accusation should, by the way, dispose of the legend, so popular in modern treatments of the trial of Christ both in Good Friday sermons and popular secular versions of the event, that Christ is innocent of any offense, and tried and condemned because of some corruption or failure or miscarriage of justice. Of the charge against him, Christ is guilty beyond any doubt.

In any case, the significant aspect of the trial is that it is not just an encounter between Christ and some men who were his enemies. The most decisive clash in all history is this one between Christ and the principalities and powers of this world, represented by and symbolized in Israel and Rome.

The understanding of principalities and powers is lost nowadays in the churches, though, I observe, not so much so outside the churches. About a year ago, for example, I was invited to lecture at the Business School of Harvard University; earlier on the same day, I also met informally with some students at the Divinity School. Since graduates of the Business School live their professional lives and work so obviously within the spheres of dominance of great corporate and commercial principalities, I decided to speak there about the meaning of the principalities. Although the Business School students were not especially theologically sophisticated, and certainly none had been theologically trained, they displayed an awareness, intelligence, and insight with respect to what principalities are and what are the issues between principalities and human beings. Yet, when the same matters had been discussed earlier with the divinity students, I found that most of them felt that such terms as "principalities and powers," "ruling authorities," "demons," "world rulers of the present darkness," "angelic powers," and the like — terms so frequently used in the Bible — were archaic imagery having no reference to contemporary realities.

It appears, in other words, to be widely believed in the churches in the United States that the history of redemption is encompassed merely in the saga of relationships between God and human beings. What there is of contemporary Protestant moral theology typically ignores any attempt to account for, identify, explicate, and relate the self to the principalities, although empirically the principalities seem to have an aggressive, in fact possessive, ascendancy in American life. Because the biblical references to principalities and angelic powers are so prominent and because the powers themselves enjoy such dominance in everyday life, their meaning and significance cannot be left unexamined.

What are principalities and powers? What is their significance in the creation and in the Fall? What is their relationship to human sin? How are these powers related to the presence and power of death in history? What is the meaning of the confrontation between Christ and the principalities? Does a Christian have any freedom from their dominion? There can be no serious, realistic, or biblical comprehension of the witness of the church in the world unless such questions as these are raised and pondered.

What are Principalities?

There is nothing particularly mysterious, superstitious, or imaginary about principalities, despite the contemporary failure to discuss them theologically. The realities to which the biblical terms *principalities and powers* refer are quite familiar to modern society, though they may be called by different names. What the Bible calls *principalities and powers* are called in contemporary language *ideologies, institutions,* and *images.*

A principality, whatever its particular form and variety, is a living reality, distinguishable from human and other organic life. It is not made or instituted by human beings but, as with humans and all creation, made by God for God's own pleasure.

In the biblical understanding of creation, the principalities or angelic powers, together with all other forms of life, are given by God into human dominion and are means through which human beings rejoice in the gift of life by acknowledging and honoring God, who gives life to all and to the whole of creation. The dominion of humanity over the rest of creation, including the angelic powers, means the engagement of human beings in the worship of God as the true, realized, and fulfilled human life and, at the same time and as part of the same event, the commitment by them of all things

194

within their dominion to the very same worship of God, to the very same actualization of true life for all things. All persons, all angels, and all things in creation have origination, integrity, and wholeness of life in the worship of God.

Just as people differ in their capacities in one sense or another, just as there are varieties in human life, so also there are varieties of principalities that can be distinguished one from another, though they all retain certain common characteristics. Let us consider various examples of principalities.

Principalities as Images

One kind of principality is designated by the word *image*. An obvious example of this sort is the image that comes to be associated with some celebrity and bears the same name as the celebrity. Thus, there was for a time the movie star named Marilyn Monroe. The person is now dead, but the image "Marilyn Monroe" is by no means dead. Not only have certain memories either personal or public survived the death of this person, but the name survives; the name, in fact, attaches to a reality that was given new life when the person of that name died. The image called "Marilyn Monroe" is not dead because there were two lives that claimed and used that name: one a principality, the other a person; only the latter died, the former is, if anything, livelier than ever.

All the talk of Marilyn Monroe as the great American "sex goddess" or as "the symbol of youth" is not just the prose of Hollywood journalists, whether they realize it or not. Marilyn Monroe, whoever she was as a person, was and is a genuine idol, an entity, bearing the same name and likeness as the person, with an existence, character, and power quite distinguishable from the person who bore the name.

An image is a very common variety of angelic power, though often of much less dignity and influence in the world than other kinds of principalities. In fact, every person is accompanied in life by an image; a person is often controlled or destroyed by that image, and invariably it survives the individual's life. . . .

Once in a while the public image of a person becomes much

195

more than just an idol, becomes a principality of such magnitude that the image is comparable to an institutional or ideological principality. Adolf Hitler, for instance, whoever was the person by that name, became and is to this day such a principality. And in terms of the relationship between Hitler the person and Hitler the principality, it may well be that long before his actual suicide the person named Hitler had been wholly obliterated by the principality named Hitler; that the person had, indeed, been possessed by a demon of that name; and that the devastation and massacre wrought in the name of Hitler was not the work of just some dark genius of the man, nor even of the man's insanity or gross criminality, but of the awesome demonic power that possessed him.

In any case, the form of principality identifiable as the public image bearing the name of a person exists independently of that person (though the person may be wholly dependent upon the principality). The form is distinguishable from the person, lies beyond control, and is in conflict with the person until the person surrenders life in one fashion or another to the principality. The principality requires not only recognition and adulation as an idol from movie fans or voters or the public, but also demands that the person of the same name give up his or her life as a person to the service and homage of the image. And when that surrender is made, the person in fact dies, though not yet physically. For at that point one is literally possessed by one's own image. The demand, then, made in the conflict between the principality and the personality is one in which the whole life of the person is surrendered to the principality and is given over to the worship of the image.

Principalities as Institutions

The institutional principalities also make claims upon human beings for idolatrous commitment in that the moral principle that governs any institution — a great corporation, a government agency, an ecclesiastical organization, a union, utility, or university — is its own survival. Everything else must finally be sacrificed to the cause of preserving the institution, and it is demanded of everyone who lives within its sphere of influence — officers, executives, employees, members, customers, and students — that they commit themselves to the service of that end, the survival of the institution.

This relentless demand of the institutional power is often presented in benign forms to a person under the guise that the bondage to the institution benefits the person in some way, but that does not make the demand any less dehumanizing. I recall, for example, the situation of a law school classmate of mine. When he was graduated he accepted a position with one of the great Wall Street law firms, an institutional power in its own right, though engaged in serving some of the great corporate principalities. During the summer, before he began work at the firm, he married. He did not consult or inform his superiors in the firm about his marriage prior to the event. Later, when he reported for work and the firm learned that he was now married, he was told that he should have consulted the employer before marrying, but, since he was married, it would be advisable for him and his wife to refrain from having any children for at least two or three years. Furthermore, for the sake of his advancement in the firm, he should and would want to devote all of his time both in the office and in his ostensibly personal life to the service of the firm, and children might interfere with this. In the end, the claim for service that an institution makes upon human beings is an invitation to surrender their lives in order that the institution be preserved and prosper. It is an invitation to bondage.

Principalities as Ideologies

Ideology is perhaps the most self-evident principality in the world at the present time. Communism, fascism, racism, nationalism: all these are principalities and powers. Humanism, capitalism, democracy, rationalism — though Americans think of these as benevolent powers — are also principalities and share all the essential characteristics of those ideologies to which America's enemies are committed.

Communism — or, more precisely Marxism as distinguished from Leninism, Stalinism, or post-Stalin Soviet communism — is a particularly lucid illustration of the nature of an ideological principality. Marxism asserts that it reveals and upholds the secret of history, that the destiny (literally, salvation) of all humanity and all nations is

197

to be found and fulfilled in the ascendancy and dominion of Marxism in the world. It claims sovereignty over all history, and the moral significance of any person's life (or, for that matter, the existence of any institution or nation) is determined in relation to the power and prosperity of the Marxist ideology. This ideology, therefore, requires of people, institutions, and nations an unequivocal and militant obeisance, a sacrifice of all other supposedly lesser causes and rights to the idol of Marxism.

Other totalitarian ideologies have, of course, represented the same sort of example of the principalities and powers that Marxism today represents. But do not suppose that the ideology of American society, though more diffuse and less systematic and theoretical than Marxism or the other totalitarian ideologies, is any different in its essential characteristics as a principality. Americans are now constantly, incessantly, and somewhat vehemently assailed with the word that the ultimate moral significance of their individual lives is embodied in and depends upon the mere survival of the American nation and its "way of life." There seems, to me at least, less and less of a public consensus about the content and style of that American way of life, just as there is an obviously increasingly intense controversy within the communist world as to what the Marxist way of life is and is to be. But that only means that the survival of the nation as such becomes the idol, the chief object of loyalty, service, and idolatry. Or, to put it a bit differently, the historic ideological realities in American history, those of capitalism and democracy, are now perhaps displaced by elementary nationalism. But in any case the preeminent factor in terms of which, it is claimed, human beings will find their own justification is in service to the nation, in the offering of all other things for the sake of national survival. Or, in the inaugural words of President Kennedy: "Ask not what your country can do for you; ask what you can do for your country."

It should be recognized that in describing the principalities and powers in terms of the realities that are nowadays called images, institutions, or ideologies, no attempt is intended to distinguish sharply the varieties of principalities. Frequently, one will have characteristics of the others. Although according to these descriptions the principality bearing Hitler's name would be called an image, this was, as has been pointed out, a principality that had the attributes of ideological and institutional principalities. For example, every nation is a principality, but it would be ridiculous to identify a nation as just an institutional power, although it is that clearly when one considers it in the sense of the governmental structures in a society. At the same time, the nation is associated with ideological powers and partakes of the nature of them — the American nation with the ideological elements of democracy and capitalism, the Soviet nation with the ideological forces called communism, some of the new nations of Africa and Asia with the ideologies of nationalism, and so on. Sometimes, too, the principality of the nation is, as it were, personified in the image of a ruler. Thus in France, DeGaulle *is,* as he himself seems fond of mentioning, France. And that is not only embodied in the constitutional institutions of the French nation but in the image of DeGaulle himself.

The Meaning of the Demonic

Like all people and all things, the angelic powers and principalities are fallen and are become demonic powers. *Demonic* does not mean evil; the word refers rather to death, to fallenness. An angelic power in its fallen estate is called a demonic power because it is a principality existing in the present age in a state of alienation from God, cut off from the life originating in God's life, separated from its own true life, and, thus, being in a state of death. In the Fall, every human being, every principality, every thing exists in a condition of estrangement from its own life, as well as from the lives of all other human beings, powers, and things. In the Fall, the whole of creation is consigned to death.

The separation from life, the bondage to death, the alienation from God that the Fall designates is not simply to be accounted for by human sin. The Fall is not just the estate in which humans reject God and exalt themselves, as if they were like God. The term does not merely mean the pretensions of human pride. It is all that and something more. The Fall is also the awareness of human beings of their estrangement from God, themselves, each other, and all things, and their pathetic search for God or some substitute for God within and outside themselves and each other in the principalities and in the rest of creation. So human beings, in their fallenness, are found sometimes idolizing themselves, sometimes idolizing snakes, bugs, other creatures, or natural phenomena, or sometimes idolizing nation, ideology, race, or one of the other principalities.

The search is pathetic because it is futile. The principalities are themselves consigned to death just as much as the people who worship them. Thus, the idolatry of the demonic powers by humans turns out always to be a worship of death.

To put it another way, that dominion that human beings receive from God over the rest of creation (including their dominion over the principalities) is lost to them in the Fall and, as it were, reversed, so that now the principalities exercise dominion over human beings and claim in their own names and for themselves idolatrous worship from human beings. People do not create the principalities nor do they control them; on the contrary, people exist in this world in bondage to the principalities. No one escapes enduring the claims for allegiance and service of the principalities. For a person to live in the state of fallenness is to endure these very claims.

Whatever other distinctions may be made among the various principalities, remember that they are themselves fallen and demonic; the substance of the claim for idolatry that all principalities assert against human life is the same. Concretely, each principality boasts that people will find the meaning and fulfillment of human life in service to the principality and to that which abets its survival; a profound concern for self-survival is the governing morality of every principality. This comes first. To this all other interests must be sacrificed; from this all else, including an individual's life and work, takes its significance; by this is a person judged.

The principalities claim, in other words, sovereignty over human life and history. Therefore, they not only compete and conflict with one another for the possession and domination of the lives of human beings, but they also deny and denounce the sovereignty of God. But do not let the arrogance of the idols conceal this fact: when a principality claims moral preeminence in history or over a person's life, it represents an aspiration for salvation from death and a hope that service to the idol will give existence a meaning somehow transcending death.

Christ and the Principalities

Although the clash between Christ and the principalities in his trial and execution is the decisive and normative encounter, it is not at all the only occasion in the historic ministry of Christ when he is confronted by the principalities. The final showdown is again and again foreshadowed in Christ's life on earth.

The apprehension with which he is regarded by the worldly authorities during the Palm Sunday celebration and during Holy Week is first exposed in the consternation and rage with which Herod received the news of Christ's coming into the world. At the same time, remember that it is part of the authentic miracle of Christmas that those who gathered at the stable to adore him do so as representatives of the whole of creation, as emissaries of all humans and all creatures and all things. Those who come to worship and honor Christ in his birth include the magi who come as ambassadors of the principalities of the world. For a moment, as it were, in the Christmas event the sovereignty of Christ over all the world is revealed, and it is in that event that the world has a glimpse of the very restoration of creation from the Fall, a foretaste of the world become the Kingdom of God.

The lordship of Christ is disclosed in the adoration in the Christmas miracle, but the hysteria and hostility of Herod at Christ's coming into the world foreshadows the later encounters between Christ and the principalities. The time of Christ's temptation in the wilderness as a particularly significant episode has already been mentioned. But, in addition to that, Christ confronts the principalities when he stills the tempest, heals the sick, frees the demoniac, upsets the traditions of Israel by eating with sinners, or shows that he is Lord of the Sabbath. And, Christ's wilderness temptation is repeated in Palm Sunday. Yet that is not the last encounter between Christ and the principalities, for he goes to cleanse the temple, and Lazarus is raised from death. Then, betrayed and forsaken to death by his disciples, condemned to death by the rulers and crucified and buried, he descends into hell — into the event in which the presence and power of death is most militant, pervasive, ruthless, and undisguised.

In some of the episodes, as in the wilderness, the crucifixion, and the descent into hell, death openly confronts Christ; in others,

Christ is visited by one or another of the principalities as emissaries of death. In all of these encounters, the principalities represent the awesome and manifold powers of death.

The victor in each specific encounter is Christ. That is important because it means that the power of Christ over death is not merely a transcendence of death as the terminal experience or as biological extinction. Thinking of the resurrection as having reference only to the crucifixion and entombment of Christ (the terminal event of his earthly life) underlies the wistful, vain, and false ideas about the immortality of the soul or life after death that so violate the gospel and corrupt the minds of many church people. Each specific confrontation between Christ and death and between Christ and one of the principalities as one of the powers of death foreshadows the resurrection, exposes and heralds the overwhelming authority over death that Christ has and holds from the beginning of time to the end of time. And the resurrection encompasses and represents all of these particular historic encounters in a single, consummate, and indeed cosmic disclosure of the triumph of Christ over death.

The resurrection is impregnated with all that has gone before; these encounters of Christ with death and its powers in history mean that his triumph over death there shown is offered for human beings and for the whole world. His victory is not for himself but for us. His power over death is effective not just at the terminal point of a person's life but throughout one's life, during *this* life in *this* world, right now. This power is effective in the times and places in the daily lives of human beings when they are so gravely and relentlessly assailed by the claims of principalities for an idolatry that, in spite of all disguises, really surrenders to death as the reigning presence in the world. His resurrection means the possibility of living in this life, in the very midst of death's works, safe and free from death.

But what of all of these notions and speculations about a life after dying, after the day of the undertaker? The Christian, the one living by the authority of and in the freedom of the resurrection, is saved from fond and wishful thinking about that. Christians have no anxiety about their disposition after their lives in this world: in fact, they know little or nothing about the matter; but they know all that they need to know, which is that the reality and truth of the resurrection has been in the present life so radically verified and realized that they are confident and joyful in leaving themselves in the judgment and mercy of God, in all things, for ever and ever.

Christ's resurrection is for human beings and for the whole of creation, including the principalities of this world. Through the encounters between Christ and the principalities and between Christ and death, the power of death is exhausted. The reign of death and, within that, the pretensions to sovereignty over history of the principalities, is brought to an end in Christ's resurrection. He bears the fullness of their hostility toward him; he submits to their condemnation; he accepts their committal of himself to death, and in his resurrection he ends their power and the power they represent. Yet the end of the claims of the principalities to sovereignty is also the way in which these very claims are fulfilled in Christ himself. The claim of a nation, ideology, or other principality to rule history, though phony and futile, is at the same time an aspiration for salvation, a longing for the reality that does, indeed, rule history. In the same event in which the pretension of the principality is exposed and undone, how and in whom salvation is wrought is disclosed and demonstrated. In Christ the false lords of history, the principalities, are shown to be false; at the same time, in Christ the true Lord of history is made known. In Christ is both the end and fulfillment for all principalities, for all humanity, and for all things.

Traits of the Principalities

THE substantive questions here become: *Who or what are the principalities and powers? How are the principalities related to the moral reality of death?*

There are two sources of insight for these questions that complement and significantly verify one another. Those sources are the biblical references to the principalities and empirical observation of the principalities. It should be remembered, as to the latter, that detached scrutiny of the principalities by humans is not possible. The fundamental reality between persons and principalities is tension and strife, and such empirical perception as human beings may have is that of victim or intended victim of the principalities.

The Powers as Legion

According to the Bible, the principalities are legion in species, number, variety, and name (e.g., Luke 8:29–33; Gal. 4:3; Eph. 1:21, 6:10–13; Col. 1:15–16, 2:10–23). They are designated by such multifarious titles as powers, virtues, thrones, authorities, dominions, demons, princes, strongholds, lords, angels, gods, elements, spirits. Sometimes the names

---

An Ethic for Christians and Other Aliens in a Strange Land, 1973, pp. 77–84, 89–90, 92–94

of other creatures are appropriated for them, such as serpent, dragon, lion, beast. A similar practice survives today, of course, where animal symbols refer to nations or institutions: the bear is Russia, the tiger represents Princeton, the donkey the Democratic Party, the pig the police.

Terms that characterize are frequently used biblically in naming the principalities: "tempter," "mocker," "foul spirit," "destroyer," "adversary," "the enemy." And the privity of the principalities to the power of death incarnate is shown in mention of their agency to Beelzebub or Satan or the Devil or the Antichrist.

The very array of names and titles in biblical usage for the principalities and powers is some indication of the scope and significance of the subject for human beings. And if some of these seem quaint, transposed into contemporary language they lose quaintness and the principalities become recognizable and all too familiar: they include all institutions, all ideologies, all images, all movements, all causes, all corporations, all bureaucracies, all traditions, all methods and routines, all conglomerates, all races, all nations, all idols. Thus, the Pentagon or the Ford Motor Company or Harvard University or the Hudson Institute or Consolidated Edison or the Diners Club or the Olympics or the Methodist Church or the Teamsters Union are all principalities. So are capitalism, Maoism, humanism, Mormonism, astrology, the Puritan work ethic, science and scientism, white supremacy, patriotism, plus many, many more — sports, sex, any profession or discipline, technology, money, the family — beyond any prospect of full enumeration. The principalities and powers *are* legion.

The Principalities as Creatures

With these creatures, as with human beings, it is never quite possible to express either the whole personality or the multiple attributes and abilities of a principality in a name, much less that of the legion of principalities and powers. The biblical practice of invoking many names or of interchanging various names, when speaking of principalities, is a help in grasping the many-faceted character and versatility of these powers. After all, what is being described and designated is a form of life, a creatureliness, which is potent and mobile and diverse, not static or neat or simply defined by what it may now or then be called. So such names as are used for the principalities, either in the biblical witness or in common talk, are necessarily suggestive, intuitive, emphatic.

A recurrent stumbling block to comprehending the principalities exists, for many people, at just this point. Human beings are reluctant to acknowledge institutions — or any of the other principalities — as creatures having their own existence, personality, and mode of life. Yet the Bible consistently speaks of the principalities as creatures. For another instance, the law (itself a principality) contains a similar recognition when it deals with various attributes of corporations, including corporate personality or existence in perpetuity or separate liability (i.e., Rev. 13).

The typical version of human reluctance to accord the principalities their due integrity as creatures is the illusion of human beings that they make or create and, hence, control institutions and that institutions are no more than groups of human beings duly organized. How do these creatures called principalities come into existence? How does an institution originate? Where does tradition come from? When is a nation born? How is an ideology created?

I am frank to admit no full answers to such queries and further to confess that I am more or less content to leave these questions unanswered. The exact origins of the creatureliness of principalities is a mystery in quite the same sense that the creaturehood of human beings remains mysterious. Within such mysteries we are not bereft of any insight, but what is knowable is partial and ambiguous, limited and fragile. Thus, we know that human beings are privy to the public inception and generation of institutions and other principalities. (In the time that has come to be regarded as the birth of this nation, some men convened and consulted and acted in concert.) Yet that human privity seems insufficient to be the whole truth; something more than the summation of human thought and activity is involved in the creature identity of principalities.

Perhaps the issue is put, with more edification, the other way around: concerted or collective human action is, in and of itself, too simple and transient to support the view that principalities are creatures made by human beings. The creaturely status of the principalities — on the contrary — comes not from humanity but from God. If that leaves, still, a large mystery, it nevertheless emphasizes that all creatures are God's creatures, that the creaturehood of principalities is essentially similar to that of human beings and is no more the handiwork of humanity than human life is. And, moreover, an understanding of the life of principalities as part of God's work of creation, and not human doing, is the biblical view confirmed empirically by the most widespread redundant and cumulative evidence that human beings do not control institutions or any other principalities.

The Fallenness of the Principalities

The principalities are numbered among God's creatures, yet they suffer the Fall as truly as human beings, as fully as the rest of creation. It is not that there are no perfect or perfectible institutions (though there are none), but rather that all institutions exist, in time, in a moral state that is the equivalent of death or that has the meaning of death. Every principality in its fallenness exists in remarkable confusion as to its own origins, identity, and office. The fallen principalities falsely — and futilely — claim autonomy from God and dominion over human beings and the rest of creation, thus disrupting and usurping the godly vocation or blaspheming, while repudiating their own vocation. This is apparent in every principality, but it is especially manifest in great ideologies like Marxism or capitalism, or in rich and powerful nations or empires, as in the Babylon parable, which often are quite literal in their preemption of God by their demands for obeisance, service, and glorification from human beings (Rev. 13:1–6).

The hostility of the fallen principalities and powers toward God and the profound confusion as to their own creatureliness which that rejection of God betrays issue in relentless aggression against all of life and, since the concern here is for ethics, especially aggression against human life in society. The principality, insinuating itself in the place of God, deceives humans into thinking and acting as if the moral worth or justification of human beings is defined and determined by commitment or surrender — literally, sacrifice — of human life to the survival interest, grandeur, and vanity of the principality.

Yet, again and again, with nations no less than other powers, history discloses that the actual meaning of such human idolatry of nations, institutions, or other principalities is death. Death is the only moral significance that a principality proffers human beings. That is to say, whatever intrinsic moral power is embodied in a principality — for a great corporation, profit, for example; or, for a nation, hegemony; or, for an ideology, conformity — that is sooner or later superseded by the greater moral power of death. Corporations die. Nations die. Ideologies die. Death survives them all. Death is — apart from God — the greatest moral power in this world, outlasting and subduing all other powers no matter how marvelous they may seem to be for a time being. This means, theologically speaking, that the object of allegiance and servitude, the real idol secreted within all idolatries, the power above all principalities and powers — the idol of the idols — is death. To many humans and, as it were, to themselves, the nations and institutions and assorted principalities may seem to be glorious, autonomous, or everlasting powers, but in fact they are themselves vassals or serfs, acolytes or surrogates, apparitions or agents of death. This is explicitly denoted in the Bible, where the principalities are named as demonic powers — as powers of death, or as tempters, or as emissaries of Satan (Rev. 12:9; cf. Gen. 3:1, 14–15).

Parenthetically, it must be noticed that this scene of the Fall, as I depict it here, is much too simplified. The principalities are not quite so coherent (how, for instance, can ideology and nationalism be distinguished in Mao's China?), neither are they arrayed in the world in settled rank or ordained order, nor are these powers noncompetitive as they confront human beings. The demonic powers are fallen, which means they do exist chaotically, apparently thriving in confusion, rivalry, and complexity. Demonic claims against human life in society are multiple, simultaneous, and competing, as anybody can realize who has endured conflicting simultaneous loyalties to family and nation and work or whatever.

An Inverse Dominion

Pretending autonomy from God, these creatures are autonomous from human control. In reality they dominate human beings. Relying upon the biblical description, I have come to think of the relationship of the principalities and persons as if the Fall means that there has been not only a loss of dominion by human beings over the rest of creation but, more precisely than that, an inversion or a reversal of dominion. So, now, those very realities of creation — traditions, institutions, nations — over which humans are said in the Genesis creation story to receive dominion and the very creatures that are called thus into the service and enhancement of human life in society exercise, in the era of the Fall, dominion over human beings (Gen. 1:26). The work of the demonic powers in the Fall is the undoing of creation (Gen. 6:11–13). The gravest effort of the principalities is the capture of humans in their service, which is to say, in idolatry of death, whatever external appearance or particular form that may assume.

Dehumanization is one term of current jargon for the reversal of dominion between persons and principalities. Specific illustrations of it from contemporary American experience abound — in the precedence, for example, of bureaucratic routine over human need in the administration of welfare or of Medicaid; in the brutalization of inmates where imprisonment is really a means of banishing people from human status, hiding them, treating them as animals or as if they were dead as human beings; in the separation of citizens in apartheid, enforced, as the case may be, by urban housing and development schemes, by racial limitations of access to credit, or by the militia; in the social priorities determined by the momentum of technological proliferation, regardless of either environmental or human interests thereby neglected, damaged, or lost; in genocide practiced for generations against Indian Americans; in the customs of male chauvinism; in the fraud and fakery and the perils to human health and safety sponsored by American merchandising methodology.

Are Some Powers Benign?

As commonplace and recurrent as such aggressions by the demonic powers against human life in society are and, literally, forever have been and so long as time lasts will be, human beings generally and, it seems, Americans particularly persevere in belaboring the illusion that at least some institutions are benign and viable and within human direction or can be rendered so by discipline or reform or revolution or displacement. The principalities are, it is supposed, capable of being

209

altered so as to respect and serve human life, instead of demeaning and dominating human life, provided there is a sufficient human will to accomplish this.

I suggest this to be, however, a virtually incredible view. It is both too naive and too narrow, incorrigible, and a stance that is both theologically false and empirically unwarranted. It really asserts that the principalities are only somewhat or sometimes fallen and the Fall is not an essential condition of disorientation, morally equivalent to the estate of death, affecting the whole of creation in time. It construes the Fall as a wayward proclivity or corruptibility in institutions and nations and other principalities. It is, moreover, a remarkable expression of human vanity, insisting that human dominion over the rest of creation, if occasionally ineffectual, is nonetheless retained if humans have the stamina to exercise it. Empirically, meanwhile, this position dismisses the enormity and interminability of human suffering of all sorts prevalent in this world, which is only properly attributable to the fallenness of the principalities and powers. War or famine or pestilence; persecution or repression or slavery — the realities that constitute the daily fortune of the overwhelming masses of human beings on the face of the earth and that symbolize, by embracing all experience that is apparently less grotesque, the threat of death for every human being — issue from the parasitical posture of the principalities toward human life. Corporations and nations and other demonic powers restrict, control, and consume human life in order to sustain and extend and prosper their own survival.

The biblical comprehension is realistic about this, exposing the wantonness of Babylon, the great nation who destroys, squanders, devours human life for the sake of her own vainglory and enrichment and power (Rev. 18:7–8, 24). . . .

Rivalry among the Powers

The scene of turmoil and confusion associated with the demonic powers becomes acute when it is recognized that these are rival, competitive powers despite the fact that, at times, they seem to confront human life as compatible or collaborating powers. All alliances among the principalities (the reciprocal arrangements of the

Pentagon, some self-styled think tanks, and the weapons industries furnish an example) are transient and expedient. Such liaisons are aptly described in Revelation by terms like "fornication," "sorcery," or "playing the wanton" (Rev. 18:7–15, 23).

From a human point of view, the principalities may in specific circumstances appear to be conspiring or collaborating together against human beings and human life (among corporations, price-fixing agreements or product control pacts furnish instances). Yet the basic conflict among all principalities remains, though it be subdued or concealed for awhile, because the only morality governing each principality is its own survival as over against every other principality, as well as over against human beings and, indeed, the rest of creation. That this singular fixation — a purpose to survive — is futile, does not diminish the fierceness of the competition and strife among principalities. It has no efficacy against death; sooner or later, in one way or another, it is empirically defeated by death so that when a nation or an institution strives so mightily to survive, it is engaged in absurd tribute to death.

People are veritably besieged, on all sides, at every moment simultaneously by these claims and strivings of the various powers each seeking to dominate, usurp, or take a person's time, attention, abilities, effort; each grasping at life itself; each demanding idolatrous service and loyalty. In such tumult it becomes very difficult for a human being even to identify the idols that would possess him or her. . . .

A Morality of Survival

The principalities and powers in this or any other society engage in their assaults against human beings and in their undoing of human life in society with extraordinary ploy and guile, deception and charade, babel and falsity (see Matt. 12:45; Luke 8:2). The Babylon episode in Revelation pictures a scene of final incongruity and distortion. The principalities thrive in chaos, as has been said. Confusion attends all the works and stratagems of these powers; after all, death is confusion in its ultimate connotation.

More than any other recent American happening, the Vietnam

war has documented and dramatized this very condition among this nation's leaders and managers. The war has exposed the process by which a principality or conglomeration of principalities beguiles and entraps people in courses of action that wantonly debilitate and destroy human life. *The Pentagon Papers* are remarkable and instructive in setting forth this manipulation, this conjuring, this insatiable appetite for human sacrifice typical of ideological and institutional powers. The public version of these claims of the demonic powers against human beings commonly sounds laudable and offers human beings grandiose promises for their safety, prosperity, virtue, even immortality. Thus, during the ordeal in Southeast Asia of the past decade, Americans have been successively induced to squander life on a scale so prodigious it appalls imagination and defies calculation for the sake of stopping the alleged threat of communist China or of securing "self-determination" for the Vietnamese or of hindering the so-called domino theory or of vindicating American "honor" or of serving the "national security" interests. And though each and all of these are shams and have long since been known as such, the hold of the military-technological-industrial complex upon the American people has remained tenacious.

The principalities have great resilience; the death game that they play continues, adapting its means of dominating human beings to the sole morality that governs all demonic powers so long as they exist — survival. To put it very plainly, concealed within the public rhetoric justifying the Southeast Asian war (and all that the war has meant as napalm, defoliation, body counts, search-and-destroy operations, saturation bombing, and as abandoned domestic needs, persecution of dissenters, political imprisonments, the alienation of the young, the moral dissipation of leaders and common citizens alike) has been the purpose of supporting and serving the Pentagon and the whole array of war principalities that the Pentagon symbolizes. To speak of the Indochinese war in terms of the relation of principalities and human beings is, bluntly, to expose the survival of the Pentagon and its satellite or adjoining principalities as the purpose of the war. This is one reason why, of course, this war has been more a symptom than a cause of the American social crisis. It is why, also, whenever the war can be said to have ended, no essential change will have been wrought in the nation.

So let it be reiterated that the theological conclusion here (the survival of the principalities is the secret purpose of the war) does not classify America's leaders as nitwits or as wicked, though some in fact be either or both, but discerns their victimization by the principalities and powers to which they are privy. Their servility to the survival interest of these powers depletes them as human beings. They become captivated, dominated, obsessed by the demonic. And let it be allowed that this same theological statement is made, and this particular example given, in order to focus upon the extraordinary magnetism and guile of the enslaving or dehumanizing capabilities of the principalities, though, analytically, this does not exhaust the matter. These relationships between the principalities and human beings, in which human life is sacrificed to sustain the demonic, and in which reputed leaders as well as ordinary folk become victims, are more intricate, more complicated, more ambiguous, more tense, more hectic than words can describe. The milieu of the powers and principalities *is* chaos.

Stratagems of the
Demonic Powers

IF THE powers and principalities be legion, so are the means by which they assault, captivate, enslave, and dominate human beings.

Yet all of the demonic claims against human life — for all their number and variegation and in spite of their dynamic qualities and even though they sponsor chaos — have a common denominator. Typically, each and every stratagem and resort of the principalities seeks the death of the specific faculties of rational and moral comprehension that specially distinguish human beings from all other creatures. Whatever form or appearance it may take, demonic aggression always aims at the immobilization or surrender or destruction of the mind and at the neutralization or abandonment or demoralization of the conscience. In the Fall, the purpose and effort of every principality is the dehumanization of human life, *categorically*.

Demonic Tactics and the Prevalence of Babel

I do not attempt, here, any exhaustive account of the ploys and stratagems of the powers that be. But I do cite some of those most

An Ethic for Christians and Other Aliens in a Strange Land, 1973, pp. 97–104, 105–7

familiar, as a matter of illustration and, moreover, in order to underscore the significance of the verbal element in the tactics that the principalities mount against human beings. That the verbal factor is so prominent among multifarious stratagems is related directly to the fact that it is the human mind that is being contested and that it is human conscience that is being threatened by the demonic. Indeed, I regard the verbal as definitive in all the ploys of the principalities.

The Denial of Truth

A rudimentary claim with which the principalities confront and subvert persons is that truth in the sense of eventful and factual matter does not exist. In the place of truth and appropriating the name of truth are data engineered and manufactured, programmed and propagated by the principality. The truth is usurped and displaced by a self-serving version of events or facts, with whatever selectivity, distortion, falsehood, manipulation, exaggeration, evasion, concoction necessary to maintain the image or enhance the survival or multiply the coercive capacities of the principality. Instead of truth as that may be disclosed empirically, the principality furnishes a story fabricated and prefabricated to suit institutional or ideological or similar vested interests (Rev. 18:23, 20:3, 10).

This ploy is commonplace commercially in American merchandising and advertising, and has been for a long time. It has lately been transported into politics and sophisticated for political purposes on a scale and with a persistence that is profoundly ominous for human beings. The contention during the Johnson presidency about "news management" documents this view. More recently, in the Nixon administration, official propaganda has been uttered in the context of a wide-ranging and systematic attack upon the media, upon newspeople, and upon citizens as auditors of news. In both of these administrations, the government's propaganda efforts have been especially concentrated upon selling a prevalent line about the Southeast Asian war. Thus, one is aware that behind both President Johnson and President Nixon have been the machinations of the principality of the Pentagon and the famous industrial-military complex. It is arguable that these two presidents have been more prisoners and victims of the demonic than sponsors of the reduction of truth to propaganda, or the marketing of official lies, or the intimidation of the media, or the denigration of the First Amendment, or the virtual abolition of credibility in the relationship of government and citizens. Meanwhile, of course, the matter has not been restricted to the Indochina war, but has affected every public issue. If citizens realize, by now, that they have been contemptuously, relentlessly importuned because of untrustworthy versions of Vietnam, they may also begin to sense how their humanity is similarly insulted by official falsehood and propaganda concerning Watergate, the cost of living, taxation, crime, product safety, certain notorious indictments, and practically anything else in which the same political principalities are implicated.

What is most significant in any of these examples is, I think, not the doctoring of the truth per se but the premise of the principalities that truth is nonexistent, that truth is a fiction, that there can be no thorough or fair or comprehensive or detached discovery and chronicle of events and that any handling of facts is ideologically or institutionally or otherwise tainted. The recent official aggressions against the media have been based upon this proposition. They take the position that the public media, by definition, have been engaged in indoctrination of a viewpoint and version that, insofar as it departs from the authorized administration line, must be either supplanted by official propaganda or suppressed.

Ominous, indeed! This presumption of the principalities that truth does not exist or cannot with some human diligence be uncovered and conscientiously communicated outreaches the subversion of the discipline of journalism. It abolishes any work of scholarship; it renders education — both teaching and learning — partisan and farcical and, in the end, condemns and banishes all uses of human intelligence.

Doublespeak and Overtalk

The preemption of truth with prefabricated, fictionalized versions of facts and events and the usurpation of truth by propaganda and official lies are stratagems of the demonic powers much facilitated by other language contortions or abuses that the principalities and authorities foster. These include heavy euphemism and coded phrases, the inversion of definitions, jargon, hyperbole, misnomer, slogan, argot, shibboleth, cliché. The powers enthrall, delude, and enslave human beings by estopping comprehension with *doublespeak,* as Orwell named it.

Orwell's prototype of the phenomenon of doublespeak declares "war is peace." That very example of doublespeak has become by way of the war in Indochina the literal watchword in America, more that a decade before Orwell's doomsday date of 1984. The plethora of doublespeak contrived and uttered because of this war has been fantastic and evidently inexhaustible. Doublespeak has been solemnly pronounced to deceive citizens, not to mention the Congress, about every escalation, every corruption, every wasted appropriation, every casualty report, every abdication of command responsibility and every insubordination, every atrocity of the war. For example, the cliché "winding down the war" has concealed the most deadly acceleration of firepower and destructive capability in the entire history of warfare on this planet. Again, in 1972, when the United Nations secretary general verified American bombing of North Vietnamese dams and dikes, potentially jeopardizing as many as five million civilians, the response of the American authorities was classic doublespeak, to wit: "The dikes are not targeted." Or, again, at the outset of the American combat involvement in Vietnam, doublespeak propagated the false conception that the U.S. intervention in Indochina with a handful of heavily subsidized mercenaries was an extension of the grand alliance of the Second World War.

If the war has furnished innumerable specific instances of the doublespeak ploy, so has American racism. In the sixties, it will be recalled, "violence in the streets" became the slogan for suppression of peaceful black protest. More recently, the so-called busing issue refers to barring black migration to white suburbs and to a presidential pledge of apartheid.

Sometimes doublespeak is overtalk, in which the media themselves so accentuate volume, speed, and redundance that communication is incapacitated (even where the data transmitted may not be false or deceptive). The auditor's mind is so insulted, inundated, or transfixed by verbal and visual technology that it is crippled or immobilized. Thus Americans had been for so long saturated on newscasts by "Vietnam" — "Vietnam" — "Vietnam" — "war" — "war" — "war" — day after day after day, that these words, relayed this way, became signals to the head to turn off.

Secrecy and Boasts of Expertise

An aspect of the delusive aura enveloping the demonic powers is the resort to secrecy. Secrecy in politics is dehumanizing per se; political secrecy begets a ruthless paternalism between regime and citizens that disallows human participation in government and renders human beings hapless against manipulation by trick or propaganda or other babel. (*The Pentagon Papers* document this so far as governmental principalities are concerned; some of the Nader reports on the automobile industry reflect the same issue as to corporate powers.)

Nowadays, Americans are told that secrecy is an indispensable principle of government. Frequently, that claim is embellished by pleas of expertise, that is, the assertion by a principality — like the Pentagon or the CIA or the Kissinger operation — that certain affairs are too sensitive or too complicated for human beings to know about or act upon. In ferocious application this really becomes a boast that bureaucratic routine or computer programming or institutional machinations are superhuman and obviate human abilities to be informed, to think, to decide, and to act, thus relegating the person to a role of spectator or acolyte, submissive and subservient to the requirements of the principality. One common and homely example is known to those who have ever tried to register a complaint or otherwise secure their rights in relation to principalities like the telephone company or the power company or a credit card outfit only to find themselves in correspondence with a machine, the convenience of which takes priority.

Surveillance and Harassment

Ancillary to secrecy in politics and commerce and in other realms is surveillance and the abolition of human privacy. The prevalence of industrial and commercial espionage; the monitoring of shoppers and elevator passengers and similar, now commonplace, so-called security precautions affecting ordinary business; the everyday atmosphere of apprehension in which people have come to live in America — all have worked to enlarge greatly the tolerance of citizens toward political surveillance and the loss of privacy. The kind of open society contemplated by the First Amendment seems impossible — and, what is more ominous, seems undesirable — to very many Americans. So there is little outrage when Senate hearings expose illegal military oversight of civilians or when the unprecedented political espionage at the Watergate is exposed or when education (if that is what it can then still be called) is conducted in so many schools in the presence of the police or other "security" forces.

It is not necessary to dwell upon such contemporary citations, however, because surveillance is a very old ploy of the principalities and not at all an innovation of electronics. One recalls that the purpose of the famous journey to Bethlehem of Joseph and the pregnant Mary was to be enrolled for a special tax applicable only to the Jews. It was not only a means by which the Roman occupiers collected revenue but was also a harassment of potential dissidents and a minute political scrutiny of a captive and oppressed people.

Exaggeration and Deception

In certain situations principalities act or overact so as to engender a belief that their conduct is warranted though no empirical justification exists. It is the audacity of the deceit, the grossness of the falsehood, the sheer excessiveness of the stratagem, the massiveness of the exaggeration that works to gain public credence or acquiescence.

In American merchandising this wantonness has foisted a huge quantity and a startling array of phony, worthless, dangerous goods and services upon purchasers. What may be more significant, such commercial deception has been so common, so widespread, and practiced for such a long time that when the same techniques are politically appropriated human resistance has already been made pliable.

This was a weapon of Nazi anti-Semitism. It was the snare of McCarthyism. This was the devious ploy summoned to defeat Congressman Jerry Voorhes and, later, Helen Gahagan Douglas. Thence the Department of Justice inherited it and has utilized it more often than one cares to recount but, most menacingly so far, to obtain public passivity to the unconstitutional mass arrests in Washington on May Day 1971.

Cursing and Conjuring

The demonic powers curse human beings who resist them. I mean the term *curse* quite literally, as a condemnation to death, as a damnation.

In earlier times, American Indians were cursed as savages in order to rationalize genocide. Somewhat similarly, chattel slavery involved cursing blacks as humanly inferior. In more recent American experience, the most effectual instance of cursing, probably, has been the official defamation of the Black Panthers through indictments that conjure images of them as bloodthirsty black revolutionaries. If, by now, most of these prosecutions have failed and the charges have proved to be false or frivolous or fantastic, the curse nonetheless survives.

From available reports, the principalities and powers of the Soviet Union employ cursing and conjuring more radically and even more recklessly than has yet happened in the United States. Their procedure involves officially diagnosing certain dissenters as insane and then confining and treating them accordingly. . . .

Diversion and Demoralization

It must be borne in mind that any effort to designate and describe or illustrate characteristic ploys of the principalities is artificial to the extent that it necessarily abstracts a particular stratagem from the havoc and frenzy within which all the powers exist and act. None of these techniques or tactics can be sharply defined; they all overlap, and, moreover, they most commonly can be cited in simultaneous use. The matter is, of course, further compounded by the intense rivalries and apparent collaborations as much as by how many of the powers besiege humans all at once. This is most pertinent to those ploys that have a distracting or diversionary aspect. That is illustrated by the political importance in contemporary American society of commercial sports. Sports engage the attention, time, and energies of multitudes of human beings, diverting them from politics as such and furnishing vicarious activity in substitution for their participation in political struggle. More than that, in circumstances where there is little citizen involvement in the realpolitik of a nation, the persecution and punishment of non-conforming persons becomes itself a form of public spectacle. For the governing authorities and for citizens who acquiesce to a spectator role, the recent American political prosecutions like those of Angela Davis or Daniel Ellsberg or Philip Berrigan serve the same purpose as the arena events involving lions and Christians in ancient Rome.

This same distracting factor is prominent, obviously, wherever scapegoats are sacrificed for the survival of principalities, whether the scapegoat be an individual (as Stokely Carmichael was for awhile in the sixties, for instance) or a class of persons (as welfare recipients have now become).

There are numberless other diversions convenient to the demonic powers, some of which may be thought of as dividends that accrue when other ploys are at work. The relentlessness of multifarious babel in America, for example, has wrought a fatigue both visceral and intellectual in millions upon millions of Americans. By now truly *de*moralized, they suffer no conscience and they risk no action. Their human interest in living is narrowed to meager subsisting; their hope for life is no more than avoiding involvement with other humans and a desire that no one will bother them. They have lost any expectations for society; they have no stamina left for confronting the principalities; they are reduced to docility, lassitude, torpor, profound apathy, and default. The demoralization of human beings in this fashion greatly conveniences the totalitarianism of the demonic powers since the need to resort to persecutions or imprisonments is obviated, as the people are already morally captive.

All of these snares and devices of the principalities represent the reality of babel, and babel is that species of violence most militant in the present American circumstances.

Babel means the inversion of language, verbal inflation, libel,

rumor, euphemism and coded phrases, rhetorical wantonness, redundancy, hyperbole, such profusion in speech and sound that comprehension is impaired, nonsense, sophistry, jargon, noise, incoherence, a
chaos of voices and tongues, falsehood, blasphemy. And, in all of this,
babel means violence.

Babylon is the city of babel. The language and liturgies of
emperor worship in imperial Rome were babel. The Nazis practiced
babel against the Jews. Babel spawns racism. In 1984, babel is the way
advanced technocracy dehumanizes persons. By the 1970s in America,
successive regimes had been so captivated by babel that babel had
become the means of ruling the nation, the principal form of coercion
employed by the governing authorities against human beings.

The State as
Preeminent Principality

THE principalities and powers, despite their several names, their multifarious appearances, or their distinguishing characteristics, share a common status as fallen creatures. They suffer and assert a singular hostility toward human life in society that expresses their own radical subjugation and subservience to the power of death.

From a human point of view, it would seem that the demonic powers are not all equal in life span or capacity for survival or in prominence or influence. Some appear to be higher or stronger or more sophisticated or otherwise greater than others. There is, it appears, a hierarchy of principalities, in which some of them have precedence over others. This is evident, beyond the scope of ordinary human observation and experience, in the way in which history treats the powers that be. The Roman Empire is thus remembered as of more importance than ancient Assyria; English colonialism in North America, vestiges of which are still notable, is interpreted as having more impact than, say, Dutch colonialism on the same continent. The same tendency is seen in how the principalities arrange themselves. A hierarchical order is accorded the principalities with the United Nations, reflected in the prerogatives of the so-called superpowers as over against other member nations.

An Ethic for Christians and Other Aliens in a Strange Land, 1973, pp. 107–11

In America, there is a similar appearance of a hierarchy of principalities: in the pantheon of sports, football is a larger commercial enterprise than, say, bowling and would seem to have a wider political influence; incumbency attributes more power, in a variety of ways, to a political party than is retained by a party out of office; the nation, together with the governmental institutions, is commonly thought of as superior to other principalities in society, like the labor unions or the professions or the universities or the corporations.

I do not know that it can be flatly concluded that there is an actual hierarchy among the principalities. The scene of the demonic powers, as human beings behold it, is so chaotic and so dynamic, so distorted and so hectic, so tense and tumultuous as to make me pause at saying that certain principalities have a greater inherent dignity than certain others. Who can say, for instance, which is the greater demonic power, the national administration of the federal government or the Mafia? or the oil industry? or the Central Intelligence Agency? or any of the multinational conglomerates? or the Chase Manhattan Bank?

So I go no further than the statement that there is an *apparent* hierarchy of principalities that fluctuates according to different circumstances, and the status orientation of which is subject to differing constructions or interpretations. It is, at the least, a convenience of thought and language to refer to such a hierarchy. Commonly, the powers are empirically regarded in such a fashion, as has been noticed, and the biblical treatment of the principalities is similar (cf. Rev. 17, 18).

Among all the principalities, in their legion species and diversities, the state has a particular eminence. The state, in this context, names the functional paraphernalia of political authority in a nation, which claims and exercises violence within a nation. The precedence of the state hierarchically among the principalities is related to the jurisdiction asserted by the state over other institutions and powers within a nation. Practically it is symbolized by the police power, taxation, licensing, regulation of corporate organization and activity, the military forces, and the like.

The paramountcy of the state among the demonic powers is probably most readily recognized in tyrannical regimes, ancient or modern. In Revelation, and elsewhere in the Bible where the state is designated as a principality of particular dignity or apparent superiority, the historical realities to which allusions are made are authoritarian or totalitarian (Rev. 13:18). In such a regime any substantive distinctions between the principality of the nation and the principality of the state are lost. The ethos of the nation is absorbed into the apparatus of authority. Or, to put it a bit differently, the spirit and tradition of the nation are abolished by the administration of the state or displaced by a fabricated version of tradition furnished by the state. For all practical purposes, in a totalitarianism, the nation and the state become merged.

By contrast (though, from a human point of view, it be a very relative matter) in nonauthoritarian societies, the distinguishable but related principalities of the nation and the state remain separated to the extent that the identity and character of the nation are embodied in tradition and inheritance, sometimes expressed constitutionally or sometimes as common law. This represents and attempts some restraint or discipline upon the exercise of authority and the functioning of the state. In a totalitarianism, what authority does *is* the law, or, alternately, one must say that in such a regime there is no law or constitutional system or the like and the law has been displaced by authority or coercive capability. Idealistically, a democratic constitution or a common-law tradition is conceived as representing and protecting human beings against the limited and defined authority of the state. That this may be more recital than practice, more illusory than real, does not alter the fact that law and authority, nation and state, name rival principalities whose tensions and conflicts may, inadvertently, if no more than that, benefit human life in society. At the same time, this does not exempt law from subjection to the power of death.

In any case, the state is much regarded historically, analytically, empirically, biblically as the archetypical principality, epitomizing the other principalities and powers, and possessing or claiming a certain special status or eminence in the seeming hierarchy of demonic powers. The state, after all, does expose the moral authority of the demonic with a directness and severity that is not so public or so obvious in the existence of most other principalities. That moral authority is death. Every sanction or weapon or policy or procedure — including law where law survives distinct from authority — that the state commands against both human beings and against the other principalities carries the connotation of death, implicitly threatens death, derives from and symbolizes death. Some of the American colonists had a kindred insight when they complained against the reign of George III to the effect that the power to tax is the power to destroy. Enumerate the usual prerogatives of the state and it becomes plain that each and every one of them embodies the meaning of death: exile, imprisonment, slavery, conscription, impeachment, regulation of production or sales or prices or wages or competition or credit, confiscation, surveillance, execution, war. Whenever the authority of the state is exercised in such ways as these the moral basis of the authority remains the same: death. That is the final sanction of the state and it is the *only* one.

The Mythology of a "Justified" Nation

THE American anxiety concerning justification is not a merely private matter but has manifold political ramifications. Perhaps the most notorious political consequence of this anxiety, expressed on a societal and cultural level in openly political terms, is the mythology (not to say fantasy) of America as the holy nation. The doctrine, which has diverse origins in the American experience as a nation, is that America is a nation with a unique destiny, bestowed upon it by God.

This has had particularly vehement lip service in the presidency of Ronald Reagan: in many instances he has pronounced America the embodiment of good, while America's presumed enemies, especially the Soviet Union, embody objective evil. Reagan thereby goes significantly beyond conventional or simplistic patriotic rhetoric. He is talking about imagined, ultimate, cosmic confrontations.

Yet what is thus alleged about America's character as a nation and about the historic destiny of the nation has a curiously familiar sound because it is, in fact, a bastard version of the biblical news about the election of Israel and then, in the New Testament, the vocation of the church as the exemplary nation or as the priest among the nations.

Politics of Spirituality, 1984, pp. 52–56, 62–65

The appropriation of the biblical tradition concerning the holy nation for application to *any* secular regime, like the United States of America, is a profound affront at once to biblical faith and to the witness to the biblical events, as well as to the church of Christ. In an earlier time in the church's life, such an offense on the part of a ruler or incumbent official — like a president — might well have provoked the sanction of anathema. Do not suppose I am one bit facetious in considering that anathema should have been, in the present day, pronounced against President Reagan for his incessant trivialization of the Bible and its content. And he has no defense against anathema in a plea of sincerity. (There are, of course, many critics who label Reagan a hypocrite because he seldom darkens a church doorway. He used to say, when asked about his absences from church services, that his religion is too private a matter to warrant church attendance. That sounds sincere enough to me, though it clearly places Reagan outside the scope of biblical faith.) In any circumstance sincerity is no defense, and sincerity in denouncing and belittling the gospel only compounds the affront. Reagan's entire well-worn story about America the holy nation, America the divine favorite among the nation, America the chosen nation is the rhetoric of fantasy, not history; of delusion, not revelation; of gross vanity, not fidelity or virtue. It is utterly anomalous — an outrage — that Reagan should hear any applause for his rhetoric or receive any adherents to his mythology about America as the "justified" nation, particularly from any constituency professing to be part of the church.

Understand, please, that I am not indulging here in a partisan comment. And I do not single out Reagan in a way that implies he is unique in his behavior and his pontifical remarks in regard to the nation's moral disposition and its ultimate destiny. There are now, and there have been for generations, Americans prominent in the political establishment, rulers and authorities of many partisan affiliations, in addition to ecclesiastical leaders and officials and hosts of preachers, who have mouthed various versions of this same fabrication about America being especially favored among nations by God. The natural and diverse beauty of the continent is taken to be a sign of that divine preference, and the same idea is then translated into the grandiose dimensions of American technological prowess and military super-power, or into "the American standard of living," or laissez-faire capitalism, or prosperity, or preeminence in science, and so on and on. The whole political discussion about maintaining America as "Number 1" among the nations, which has, notably, developed since the frustration of American superpower in Korea and then, grotesquely, in Vietnam, and subsequently in Lebanon and in Latin America, is part of this pathetic syndrome. The basic impression is that God has so favored America that God has rewarded America — by making and keeping the nation as "Number 1" — in advance of the judgment.

That is only one of the ways in which this fantasizing about the nation works havoc (mainly in the form of mockery and ridicule) with biblical faith. For any professed church folk to be privy to these shibboleths about the nation is scandalous; for the president or adjacent high authorities to indulge and propagate the same is dangerous; for this credo to become widely accepted among the general citizenry borders on some sort of mass hallucination.

So Reagan is mentioned here by name because he has been an incumbent president and, in that capacity, has brought himself into the matter and extended the topic to greater extremities of rhetoric and myth than ever before. But, in naming him, we must keep in mind that there are legions more, among the American people and among those who purport to rule this society. Most sad to say, in these same ranks are multitudes of church-related folk, some hapless, some guileful, articulating these same themes.

I wish this whole matter were innocuous, just an irritation occasioned by careless and excessive language, a mere distortion of some elements of America's past, an issue of "civic religion," which, though intellectually corrupt and bankrupt in terms of spirituality, is unlikely to disrupt society in a practical manner. But this is not an innocuous cause; it is one both pernicious and perilous for society and one rapidly becoming a crisis.

I do not give much credence to conspiratorial interpretations of history, but I apprehend that the truth is that there are persons and organizations and financing resources seeking to transmute the mythology and rhetoric concerning America the holy nation into a political and ideological movement to "convert" America into a so-called Christian nation. Some of these powers speak of restoring America as a "Christian nation" — in blatant falsification of American history as well as remarkable distortion of what it means, in biblical perspective, to be Christian. . . .

The problem of America as a nation, in biblical perspective, remains the elementary issue of repentance. The United States is, as all nations are, called in the Word of God to repentance. That, in truth, is what the church calls for, whether knowingly or not, every time the church prays *Thy Kingdom come.*

America needs to repent. Every episode in the common experience of America as a nation betells that need. If such be manifest in times of trauma and trouble — such as now — it is as much the need in triumphal or grandiose circumstances.

The nation needs to repent. If I put the matter so baldly, I hope no one will mistake my meaning for the rhetoric of those electronic celebrity preachers who sometimes use similar language to deplore the mundane lusts of the streets or the ordinary vices of people or to berate the constitutional bar to prayer, so-called, in public schools while practicing quietism about the genocidal implications of the Pentagon's war commerce or extolling indifference toward the plight of the swelling urban underclasses.

Topically, repentance is *not* about forswearing wickedness as such; repentance concerns the confession of vanity. For America — for any nation at any time — *repentance means confessing blasphemy.*

Blasphemy occurs in the existence and conduct of a nation whenever there is such profound and sustained confusion as to the nation's character, place, capabilities, and destiny that the vocation of the Word of God is preempted or usurped. Thus the very presumption of the righteousness of the American cause as a nation *is* blasphemy.

Americans, for some time now, have been assured, again and again, that the United States will prevail in history because the American cause is righteous. Anyone who believes that has, to say the very least, learned nothing from the American adventurism in Vietnam. Then, a succession of presidents made similar pronouncements, but America suffered ignominious defeat nonetheless. And if in the last few years some sense of guilt about Vietnam has begun to surface, this has been, for the most part, a strange and perverted sentiment because it has attached not to the crimes of American intervention in Southeast Asia — to massacre, despoilment, and genocide — but to the event of American defeat. To feel guilty because America lost, rather than because of what America did, is another, if macabre, instance of false righteousness. That is only the more underscored when the unlawful invasion of Grenada is examined as an attempt to fantasize the victory for American superpower that was missed in Vietnam.

Furthermore, the confusion of a nation's destiny and of a nation's capabilities with the vocation of the Word of God in history — which is the *esse* of blasphemy — sponsors the delusion that America exercises domination over creation as well as history, and that it can and should control events in the life of creation. Other nations, ancient and modern, as has been mentioned, suffer similar delusions, but if there ever has been a nation that should know better (that is, that should repent), it is America, if only because of the American experience as a nation and a society in these past few decades.

After all, it is only in the period since, say, Hiroshima, in which American power, rampant most conspicuously in the immense, redundant, overkill nuclear-weapons arsenal, has been proven impotent, because if it is employed, it portends self-destruction, and if it is not, it amounts to profligate, grotesque waste. In either instance, American nuclear arms are rendered practically ineffectual in dominating events, but they still mock the sovereignty of the Word of God in history.

Much the same must, of course, be said of the nation's society and culture, which has become, as I have earlier remarked, overdependent upon the consumption ethic, with its doctrines of indiscriminate growth, gross development, greedy exploitation of basic resources, uncritical and often stupid reliance upon technological capabilities and incredible naivety about technological competence, and crude, relentless manipulation of human beings as consumers. Increasingly, now, people can glimpse that this is no progress, no enhancement of human life, but wanton plunder of creation itself. People begin to apprehend that the penultimate implementation of the American consumption ethic is, bluntly, self-consumption. In the process, it has become evident as well that the commerce engendered by the American consumption ethic, together with the commerce of weapons proliferation, relates consequentially to virtually every injustice of which human beings are victims in this nation and in much of the rest of the world.

And so I say the United States needs to repent; the nation needs to be freed of blasphemy. These are, admittedly, theological statements. Yet I think they are also truly practical statements. America will remain frustrated, literally demoralized, incapable of coping with its concrete problems as a nation and society until it knows that realism concerning the nation's vocation that only repentance can bring.

One hopes repentance will be forthcoming. If not, it *will* happen: in the good time of the judgment of the Word of God.

Science and Technology:
A Biblical View of the Arms Race

I do not cease to give thanks for you, remembering you
in my prayers . . . that you may know . . . what is the
immeasurable greatness of his power in us who believe,
according to the working of his great might which he
accomplished in Christ when he raised him from the dead
and made him sit at his right hand in the heavenly places,
far above all rule and authority and power and dominion,
and above every name that is named, not only to this age
but also in that which is to come; and [God] has put all
things under his feet and has made him the head over all
things. . . .

EPHESIANS 1:16, 18a, 19–22

Finally, be strong in the Lord and in the strength of his
might. Put on the whole armor of God, that you may be
able to stand against the wiles of the devil. For we are not
contending against flesh and blood, but against the principalities, against the powers, against the world rulers of this

---

Waging Peace, ed. Jim Wallis, 1982, pp. 109–13

present darkness, against the spiritual hosts of wickedness
in the heavenly places. Therefore take the whole armor of
God, that you may be able to withstand in the evil day,
and having done all, to stand.

EPHESIANS 6:10–13

If human beings today are to realistically comprehend or sanely
confront the nuclear issue, it is imperative to expose the mythology
— and to dispel the mythological aura — that shrouds the realm of
nuclear policy. The prospect of nuclear war must no longer be preempted by military, scientific, or diplomatic professionals or similar
putative experts; the subject must no longer be withheld from the
scrutiny of the conscience and the common sense of ordinary people.
Insofar as the prevailing nuclear mythology inhibits that, it must be
exorcised.

The primordial mythology of nuclear power has complicated
origins in various aspects of American culture and is compounded by
certain historic events. Perhaps the most conspicuous cultural feature
has been a profligate idolatry of science, fostering gross overestimations
of the capabilities of science and technology, together with an uncritical, indeed wanton, imposition of the scientific method, so-called,
throughout society. These circumstances have, in turn, issued in a
literally fantastic attitude that technical capability should be implemented just because it exists, without the exercise of human discretion
as to the moral character of any particular venture. Views such as these
are secreted in a belief, inculcated profusely in the culture since the
start of this century, that science is morally neuter or, to put it in
some traditional theological terms, that science as a principality somehow enjoys exemption from the Fall. This naivety, incredible though
it be, is commonly associated with the superstition that science can,
eventually, supply remedy for any peril or problem wrought from
stupid or untimely or inappropriate implementation of any specific
technical capability.

The consequences, practically, of these foolish verities have been
multifarious, nefarious, and often grotesque in the nuclear realm as
well as elsewhere. Thus, to mention a single item only, hundreds of
thousands of hapless Americans now await tardy rescue from jeopardies

unprojected or, anyway, unforewarned by commercialized science, fomented by reckless, premature, or otherwise improvident disposal of toxic wastes.

In Hiroshima (which is simultaneously the primeval and the penultimate event of nuclear history) such ideas sponsored within the pantheon of science converged with the shibboleths spawned initially by the Second World War. These were quickly enough extended and embellished to suit the cold war, and they survive still, in substantially this latter form, in the Pentagon, the intelligence apparatus, and the self-styled national security authorities. The upshot has been the much-boasted connection between zeal for American nuclear preeminence and a fancied holy destiny for postwar America, the asserted efficacy of superpower in determining history and in domineering the life of creation, and the extraordinary, if nonetheless self-evident, contradiction embodied in the doctrine of nuclear deterrence.

Events have by now intervened and surpassed the heavy myths wrought from Hiroshima: American nuclear preeminence has been dissipated and perhaps was, all along, illusory. The inherent impotence of superpower to feign sovereignty in history and domination over the existence of creation has been verified in one calamity after another befalling the professed superpowers (such has been the redundant lesson in Korea, Vietnam, Afghanistan, Poland, Central America). At the same time, the doctrine of deterrence seems overwhelmed by the already common public skepticism it entices.

Meanwhile, the fundamental proposition that rendered the making and use of nuclear weapons thinkable in the first place — the curious hypothesis that science is morally innocuous — continues to be refuted categorically, day after day, not only because of the probability of nuclear apocalypse but also because of the plethora of other perils, contaminations, and plagues produced and promoted in the name of science as safe and beneficial to life. In short, in the present age history itself confirms the radical moral ambiguity of science and of all that science does and claims: history verifies and tells the truth that science is a fallen principality.

The disintegration of the mythology abetting the nuclear weapons race exposes the moral chaos in this world, which *is* the Fall as it affects institutions, nations, systems, regimes, bureaucracies, corporate

235

enterprises, ideologies, and the whole further array (more exactly, *dis*array) of principalities and powers. The collapse of that myth structure seems to have rendered Alexander Haig, erstwhile president of United Technologies, Inc., incurably hysterical, but it is nonetheless liberating for human beings who have harbored throughout the nuclear darkness faculties of conscience and sanity.

To their experience the blunt admonishment of the Letter to the Ephesians sounds familiar wisdom concerning the character of the principalities and powers, their diversity, disparity, and versatility, their virtually irresistible momentum, and, most ominously, their predatory attitude toward human beings and toward human life. Ephesians recites an absolutely crucial insight for anyone worried about nuclear power: the enemy, which is in truth death pervasive throughout creation, is manifest in institutions and nations, thrones and authorities, dominions and realms, administrations and myths, principalities and powers. And even though there be flesh and blood (that is, human beings) idolatrous of death, the power of death is never *merely* vested in wicked people. I suppose Alexander Haig can take comfort in that fact.

That explains, in part, why the Ephesians' designation of the alienation and hostility of the fallen principalities and powers toward fallen human life, and the fallen existence of the rest of creation, is so vehement. Ephesians bespeaks a warfare between the powers and human beings in which human life has no safety and no respite and, finally, no salvation except that which is known in the sovereignty of the Word of God in history as that is acknowledged, upheld, and honored here and now.

Another manner in which to speak of the predatory character of the conglomerate of principalities identifiable as the nuclear reality is straightforwardly in terms of the volume and extremity of violence that nuclear weapons concentrate. This is a violence of such dimensions that it obliterates aggressor as well as victim. Nuclear power is not only utterly destructive; it is, manifestly, utterly self-destructive. Moreover, it is not only visibly, quantitatively, physically destructive; it is psychologically, qualitatively, morally destructive. Actually, I believe any violence is inherently suicidal, but whatever argument there may be about that, the nuclear violence forecloses dispute: nuclear weapons are definitively suicidal.

Surely that has been the message of the Second World War, summed up in Hiroshima. That involved such sustained, debilitating, and, at last, diabolical violence that it consumed those who commissioned it on each side, ostensible victors no less than notorious vanquished. For America in the Second World War, the means of military conquest became morally suicidal for the nation and politically suicidal for democratic society and constitutional government. The policies of official violence that rule the nation (the paramilitarization of the police, the usurpation of the economy by Pentagon procurement, the unlawful, often criminal, practices of so-called intelligence and security agencies, to mention only a few features of the American technocratic regime that now prevails) in truth were authorized by Hiroshima.

In the nuclear issue, odd as it may sound to say, more than human lives are at stake, more than human survival is at issue. The nuclear principalities and powers threaten human extinction — and indeed the literal ruin of creation — in a way that incarnates the boldest offense of which any creature is capable, namely, *blasphemy* (cf. Rev. 13). Blasphemy is much more than a profaning of the name of God. It is more than incantation or curse. Blasphemy is peculiarly the temptation of the principalities — the nations and the corporate powers, science or commerce — in contesting the sovereignty of the Word of God in this world, in challenging and opposing the authority *now* of Jesus Christ as Lord of history, in gainsaying or evading accountability to human life and the life of the rest of creation, and in usurping and disrupting the vocation of the Word of God in judgment of these same nuclear principalities and powers. In this context, the very existence of the nuclear principalities, joined with the weapons in which they trade, is both essentially blasphemous and consummately blasphemous.

This is why a nuclear freeze, so-called, is but a phrase, not a policy. A nuclear freeze is not only not enough, as a reaction of nations and persons to the imminent nuclear threat; it is also gravely suspect as an arrogant co-option, at the instigation of the nuclear principalities, of the antinuclear sentiment and of the antinuclear movements. Nuclear freeze invites hallucination of a finale to the nuclear weapons proliferations and escalations in circumstances in which, in reality, nothing significant has changed.

On the other hand, even discredited nuclear mythology seems to retain enough influence to preclude American consideration of what is usually called "unilateral disarmament." Although it is seldom elaborated concretely, unilateral disarmament is assumed and asserted to be a radically foolhardy course. I do not know (I forebear to guess) what Alexander Haig and his ilk may mean when they discharge the phrase, but I do not find it foolish to contemplate disassembly of the establishment of nuclear principalities or disarming of warheads that so poignantly and immediately jeopardize our own lives as well as terrorize others. To my mind, this single allegedly unthinkable option — unilateral disarmament — is the only policy expressing hope. That is because I understand its potential to be penance for blasphemy.

Then, after repentance and its works, Americans might even act upon that wise proposal of Admiral Rickover to dismantle the Pentagon.

Medicine

I HAD not had reason for any such confidence [in the medical system] until then. By the time I entered Roosevelt Hospital, in fact, my morale was something like that of the woman with the hemorrhage, described in the Gospel according to St. Mark, "who had suffered much under many physicians, and had spent all that she had, and was no better but rather grew worse." It commonly requires a piteous effort to locate a conscientious doctor in the city. To obtain a doctor at all is a notorious problem among the poor, as I had learned secondhand, while living in East Harlem, from the recurrent troubles that my neighbors and clients encountered in seeking medical assistance or hospital care. Lives were — they still are — daily being jeopardized, impaired, or, often, lost because of underequipped, overtaxed, understaffed hospital and health facilities and because of the unavailability or absence of surgeons, physicians, nurses, and other medical personnel. Allow, on top of this, for the staggering patient load (the numbers of human beings in need of attention would be even greater) and for haste, misdiagnosis, and other human error, and the conclusion is inescapable that the public health bureaucracy has not only failed the poor of this society but is actually inimical to the health of the poor. . . .

For the middle classes this is only occasionally, and then, only

---

Second Birthday, 1970, pp. 24–26, 31–34

partially, mitigated by gambling on insurance schemes. In America, hospitalization is a disagreeable luxury, and the significant difference between the poor and the bourgeoisie is not in effectual insurance protection for either, or in the capability of the middle classes to afford what the poor cannot buy, but in the facility of the middle classes in obtaining credit. Accelerating inflation and easy access to expensive credit — a combination that is active in other realms of society as well as health — work together to make the purchase price of medical and hospital care for the middle classes their indefinite indebtedness. The ethics of class dictates that a contrary public illusion be maintained, but the truth is that in this way, and in some others, the American bourgeoisie become empirically more impoverished than the poor. At that point, the poor may still complain of their neglected or wasted health, but at least they retain a certain dignity as human beings, while the middle classes are consigned to a ridiculous and far more ignominious poverty. . . .

The most basic issue is, manifestly, that health has become *primarily* a commercial enterprise in this land. There is ample documentation of the subversion of human health by the commercialization of the medical profession and its satellite disciplines, occupations, and industries. That is to be found, not only in the frequency of occurrences nor merely in the broader context, which has been mentioned, of the problems of availability and accessibility for both poor and middle classes or of the fact that, generally, neither poor nor bourgeois people can actually afford the health care they need when they need it. Much more can be cited: the gross abuse of Medicare and Medicaid through fraudulent collection of fees for services never rendered and, sometimes, for fictitious patients; the similar, familiar, if more discreet, padding practices that have become virtually customary by doctors and hospitals where private insurance schemes are applicable; the inversion of priorities in medical research occasioned by the profit motive; the vain emphasis often given to cosmetic, as distinguished from organic, procedures in surgery; the diverting of private monies given for health purposes to the maintenance of the health-charities bureaucracy with its elaborately wasteful promotional and fund-raising apparatus; the scandals, exposed partially through Senate inquiries, in prescribing, labeling, pricing, and marketing drugs and pharmaceuticals; the commercial indoctrination of both the sick and the well to purchase and use potents, tonics, pills, symptomatic remedies, and assorted pseudomedicines, frequently abetted by specious professional endorsements. The health business, in its various branches, is one in which a primitive laissez-faire ethic still dominates with all the comparable cruel and savage consequences for human life that the same ethic has fostered in other realms where it has been allowed without bridle, and, lately, this process has been accentuated by the attempts, substantially successful, of the American Medical Association to politicize the doctors in order to enhance their commercial advantages.

This is, admittedly, a victim's diatribe that omits compliments, which some physicians and surgeons deserve, and does not mention the generosity of some hospitals or the selflessness of many hospital personnel of all sorts or the dedicated imagination of many in research or the honesty and viable conscience of others in the health industry. I do not ignore any of these. . . . Yet it does not honor that esteem to gainsay or to minimize the corruption, which the commercialization of health care in America has wrought. Moreover, I can complain as I have about the doctors and their associates because, as a lawyer, I am mindful that my own profession is about equally vulnerable to analogous indictment. The devotion of the legal profession for generations to commercial interests, at the expense of service to the remainder of the community and, especially, to the profound deprivation of the poor in their legal rights and causes, has become, by now, notorious and has been significantly responsible for bringing this nation to the brink of insurrection and a totalitarian repression. The intent of my own practice as a lawyer has been to oppose that. It is by this same authority, in the context of what I learned in illness and what I observed as a patient, that I can protest, without arrogance, I trust, the precedence that greed has gained over health in American society.

The Law as an Aggressor

THE delusion that captivates so many humans and specifically so many Americans, that the principalities are somehow exempted from the Fall and vouchsafed from death and thus are viable or can be so rendered, is directly relative to the victims of the demonic powers. Human beings do not readily recognize their victim status in relation to the principalities. To illustrate concretely: the American legal system, a principality, has seemed to me — a white, middle-class, Harvard-educated lawyer — to be civil and fair; to be viable, both theoretically and, *so far as I have been concerned,* practically. Only recently, and only once, so far, have I had occasion to see myself as a victim rather than as an apparent beneficiary of that system. That one event in which I felt I was being assaulted and violated as a person by this system, being victimized by the principality, being threatened with death, was in the utterance of charges, without support in fact or law, against me in connection with my friendship and hospitality for Daniel Berrigan. Even in those circumstances, I could muster an apologetic for the legal system. That is, I could conclude that the attempted prosecution was a political matter, an aberrant use of the law, a form of harassment, and take comfort that the charges were found insufficient and improper by the court and dismissed. So, even in the Block Island case, it is difficult for me to

---

An Ethic for Christians and Other Aliens in a Strange Land, 1973, pp. 84–86

regard myself, in relation to the legal system, vis-à-vis *that* principality as a victim.

My inability or reluctance to visualize myself as suffering
the aggressions of the principality against human life is not, however,
definitive as to this characteristic of all principalities. How must this
same American legal system have seemed to George Jackson, who
died under such ambiguous circumstances in San Quentin after a
dozen years confinement issuing from conviction for a theft of $70?
Another aberration? One wishes that might be true, but the facts
are persuasively contrary. American blacks have consistently, for all
the generations in which there have been American blacks, been
dealt with by the legal system in the same way that this principality
disposed of George Jackson. How viable was the Bill of Rights at
the time of its ratification to a black chattel slave? Aberration? There
is no other honest way to describe the relation between the law in
America and American blacks, between this principality and these
human beings, than in terms of the aggressions of the legal system
against human life. For blacks in the USA (to cite no other non-
whites of which the same must be said) the law, in a quite overwhelming sense, in the legislatures, in the courts, in law enforcement
and administration is now, as it always has been, an enemy: a harasser,
an invader, an oppressor. And this is the law's reality not only in
notorious circumstances, like chattel slavery or the era of the lynch
mobs or the generations of voter intimidation and disenfranchise-
ment or in the assassinations of black leaders or in the vindictiveness
of welfare policy or in the official persecution of black politics or
in the ingenious and tireless evasions of school desegregation (contrived as much in the White House as in any school board) or in
the sometimes fatal abuse of black prisoners but also, and perhaps
more significantly, in the apparently petty, routine, daily assaults and
importunities that blacks suffer under the guise of legality. Any talk
of injustice for blacks as merely occasional or aberrant is, simply,
racist sophistry.

On the other hand, if the law's aggressions against blacks are
admitted and, for the sake of maintaining the illusion that institutions
are or can be made truly viable, it is suggested that the law in America
remains, nonetheless, viable for white citizens or that there are in fact
racially identifiable two legal systems, then the most crucial issue

respecting the supposed viability of principalities emerges. If the American legal system seems viable for me and other white Americans but is not so for citizens who are black, or for any others, then *how,* as the dual commandment would ask, in the *name of humanity, can it be affirmed as viable for me or for any human being?*

Money

IDOLATRY, whatever its object, represents the enshrinement of any other person or thing in the very place of God. Idolatry embraces some person or thing, instead of God, as the source and rationalization of the moral significance of this life in the world for, at least, the idolater, though not, necessarily, for anybody else at all. Thus human beings, as idolaters, have from time to time worshiped stones and snakes and suns and fire and thunder, their own dreams and hallucinations, images of themselves and of their progenitors; they have had all the Caesars, ancient and modern, as idols; others have fancied sex as a god; for many, race is an idol; some worship science, some idolize superstition. Within that pantheon, money is a most conspicuous idol.

The idolatry of money means that the moral worth of a person is judged in terms of the amount of money possessed or controlled. The acquisition and accumulation of money in itself is considered evidence of virtue. It does not so much matter how money is acquired — by work or invention, through inheritance or marriage, by luck or theft — the main thing is to get some. The corollary of this doctrine, of course, is that those without money are morally inferior — weak, or indolent, or otherwise less worthy as human beings. Where money is an idol, to be poor is a sin.

This is an obscene idea of justification, directly in contradiction

Dissenter in a Great Society, 1966, pp. 40–47

with the Bible. In the gospel none are saved by any works of their own, least of all by the mere acquisition of money. In fact, the New Testament is redundant in citing the possession of riches as an impediment to salvation when money is regarded idolatrously. At the same time, the notion of justification by acquisition of money is empirically absurd, for it oversimplifies the relationship of the prosperous and the poor and overlooks the dependence of the rich upon the poor for their wealth. In this world human beings live at each other's expense, and the affluence of the few is proximately related to, and supported by, the poverty of the many.

This interdependence of rich and poor is something Americans are tempted to overlook, since so many Americans are in fact prosperous, but it is true today as it was in earlier times: the vast multitudes of people on the face of the earth are consigned to poverty for their whole lives, without any serious prospect whatever of changing their conditions. Their hardships in great measure make possible the comfort of those who are not poor; their poverty maintains the luxury of others; their deprivation purchases the abundance most Americans take for granted.

That leaves prosperous Americans with frightful questions to ask and confront, even in customs or circumstances that are regarded as trivial or straightforward or settled. Where, for instance, do the profits that enable great corporations to make large contributions to universities and churches and charity come from? Do they come from the servitude of Latin American peasants working plantations on seventy-two-hour weekly shifts for gross annual incomes of less than a hundred dollars? Do they depend upon the availability of black child labor in South Africa and Rhodesia? Are such private beneficences in fact the real earnings of some of the poor of the world?

To affirm that we live in this world at each other's expense is a confession of the truth of the Fall rather than an assertion of economic doctrine or a precise empirical statement. It is not that there is in every transaction a direct one-for-one cause and effect relationship, either individually or institutionally, between the lot of the poor and the circumstances of those who are not poor. It is not that the wealthy are wicked or that the fact of malice is implicit in affluence. It is, rather, theologically speaking, that all human and institutional relationships are profoundly distorted and so entangled that no person or principality in this world is innocent of involvement in the existence of all other persons and all institutions. . . .

The idolatry of money has its most grotesque form as a doctrine of immortality. Money, is, then, not only evidence of the present moral worth of a person but also the way in which a life gains moral worth after death. If someone leaves a substantial estate, death is cheated of victory for a while, if not ultimately defeated, because the money left will sustain the memory of the person and of the fortune. The poor just die and are at once forgotten. It is supposed important to amass money not for its use in life but as a monument in death. Money thus becomes the measure of a person's moral excellence while alive and the means to purchase a certain survival of death. Money makes people not only moral but immortal; that is the most profound and popular idolatry of money.

To the Christian conscience, all ideas of immortality — along with all notions of self-justification including that of the mere acquisition of money or other property — are anathema. The gospel of Jesus Christ is not concerned with immortality but with the resurrection from death; not with the survival of death either in some "afterlife" or in the memorialization of life after death. The gospel is, instead, distinguished by the transcendence of the power of death here and now within the precincts of life in this world. The gospel discerns and exposes *all* forms of idolatry as the worship of death, and, thus, the gospel recognizes and publicizes the idolatry of money or property in any form as both false and futile. False because where money is an idol — that is, where money is thought to impute great or even ultimate moral significance to the one who holds it — it preempts the place of God; futile because money, and everything whatsoever that money can buy or build or do, along with those who lust after or gain money, dies. Where money is beheld as an idol, in truth the idol that is secreted in such worship is death. The gospel is about resurrection and it is that which unmasks the fraudulent association of all promissory doctrines of immortality with idolatry in one or another fashion. The gospel, in other words, has to do with the readily available power of God's grace to emancipate human beings in this life from all idols of death, even money — and even in America.

It is the freedom from idolatry of money that Christ offers the rich young man in the parable. Remember, it is not that money is inherently evil or that the possession of money as such is sin. The issue for the Christian (and ultimately, for everyone) is whether a person trusts money more than God and comes to rely on money rather than on grace for the assurance of moral significance, both as an individual and in relationship with the whole of humanity.

As a Christian I am aware — with more intimate knowledge and, therefore, with even greater anguish than those outside the church — that the churches in American society nowadays are so much in the position of that rich young man in the parable that they are rarely in a position to preach to prosperous Americans, much less to the needy. Even where the churches are not engaged in deliberate idolatry of money, the overwhelming share of the resources in money and other property inherited by and given to the trust of the churches ends up being utilized just for the upkeep of the ecclesiastical establishment. Appeals are still being made that to give money to the churches is equivalent to giving money to God. Of course anyone, who cares to, or who is free to do so, can see through such a claim: it is just a modern — albeit less candid, yet more vulgar — sale of indulgences, an abuse against which there is a venerable history of protest beginning with Jesus himself when he evicted the money-changers from the temple.

Freedom from idolatry of money, for a Christian, means that money becomes useful only as a sacrament — as a sign of the restoration of life wrought in this world by Christ. The sacramental use of money has little to do with supporting the church after the manner of contributing to conventional charities and even less with the self-styled stewardship that solicits funds mainly for the maintenance of ecclesiastical salaries and the housekeeping of churchly properties. The church and the church's mission do not represent another charity to be subsidized as a necessary or convenient benevolence, or as a moral obligation, or in order to reassure the prosperous that they are either generous or righteous. Appeals for church support as charity or for maintenance commonly end up abetting the idolatry of money.

Such idolatry is regularly dramatized in the offertory, where it is regarded as "the collection" and as an intermission in the worship of the people of the congregation. Actually, the offertory is integral to the sacramental existence of the church, a way of representing the oblation of the totality of life to God. No more fitting symbol of the involvement of Christians in the everyday life of the world could be imagined, in American society at least, than money, for nearly every relationship in personal and public life is characterized by the obtaining or spending or exchange of money. If then, in worship, human beings offer themselves and all of their decisions, actions, and words to God, it is well that they use money as the witness to that offering. Money is, thus, used sacramentally within the church and not contributed as to some charity or given because the church, as such, has any need of money.

The sacramental use of money in the formal and gathered worship of the church is authenticated — as are all other churchly sacramental practices — in the sacramental use of money in the common life of the world.

No end of ways exist in which money can be so appropriated and spent, but, whatever the concrete circumstances, the consistent mark of such a commitment of money is a person's freedom from idolatry of money. That includes not simply freedom from an undue affection for money but, much more than that, freedom from moral dependence upon the pursuit, acquisition, or accumulation of money for the sake of justifying oneself or one's conduct or actions or opinions, either to oneself or to anybody else. It means the freedom to have money, to use money, to spend money without worshiping money, and thus it means the freedom to do without money, if need be, or, having some, to give it away to anyone who seems to need money to maintain life a while longer.

The charity of Christians, in other words, in the use of money sacramentally — in both the liturgy and in the world — has no serious similarity to conventional charity but is always a specific dramatization of the members of the Body of Christ losing their life in order that the world be given life. For members of the church, therefore, it always implies a particular confession that their money is not their own because their lives are not their own but, by the example of God's own love, belong to the world.

That one's own life belongs to the world, that one's money and possessions, talents and time, influence and wealth, all belong to the whole world is, I trust, why the saints are habitués of poverty and ministers to the outcasts, friends of the humiliated and, commonly, unpopular themselves. Contrary to many legends, the saints are not spooky figures, morally superior, abstentious, pietistic. They are seldom even remembered, much less haloed. In truth, all human beings are called to be saints, but that just means called to be fully human, to be perfect — that is, whole, mature, fulfilled. The saints are simply those men and women who relish the event of life as a gift and who realize that the only way to honor such a gift is to give it away.

Race as a Principality
in the Church

TO NO principality — unless it be to those of commerce and finance, which are often allied with and committed to racism — have the American churches been more notoriously and scandalously and complacently accommodating than to the principality of racism.

Racial discrimination and segregation, though often in ingenious guises, still mars the lives of most congregations of most denominations. And this condition persists even in the face of the significant political and legal changes taking place in the nation in the relations of the races.

These congregations that condone or practice segregation and discrimination represent not just an open defiance of what has at last become a public policy favoring integration in public and quasi-public life — transportation, education, housing, employment, and most public accommodations — and not just a failure to treat conscientiously the meaning of baptism as the sacrament of the unity of all people in Christ. They also represent a surrender to the principality of racism and to its claim that its survival and continuance is of such importance as to take precedence over both the law of the land and the integrity of the church as church. Let us not suppose for a moment that it is

---

Free in Obedience, 1964, pp. 72–82

only some of the predominantly white denominations that give themselves over to racial segregation; some Negro denominations do exactly the same. And, above all, let us not think that surrender to the principality, the demonic power, of racism is an issue only for congregations in the South; it is as much an issue in congregations in the North, although in a more subtle and less vulgar form.

Do not assume, either, that the churches and people of the churches who have entered the service of racism all suffer from obstinacy, ignorance, hatred, or pathological disorder. Many church people, church groups, and churches with the most benign intentions and socially liberal impulses are also accomplices to the idolization of racism. For example, if one examines the pronouncements of preachers and church assemblies over the past thirty years (before that, there was silence about race in the churches in America, unless one goes back to the Reconstruction period and to the Abolitionist movement before and during the Civil War) it is difficult to locate a coherent, theologically substantive, or authentically prophetic statement about the relations among the races either in society or in the churches. What can be found aplenty are empty promises, theological superficialities, and pietistic indifference. What can be found, usually, are recitations of the most elementary humanistic propositions about equality and liberty. And while these premises of humanism are influential ideas in the ethos of the American nation, they come nowhere near embodying or expressing the concern of the gospel for the races and sorts and conditions of human life, nowhere near representing and upholding the character of the church as the community in history in which the unity of all human beings in God and in the worship of God is already manifest. Insofar as the churches in America, in other words, have in practice followed society in the evolution, now become revolution, in race relations and have simply imitated or repeated the slogans of humanism, they have forsaken or suppressed the unique word that they exist to proclaim, to serve, and to be. And they become by default — by silence, indifference, and irrelevance — handmaidens of the principality of racism, for the principality of racism is as well served by appeasement as by idolatry.

Within the last year there has stirred among the churches and the church hierarchy a sudden realization, a frightful consternation, that humanistic and pietistic benedictions entreating "better race relations" were not and are not sufficient to contain or mitigate the Negro revolt. It dawned at last upon at least some of the American churches that an insurrection had begun, that the cause of "good race relations" had turned into a desperate and bitter racial crisis. The dawn came at about the same time for the president, too, and for the commercial and journalistic and educational powers of the white establishment in America. Emergency meetings at the highest ecclesiastical echelons were summoned. Church budgets were loosened to provide funds in both indirect and direct support of the civil rights movement. Clergy were now authorized to participate in demonstrations and other forms of direct action. Red tape was out. The ecclesiastical authorities and common churchfolk began asking, many for the first time, "What do the Negroes want?" and began calculating what concessions might be offered to the insurrectionists (not realizing that the question "What do they want?" is no generosity but, in fact, contains the seed of white supremacy; the very question assumes that the whites, in the churches or in society, remain and should remain in control, in the role of deciding and ruling). In brief, the sudden excitement in the churches and within the leadership of the churches over the racial crisis seems to arise from an anxiety over the survival of white ascendancy in the churches and in the leadership of the churches rather than from either compassion for the people of color or passion for the gospel that is the means by which all people may dwell in reconciliation.

I have with my own ears heard more than one ecclesiastical leader of a predominantly white denomination admit that the very recent concern of the leaders of these churches in the racial crisis is a recognition of the fact that integration in American public institutions is now imminently inevitable. Therefore, it is important for the churches to intervene swiftly enough so that when the day of certain victory of the Negro revolt comes the churches will be found to be on "the right side," which means, if such comments are taken at face value, on the side that is going to win.

This last-minute involvement of the churches and their leaders in the racial crisis seems to be motivated mainly by fear, but that does not necessarily vitiate it. This involvement can be for some churches and church people in America — and one may hope that it will be, despite what prompts it — a means of seeing how racism in any of its manifestations divides the church, how it is in fact one of the powers of death at work in the world, and how it can only really be met in the freedom from death with which Christ has set people free.

The point here is not to question the sincere motivation of any leader or church now finally involved in direct action in the racial crisis; their own words and actions will speak for them. The point *is* to emphasize how deeply and terribly the American churches are compromised in many instances and places to the principalities that rule American society, especially those of race and class and status. The complexity of the implication of the churches with the causes of the principalities is very great. A congregation or denominational board, for example, may not indulge in praise or other open service to the principality of racism; but it may nonetheless be beholden to the principality by virtue of the fact that the capital assets of the congregation or board are invested in commercial, industrial, or real estate enterprises that profit from and support racism in one form or another.

Any honorable and effective attempt on the part of the churches to free themselves of complicity with racism is bound to involve them also in a rigorous and selfless scrutiny of their commitments to, and vested interest in, the principalities of finance and commerce in order to find out whether and how far their investments represent a de facto service of racism. As a matter of fact, some churches and boards have, in the recent past, examined their investment portfolios with this issue in mind. And a few have exerted pressure on enterprises in which they hold substantial investments for policy changes in the hiring of Negroes, advertising, and the like. But most have not yet done this. One major denominational body, after considering such action, decided that it was inappropriate for a church body to employ economic pressure as a tactic, despite the massive evidence that such pressure has been the single most effective weapon in the integration struggle. One trustee on this particular board put it this way: "The responsibility of the trustees is to invest the funds of the church to make money."

Undoing the complicity of the churches with racism will also lead, as we have previously observed, to agonizing reappraisal of other issues and commitments. The same churches and church people will have to confront their fondness for the ideology of the industrial revolution, and for those that have become shrines of this form of secularism there will indeed be traumatic readjustment.

254

The University and the Seminary

Grace, mercy and peace from God . . . and Christ Jesus our Lord.

As I urged you when I was going to Macedonia, remain at Ephesus that you may charge certain persons not to teach any different doctrine, nor to occupy themselves with myths and endless genealogies which promote speculations rather than the divine stewardship which is in faith; whereas the aim of our charge is love that issues from a pure heart and a good conscience and sincere faith. Certain persons by swerving from these have wandered away into vain discussion, desiring to be teachers of the law, without understanding either what they are saying or things about which they make assertions.

1 TIMOTHY 1:2b–7

There is no standing that I have or assert for remarking upon the present condition of theological education in America. I am only a visitor and observer, and both victim and beneficiary. I behold theological education from the outside rather than the inside. What I

"Myths, Endless Genealogies, the Promotion of Speculations and the Vain Discussion Thereof," *Sojourners,* August 1977, pp. 12–13

notice, mainly, are some consequences of the current mode of the enterprise.

Now and then I am called upon to preach in seminaries and congregations or to lecture in so-called religious studies programs in colleges and universities. I hear some news concerning theological education, especially where my own books are used in courses and classes. (Vanity, perchance, prompts an opinion that these usually enter curricula belatedly — five or ten years after publication, creating a curious lag in any dialogue between critical reader and author, and causing them to be treated as if they were posthumous rather than contemporary or history rather than theology.)

I have pastoral relationships with seminarians and theological students, faculty, postulants, clergy both female and male, along with an ecumenical host of disenchanted or rebellious or frustrated or angry or saddened clergy dropouts. It is my fortune to keep communication with many earnest biblical people scatted along the margins of the churches of American Christendom in experimental ministries, par-acongregations, households, communities, and ad hoc efforts.

This recitation is to acknowledge the scope — or limits — of my impressions of theological education. There may be other vantage points for viewing theological education that might warrant views quite different from my own.

As I understand and use the term, theological education encom-passes the preparation and qualification of those to be ordained in the churches as priests, preachers, and pastors; the pursuit of scholarly and academic work including that which relates theology to the arts and sciences, as well as other disciplines and professions commonly rep-resented in the university; and the nurture and edification of the people of the churches in the biblical faith.

Although these are distinct aspects of theological education, they are not severable but interdependent and reciprocal. One cannot be substituted for the others; one cannot compensate for the neglect or omission of either of the others.

The appropriate distinctions have not been kept, however, and the reciprocity essential among these different tasks has suffered. Theo-logical education in each of the three spheres mentioned is confused, vulnerable to vogue or fad, sometimes dilettantish or glib, worldly, and incoherent.

The particular cause for this, it appears to me, is the cooption of the seminaries by the prevailing ideology of the American university. As a consequence, the vocation of the seminary in readying persons for the ordained ministry is diluted.

Developments in the past thirty years in the sciences, notably in physics, chemistry, mathematics, and, lately, biology, are enough to expose the falsehood of the claim — so dominant for so long in the university — that the methods of science are objective or neutral. The fact is now being redundantly verified — in the environmental crisis as much as the arms race — that methodology *always* involves values, priorities, goals.

Indeed, ideology is inherent in methodology. Scientism, if elaborated, discloses a doctrine about ultimate truth — namely, that truth is divisible rather than whole and may be ascertained in fragments while being ignorant of the implications of a part for the rest. Even while the fraudulence of such a doctrine, implicit in the scientific method, is being confirmed practically, the university still largely clings to the doctrine and futilely attempts its application in all the arts and disciplines.

The seminaries have generally been so covetous of academic recognition and so anxious for locus within the ethos and hierarchy of the university that they have not noticed how alien and hostile those premises are to the peculiar vocation of a seminary. Thus the seminaries succumb to disseminating ideological renditions of the faith that demean the vitality of the biblical witness by engaging in endless classifications and comparisons of ideas. All this eschews commitment and precludes a confessional study of theology.

Do not misunderstand me: I am insisting that the indispensable credential for ordination as priest or pastor is that the person called to such office be a confessing Christian, as distinguished from a religious inquirer or a theological debater or, for that matter, a scholastic. This credential is, or should be, the task of the seminary. As such, the appropriate location of the seminary is within the church, the Body of Christ, and not within the university. The seminary's manner in the preparation and qualification of those to be ordained should exemplify the church rather than imitate the university. To me that implies a far more modest and flexible scope for seminary studies than that which pertains in the model of a professional graduate school.

It is that model that has harmed the nurture of the laity by fostering a pseudoprofessionalism — in fact, a form of clericalism — among the ordained, with many of the worst features of secrecy, prerogative, asserted expertise, vested status, and paternalism familiar to the secular professions. In short, the enthrallment of the seminary with the ideology of the university sponsors a professionalization of the ordained ministry that aborts the edification of the people of the church and that contradicts the servant character of the clergy's vocation.

This does not suggest that theological studies should not be represented with the university. Theology belongs in undergraduate and graduate echelons, whether on competitive or apologetic terms with other disciplines. Any university without such is to that extent diminished and deprived. But the theological and religious studies of the mature university do not furnish the confessional basis for equipping those to be ordained in the churches. The captivity of the seminary in the university has occasioned a radical secularization of the ordained ministry in the church in America.

At the same time, I advocate no curtailment of the work of biblical scholarship. Yet that endeavor is more apt to flourish under unique auspices, separate from (though not indifferent to) either the university or seminary — for instance, in guilds of scholars, or orders, or (assuming certain reforms) monasteries.

But now I anticipate too much: first of all the seminary must be reclaimed for the church of Christ.

The Constantinian Status Quo

BY THE accommodation [of the Constantinian Arrangement], signaled by the conversion of the emperor and the establishment of Christianity as the official "religion" of the Roman empire, a comity between church and nation was sponsored that, in various elaborations, still prevails in the twentieth century. The incidents that occasioned the Constantinian Arrangement, as such, are not as significant for contemporary Christians, or for either church or state today, as the ethos spawned and nourished by that comity and the mentality that has been engendered and indoctrinated by it over so long a time. It is, put plainly, an ethos that vests the existence of the church in the preservation of the political status quo. This inbreeds a mentality, affecting virtually all professed Christians, and most citizens whether Christians or not, which regards it as normative for the church's life to be so vested. And that has caused radical confusions in the relations of church and nation, church and state, church and regime. It has encouraged and countenanced stupid allegiance to political authority as if that were service to the church and, a fortiori, to God. Venerable though it be, this accommodation, and the way of conceiving of the juxtaposition of church and political authority that it has inculcated for so very long, accounts more than anything else for the profound secularization of the church in the West and for the inception of Christendom as the worldly embellishment of Christianity.

Conscience and Obedience, 1977, pp. 48–51

To put the same matter the other way around, it is the Constantinian Arrangement that has fostered, in numerous versions and derivations, through the centuries, such a religioning of the gospel that its biblical integrity is corrupted and such an acculturation of the church that it becomes practically indistinguishable from the worldly principalities so that both gospel and church become adjuncts or conveyances of civil religion and of a mock-sanctified status of political authority. In consequence, contemporary Christians inherit the heaviest possible presumption of legitimacy favoring incumbent political rulers and regimes, and with that a supposed preemptive duty of obedience to them that has been challenged only spasmodically.

I do not judge — I have neither vocation nor capability for that — the complication of factors that weighed on the side of the church concluding this comity with the empire. One may speculate about various influences: the arrangement ostensibly brought an end to the long era of the church's persecution, for one consideration. Moreover, the mission to evangelize the world might readily have been supposed implemented by the conversion of the emperor. At that, there is some evidence in St. Paul's career as an evangelist — as early as when he wrote Romans — that he aspired himself to confront and convert the emperor though his apologetic was heard only by lesser officials like Felix, Festus, and Agrippa, and he is said to have converted only certain of Caesar's soldiers, his jailers, not Caesar himself.

The query occurs, indeed, whether Paul had so strenuous an aspiration to convert the emperor that this determined the substance of Romans 13:1–7.

There were other influences, too, including the effort, particularly in the first century, of the church to distinguish itself from the Jewish sects and notably from the zealotic parties of Judaism in the eyes of the ruling authorities.

These are all solemn considerations, and I do not ridicule them insofar as they may have been inducements arising in the early and apostolic eras of the church sanctioning eventually the Constantinian Arrangement. Anyway, history cannot be undone, this comity, whether misfortune, or worse, or not, is part of the inheritance of contemporary Christians — an immensely important happening that cannot be erased. That is why I treat it, here, as a political and theological issue, and why I suggest that, though history cannot be retracted, the inherited political and theological stance for the church, signified in the Constantinian accommodation, must be transcended: contemporary Christian people can be emancipated from the indoctrination of the Constantinian mentality and a biblical integrity can be renewed in the church.

I construe the Constantinian comity as the historic reversal of the precedent established in the apostolic church regarding relations with political authority. In the first century, the imperial authorities permitted a comity with various religious sects (including those of the Jews except for the zealots who advocated rebellion against the Roman rule) that safeguarded the practice of religion and religious premises and prerogatives of religious leaders so long as these were politically innocuous and did not disrupt or resist political authority. The church in the apostolic period could have conformed and become a beneficiary of this sort of comity, and controversy preoccupied the church and the apostles of the church about this. One formulation of the dispute concerned whether the church was, indeed, a sect of Judaism or whether it was distinguished in a way that required the church's faith and message to be dispersed throughout the world. Much of the deliberation of this issue revolved, of course, around St. Paul and the question of his authority as an apostle and his arguments for preaching the gospel to the gentiles. It is the persuasion of Paul, and the acceptance of his apostolic authority, together with the vision that St. Peter suffers concerning the ecumenical scope of the mission of the church in this world, that establish that the church is no mere sect, among many sects, and that the church cannot afford the accommodation with political authority that the sectarian comity conveyed. Rome perceives the calling of the church to the ecumenical mission accurately to be a threat to its political hegemony and, thereafter, the intimidation, defamation, and harassment of the church escalates into persecution.

In this light, the promulgation of the Constantinian Arrangement represents a reversal, both politically and theologically, of the apostolic precedent of the juxtaposition of the church and political authority. The issue ever since, through both the glory and the tragedy of the church's presence in the world, has been whether the church can be free of the Constantinian comity and whether the apostolic precedent can be revived, and that not so much for the sake of the church as for the sake of the world.

The Church as Principality

SOMETIMES the church dishonors the freedom that God has given it by supposing that the public freedom that the nation accords the institutional existence of the church is essential to the proclamation of the gospel and its service and witness in the world. Sometimes the church yields or gravely imperils its integrity as the church by becoming the handmaiden of the ruling principalities of race, class, or commerce. At other times the church becomes so preoccupied with the maintenance and preservation of its own institutional life that it, too, becomes a principality. Within American Protestantism, where the church is radically divided into sects and denominations, this last situation is most acute and apparent.

When churches are principalities they bear the marks essential and familiar to all other principalities of an institutional and ideological character. The moral principle that governs their internal life, like that which governs a corporation or university, is the survival of the institution. To this primary consideration, all else must be sacrificed or compromised.

Churches and church bodies may be principalities in a variety of forms. A single congregation or parish may be a principality. Or a great denominational headquarters may be one. The tradition of a given church, in much the same way as in society, may rule as a principality.

Free in Obedience, 1964, pp. 95–99

The image of a church leader or ecclesiastical authority may be a principality. Committees, commissions, and councils that burgeon into vast bureaucracies may be principalities. In all these situations the churchly principality invites the world to serve its own preservation and prosperity, seeks and needs the service of humans for its own survival, and, indeed, demands that they regard it as an idol.

The demonic character of a churchly principality cannot be hidden by the simple retention of some of the condiments of the Christian faith. Thus, much of what is now discussed and practiced in the American churches as the witness of the church does not really pertain to the witness of the church to the life and action of God in the world, but rather to the witness of the church to itself as churchly institution. And while there may be a legitimate witness to the church as Christ's Body, service to the institution is not synonymous with it and certainly not synonymous with witness to the Word of God.

In some times and places, the churchly institutions make extravagant demands of homage and service both upon human beings and other principalities. For example, in some societies, including some regions of this country where a particular sect or denomination has achieved such political and economic power that it dominates the government, the state may be required to defend its property, safety, and even its doctrines. Apart from such local exceptions, however, the churchly principalities do not have that much dignity vis-à-vis other principalities, although they still exist and can be identified in American life.

Such churchly principalities stifle and suppress Christians who resist putting the institutional self-interest before their freedom in the gospel. One might cite dozens of specific cases of this. I mention only one here to illustrate the problem, because I know at first hand the extraordinary measures that were taken to conceal what happened. The incident involved a clergyman who had worked for some years, mainly in the deep South of which he was a native, in the racial crisis. This Christian minister recognized that more was involved theologically and confessionally in the racial crisis than recitations of humanistic ethics and assurances of good intentions, or programs of study about "race relations" and the annual observances of Race Relations Sunday. He, therefore, used his access to white Southerners to preach the gospel, to go among his native people as an evangelist and apologist. He understood that as a person has his own life renewed in the life of Christ, he is set free to love himself and *all* human beings. He knew that the reconciliation wrought by Christ encompasses the only real reconciliation there can be among those of different races. As he saw it, the racial crisis had more to do with the meaning of Christ for human life than all of these programs and pronouncements and conferences and committees. He thought that race also had something to do with the renewal of the church.

But it came to pass that he was summoned by his superiors and colleagues within the churchly institution and told that he had become a great embarrassment to the institution because some people were beginning to think that the institution had no "positive program" in "race relations"; besides, the institution could not afford to have someone on its staff who was just going here and there preaching the gospel. There had to be a "positive program"; in other words, the priority in the preacher's work had to be that which would gain recognition for the institution, enhance its prestige, and prove that it was doing something. Homage to the churchly principality had to come before esteem for the gospel.

One of the serious issues for laity when confronted with the claims of such a churchly principality for homage and service is that the laity who do enter into such service are dissipated in it and are thereby diverted from their witness to and against the principalities of commerce and politics to which they are exposed in their daily life and work. They are dissipated not because the struggle against a churchly principality is any different as witness than that against any other principality, but because they will find no courage for the struggle if all that they know or are involved in, in the name of the church, is some churchly principality.

It is worth repeating that to discern that there are churchly principalities such as these mentioned does not in itself reflect upon the sincerity or motives of any person related to such institutions. Rather, it is to recognize that this is, after all, a fallen world, and church institutions are not exempt from the Fall, though there be another sense in which the church is free from the bondage to death that characterizes the Fall. It is important to note also that on the part of many who are privy to the churchly principalities there is a certain naivety about their personal capability to change and reform the institution. Indeed, the void in Protestant moral theology in accounting for and treating the principalities and powers is nowhere better illustrated than in situations where the notion continues to prevail among church bureaucrats that they control the institution; whereas, in truth, the principality claims them as slaves.

This does not mean that Christians should be loath to work in churchly institutions, but it does mean that those who do should be aware of the reality that confronts them and should not be romantic about it because the principality bears the name "church." Above all, they should be prepared to stomach the conflict that will surely accompany their use of the freedom from idolatry of even churchly principalities that Christ has secured.

Does America Need a Barmen Declaration?

THE consideration of a question such as *Do we need a new Barmen Declaration?* or *Do Americans now need a Barmen Declaration?* at once discloses how history is comprehended. The very way the issue is framed furnishes temptation to suppose that history repeats itself in an eventful manner, so that the current American political circumstances are beheld as constituting a recurrence of those in Germany forty years ago and are, in turn, thought to warrant a response analogous to that of the Barmen Confession.

To succumb to this temptation stereotypes history. It reduces history to redundancy. It represents a modified predestinarianism that deprives creatures — both persons and principalities — of responsibility for decisions and actions at the same time that it narrows and ridicules the militant judgment of God in history. As a conception of history it is categorically unbiblical and, furthermore, it is dull.

For all of that, the present American crisis is sufficiently bewildering to entice many citizens to treat history in just such a simplistic, imitative manner. In this vein, Nixon is compared with Hitler; Amerika is named fascist; Watergate is equated with the Reichstag fire.

Christianity and Crisis, December 24, 1973, pp. 274–76

I reject this view of history as false, misleading, escapist. I esteem history as ambiguous, versatile, dynamic.

I do not imply that there are no appropriate comparisons to be ventured or no significant similarities to be noticed. But I find that history "repeats" itself as parable rather than analogue and that the edifying similarities are topical rather than eventful, having to do with perennial issues embodied in changing circumstances from time to time instead of with any factual duplication transposed from one time to another.

As a practical matter, this means that for some American church people today to recall Barmen and to inquire as to its relevance requires attention as much to situational differences and analytical distinctions as to any apparent similarities.

Or — to put this concern in other words — we must not address the question of the need for a new Barmen in a way that relieves us of making the decisions we must make. It would be a grandiose paradox to recall the Barmen Confession in a way that abets default on our part in America now. Under this rubric I offer these remarks concerning both the political situation and the church situation in the United States today in reference to the precedent of the Barmen Confession.

One important distinction between Germany in 1934 and America now is that Germany then was arising as a nation from the calamity of defeat in World War I. She was a nation regaining her vanity after the most profound humiliation of her history. She was on the ascendancy (again); indeed, Germany in 1934 was a nation on the verge of blitzkrieg, conquest, plunder. And her hope, fantastic as it may now seem, outreached the glory of triumph in war over enemies who had once subjugated her millennial pretensions of world domination.

The contrast with contemporary America is startling. America is now rapidly losing world preeminence. The nation is in decline in virtually every sense in which such matters are commonly calculated — morally, monetarily, culturally, ideationally, militarily, productively, environmentally. Her power — her superpower — proves preposterous and ineffectual and is more mocked than feared elsewhere in the world. Her vanity is confounded; the popular myths about her destiny are ridiculed and doubted; her citizens are sullen, bemused, despairing, vulnerable.

In 1934 Germans were becoming excited and enthralled with the Nazi ambition for their country, and they were being mobilized in that cause. Americans have lately become demoralized, distracted, apprehensive as to *any* cause — especially that of the nation — except, perhaps the purchase or pursuit of individual safety and survival in the most mundane connotations of those terms.

More concretely, in comparing the Nazi totalitarianism and the totalitarianism that threatens America, there is in the latter official propaganda and heavy deception, but there is not the pervasive ideological ambience that marked the German scene in the thirties. Americans have never been regarded as ideologically sophisticated anyway, but now technology has practically displaced the political function of ideology.

In contrast to the Nazi reality, political authority in America has little need to launch indoctrination or practice much ideological manipulation because the available means, furnished by technology, of transmitting information have transfixing capabilities to paralyze human comprehension. Even the truth can be dispatched in the American technocracy with such acceleration and redundancy that it estops human beings from hearing or understanding it. Or, as another instance, how can the right of privacy be safeguarded and honored in a society where technology has made surveillance, both private and public, cheap and accessible to virtually any institution or person? Does not the technical capability for ubiquitous surveillance of citizens in itself render a constitutional right of privacy quaint?

Related to the displacement of ideology by technology has been the transplantation in America of the long entrenched commercial ethic into politics. Not only surveillance but secrecy, manipulation, fabrication, fraud, espionage — all familiar in business practice for generations — have now become politically commonplace. Rationalizing such tactics is a reverence for property as the rudimentary value in society, taking precedence over human life and justifying any expedient abuse of human beings.

It is the transfer into politics of this ethic — that property bears intrinsic worth and that human beings have moral significance only insofar as it may be imputed to them because of their relationship to property — that occasions remarks like that of John Mitchell, erstwhile attorney general of the United States, that in the Watergate scandal he was innocent of offense since he had not stolen any property. In much the same way Richard Nixon — apparently oblivious to constitutional misdemeanors that involved specific aggressions against persons and that, in principle, mean contempt for all persons living under the American government — has assured citizens that he is not a crook but has earned whatever property he possesses.

In short, the political implementation of the property ethic in a late technocratic society spawns totalitarianism in America in the seventies, as distinguished from the joinder of ideology and national vanity that characterized Germany in the thirties. The assault upon human sanity and conscience would seem no less in the American circumstances than in those in Germany, however, and where some sense of human outrage does survive, some similarities between America today and Germany then begin to emerge.

There are relatively few dissenters and resisters, for one thing, and where they speak and act, they suffer defamation and persecution. In recent years in the United States, it is not only political prosecutions, trials, and imprisonments that document this fact but the less visible economic coercions, such as those exerted against students and faculty following the Kent State infanticide, which chiefly accomplished the quietism the campuses have suffered ever since.

There is a kind of psychological dividend for the regime, whether Nazi or American, in this state of affairs. For every person politically prosecuted or conformed by coercion there are numberless others, geometrically accrued, who are sufficiently intimidated by the fate of the more conspicuous victims to acquiesce. This is, precisely speaking, the secret of such success as totalitarianism anywhere, at anytime, attains.

Not to be, any longer, overlooked is the issue of the pathology of political leaders. In retrospect much significance has been attributed to it in the Nazi emergence in Germany, but it is more the problem to consider this aspect contemporaneously. If Christians — if no one else — were now earnest about the pathology of Richard Nixon as president, I venture, without pretensions toward psychobiography, that they would be attentive to matters peculiarly within the pastoral care and competence of the Christian witness. That is to say, they would be concerned with how guilt becomes arrogant motivation, with how delusive power victimizes a person, with the futility of flagellation, with the reality of truth and the redemptive power that adheres in telling the truth, with healing, with exorcism, with confession, with forgiveness and, indeed, with God's own judgment of persons and nations.

For Germans and Americans, at the center of the profound social changes they both have suffered or suffer is the matter of law and authority. If this issue takes many forms, it nevertheless can be succinctly stated: it is the problem of authority usurping the law, of authority merging with the law, of authority displacing the law, of authority become a law unto itself, of unaccountable authority, of the very premise of government become the exercise of authority per se, of authority abolishing law and of coercion substituting for order, and of all persons made vulnerable to political aggression.

In this connection Nazism is sometimes represented as a revolution for the German nation. Whether, analytically, that be the case or not, America has been enduring a counterrevolution for the past quarter-century that the Nixon administration has epitomized but did not instigate. It is a counterrevolution with respect to the social ethic of the American revolution, in which the governing institutions have been usurped or set aside by the power of extraconstitutional agencies (like the CIA, the White House plumbers, the Pentagon, the secret police operations, the industrial-technocratic complex) that have come to function as a secret, second government beyond the reach of public control. It is this that renders the contemporary American political situation chaotic. If there be a sense in which it can be said that Hitler saved Germany from anarchy, it must also be said that Nixon feigns to rule where anarchy has become predominant political reality.

The churchmen who gathered at Barmen made their confession of the gospel as an exposure of and rebuke to the "doctrinal monstrosities" of Nazism's so-called positive Christianity.

In America we have nothing so definitive or so self-conscious as "positive Christianity" was in Germany in 1934. The American civil religion has grown and has become diffuse and vague. It represents a loose and jumbled collection of memories and myths and other notions permeating the national ethos, and it lacks the coherence and formality that the Nazi version of "positive Christianity" had. Yet this does not imply that the civil religion here is less pernicious or any less hostile to the gospel. One monstrous doctrine, for example, of American civil religion is the false and uncritical identification of the American churches with incumbent political authority and, beyond that, with the national vanity claiming a unique or divinely named destiny for America.

Associated with this grossly unbiblical view is the redundant assertion of America's moral superiority, as among the nations, commonly said to be verified by war and weapons capabilities, productivity, and consumerism. And this moral pretension, in turn, requires an endless supply of scapegoats and other victims to explain away whatever goes wrong or otherwise detracts from the supposed national preeminence. Thus we are implicated in constant denials of corporate responsibility in society, as in casting upon Lt. Calley the burden of common guilt for the genocide of the Indochina war.

If there are American Christians inclined to utter a new Barmen Declaration, a place to begin is with "doctrinal monstrosities" such as these, which remain virtually unchallenged among the American churches.

Another issue at Barmen sharply contrasts with American circumstances. The Nazis not only had sponsored a widespread propagation of their positive Christianity, but had also engaged in blunt ecclesiastical interference, directly subverting the government of the German churches. The effort was organized under a Reichsbishop whom the Nazis foisted upon the churches, and by the time of the synod at Barmen more than eight hundred pastors had been ousted from their pulpits by the regime's church administration.

Here there is no similar ecclesiastical meddling — perchance because the churches in America are more innocuous — nor does there need to be. Instead, there is an elaborate American comity by which political domination of the churches is sanctioned by the status of church property holdings. Thus, tax exemption for the churches inhibits a critical political witness by the churches. Thus, a presidential assurance of aid to church-related schools can insure the silence of the ecclesiastical hierarchy on certain public issues. In short, the dependence of the American churches upon property renders the churches so utterly vulnerable to political manipulation as to obviate a more direct ecclesiastical interference.

For all of this, if it is concluded that something like a Barmen

Confession is appropriate now in America — and, it must be said, confession of faith is *always* apropos — there remains a question of how such a confession could happen. Who is there to confess? At Barmen the churches at least had a unity and cohesion sufficient to convene a synod that could speak out. The inherited churches here exist in such disarray, such disunity, such incoherence as to supply the inference that they have, as yet, no capability of confession.

Another Barmen Declaration may be timely, but we cannot overlook the fact that the very idea of such a confession is unAmerican — disruptive of that basic comity thought necessary to the nation's religious and ecclesiastical pluralism. Nor can we gainsay the depth with which it is embedded in the American mentality that anything like a confession of faith is a matter of resolute privacy (which is the reason the content confessed typically affirms "Jesus saves" but not "Jesus Christ is Lord"). On the other hand, a doubt lingers as to whether the so-called social activists from the nation's churches are able to distinguish between some mere political manifesto and a historic confession of the gospel.

Perhaps the answer to the question about any new Barmen Declaration is to be found in another way altogether. Perhaps the question is answered in what actually happened to those who signed the Barmen Confession. Every one of them was executed, exiled, or imprisoned.

When American churchpeople are ready for such consequences, we will be enabled to confess the faith. Ironically, if we are not able to confess we will certainly suffer the same consequences — ignominiously.

Acolytes of the Demonic Powers

IF THERE be knowing victims of the principalities, if there indeed be saints and prophets, there are many victims who do not realize it, and there are persons who are eager slaves to these idols. Often these acolytes of the demonic seem oblivious to how the principalities tyrannize and corrupt their humanness. In Revelation, the kings and merchants and traders seem startled and bewildered at Babylon's doom (Rev. 18:9–17). There are those who actually define their humanity as nonhuman or subhuman loyalty and diligence to the interests and appetites of the principalities. There are many who are dumb and complacent in their captivity by institutions, traditions, and similar powers. There are persons who have become automatons. There are humans who know of no alternative to an existence in vassalage to the principalities. There are people who are programmed and prop-agandized, conditioned and conformed, intimidated and manipulated, fabricated and consigned to role-playing. There are human beings who are demonically possessed.

There are spectacular or extreme examples of dehumanized obeisance to the demonic — such as the Emperor Domitian or, per-haps, King George III or Hitler or Stalin. But what may be of greater significance in the present American situation are more ordinary

An Ethic for Christians and Other Aliens in a Strange Land, 1973, pp. 87–89

persons whose humanity is jeopardized or humiliated by the routines of technocracy — like assembly-line workers or salespeople or consumers or promoters or bureaucrats or suburbanites. The servility to ideological, racial, class, or institutional powers of victims such as these is so numerous and commonplace in mass society that it is seldom challenged or, for that matter, much noticed.

Beyond those who are rendered virtual robots are those called leaders.

The unrelenting, manifold, versatile, ingenious aggressions of the principalities against human life in society, the victimization of human beings — sometimes brutally, sometimes subtly; sometimes meeting resistance, sometimes with ready assent — by the demonic powers exposes a crucial aspect of the contemporary American social crisis. The American problem is not so simple that it can be attributed to a few — or even many — evil persons in high places any more that it can be blamed on long-haired youth or on a handful of black revolutionaries. Besides, our persons in high places are not exceptionally immoral; they are, on the contrary, quite ordinarily moral. In truth, the conspicuous moral fact about our generals, our industrialists, our scientists, our commercial and political leaders is that they are the most obvious and pathetic prisoners in American society. There is unleashed among the principalities in this society a ruthless, self-proliferating, all-consuming institutional process that assaults, dispirits, defeats, and destroys human life even among, and *primarily* among, those persons in positions of institutional leadership. They are left with titles but without effectual authority; with the trappings of power but without control over the institutions they head; in nominal command but bereft of dominion. These same principalities, as has been mentioned, threaten and defy and enslave human beings of other status in diverse ways, but the most poignant victim of the demonic in America today is the so-called leader.

It is not surprising, thus, to find — in addition to the ranks of those whose conformity to and idolatry of the principalities means that they are automatons or puppets — some persons, reputed leaders attended by the trappings of high office, who are enthralled by their own enslavement and consider themselves rewarded for it, and who conceive of their own dehumanization as justification or moral superiority.

Nixon: How to Stop the War (and Other Outrages) by Working within the System

MY TEXT is Article II, Section 4, of the Constitution of the United States of America:

> The President . . . shall be removed from Office on Impeachment for, and Conviction of, Treason, Bribery, or other high Crimes and Misdemeanors.

My plea is that all protests against the war be converted, now, and become concentrated in a fresh, insistent, specific, immediate, irresistible citizens' demand for the impeachment of the President of the United States.

Impeachment is an extraordinary remedy. In the American system it has origins in the twin doctrines of the Declaration of Inde-

---

An address given prior to the Watergate revelations at both the First Unitarian Church of Providence and at Saint Stephen's Episcopal Church, April 30, 1972.* *Commonweal,* May 26, 1973, pp. 280–81. This was apparently first uttered at an antiwar rally at Princeton University. So *Simplicity of Faith,* p. 77.

pendence that incumbency does not in itself legitimatize rulers and that a people shall not indefinitely suffer arbitrary, capricious, vindictive, lawless, or criminal authority but have means of removing unfit rulers. Impeachment, in America, is the constitutional recourse that renders revolution needless.

Impeachment is an extraordinary remedy appropriate to the extraordinary circumstances in which Americans now live.

The fact is ordinary protest has been exhausted; verbal dissent is ignored; congressional action has only prompted presidential defiance; non-violent civil disobedience has become counterproductive; violence has never been either morally defensible or practically effectual and only further incites official violence; demonstrations and petitions, sit-ins and marches are redundant; ordinary protest will not stop the war. We have all beheld, within these few weeks, how the familiar forms of protest become, at the most, a kind of weeping and wailing — therapeutic, perhaps, for those who mourn but no relief for the nation.

This is something that citizens have known, whether or not it has been admitted, for a long time. Some of us have realized this for as long as eight years, since we first voiced dissent about the war. All of us have known this since the Nixon regime took power, which is to say, since opposition to the war became the convinced sentiment of the majority of Americans. Indeed, in the entire saga of the incumbent administration, the single instance in which the president can be said, with complete confidence, to have been candid — to have been guilelessly, unambiguously, unequivocally, undeceptively truthful — was the day, three years ago, when he told us that he would not heed *any* protests; when he, thus, pronounced the astonishing doctrine that the president is unaccountable to the American people.

This president has verified his intransigence ruthlessly, as his administration has sought to obliterate dissent from his policy while muting the will of the majority of the people:

- by unconstitutionally making war,
- by enlargements of that illegal war in Asia, sometimes clandestine, often fantastic and brutal,
- by defying and frustrating the constitutional prerogatives of the Congress,

276

- by brazen misuse for war of funds otherwise appropriated,
- by impugning the loyalty of presidential candidates and other political opponents,
- by flaunting contempt for the First Amendment while seeking to intimidate and manipulate the media,
- by maliciously imputing violence to all protest,
- by unprecedented political abuse of due process of law through illegal surveillance of civilians, and similar harassments, and the utterance of false, fake, and defamatory charges,
- by sanctioning unconstitutional mass arrests and political detentions,
- by repeated attempts to demean and usurp the courts and to discredit publicly their constitutional authority,
- by abdicating command responsibility in seeking to suppress the scandal of the My Lai massacre,
- by dishonoring Vietnam veterans, rendering POWs pawns of the corrupt Saigon oligarchy, recklessly endangering American troops by countenancing the complicity of so-called allies in the Indochina drug traffic, and seeking punishment for the young in exile,
- by deliberately deceiving the people and failing the presidential oath.

In all of this, for all these years, (to adapt a phrase) the message has been perfectly clear. We Americans suffer a regime that is essentially lawless, that acts as a law unto itself, whose conduct renders it illegitimate, that seeks to maintain its authority even if it must dismantle and destroy the constitutional system, that has shown itself to be irrevocably beholden to violence and coercion, both physical and psychological, as much at home as abroad.

Two years ago, in the aftermath of the Cambodian "incursion," during the last widespread antiwar protests, we glimpsed the extremities of the violence that the Nixon rule sponsors in the infanticide at Kent State.

Subsequently, a quietism settled over the nation's campuses. (Quietism is a name with historic connotations, referring to the "quietist movement" in Nazi Germany through which acquiescence was practiced to the Nazi criminality. I am using the term here deliberately.)

Some attribute high motives or esoteric reasons to explain the quietism of the past two years: the students had recovered a zeal for study, it has been said, or some desired to pursue mystical exercises. I find a much more straightforward explanation. Most students got the message that with this government protest provokes persecution. In the months immediately following Cambodia and Kent State, the federal authorities drastically cut aid for scholarships and research and other subsidies, withdrew guarantees for educational bank loans, stopped funding student employment. And students understood that message: dissent endangers survival. There has been quietism not because there has been approval of the government — and certainly not because very many have been so bemused as to believe the fraudulent official rhetoric about "winding down the war" while the war has been constantly spread geographically and, through automation, geometrically. There has been quietism because there has been fear — because the economic pressures for political conformity have been successful among the young just as inflation, unemployment, taxation, and indebtedness have been manipulated to preoccupy, benight, and neutralize so many older citizens.

Within these last weeks, the quietism on the campuses has been breached by the further mindless outrages in Indochina. If today's protests amount to no more than mourning, then let the students weep — let all citizens weep and wail — but *never again* must quietism be practiced in America.

Let it be emphatic that none of this has anything to do categorically with partisanship — with stereotypical party politics — with the Republican vs. Democratic thing. That has, long since, been surpassed by events. In those events, concentrated so much in the war, we ought by now to have learned something. We ought to have learned that the issue is not the war or that the issue is no longer the war. The war has become the grotesque symptom of the most rudimentary social issue — whether authority is subject to law, whether incumbency validates authority, or whether authority can still be required to function constitutionally, whether, in short, the president is accountable.

I am mindful, in these remarks, that the American crisis is one that transcends these events. America would be, now, in crisis even if we had been spared the Nixon presidency. The profound issue of this country is whether a constitutional system is feasible, at all, in an advanced technological society. What we confront is no mere regurgitated McCarthyism, nor an American neo-Nazism, but the threat of technological totalitarianism such as Orwell foretold. That issue has been with us, noticeably, since Hiroshima — since the Pentagon and the CIA and the famous military–industrial–scientific principality preempted foreign military policy, seized the budget, discounted domestic needs, virtually incapacitated the Congress, and captivated the presidency.

But I am also mindful that we have not been spared the Nixon regime and that the constitutional crisis can no longer be gainsaid or evaded. *Any* chance that the nation has of coping with these fundamental institutional issues requires the removal *now* of this president and the repudiation of his kind of regime.

Although Americans are much demoralized and feel impotent, I still think the system can be redeemed by utilizing the Constitution, and so I plead (in this day of heavy euphemism and coded language) that the present outcry to "stop the war" be translated "impeach the president."

If it is true, as has been said, that this war is not worth the sacrifice of one more American life, or if, as I would amend the statement, this war has never been worth the sacrifice of a single human being, then each day that Richard Nixon remains in office is an abomination to the Lord.

An Open Letter to the
Presiding Bishop

Dear Bishop Allin:

In the Body of Christ each baptized person has pastoral charge of all the members and each becomes responsible, in his or her ministry, to all the others. The integrity of the life and witness of the whole church is nurtured in this elementary interdependence of the various members of the Body of Christ, as St. Paul's Letters to the Corinthians and the Ephesians especially emphasize. As Christians, each of us is called to care for one another, to counsel one another in charity and candor, to exhort one another.

Accordingly, the Anglican tradition has insisted, from its inception, that those installed in ecclesiastical office are accountable to those over whom they exercise the authority of such office.

I uphold that aspect of Anglicanism, and, heeding the Letters, I am prompted to write to you, in the aftermath of the general convention lately convened in Denver, about your demeanor as the presiding bishop. At the same time, I write out of concern, long felt, for you as a human being. Probably I would forbear this open letter, lest it intrude upon your business or arouse a defensive response or otherwise vex you, if it brought you only my own view. As it is,

---

The Witness, January 1980, pp. 10–11

however, my own observations are also shared throughout the church by devout, knowing, and earnest people, both laity and clergy. This has been confirmed to me in the last few years when I have visited congregations, clergy conferences, and other church events, and it was repetitiously confirmed to me at Denver.

For these years of your incumbency as presiding bishop, I have hoped, as have so many others, that you would sometime evince a strong and definite conviction concerning the mission of the church in this world and, particularly, that of the Episcopal Church in contemporary U.S. society. None has been forthcoming. Instead, you have again and again manifested an absence of conviction, a failure of candor, a spirit of confusion, a doublemindedness, a tendency to tailor utterance to the circumstances of the moment. Your image of ambivalence and elusiveness was noticeable throughout the controversy attending the ordination of women, after your initial hysteria about the Philadelphia ordinations subsided. It was not until after the general convention had acted definitively that you confided your skepticism about the vocation of women as priests, and then you did so in a manner that seemed calculated to incite defiance or circumvention of the law of the church. In consequence, the so-called conscience clause has been inflated far beyond the scope of conscientious dissent or protest into a virtual act of nullification that jeopardizes the efficacy of canon law and scandalizes the very polity of the Episcopal Church.

All of this had been foreshadowed, of course, in the Wendt trial in the ecclesiastical court in the diocese of Washington, when in violation of your canonical duty you defied the subpoena of the court to appear and testify, and were thereupon duly adjudged in contempt of that court. You have done nothing to purge yourself of that contempt.

There are those who refer to you as a "conservative," but that is hyperbole. Such disrespect for the law of the church as you have shown and encouraged is not a conservative trait.

I attribute this behavior, rather, to a lack of conviction, or to expediency, which, lamentable in any circumstances, is essentially incongruous to the office you hold. That is why I have mentioned, now and then, that I would much prefer as presiding bishop a vigorous and principled reactionary. At least, then, there could be disagreement and dispute in the church that would be candid and wholesome. As it is, instead of leadership, in these past six years, there has been aimlessness.

Yet aimless is not the same as harmless. You have not been in a situation of the bland leading the bland if only because so many have suffered so much harm on your account, whether by reason of deliberate intent or omission. After all, it cannot be overlooked that your improvidence occasioned the imprisonment of two church employees, facilitated the subsequent imprisonment of seven other Hispanics, and seriously impaired the constitutionally sanctioned freedom of the churches in this country. Nor can the countless hassles, obstacles, and discriminations encountered by women qualified and called to ordination as priests be overlooked. Nor can the cruel and hypocritical attitude toward the ordination of homosexuals. Nor can the neglect of all the other issues between the church and this society whilst the dissipation of sham debates and churchy charades continues.

Leadership could have made a difference in all of these matters, but, alas, the Episcopal Church has been deprived of leadership. When you were elected at the Louisville general convention a void opened in the leadership of the Episcopal Church, which has been filled by management. In the church, as with other principalities and powers, management is preoccupied with institutional preservation and with condiments of statistical prosperity. To management, substantive controversy is perceived as threatening per se, rather than as a sign of vitality, and conformity to the mere survival interest of the institution gains domineering priority. In the church, such a governance stands in blatant discrepancy with the image of the servant community whose life is risked, constantly, resiliently, for the sake of the renewal of the life of the world. In the church, to put it another way, such a managerial mentality capitalizes the worldliness of the church. The church becomes most conformed to this world where the church is most preoccupied in the maintenance of the ecclesial fabric.

If a management regime in the church, so inverted and so trite, persists for long, it renders the church self-indulgent, supercilious, self-serving, and silly. At Denver, one sign that the credibility of the Episcopal Church nears that point was the three-page spread in the *Denver Post,* published at the end of the first convention week, which highlighted, as news of the Episcopal Church in solemn assembly, the brisk trade in Amish cheeses that was happening in the Exhibit Hall.

The suppression of issues pertinent to the servanthood of the church in the world is symbolized prominently in the emergence of the urban bishops' coalition. That effort holds promise of reclaiming a viable witness on the urban scene. I applaud the coalition and such headway as happened at Denver through its efforts, but the point not to be missed is that it should never have been necessary to undertake such a campaign in the first place; the church at large should have been open to and committed to the urban priority so as to obviate the extraordinary program the coalition has had to mount.

Beyond all this — the default on issues, the harm done persons, the playing at church, the mentality of management, the lawless attitude, the leadership void, the absence or ambiguity of conviction — is the consequence for you as a human being. I believe, Bishop Allin, you are the most poignant victim of the present malaise of the Episcopal Church. In that perspective your role is more symptomatic than causal. I do not for a moment consider that you are to blame for everything that is amiss now in the church. At the same time, though, you *are* blameworthy because you *are* the incumbent presiding bishop.

There is a certain Anglican (or, perchance, merely English) etiquette that sometimes inhibits the telling of the truth. It causes people to say privately what they will not speak publicly or otherwise to be coy or euphemistic. That etiquette does not hinder me from writing to you. I verify my regard for you as a person and evidence my respect for the office you hold by telling the truth to you.

During the general convention it was reported that you remarked that you long to return to the parish ministry. I take your word at face value. And I say to you: the time is *now* to implement your impulse. As your brother in Christ, I appeal to you to resign forthwith as presiding bishop.

Faithfully yours,
William Stringfellow

The Politics of Pastoral Care: An Ecumenical Meditation concerning the Incumbent Pope

Now Peter and John were going up to the temple at the hour of prayer, the ninth hour. And a man lame from birth was being carried, whom they laid daily at the gate of the temple which is called Beautiful to ask alms of those who entered the temple. Seeing Peter and John about to go into the temple, he asked for alms. And Peter directed his gaze at him, with John, and said, "Look at us."

And he fixed his attention upon them, expecting to receive something from them. But Peter said, "I have no silver and gold, but I give you what I have; in the name of Jesus Christ of Nazareth, walk." And he took him by the right hand and raised him up; and immediately his feet and ankles were made strong.

And leaping up he stood and walked and entered the temple with them, walking and leaping and praising God. And all the people saw him walking and praising God, and recognized him as the one who sat for alms at the Beautiful

The Witness, February 1984, pp. 12–14

Gate of the temple; and they were filled with wonder and amazement at what had happened to him.

THE ACTS OF THE APOSTLES 3:1–10

And as [Peter and John] were speaking to the people, the priests and the captain of the temple and the Sadducees came upon them, annoyed because they were teaching the people and proclaiming in Jesus the resurrection from the dead. And they arrested them and put them in custody. . . .

THE ACTS OF THE APOSTLES 4:1–3*a*

In the earliest experience of the apostolic church, during the period promptly after Pentecost . . . long before the church acquired an ecclesiastical polity resembling what now prevails . . . when the orders and ministries of the church were simply authorized charismatically and functionally . . . prior to the conformity and decadence sponsored by the Constantinian Arrangement . . . the precedent for the office and service of those who would, later on, be called and ordained as bishops was established. So it is that the vocation of a bishop is illuminated in the Acts of the Apostles.

I have participated during the last few years in the endemic dismay of churchfolk — both within and outside of the Roman Communion — at the ambivalent, and poignant, behavior of Pope John Paul II.

Perchance I should mention before further comment, that I remember circumstances when I, as with many other non-Roman Christians, thought it impudent publicly to volunteer my views of any pope's conduct. That vain etiquette, however, has been obviated by, among other things, John Paul's own construction of the ecclesiastical primacy of the papacy.

Hence, in the midst of my repeated bewilderments and multiplying disenchantments with John Paul, I turn to the Acts of the Apostles to ascertain what I can from this elementary source about what a bishop is (or is supposed to be) according to ancient experience.

What is to be found and confirmed in Acts is a priority of

pastoral care epitomized in the function and ministry of bishop. Administration, which so preempts the attention of contemporary bishops, is, in Acts, a matter, at most, of quaint allusion. It is merely one specification of the pastoral office. At the same time, teaching in Acts virtually always has the particular connotation of "teaching and proclaiming the resurrection from the dead." It is more prominent than administration, yet it has the same emphatic aspect of nurture. Teaching is a feature of pastoral care. Much the same can be affirmed from Acts concerning the confrontation with the world and the discernment of the needs of the world, as the texts cited indicate.

In brief, the apostolic ministry begins in pastoral concern for each member of the whole church and reaches into the very interstices of the body of the church. Simultaneously, it addresses the worldly regimes of the principalities and powers, as well as all people everywhere, at once exposing every need and vouching for the redemptive vigilance of the Word of God in the world. Thus, a bishop (as I am sure many bishops realize) is dialectically positioned between church and world. This is really not a situation of grandeur. Maybe that is why, too often, where the office of bishop has been rendered grandiloquent it has lost pastoral integrity for either church or world.

While I name pastoral care as the venerable characteristic of the ministry of a bishop, I trust it is understood that there are no particular psychological or similar implications assumed. Pastoral care has acquired narrow, partisan, and self-serving connotations in certain ecclesial precincts nowadays associated with assorted therapies. Possibly such have some worldly legitimacy, but, recalling Acts concretely, none furnish substitute for the new life exemplified in Jesus Christ and informed by the vitality of the Word of God in the Holy Spirit. None do more than foreshadow the new humanity in Christ that constitutes the exact vocation of the church. Bishops have reason for both gratitude and cheer. They are not called to be amateur or ersatz therapists of any sort: they are called, rather, to be pastors for the whole church in this world.

Yet if the pastoral ministry pertinent to a bishop's office is free of heavy psychological or personalistic or indulgent implications, it must be openly acknowledged that pastoral care *does* have political significance. In this regard the whole Bible is redundant, and the book of the Acts of the Apostles is most notably so. Thus, the episode first related in Acts concerning the activities of the apostles following their own renewal as persons and as a community in the Holy Spirit, at Pentecost, is archetypical of the episodes reported later on in the book. Acts is, simply, the chronicle of the confrontations between the apostles and the apostolic church and the ruling authorities. The witness and ministry *pastorally* of the new Christians is beset by hostility, harassment, surveillance, arrest, imprisonment, sometimes execution, persecution. Over and over again, the story of that experience that composes Acts is essentially the same as that which Peter and John knew in the first reported incident involving the healing of the lame beggar at the gate of the temple called Beautiful. . . .

From the earliest experience of the church, the apostles are poised against the rulers of this world. That is the basic posture in the relationships of church and worldly regimes. I believe this is a clue to the political character of authentic pastoral care, especially as the pastoral ministry is vested in the office of bishop. One lesson to be learned from the arrest of Peter and John in consequence of their care for the beggar and their witness, thus, to the world, is that when bishops are most conscientious pastorally, they are apt to be most cogent politically.

Some bishops seem, lately, to return to this discernment (after the prolonged manipulation of bishops and of the whole church via the Constantinian Arrangement and its derivations). The American Roman Catholic bishops' pastoral letter on nuclear reality is a particularly significant example. Other bishops, including some Episcopalians, now repudiate the "just war" sophistry that has so benighted Christendom in the West for so long.

There seems, however, to me to be such diffidence on these matters on the part of the incumbent pontiff as to raise a query about whether John Paul — reputed chief pastor of all in both church and world — comprehends the inherently political character of pastoral ministry as elucidated in Acts in incidents like that of the arrest of Peter and John.

At the least John Paul appears radically ambivalent. One specific source of disillusionment with his behavior is, on the one hand, his bold and passionate pastoral involvement in Poland — and the manifold and continuing political ramifications of that care; coupled, on the other hand, with his paternalistic and caustic attitude toward the need for a comparable ministry and witness in Central America.

Meanwhile, especially on the American scene, John Paul sponsors the interminable suppression of women, particularly the religious, and exacts "loyalty oaths" favoring male dominance ecclesiastically from nominees to the episcopacy. In that context, his views concerning both sexuality and sex invite ridicule. To put it directly, does the pope seriously suppose that scoldings condemning masturbation as "a very grave moral disorder" deflect attention from the oppression of women or merit more notice and effort than the threat of nuclear obliteration, about which the pope has been cautious, if not equivocal?

Papal utterances concerning the sanctity of life sound hollow or hypocritical to many people who note the quietness or coyness of the Vatican on Grenada, or El Salvador, or, for that matter, Lebanon, or the increasing probabilities of nuclear calamity. And, to me, most ominous and alarming are the official papal inquests into some of the women's religious orders. These parallel investigations affecting the archbishop of Seattle (who has refused to pay taxes for war) and kindred bishops, and the attempts to manipulate the governance of the Jesuits. Are these what they seem to be — attempts to intimidate factions or persons or powers within the church who are apt to be critical of the pope and his ambivalent politics?

It is a melancholy scene that attends John Paul, one in which a politics is practiced that has a kind of antipastoral emphasis or in which a pastoral ministry is professed that is antipolitical. There may be no *timely* remedy for this extraordinary shortcoming or confusion in the ministry of John Paul. But I commend, to one and all, that a fit remedy is awaiting application. It is in the politics of pastoral care articulated in the Acts of the Apostles.

Kissinger: The Price of Power

SEYMOUR Hersh's book, *The Price of Power: Kissinger in the Nixon White House,* verifies the macabre reciprocity that constitutes the relationship between Henry Kissinger and Richard Nixon. Theirs is a connection that, a decade or so ago, pursued genocide as a matter of high policy in Vietnam and Cambodia, and that was poised to execute a similar course against the PLO in the Middle East. Meanwhile these two, in cahoots, brazenly defied constitutional restraints upon executive abuses, openly ridiculed and then subverted the rule of law as such, and instigated — in the language of a bill of impeachment — "high crimes and misdemeanors" that were to become both the most conspicuous activity and the historic legacy of the Nixon presidency.

Like most persons of pathological ilk, Kissinger and Nixon are incorrigible: they are still at their obnoxious games. Notice that the former attempts to use the Presidential Commission on Central America to publicly rehabilitate the latter, while both angle to fill the vacuum in foreign policy sponsored by Ronald Reagan with their putative respective expertise.

Hersh, a Pulitzer Prize–winning journalist, has marshaled a plethora of new or previously unrevealed material that shows how

---

"High Crimes and Misdemeanors: The Macabre Era of Kissinger and Nixon," *Sojourners,* January 1984, pp. 12–14

ruthlessly, relentlessly, and — most of all — pathetically Kissinger and Nixon exploited one another while one was the so-called national security adviser and the other was the so-called president. The Hersh documentations and disclosures at once embellish and expand the common knowledge that U.S. citizens were finally required to confront during the preliminary impeachment hearings.

That those proceedings were aborted, that the system was not allowed to run its lawful course, by some perfidious deal imposed on hapless Gerald Ford by Nixon should not divert or dilute public recollection and recognition of how inimical the liaison of Kissinger and Nixon is to both constitutional government and, simply, human decency. If for no other reason, the Hersh book is timely and significant insofar as it replenishes the public memory of the jeopardy and scandal that Kissinger and Nixon wrought by the sheer concentration of wickedness and wile.

The straightforward truth is that Nixon is a barbarian, Kissinger a predator. Their official conduct, jointly and respectively, is redundantly distinguished by violence, savagery, lust, malevolence, avarice, and an overwhelming contempt for human life, including their very own claims to being human. Their official demeanor is at once literally and figuratively soaked in the blood of their victims, who are legion and who are, for the most part, nameless but who include, prominently, most Americans.

In such remarks as these, I am not cursing. I do not even indulge in hyperbole. On the contrary, I am speaking quite precisely, and I am suggesting that the vicious tactics and death-dealing qualities so evident in Kissinger and Nixon are most tellingly exposed in their bizarre association, in their assorted manipulations and versatile abuses of each other, even more than in the manifold atrocities for which they share public responsibility (though they have so far escaped public accountability).

Furthermore I do not, by emphasizing their guilty connection, intend to lump Nixon and Kissinger indiscriminately together in a way that minimizes their distinctive and different characteristics and capabilities. For example, I recognize the remarkable moral consistency of Richard Nixon. It is virtually unrivaled among American politicians.

I recall the first degenerate campaign effort in 1946 of Nixon against Congressman Jerry Voorhis. All that has transpired since in Nixon's career was inherent in that initiation. The only significant change has been in the multiplication of his prey. Morally, thus, there is a solemnity about Nixon that contrasts with Kissinger.

Kissinger has both a wit and a glib intelligence but seems morally inarticulate. He is, as Hersh profusely illustrates in his book, the penultimate opportunist, a person bereft of moral sensibilities, one so morally incapacitated that one's humanness itself is brought into doubt.

It will suffice here to say that Nixon and Kissinger are no ordinary scoundrels. The public evidence (spare us, Lord, the private intelligence) is of two men so obsessed with their own vanity — in the sense that the Bible so often mentions vanity — that the obsession has become idolatrous, and everything else is preempted by it.

But how, then, have either of them retained public credibility for so long? The answer is that each has succeeded in shifting credibility from a connection with truth to a dependence upon marketing technics. The shift is from that which is credible because it derives somehow from the truth to that which is credible because people can be coerced, induced, conditioned, or programmed to believe it whether or not it has any significant relationship with the truth. Often, in the present U.S. culture, especially in the commercial realm, credibility is achieved simply by the technics of repetition, redundancy, and volume. (That is a reason why the shibboleths of the cold war are still potent.)

Kissinger and Nixon have each mastered this process. Hence citizens are confronted with the proposition that Richard Nixon is, whatever else he is, a great foreign policy expert; one whose "input" ought not to be lost to the nation just because he is, as he put it, "a crook." Yet the proposition, in its generic version, originates in Nixon's own mouth. It has been reiterated for a score of years in Nixon press handouts. It has no independent or objective source; it is an utterly self-serving fabrication that has been repeated so much that multitudes suppose it to be credible.

The Hersh book massively refutes the concoction that Nixon is an expert in anything, save deception. Meanwhile, in Kissinger's case, credibility accrues along with some public esteem, if not affection, for the extraneous reason that Kissinger has been skillful in playing the role of celebrity. That attracts, indeed fascinates, many and can take the place of credibility based upon truth and the telling of the truth. The phenomenon is part of a broader scene in which, in American public life, theatrics have been substituted for substance. Kissinger's self-heralded "shuttle diplomacy" is a peculiarly dangerous example of that.

Where the definitive relationship is between credibility and marketing, rather than between credibility and truth, every policy question becomes a public relations scam. That is what has been done by Nixon and Kissinger in their notorious collaboration. And, thus, the secret bombing of Cambodia came to pass and, more than that, a real live movie star became president.

In the Hersh book, as in all versions of the Faustian story, the question recurs: What is the price of power? The answer in the Kissinger/Nixon translation is conscience: the conscience must be discarded. This is a very high price. Those who pay this price are, the Bible avers, consigned to perdition forevermore.

IV. LIVING HUMANLY

Healing

MOST church people, to mention no others, I am afraid, have become so unbiblical in their minds that they think *miracle* means *magic,* and they seem to suffer fakers and fools gladly, at least they patronize them in various ways even when the hocus-pocus is ostentatious and transparent, even where obvious commercial advantage is taken, or even, sometimes, where a disavowal of legitimate medical practice is involved. Church people are often so deeply imbued with a fairy-tale version of the gospel, from the corruptions of Sunday school and the like, that they would rather be conned than relinquish their fables.

I was bothered to hear so many who are close to me and who had known of the crisis in my health invoke the language of miracles about my healing. I would not have volunteered that name myself just because of the false connotation of supernatural tricks attached to it. There was no miracle in any sense such as that in my being healed.

Still, I knew that miracle is a more versatile symbol that can be meant without gainsaying the arts of surgeons and physicians, and without real comparison to the business of conjurers or the doctrine of wizards. I realized that what miracle signified to all who had invoked it about my survival was a gratitude for my recovery from death. They bespoke the splendor of the mysteries of healing and of love.

Second Birthday, 1970, pp. 200–203

When all due allowances have been made for doctors and for medicine, it is when these mysteries — healing and love — are joined that, in fact, a miracle happens.

What is involved, then, whatever else is implicated, is self-love. The love of others is there, but that alone cannot suffice, as potent as it may be. Self-love is decisive. I do not mean, by that, a strenuous will to live. I refer to a reality that is, indeed, rather the opposite: a love of self that, esteeming life itself as a gift, expects or demands no more than the life that is given and that welcomes and embraces and affirms that much unconditionally. I mean self-love that emulates and, in the end, participates in, the love of God for life.

The evening next after my return to the island from the hospital, Anthony and Bengt and I had a meal together. It was an unexpected celebration. It recalled for all of us the meal we had shared just before I left the island to enter the hospital. That previous meal was similar to a wake. My friends were both persuaded it was the last time we would have a meal together. They were prematurely mourning. I had my accustomed distress for the illness, but I did not have their apprehension and my morale was good.

It was during the second meal that Bengt first pressed the idea of writing this book. He insisted it need not be morbid or grisly or vain. "We were both sure that you would die," he mentioned the other, earlier meal, "but you didn't feel that way that night." Bengt has a habit of protesting a lack of sophistication whenever he is about to say something truly sophisticated. "I am just a seaman," he continued, "but I think it was faith. I call that faith. You had faith." It seemed an accusation. "You have to write about faith."

Well, one can write of faith and, thus, as here, speak of prayer and providence, vocation and freedom from time, work, and dominion, recall and absolution, healing and love, the transcendence of death in many ways and eucharist for life. Or, one can be succinct: life is a gift that death does not vitiate or void: faith is the acceptance, honoring, rejoicing in that gift. That being so, in my own story, *it did not matter whether I died.* Read no resignation or indifference into this confession. It is freedom from moral bondage to death that enables a person to live humanly and to die at any moment without concern.

Conscience

SOME days following Father Berrigan's unwanted departure from Block Island, a telephone call was received from a prominent clergyman, the senior minister of a comfortable, rich, white, Protestant congregation in that part of the country that has come to be known as "middle America." The voice on the phone seemed somehow excited — titillated, in fact — as an invitation was conveyed to visit the congregation to speak about "the crisis of conscience" that, it was presumed, we had recently suffered in connection with Berrigan's visit to our household. The message struck both of us, at the time, as slightly morbid — this minister was, evidently, looking for a dramatic entertainment for his congregants in which the excruciation of deciding whether or not to receive Berrigan, the criminal priest, would be related with suitable anguish. Protestants in America have this notion that the exercise of conscience is a form of self-torture — perhaps that partly explains how immobile and moribund conscience is in the churches.

The idea behind the proposal also impressed us as amusing, since neither of us had endured any epic of conscience regarding our friend Dan. The friendship among the three of us authorized — on the most straightforward and elementary human level — Dan to visit us whenever he wished to do so. At the time he became a fugitive, as has been

---

Suspect Tenderness, 1971, pp. 97–103

indicated, it was mentioned casually that he might turn up at our home. There was no anguish or other anxiety involved in that brief conversation. Dan's peculiar legal status did not diminish our esteem for him and raised no issue about whether he would be welcome. There being nothing of substance to consider about that, it was not discussed.

Crisis of conscience, indeed! That clergyman on the telephone betrays an ignorance of what conscience is.

This incident is not included here to ridicule the minister in question but as an illustration of a widespread misapprehension of the meaning of conscience that exists within American society and, most strangely and inappropriately, within the extant churches in the United States. It is a matter previously alluded to when criticism was made of those inclined to put down or evade the Berrigan witness by naming Daniel and Philip as prophets or martyrs, with the insinuation that they have indulged conscience idiosyncratically.

If conscience is no more than individualistic insight, void of social context, isolated from historical connections, without the discipline of human experience other than that of a single person, then we would argue that there is no such reality as conscience at all. We would, of course, allow anyone who likes it to hold this view (though it seems to us manifestly nonsensical); our dispute is specifically with those who in such a fashion eliminate conscience so far as the Christian faith and community are concerned.

Conscience, in the gospel, as well as in the actual experiences of the early Christians, refers to the new or restored maturity of human life in Christ. A person who becomes a Christian — speaking of that event in its biblical connotations as distinguished from any particular church traditions — suffers at once a personal and a public transfiguration. One's insight into one's own identity as a person is, at the same time, an acceptance of the rest of humanity. One's reconciliation, that is, the experience of forgiveness, is profoundly private, but, simultaneously, this reconciliation is radically — even cosmically — political, incorporating one's own humanity into the whole of humanity and, indeed, the whole of creation. If in religionizing Christianity and in domesticating the church of Christ in America, many churchfolk have been deprived of this news of the political character of conversion, the truth remains unperturbed in the Bible, particularly in the evidence there of the style of life of the first-century Christians. The story of Ananias, who distrusted and dishonored this extraordinary covenant in Christ and, at doing so, "fell down and died," is one of the most striking citations, though there are many others.

Baptism, as practiced in the apostolic church, was the manner in which this corporate or political dimension of personal reconciliation was solemnized and publicized. The renewal of this person being baptized was understood to be relevant and good news for all persons everywhere, not just for others of the church. Each time a person was (is) baptized, the common life of all human beings in community was (is) affirmed and notarized.

The baptized, thus, lives in a new, primary, and rudimentary relationship with other human beings signifying the reconciliation of the whole of life vouchsafed in Jesus Christ. The discernment — about any matter whatever — that is given and exercised in that remarkable relationship *is* conscience. In truth, the association of baptism with conscience, in this sense, is that conscience is properly deemed a charismatic gift.

Although to various others, conscience may be a synonym for personal convenience, rationalization, eccentricity, or even whim, as far as the Christian faith is concerned to deride or dismiss conscience in any such ways as these amounts to a denunciation of the Holy Spirit, a denial of its militancy, perhaps even a secret denial of its existence. To ignore or suppress conscience is to gainsay effectually the vitality of God's concern for human life in society here and now.

The inescapable issue in conscience for Christians is what has here been called the social or political context in which conscience is exercised; that social or political element in conscience refers concretely to the activity of the Holy Spirit historically upon the community of believers and the members of the community evoking their experience of renewed humanity for the sake and service of human life in the world. The initiative in conscience belongs to God; the authority of conscience is the maturity of the humanity of the Christian; the concern of conscience is always the societal fulfillment of life for all. Still, the Christian community is diverse and dispersed, its members have different capabilities and locations, and the Holy Spirit is versatile, while the needs of the world, in the sense of humanizing life for mankind, are multifarious and cumulative and, not infrequently, contradictory. The exercise of conscience, therefore, is not the same thing as the arrival at consensus. In specific circumstances within a particular segment of the body of Christians, there may be a coincidence of conscience and consensus, but there may also be conscientious fitness not attended by consensus or there may even be many simultaneous voices of conscience, some of which seem inconsistent one with another. That conscience is not mechanical or narrow but free in its use and far-reaching, we take to be a tribute to the vigor and versatility of the Holy Spirit, as well as a sign of the imagination and seriousness with which Christians are called to regard and become involved in history.

Pietists, among them some partisans of natural law, will complain that this comprehension of functioning conscience within the Christian witness makes evaluation of any particular action, which is said to be conscientious, difficult. That we readily concede; it is, in fact, impossible, and we gladly recall that the prerogative of judgment of conscience is vested in God, not in human beings, not in laws, not in the state, not in the ethics of culture, not in the church, and certainly not in the churches, sects, and denominations. What transpires, in decisions and actions of conscience, on the part of a Christian or of some community of Christians or of many Christians positioned diversely, is a living encounter between the Holy Spirit and those deciding and acting in relation to human needs in society. If either those who act or those who stand apart from the action presume judgment of what is said and done, they negate the viability of that encounter. The practice of conscience, thus, is an extraordinarily audacious undertaking, disdaining all mundane or conventional prudential calculations and confessing the exclusivity of God's judgment and trusting God's judgment as grace. Conscience requires knowing and respecting one's self as no less, but no more, than human. The exercise of conscience represents — as 1 Peter remarks — living as a free human being.

How, in historic, actual circumstances, conscience may err remains, mercifully, God's secret insight, but that conscience may err becomes no excuse for any default, abstention, or silence, or for any substitution of prudence for conscience, since none of these common recourses are spared God's judgment either, though each of them exposes those who would retreat into them as those who are not free as human beings and who are very impudent toward God.

To ease the issue of God's judgment or to feign to evade God's judgment many construe the use of conscience as an abstract and a priori problem and, hence, indulge, often ingeniously, in hypothetical speculations about what decision should be had in imagined situations. They seek, we suppose, in this manner to anticipate contingencies and prepare in advance to meet them and, we suspect, hope to reduce the trauma of decision-making and, as it were, minimize the pertinence of judgment. Yet conscience, at least in its Christian form, is *never* a hypothetical game, and to turn it into such an indulgence both abuses history by taking persons and events less seriously than in their actuality and devalues the judgment of God, which always concerns and addresses that which is historically concrete.

Thus, after Berrigan's presence in our home while a fugitive, we have been frequently asked if we would receive other fugitives — Angela Davis? Timothy Leary? a Quebec terrorist? a draft dodger? — to which we have replied that we do not know what we would decide to do if confronted with any such questions. We await, in conscientious decisions, the real situation. We welcomed Dan. The controlling circumstances in that action did not happen in August of 1970, but long before, in 1964, when Berrigan and Towne and Stringfellow first met and became friends. Just so is every conscientious act historic, in living context, serious, free of advance restriction or hypothetical commitment, and wholly vulnerable to God's judgment.

Assuming that the word *inspiration* can be used without its sentimental or indefinite connotations, we would say that conscience involves a conjunction of inspiration with common life or, put theologically, conscience is the access of the Holy Spirit to human beings in their decisions and actions in daily existence.

Discernment

THE gift of discernment is basic to the genius of the biblical life-style.

Discerning signs has to do with comprehending the remarkable in common happenings, with perceiving the saga of salvation within the era of the Fall. It has to do with the ability to interpret ordinary events in both apocalyptic and eschatological connotations, to see portents of death where others find progress or success but, simultaneously, to behold tokens of the reality of the resurrection or hope where others are consigned to confusion or despair. Discerning signs does not seek spectacular proofs or await the miraculous, but, rather, it means sensitivity to the Word of God indwelling in all creation and transfiguring common history, while remaining radically realistic about death's vitality in all that happens.

This gift is elemental to the work of prophetism as that is known and practiced within the confessing community; indeed, it is discernment that saves prophecy as a biblical vocation from either predestinarianism on the one hand or occult prediction on the other. At the same time, discerning signs is directly related to the possibility of celebration in a sacramental sense, to the vitality of the worship of the people and the quality of that worship for coherence and significance as the worship of God rather than hoax or superstition.

Proximate to the discernment of signs is the discernment of

An Ethic for Christians and Other Aliens in a Strange Land, 1973, pp. 138–43

spirits. This gift enables the people of God to distinguish and recognize, identify and expose, report and rebuke the power of death incarnate in nations and institutions or other creatures, or possessing persons, while they also affirm the Word of God incarnate in all of life, exemplified preeminently in Jesus Christ. The discernment of spirits refers to the talent to recognize the Word of God in this world in principalities and persons despite the distortion of fallenness or transcending the moral reality of death permeating everything.

This is the gift that exposes and rebukes idolatry. This is the gift that confounds and undoes blasphemy. Similar to the discernment of signs, the discernment of spirits is inherently political while in practice it has specifically to do with pastoral care, with healing, with the nurture of human life, and with the fulfillment of all life.

The powers of discernment are held by St. Paul to be those most necessary to the receipt and effectual use of the many other charismatic gifts (1 Cor. 12). Discernment furnishes the context for other tasks and functions of the people of God. It safeguards against covetousness, pride, trick, exploitation, abuse, or dissipation (1 Cor. 13, 14). Moreover, discernment represents the fulfillment of the promise of Jesus Christ to his disciples that they would receive authority *and* capability by the Holy Spirit to address and to serve all humanity (John 15:18–26). Discernment is bestowed upon them, and those gathered with them, in Pentecost, wherein the church is born and the Jerusalem vocation is renewed. And discernment is thereafter always evident in practice wherever the church is alive (see Acts 2:14–21).

These are awesome gifts. They have seemed, perchance, all the more so because the powers of discernment are nowadays so seldom invoked, so little practiced, so erratically verified in the demeanor of the conventional American churches. As with other gifts of the Holy Spirit mentioned in the New Testament, discernment of both signs and spirits has somehow become regarded as something rare and unusual — bizarre, even esoteric, occult, or spooky. We admit discernment as an attribute of the primitive church but readily suppose that it has disappeared or has been so diluted in the succession of centuries since the apostolic era that it can no longer be expected to be apparent in any but the most exceptional circumstances.

I have a quite different view of the gifts of God to the church and to the members of the church. I regard none of the charismatic gifts —

least of all discernment — as fantastic or outlandish but, on the contrary, as commonplace and usual marks of the church. Pentecost, in other words, typifies the event of the church, and that not only during the apostolic period but thereafter. The manifestation of the multifarious charismatic gifts, including, most particularly, the exercise of the powers of discernment, is definitive of the church. No assembly, institution, or congregation professing to be of the church of Christ can be regarded seriously in that profession if these powers and works are not evidenced. If today there is hesitance or inhibition in apprehending the practice of discernment within any of the American churches, it is not because the Holy Spirit has begrudged a gift but, more likely, because there has been too much timidity in practicing discernment. The problem is not want of accessibility to the Holy Spirit but, rather, that the gift has been rejected or abandoned. Indeed, as ancient baptismal affirmations declare, discernment is the elementary, common, and ecumenical gift intrinsic to the authority that every Christian receives, essential to the efficient use of all other charismatic gifts, characteristic of the mature Christian witness in the present day no less than long ago. There are, of course, risks of vanity and temptations of abuse in the discernment of signs and of spirits, as there are with respect to any of the charismatic gifts; but that does not absolve lassitude or excuse indifference or rationalize inaction or condone equivocation. What chiefly hinders discernment in the contemporary churches is not so much arrogance as it is ingratitude. It is not that church people are too proud but that they are not bold enough; it is not even very pertinent to this issue that American Christians are apostate, since what is more relevant is that they are adolescent in biblical faith.

Discernment of spirits and discernment of signs generally coincide in the same circumstances or appear as particular versions or dimensions or emphases in the same event. Both have to do with the recognition and exposure of the moral presence of death in history and with the confrontation of the power of death with the Word of God. Thus, to follow my own counsel against timidity in practicing discernment and to supply concrete examples, I must pose the question: What can the biblical mind perceive in a society, in America now, overrun with the violence of babel?

In the midst of babel, speak the truth.

Two major blunders based upon false perceptions or delusions have repeatedly been indulged by Christians, as well as other citizens, who have sought to resist official violence and to refute babel. One is the presumption of rationality in the nation's leaders. That presumption is often coupled with the superstition that incumbency in high office, notably in the White House, somehow enhances the faculties of sanity and conscience, whereas the evidence is that occupancy of the presidency or similar heights is a pathetically dehumanizing ordeal, harmful to both sanity and conscience. This has become acutely obvious in the past decade during which the idolatry of death as the nation's moral purpose has been so grotesquely magnified in the Indochina war.

It is more accurate, more truthful, to perceive the president as a victim and captive of the principalities and powers. (*The Pentagon Papers* document and detail the process by which presidents and other officials are victimized by demonic powers.) In fact, the captive status of the person occupying the office has by now reached such proportions that the presidency has become a pseudomonarchy functioning as an elaborate façade for an incipient technocratic totalitarianism. That sham points to the second tactical error: imputing malice to the nation's reputed leaders. If Mr. Nixon or General Westmoreland or John Mitchell, or any of their predecessors or any of their successors, can be said to be wicked men, that is of much less moral significance or political relevance than the enthrallment of men such as these with the power of death and their entrapment and enslavement by the powers and principalities in relation to which they nominally have office. The critical question is not whether these "leaders" bear malice, but whether they are captivated and possessed by the violence of babel.

And if they are, if that is what can be discerned, what then? If this nation and its reputed leaders be sorely beset so specifically by the demonic, what befits the Christian witness?

In the face of death, live humanly. In the middle of chaos, celebrate the Word. Amidst babel, I repeat, speak the truth. Confront the noise and verbiage and falsehood of death with the truth and potency and efficacy of the Word of God. Know the word, teach the Word, nurture the Word, preach the Word, define the Word, incarnate the Word, do the Word, live the Word. And more than that, in the Word of God, expose death and all death's works and wiles, rebuke lies, cast out demons, exorcise, cleanse the possessed, raise those who are dead in mind and conscience.

Exorcism

IF, IN modern Christendom, exorcism as a gift of the Holy Spirit has been generally regarded with apprehension and suppressed, it nevertheless had venerable prominence in the biblical tradition. Not only did Jesus exorcise, but it was part of the Messianic expectation in Old Testament Judaism that the Messiah would have this power. Furthermore, in the primitive church, exorcism, being one of the gifts specifically promised by Jesus for the mission of the church, was widely and effectually practiced, according to the New Testament (Acts 10:38; 13:10). Indeed, in the ancient church, liturgical forms of exorcism were commonly in use as a preparation for baptism (1 Pet. 5:8; James 4:7). Vestiges of that early practice survive in baptismal rites to the present time, though I find little evidence that these are taken very seriously in instruction for baptism.

Still, exorcism cannot be dismissed as some quaint residue, if only because of its biblical status. Some psalms are liturgical exorcisms. In the Jewish tradition of exorcism, as has been earlier mentioned, there is the story of Moses exorcising the pharaoh. It seems to me that this citation alone is sufficient to show the contemporary relevance of the gift and the necessity for its practice. And, in fact, exorcism is far more widely implicated in witness today than is usually acknowledged directly, the Lord's Prayer itself being a form of exorcism.

An Ethic for Christians and Other Aliens in a Strange Land, 1973, pp. 149–51

Whether many who redundantly and ceremoniously recite the Lord's Prayer are cognizant of it or not, the fact remains that the invocation of the name of God, followed at the end of the prayer by the plea to "deliver us from evil" or "from the evil one," constitutes an act of exorcism (Matt. 6:9–13).

All that has been affirmed about the political connotations of healing must be reaffirmed, of course, about this specific kind of healing. The political significance of exorcism is rendered even more emphatic by the content of the Lord's Prayer and by the political circumstances of the impending condemnation of Christ that attended his commendation of this prayer to his disciples.

Politically informed exorcisms that I believe to be as exemplary as that involving the pharaoh do still occur, if occasionally. This, indeed, was the witness of the Catonsville Nine, when they burned draft records in May 1968. As those attentive to their trial or those who have read or seen the play about the trial can apprehend, the action at Catonsville was a sacramental protest against the Vietnam war — a liturgy of exorcism, exactly. It exposed the death idolatry of a nation that napalmed children by symbolically submitting the nation to the very power upon which it has relied, by napalming official pieces of paper. It is relevant to understanding the significance of the Catonsville action that the Berrigan brothers and others of the defendants had been involved over a long time, particularly since the extraordinary papacy of John XXIII, in the renewal of the sacramental witness in the liturgical life of Christians. They had become alert to the social and political implications of the Mass as a celebration and dramatization of the reconciliation and renewal of creation or as a portrayal and communication of the Jerusalem reality of the church of Christ loving and serving the world. The Catonsville action is, thus, a direct outreach of the renewal of the sacramental activity of the sanctuary, a liturgy transposed from altar or kitchen table to a sidewalk outside a Selective Service Board office, a fusion of the sacramental and the ethical standing with the characteristic biblical witness.

Prayer

WHEN I mention that I needed to pray, I am referring to prayer in what I understand to be its most essential, simple, and rudimentary reality, as a relationship in which the authentic (or, one could say, *original*) identity of a person is affirmed in the Word of God by the Word of God. Prayer, as I mean it, has its integrity in recall of the event of one's own creation in the Word of God.

Prayer, in this significance, is distinguished from the vulgar or profane connotations that have, unhappily, accrued to the term. Prayer, for instance, has nothing, as such, to do with utterance, language, posture, ceremony, or pharisaical style and tradition. Prayer is *not* "talking" with God, to God, or about God. It is *not* asking God for anything whatsoever. It is *not* bargaining with God. It has *no* similarity to conjuring, fantasizing, sentimental indulgence or superstitious practice. It is *not* motivational therapy, either. It is *not* inspirational. It does *not* seriously resemble yoga, "transcendental meditation," or any other inverted exercises.

More definitively, prayer is *not* personal in the sense of a private transaction occurring in a void, disconnected with everyone and everything else, but it is *so* personal that it reveals (I have chosen this verb conscientiously) every connection with everyone and everything else in the whole of creation throughout time. A person in the estate

---

Simplicity of Faith, 1982, pp. 67–68

of prayer is identified in relation to alpha and omega — in relationship to the inception of everything and to the fulfillment of everything (cf. Rom. 1:20, 1 Cor. 12:12–13, Rev. 22:12). In prayer, the initiative belongs to the Word of God, acting to identify or to reiterate the identity of the one who prays.

Simultaneously, prayer recognizes the identity of God and specifically acknowledges the *godliness* of God. In prayer, construed as a state of being (and not as a religious act), the one who prays is engaged in merely affirming who God is in relation to the acceptance of his or her own humanness.

Now prayer, and the manifold implications of prayer signifying relationships with the totality of the life of the rest of creation, is the characteristic attitude of the Communion of Saints. I refer, when I use that curious and venerable title, to the entire company of human beings (inclusive of the church but transcending time and place and thereby far more ecumenical than the church has ever been) who have, at any time, prayed and who will, at any time, pray; whose occupation, for the time being, is intercession for each and every need of the life of this world. As the Communion of Saints anticipates, in its scope and constituency, the full assemblage of created life in the Kingdom of God at the end of time, so prayer emulates the fullness of worship when the Word of God is glorified eternally in the Kingdom.

Prayer, in quintessence, therefore, is a political action — an audacious one, at that — bridging the gap between immediate realities and ultimate hope, between ethics and eschatology, between the world as it is and the Kingdom that is vouchsafed.

Sanctification

WHILE I do not wish to magnify semantic or rhetorical issues or to dwell much on them, both sanctification and holiness bring freight and are often subject to inflated connotations. In any case, by sanctification I mean the endeavor by which a person is sanctified or rendered holy. The endeavor is not one of the person so affected but, quite the contrary, is an effort of the Word of God, which *elects* the one made holy and which, I believe, offers similar election freely to every person. To be more precise about it, *sanctification is a reiteration of the act of creation in the Word of God.* Thus sanctification refers to the activity of the historic Word of God renewing human life (and all of created life) in the midst of the era of the Fall, or during the present darkness, in which the power of death apparently reigns. Holiness designates the essential condition of a person who confesses that he or she has suffered the renewal of his or her being, or selfhood, in the Word of God and is restored to wholeness as a human being. While there *is* an implication, in being holy, of incessant repentance, there is no implication of perfection or of any superior moral status. Among humans, holiness may involve a relatively more profound experience of being human, but it does not indicate as such the exceptional or the extraordinary. To the contrary, holy connotes the holistic in human life and, in that connection, the normal, the typical, the ordinary, the generic, the exemplary.

Politics of Spirituality, 1984, pp. 30–35, 41–42

I am aware, of course, that sanctification is ridiculed and holiness is belittled — and the saints are defamed and scandalized — when especial moral worth or purity or achievement is imputed to being holy. This is, in reality, a condescension of those conformed to the world, their form of dismissal, an excuse for others to cop out in a manner that pretends to recognize and flatter the saints.

Within my own memory, probably the outstanding incident of this pretentiousness happened on the day in 1970 when Daniel Berrigan (the Jesuit who had become both celebrated and notorious for his resistance to the war in Southeast Asia), then being sought by the federal authorities as a fugitive (as Dan puts it) from injustice, was seized by the FBI at the home of Anthony Towne and myself on Block Island. The event was heavily covered by television and other media, and that evening, on one of the Providence TV newscasts, an interview was conducted, about Dan's capture, with another prominent Jesuit who was in the jurisdiction. He was John J. McLaughlin, a candidate in the Republican Party for the United States Senate. This was, of course, before strictures against priests in public office were widely pronounced by the pope. (McLaughlin lost and later achieved some prominence on the White House staff as casuist for President Nixon, but after a while he quit the Jesuit order.) In the interview on television the day that Dan was seized, Father McLaughlin delivered a long and verbose comment about those who work for change from within the system and those who work for change from outside the system. But then, as if summing up the contrast, he declared, "Of course, you must remember that Dan is a poet!" With that accusation, he not only dismissed the Berrigan witness against the Vietnam war but also banished Dan from the company of ordinary folk. Dan is different from other people: Dan is a poet; Dan is eccentric; what applies to Dan does not have relevance or weight for other persons. More than that, at the conclusion of this sophistry is the notion that because a poet is considered idiosyncratic, an ordinary human (i.e., a nonpoet) is excused from the claims of conscience that may be thought to influence the poets.

McLaughlin's evasion of conscience aside, being holy, as I have stressed, or becoming and being a saint, does not mean being perfect but being whole; it does not mean being exceptionally religious or being religious at all; it means being liberated from religiosity and religious pietism of any sort; it does not mean being morally better, it means being exemplary; it does not mean being godly, but rather being truly human; it does not mean being otherworldly, but it means being deeply implicated in the practical existence of this world without succumbing to this world or any aspect of this world, no matter how beguiling. Being holy means a radical self-knowledge; a sense of who one is, a consciousness of one's identity so thorough that it is no longer confused with the identities of others, of persons or of any creatures or of God or of any idols.

For human beings, relief and remedy from such profound confusion concerning a person's own identity and the identity and character of the Word of God becomes the indispensable and authenticating ingredient of being holy, and it is the most crucial aspect of becoming mature — or of being fulfilled — as a human in this world, in fallen creation. This is, at the same time, the manner through which humans can live humanly, in sanity and with conscience, in the fallen world as it is. And these twin faculties, sanity and conscience — rather than some sentimental or pietistic or self-serving notion of moral perfection — constitute the usual marks of sanctification. That which distinguishes the saint is not eccentricity but sanity, not perfection but conscience.

These are all considerations that impinge upon why I commonly use, herein, and have used, for more that a decade, in other books or public utterances, the *Word of God* as the name of God, in preference to the mere term *God*.

In American culture and, I suspect, everywhere else, the name of God is terribly maligned. For one thing the name *God* is seldom any longer used as a name, and that in itself is a literal curse addressed to God. To take a very obvious and familiar example, when Ronald Reagan, in his pronouncements on the school prayer issue and otherwise, says "God," it is difficult to fathom what he may be fantasizing, though it would appear, at most, that he is imagining some idea of god. Sometimes he himself clarifies that by inserting a prefix and speaking "his god" or "our god" or, also, "their god," while mentioning, as Reagan perceives the situation, an alien or enemy people.

Yet *no* idea of god is God; no image of god is God; no conception of god, however appealing or, for that matter, however true, coincides with the living God — which the biblical witness bespeaks — present, manifest, militant in common history, discernible in the course of events through the patience and insight of ordinary human beings. The living God, whose style and character the Bible reports, is subject now, as in the biblical era, to the witness of human beings, to their testimony describing what they have beheld of the intent, involvement, self-disclosure, effort, and concern of the Word of God in this world. And so, with as much standing or authority as our predecessors in the faith had long ago, biblical people in this day attest to God as revealed in this history, as the *Word of God,* the very same One to whom the biblical witness refers and in which the biblical witness so much rejoices.

When, therefore, I use here this name of God, it is deliberately intended to invoke the scriptural saga of the Word of God active in common history from the first initiative of creation. Simultaneously I refer (as, so to say, both Isaiah and John insist), the selfsame Word of God incarnate in Jesus Christ. At the same time, I mean to recall the Word of God permeating the whole of creation and ready to be discerned in all things whatsoever in the fallenness of this world; and, again, the Word of God as the Holy Spirit, at work contemporaneously, incessantly agitating change in this world (as the event of Pentecost and the Acts of the Apostles each verify).

The restoration of the original identity of a person — in all its particularities and all its relationships, in the totality of its political significance — the renewal of a person's wholeness, which is the initiation into holiness, is utterly the effort of the Word of God. There is no interpretation that is attributable to a person's ambition, attainment, discipline, works, or merit. The renewal of creation, including the restoration of integrity to persons, is a matter of the grace of the Word of God. It is a generous gift indeed, as I have already mentioned, encompassing the restoring of relationships within a person and between that person and all other persons, all principalities and powers, nature, and the residuum of creation. The gift is also precocious because it is offered *now,* in the midst of the Fall, in a way that disrupts, challenges, and resists the apparent sovereignty of the power of death in this world. That means, in turn, that this is an experience that shatters time and liberates people from the confinement of time by at once recalling all that has gone before and anticipating all that is to come.

Instead of being somehow transported "out of this world," rather than indulging abstinence, evasion, or escapism, rather than fabricating some isolation or separation or privatism, the irony in being holy is that one is plunged more fully into the practical existence of this world, as it is, than in any other way. . . .

Holiness is not an attainment, in any sense of the term, but is a gift of the Word of God. Holiness is not a badge of achievement for a saint but is wrought in the life, in the very being, of an ordinary person by the will of the Word of God. Holiness, from the vantage of the person who may truthfully be said to be holy, is, in the most elementary meaning, the restoration of integrity and wholeness to a person. That inherently involves, for that person, repentance — utter repentance, encompassing and comprehending the whole of that person's existence, even recollecting one's creation in the Word of God by the Word of God. It involves, as well, a prospective or continuing living in repentance unto the very day of the judgment of the Word of God in the consummation of the history of this world. But such radical repentance does not imply, much less require, self-denial or any sort of suppression or sublimation of self. Quite the contrary: in becoming and being sanctified, *every* facet, feature, attribute, and detail of a person is exposed and rejuvenated, rendered new as if in its original condition again, and restored. Thus, instead of self-denial, what is taking place is more nearly the opposite of self-denial: in place of denial there is fulfillment.

The experience of St. Paul is edifying in this respect, particularly since Paul has furnished us with more news of his experience in becoming and being a saint than any other New Testament character. To take a straightforward example, Paul in his early career boasted that he was the most zealous of those who persecuted the gospel and confessors of the gospel. From that we know that Paul had a quality, perchance even talent, that is described as *zeal*. Later on, Paul becomes the most zealous apologist for the gospel, even aspiring to confront the emperor with his advocacy. Lo! Paul retains this quality of zeal, save now, when he has become the great apologist, this aspect of his personhood is turned around, renewed, matured, restored to him in something like its original integrity in his own creation in the Word of God. The zeal of Paul does not have to be excised in order for him to become and be a saint, although he had engaged this zeal of his to harass and harm and inhibit the gospel. Had his zeal been somehow suppressed or extinguished, it would then have been less than the person Paul implicated in conversion and in becoming holy. And *that* becomes a self-contradiction: it is only the whole person, fully repentant, without anything withheld, denied, secreted, who can be holy.

On the Charismatic
and the Demonic

IT IS not a fortuity that there is so much excited contemporary interest in the demonic and in the charismatic.

Biblically, the two are treated in proximity, one seldom mentioned without reference or allusion to the other. Particularly in the New Testament, the relationship of the demonic and the charismatic appears dialectical and, often, paradoxical. That, in itself, is a clue that the association of the demonic and the charismatic is basic and profound.

At the same time, in the ordinary, everyday existence of this world, the significance of the charismatic and the demonic for each other is confirmed — most conspicuously — in the confusion concerning phenomena manifested either by exercise of charismatic gift or by invocation of demonic power. It is commonplace for one to be mistaken for the other. There mere immediate consequences or the apparent effects of the engagement of charismatic authority or of reliance upon demonic capability as such are not conclusive, much less definitive, as to whether, in truth, the charismatic or the demonic is at work. Perhaps that is why St. Paul esteems discernment as the characteristic gift of faith in Jesus Christ.

This circumstance of the popular confusion, and the easy con-

---

Preface to a book, *Grieve Not the Holy Spirit,* unpublished

fusion, of the demonic and the charismatic largely accounts for the fact that the present public fascination with the demonic and the charismatic occurs simultaneously. The aspect of sheer fascination contributes to the confusion, I suspect, especially where it is a morbid interest or, simply, superstitious, or a matter of religious, commercial, or similar vogue. American religion, as much as American business, has always been characterized by the promotion of fad, and the surfacing of the demonic and the charismatic topically in the culture at this time is an instance of that sort of exploitation.

For all of that, I suggest that the current intrigue with the demonic and the charismatic (exampled by the theatrical and literary revivals of Dracula or of Sherlock Holmes, and by multifarious phenomena of tongues and language, by the practice of sorcery as well as the occurrence of healings, by exploitation films, books, and television programs) is much more that a superficial sign of the times. It is the history that people have lately suffered — the threat of nuclear arms and nuclear energy, the evident impotence of superpower, the warfare between remote and imperious institutions and human beings, the incompatibility of environmental survival and the accustomed standard of living, the accrued and aggravated guilt of the Vietnam genocide, the lawless decadence of governmental authorities, the relentless attrition of inflation — that renders coping with the demonic and comprehending the charismatic relevant now and, even, urgent, and, incidentally, exploitable.

I believe the present agitation over the charismatic and the demonic to be a true sign of this age and of the age to come. (This book explains that belief and commends it to you.)

The effort here is to reclaim the biblical relationship of the demonic and the charismatic and, by that effort, to divest both of the secular myths, deceptions, falsehoods, and frauds that encumber each of them, to dispel the confusion of the one with the other, to, if you will, exorcise the names — *demonic* and *charismatic* — and thus expose the realities or powers to which the names refer, and, then, to publish and reaffirm the significance of each for the other.

I am using these terms, let it be clear immediately, in a generic sense: *demonic* refers to any, and every, agency of death, in whatever guise or form, however subtle or ingenious, howsoever vested or manifested; *charismatic* refers to each and every gift, talent, capability,

317

and limitation of persons, within the whole body of humankind in this world, as these are bestowed and renewed in the Word of God. As shorthand, with all its imprecision, one might think of the demonic as anything whatever that dehumanizes life for human beings, while the charismatic is that which rehumanizes life for human beings within the context of the whole of fallen creation.

When I stress that the biblical knowledge of the demonic and of the charismatic is straightforward, commonplace, and familiar — unencumbered by the exaggerations of supernaturalism or undistorted by superstitious indulgences — I am, at the same time, alleging that the churches of American Christendom have been suppressing the biblical testament about both the demonic and the charismatic and, in doing so, have been misrepresenting the activity of the Word of God and the Holy Spirit and misconstruing the routine of the Christian life. Where that suppression has not been accomplished by neglect or omission of the subject, it has been done by adaptation of worldly images of the demonic, witches and hobgoblins, and by captivation with secular imitations of the charismatic, celebrities, "super star." In either case, instead of learning and practicing the biblical attitude toward the demonic and the charismatic, the churches, for the most part, have sanctified and spread superstition and maintained, among the people of the churches, both ignorance and vice concerning the demonic and the charismatic.

The apostasy has complicated configurations, depending upon which sect or denomination is specified, and, no doubt, it has origins in ecclesiology, and in the culture, comparably complex. Scrutiny of all that would support, I think, a conclusion that religiosity and superstition reinforce polity and induce compliance to the prevalent regimes in society. In the process, acknowledgment of the Word of God militant in common history — and the actual worship of God on the part of human beings — is usurped by the idolatrous mystique attributed to the churchly institution as custodian of extraordinary secrets or as mediator of assorted dispensations and practically magical gratuities.

The whole matter comes to acute focus in the cursory and profane regard that the Word of God as the Holy Spirit suffers, generally, within the churches. . . .* In the Bible, the Holy Spirit is

---

* What is omitted here is the account of his experience of confirmation that subsequently found its way into *The Politics of Spirituality*. See above, pp. 23-24.

no term summoned simply to fill a void, or to enthrall rather than instruct the laity, or achieve some verbal sleight-of-hand because comprehension is lacking. Biblically, the Holy Spirit names the faithfulness of God to creation. Biblically, the Holy Spirit denominates the militant presence of the Word of God inhering in the life of the whole of creation. Biblically, the Holy Spirit is the Word of God at work historically, pervasively, existentially, renewing, incessantly, the life of this world. By virtue of this redundant affirmation of the biblical witness, the false notion that the Holy Spirit is somehow possessed by and enshrined within the sanctuary of the church is refuted.

The biblical news of the Holy Spirit prompts the expectancy of encounter with the Word of God in any and all events in the common life of the world. It is the biblical saga of the Word of God as Agitator, as the Holy Spirit, that assures me that wheresoever human conscience is alive and active that is a sign of the saving vitality of the Word of God in history, here and now.

This is a way of saying that in dealing with the demonic and the charismatic in their biblical connection, we are spared adventures into occult, paranormal, or supernatural realms, and, instead, we are confronted with the mundane involvement of the Word of God in the vocation of human life in society. Attention turns to the Holy Spirit working, characteristically, existentially and historically, and to the significance of that effort of the Word of God for the everyday decisions and actions of persons. Contrary to every pagan interpretation of the demonic or of the charismatic, the concern, biblically defined, thus is ethics.

I have mentioned this elsewhere, specifically, in *An Ethic for Christians and Other Aliens in a Strange Land,* in a section on the political significance of the charismatic gifts that I now think too succinct and, perchance, cryptic. And there are some allusions to the same matter in *Conscience and Obedience: the Politics of Romans 13 and Revelation 13 in Light of the Second Coming,* which seem, however, rather heavy. (Though it was not so preconceived, this book, with the other two, composes a trilogy. Anyway, they have that coherence now in my own head, and I hope the experience of the reader is similar.)

I consider by the way my (other) books, especially these two just cited, to be intrinsically cheerful — glad in the gospel, informed

319

by hope. (I affirm as much of this book.) I am, thus, dismayed when I hear reports that some suppose me pessimistic — a doomsayer of some sort. I attribute this misapprehension of what I write (and do) to the concentration in my work upon the nature, scope, and potency of the demonic in the common existence of this world affecting the principalities and powers as well as persons. Albeit a biblical theme, it is not one that has generally received the attention it merits in the American milieu, either secular or religious. I realize that news of the power of death may be hard to hear; yet talk of the resurrection from death is gratuitous or facetious unless or until the fullness of the reality of the power of death is risked. The goodness of the good news is relative to the veracity of the bad news. This is why I often warn people not to be religious — not to be deceived that any species of pietism has any efficacy whatever against death's power. And why I remain wary that any version of success that professed Christians pursue is equivocal, vain, and supercilious. Or why I plead that religious enthusiasm, whether self-generated or otherwise induced, not be mistaken for joy.

I believe we are beneficiaries of a hope, which transcends death now, wrought in the vitality of the Word of God in this life in this world. The joy of living in that hope is manifest in patience, steadfastness, resilience, or in the sense of being justified by the sufficiency of the grace of the Word of God.

The Day of Saint Stephen, 1977   William Stringfellow
Block Island, Rhode Island

The Marks of Involvement

IT IS sometimes asserted that the church should concern itself only occasionally in public affairs, where society is confronted with a "moral" issue. The problem with that view is that it oversimplifies the moral conflict in the world. There is no issue in society that is not a moral issue in both the transient human sense and also as one that God judges. In a fallen world, all human beings live at each other's expense, and every decision and action, even those that seem trivial or only private or unambiguous, is consequentially related to the lives of all other human beings.

What you or I decide and do affects all other people, and every decision or action or omission is thus not only a moral but a theological issue, a sacrament of one's responsibility for and love for one's self and others, or else a sign of one's disregard for and alienation from one's self and everyone else. Indeed, on the Last Day, though not before, God's own judgment of every act, word, and deed of every person will expose the true moral disposition of each in relationship to all. Meanwhile, each of us must make our own decisions, knowing that each decision is a moral decision with consequences for all other people but not knowing what many of those consequences are or will be until we are judged by God's mercy. Meanwhile, all Christians, remembering their baptisms, must

---

Dissenter in a Great Society, 1966, pp. 160–64

take their stand in the practical affairs of this world in fear and trembling.

But if there is no option of withdrawal, if silence is a form of involvement, if default abets the winning side, if all are in fact involved, how shall Christians and how shall the church be responsible in their political involvement? How shall they be involved and yet remain unstained by the world?

Surely the answer to that is: in the very manner of Christ's own ministry in this world.

There is no convenient set of rules, no simple blueprint, no simplistic ethics of decision for the Christian. The Christian witness in society does not consist of praising and practicing the "Golden Rule," which, after all, is a secular ethic of self-interest that demeans the essence of the gospel. But there are at least some clues about the style of witness characteristic of the Christian life in the world, both for the church as such and for the individual member of the church.

(1) *Realism:* Christians are those who take history very seriously. They regard the actual day-to-day existence of the world realistically, as a way of acknowledging and honoring God's own presence and action in the real world in which human beings live and fight and love and vote and work and die. And Christians know, more sensitively and sensibly than other people, that this world is a fallen world, not an evil world but the place in which death is militant and aggressive and at work in all things. Christians know that in this world in which, apart from God's work in all things, death is the only meaning, all relationships have been broken and all human beings suffer estrangement from one another and alienation from themselves. Of all people, Christians are the most blunt and relentless realists. They are free to face the world as it is without flinching, without shock, without fear, without surprise, without embarrassment, without sentimentality, without guile or disguise. They are free to live in the world as it is.

(2) *Inconsistency:* Christians, in their fidelity to the gospel in their witness in this world, will appear inconsistent to others in public views and positions. They cannot be put into a neat pigeonhole, their stances and conduct are never easily predictable. Christians are nonideological persons in politics, and there is no other label appropriate for them than Christian. They know that no institution, no ideology, no nation, no form of government, no society, can heal the brokenness or prevail

against the power of death. And though Christians act in this world and in particular circumstances in a society for this or that cause, though Christians take their stand and speak out specifically, they do so not as servants of some race or class or political system or ideology but as an expression of their freedom from just such idols.

(3) *Radicalism:* That means, of course, that the posture of Christians is inherently and consistently radical. (I do not use the word in any of its conventional economic or political connotations.) Christians are perpetually in the position of complaining about the status quo, whatever it happens to be. Their insight and experience of reconciliation in Christ are such that no estate in secular society can possibly correspond to, or much approximate, the true society of which they are citizens in Christ.

They are — everywhere, in every society — aliens. They are always, in any society, in protest. Even when a cause that they have themselves supported prevails, they will not be content but will be the first to complain against the "new" status quo.

For example, many Christians at the present time in the United States are deeply and actively involved in the struggle to achieve integration in American public life. Christians in that struggle, however, will characteristically be the first to recognize that integration of American society, as much as it is absolutely essential to the survival of this nation, is in no way to be confused with or identified with the Kingdom of God. Integration, from a Christian point of view, must be counted as a modest, conservative, attainable, and necessary social and political objective in this nation at this time. It is by no means the measure of reconciliation among human beings in this world.

(4) *Intercession:* Christians are concerned, politically, for all people in all the diversity of problems and issues of public life. Characteristically, the sign of the inclusiveness and extremity of Christian concern is represented and embodied in their specific care for those who, in a given time in society, are the least in that society, for those whom all the rest have ignored or forgotten or cast out or otherwise have abandoned to death.

The venerable ministry of Christians for the poor since the very days of the New Testament, for instance, is not simply compassion for their endurance of unemployment or hunger or cold or sickness or rejection by society but is also, at the same time, a way of caring for all others in society who are not poor or who have some security from the assaults of poverty. Christians know that their passion for the world, their involvement in society, their stand in politics, and their witness in the present age encompass even their own enemies, even those whom they oppose in some specific controversy, even those who would deny the freedom of their witness, even those who hate them, and especially those who are threatened by Christian witness.

The Christian political witness, for the individual Christian and for the body of the church, means demonstrating in and to the world what the true society is by the living example of the society of the church.

The Christian political witness is affirming and loving the essential humanity of all in Christ in the midst of humanity's abdication of human life and despite the whole array of death's assaults against human life.

The Christian political witness is the audacity to trust that God's love for this world's existence is redeeming, so Christians are human beings free to live in this world by grace in all practical matters and decisions.

That is why the church of Christ is the only society in this world worthily named great.

Reparations: Repentance as Necessary to Reconciliation

And if ye shall perceive your offenses to be such as are not only against God, but also against your neighbors; then ye shall reconcile yourselves unto them; being ready to make restitution and satisfaction, according to the uttermost of your powers, for all injuries and wrongs by you to any other; and being likewise ready to forgive others who have offended you, as ye would have forgiveness of your offenses at God's hand; for otherwise the receiving of the holy Communion doth nothing else but increase your condemnation.

> an exhortation or warning for the celebration
> of the Holy Communion in *The Book of Common Prayer*

The reparations demand of the National Black Economic Development Conference has been heard in the white churches and synagogues with a mixture of resentment and dismay. There is resentment at what whites regard as a disruption of the sacred activities of their

---

In *Black Manifesto: Religion, Racism, and Reparations,* Robert S. Lecky and H. Elliot Wright, eds., 1969, pp. 52–60, 63–64

sanctuaries, a defiling intrusion upon what they have supposed is their most earnest and innocent effort, their worship. There is dismay because the direct implication of the reparations Manifesto is a challenge to the integrity of white worship and an exposé of those who still attend such worship while countenancing the inherited and continuing alienation of the races in this land and in most of its churches. This black demand, unlike others that have been uttered heretofore, seems to invert everything so far as the white synagogues and churches are concerned. Up to now white religion might have been questioned for doing too little and for doing that too late, for an insufficient generosity, for a resilient apathy, for tardiness, for a condescending spirit, but never before in an effective way have the very presuppositions of white religion in America been contested so that what has been assumed to be holy is seen as unsanctified, or so that shrines can with justification be violated, and so that white guilt — accumulative, inherited, corporate guilt — is at last dramatized as the central racial issue in the nation and, particularly, in white religion. . . .

Although the publicity attendant to the promulgation of the reparations Manifesto and to the early presentations of it in white sanctuaries has tagged this as a radical or militant move, the truth is that reparations is such an old, established, and much utilized remedy in the law that its invocation in the name of American blacks must be counted as a conservative tactic and one that, if anything, is long overdue. In ordinary commerce, for example, reparations are the essential element of compensatory damages; in the relations of nations in the aftermath of war, reparations are a traditional resort. Reparations are a *limited* remedy, it must be remembered, appropriate where some harm or injury or wrongful loss has been suffered for which restitution monetarily can to some extent restore parties wronged to their position prior to the injury or other loss. Legally, reparations are to be distinguished from punitive damages, which — in addition to any attempt at restitution — impose costs upon the culpable party as a penalty or punishment. The conservative posture of the Black Manifesto is proved at just this point. From three and a half centuries of chattel slavery, segregation, and systematic exploitation, a simply overwhelming case can be argued for exacting punishment against American whites, but the Manifesto does not speak punitively and adheres to the idea of reparations, where some measurable basis for damages, some element of compensation, is controlling.

Reparations . . . have been considered and utilized in and by this society not only in the contractual and other business affairs among and between corporations and persons but also by the national and other echelons of government. Falsely convicted and imprisoned persons receive reparations as some gesture from the state to make up for their loss of freedom and income. Whole classes or categories of people have been paid reparations for wrongs visited upon the group, as has occasionally been the case for some of the Indian tribes and as was notably the precedent in compensation proceedings finally instituted on behalf of Japanese-Americans who had been wrongfully deprived of their freedom and property by internment during the Second World War. Reparations are still being adjudicated and awarded to victims of Nazism, particularly those who were in concentration camps, and the United States has consistently supported this as a propitious if only partial recourse in these circumstances. The precedent of reparations for those who suffered so brutally from Nazism and for some of their heirs may well be construed as the situation most comparable to that of the American blacks. . . .

Yet if reparations do not represent a radical measure in American experience, privately or publicly, the remedy does raise two matters of peculiar significance in the relationships of blacks and whites. . . . One of those issues is, of course, the inherent recognition in any reparations plan that an injury has been inflicted or a wrong committed by one against another. There has been *no necessary acknowledgment* of responsibility — much less confession of guilt — on the part of white society, or its people, or any of its institutions, including those religious, in any of these racial programs under either governmental or private auspices. . . .

At the same time, in this remedy the utilization and disposition of a reparations award lies wholly within the control and discretion of the injured party. Up to now, virtually all civil rights, antipoverty, and related enterprises undertaken by the governments, the universities, the unions, businesses and industries, the social-work bureaucracies, and the churches have vested control over funding and policy in the whites. If the racial crisis seems not to have been mitigated but in truth aggravated, despite such prodigious exertions by white society, it is because of the anomaly of trying to relieve the victims of a system by perpetuating their dependent and subservient role in that system. Reparations would rectify this by vesting control in the blacks. . . .

Why should the churches and synagogues pay reparations? The white ecclesiastical institutions in America are and have long been directly implicated in profiteering from slavery, segregation, and other forms of white supremacy through the investment and management of their endowments and other holdings in the American economy. The predominant social witness of the churches racially, for generations, has been incarnated in the wealth and property of white religion and not in the redundant preaching or pronouncement about racial justice. Indeed, such utterances — made in the context of white racism institutionalized in church economics — can only be construed as gratuitous hypocrisy. The wonder of it all is how a people can so deceive themselves; perhaps they only can when the deception is practiced in the name of God.

The churches and synagogues, in a sense, volunteer as the initial targets for reparations because they claim a surrogate vocation in society as custodian of the conscience of the nation. An issue raised with the churches is thus raised symbolically for all institutions and persons in society and, presumably, it is thus raised in the place of the most mature moral sensitivity, experience, and alertness. . . .

Theologically, reparations is a means of validating repentance. The citation from *The Book of Common Prayer*, rendered above, puts succinctly that which is generally the view in both of the great biblical faiths to which American white religion asserts connection. It is proper and appropriate for the Black Manifesto to be first of all heard in the white congregations and assemblies *just because* it is there where it has been taught that repentance requires "restitution and satisfaction, according to the uttermost of your powers, for all injuries and wrongs by you to any other."

. . . Whites in either church or synagogue might wish that there be no such thing as corporate guilt, but the insight of the Bible is emphatically contrary. The second chapter of Genesis is radical in its conception of corporate guilt. The doctrine of the Fall is that human beings are consequentially related to one another in all things throughout all of time, so that each person bears moral responsibility for that which befalls every other person. In the New Testament, one of the cosmic dimensions beheld in the drama of the Crucifixion is the corporate guilt of all humanity throughout the ages (and not the particular guilt of some hapless Pharisees or soldiers contemporaneous with the event). And St. Paul remains zealous to remind us that not one person is innocent of any of the commandments according to the authority of Israel's witness.

White religionists of all varieties on the present scene may clamor, if they wish, about their innocence in the centuries-old brutalization of American blacks, but let not one indulge the notion that there be warrant for such a wish in the Bible.

Reparations also offer an extraordinary opportunity to the white ecclesiastical establishment to be saved from the importunities of other institutions, especially the state. The last years have seen two developments that are ominous so far as the prospect for the churches retaining some freedom and integrity vis-à-vis the state is concerned. One is the accelerating depletion of the human constituency of the great denominations. This trend, occasioned by deaths, dropouts, and the refusal of the young to affiliate with institutional religion, coincides lamentably with burgeoning totalitarian tendencies in the state, both in the national government and in the governments of many localities, notably in the great urban jurisdictions. The transformation of the local police from civilian to military functions, the assault upon the independence of the courts, the increasing surveillance of citizens, the instigation of political prosecutions, the preparations for "preventive detention," the Pentagon's primary initiative in suppressing black protest and quashing other dissent — are but some few specific evidences of the emergent American totalitarianism. On such a scene the great, white ecclesiastical institutions are to be found with a dwindling and ineffectual constituency but at the same time with a staggering wealth fully capable of maintaining the ecclesiastical fabric even though the pews are depleted. Such churches, I suggest, become anxious about their role and influence in society and become utterly vulnerable to manipulation by other institutions and, most perilously at this moment, by the state. Analogically, the white ecclesiastical establishment in America is becoming as defenseless against the state as the Dutch Reformed Church is in South Africa or as pliable as most of the churches became in Nazi Germany. It is the wealth of the American white churches that is decisive (though not exclusive) in their vulnerability, and in this light the reparations Manifesto unwittingly, I suppose, affords these churches an opportunity (perchance a final one) to free themselves as institutions by divesting themselves of the burden of their wealth. . . .

In that process let it be remembered that the underlying issue is reconciliation and the categorical necessity of repentance in reconciliation. The chief obstacle now to an effectual reparations program is that white Christians and Jews loathe repentance: they are deceived into supposing they have nothing to repent of, or they are afraid they may repent too much.

There are none who have nothing to repent of, not even one. And it is just as impossible to repent too much as it is not possible to forgive too much.

An Exhortation to Integrity

WHAT disturbs me most about the public emergence of Christians who
are homosexuals is the exaggeration of the significance of sexuality and
sexual preference per se that these circumstances have occasioned in the
Episcopal Church and in the churches generally in America.

The matter of sexual proclivity and the prominence of the sexual
identity of a person are both highly overrated.

If this notoriety can be attributed to the enthusiasm of certain
homosexual zealots, it can also be blamed on those within the church
who seek scapegoats or need victims to persecute in order to tran-
quilize their anxieties and their skepticism concerning their own
justification.

This has placed us all in a situation in this convention where
there is danger of an overkill reaction, particularly as far as sexuality
and the priesthood is concerned.

I have already expressed myself in an article in *The Witness* (July
1979) on sexuality and the priesthood, and do not repeat those
observations here, save to reiterate that the issue is *not* homosexuality
but sexuality in any and all of its species and that, as much as I can
discern, sexuality is as extensive and diverse as human life itself. There
are as many varieties of sexuality as there be human beings.

An address to the National Convention of Integrity, St. Thomas Church,
Denver, September 7, 1979

I commend you to consider sexuality in the context of conversion — in the context of the event in which one becomes a new person in Christ.

In that event, whatever else must be said of it, all that a particular person is, sexuality along with all else, suffers the death in Christ that inaugurates the new (or renewed) life in Christ. One dies to self — every talent, every gift, every capability, every attribute, every limitation, every feature or facet of our personhood, every detail and item of our biography and inheritance suffers that death in Christ. It is a death of personality, intelligence, emotion; of the psychic and the physical, of what the Greeks called "body and soul" or "flesh and spirit." And it is a death to distortion, confusion, illness, idolatry, brokenness, ambiguity, corruption, dissipation as to all of these. It is so truly death, that on the day of the undertaker there is, for one who has already died in Christ, no surprise — nothing new concerning death to be confronted.

But that death in Christ in which we are restored for new life does not involve the denial or suppression or repression of anything that we are as persons. It involves instead the renewal of our persons in the integrity of our own creation in the Word of God.

Thus, behold St. Paul — about whose conversion we know more than any of our predecessors in the gospel (since he wrote of virtually nothing else!). Among other things, Paul was a most zealous man. He possessed the attribute and gift of zeal. He boasted, before his life in Christ, that he was the most zealous persecutor of the gospel; he boasted in his new life in Christ that he was the gospel's most zealous apologist. Both before and after, as it were, he is still Paul, the extraordinary zealous person. His zeal is not repressed or rejected in his conversion; it is renewed and accepted.

The new life in Christ means, for our minds and our bodies and for any of our abilities, that we have the exceptional freedom to be who we are and, thus, to welcome and affirm our sexuality as a gift, absolved from guilt or embarrassment or shame; to be liberated in our sexuality from self-indulgence or lust; to be free to love with wholeness as persons and to recognize and identify and embrace the same wholeness in others; to be freed to enjoy, to celebrate, to play, to have fun in our own creation in relationship to others and to the rest of creation.

Thus I am disturbed because the church treatment of homosexuality seems to be largely in a void — separated out from the broader context of human sexuality in its marvelous diversities. (In this, in truth, the church is retrogressive — far behind where society currently is.) More than that, the church treatment of homosexuality largely rests upon false stereotypes that, at once, demean or deny the individuality of sexuality and furnish pretext for a kind of vehement and hysterical defamation. The purpose, all the while, of such stereotyping and slander is evident: it is a way of covering up the sustained hypocrisy and pastoral default that has so far, for so long, characterized the situation of homosexual clergy especially in their relations with ecclesiastical authority.

If homosexuals are needed as victims and scapegoats for such purposes, the wider ecclesial and political implications of being consigned to such a fate must not be overlooked. This same device

- aborts conscientious ministry to others, to laypeople, and to those outside the church so far as sexuality is concerned;
- distracts from other issues that claim and deserve the attention of the church — like those signaled by the Episcopal Peace Fellowship or the vexing problems related to church investments and endowments;
- suppresses attention to other aspects of our humanity vulnerable to lust — about which the New Testament is often caustic — like gluttony, the dissipations of success, the idolatry of lucre;
- imposes a superficial conformity and quietism among clergy out of fear of exposure or, worse, of slanderous assault;
- is silent about the league of the church with fallen principalities and powers — including, notably, the worldly institutions of family and marriage, profoundly distorting the gospel's view of these powers.

Dear friends:

I have come here to make these few remarks by way of exhorting you:

- be urgent, but do not boast;
- resist hypocrites, eschew temptation;

- insist that everyone regard you as a person, accede to no stereotype;
- whenever homosexuality is mentioned, be certain sexuality is first considered;
- embrace your witness as an intercession for others; conduct yourself becomingly as a new person in Christ, and, most of all,
- love yourself, in that way you will be enabled to love others and honor the Word of God that loves you.

An Authority over Death

As I regard myself, I have never been especially religious, and, having been reared as an Episcopalian, the pietism of which I may be guilty has been ambiguous — a casual matter and an inconvenience more than a matter of consistency or fixed conviction. Still, as a younger person, particularly while an undergraduate, I had been precocious theologically, and instead of being attentive to whatever it was that students, in those days, may have been interested in, I concentrated much, in the privacy of my mind, on theology and upon what might be called theologizing.

I do not mean that I often studied or even read the works of theologians, because I did not do that, but I did begin then to read the Bible, in an unordered and spontaneous way, and I did begin, thus, to be caught up in a dialectic between an experience with the biblical witness and my everyday existence as a human being. I recall, in this, that there seemed to me to be a strong opposition between both the biblical story and my own life, on one side, and religion and religious moralism, on the other. After a while that opposition took on greater clarity, and I could discern that the former has to do with living humanly, while the latter has to do with dying in a moral sense and, indeed, with dying in *every* sense.

Suspect Tenderness, 1971, pp. 69–76. A sermon preached October 20, 1970, at Stringfellow's home church, St. John's Episcopal, Northampton, Massachusetts, in the aftermath of Dan Berrigan's capture on Block Island.

To anyone who knows this about me, it will come as no surprise to learn that in the immediate aftermath of the seizure by the federal authorities of Daniel Berrigan, at *Eschaton,* the home that Anthony Towne and I share on Block Island, I spent what time our suddenly hectic circumstances would afford with the New Testament. This was no exercise in solace; neither Anthony nor I had any regret or grief to be consoled, and we had each beheld the serenity of Dan as he was taken into the anxious custody of the FBI. The coolness of Berrigan had been a startling contrast to the evident shame and agitation of the agents, and we both understood that, whatever Dan was suffering in his transition from fugitive to captive, he had no need for pity or remorse, least of all from us.

To open, then, the Bible was an obvious, straightforward, natural thing to do. Berrigan had done something similar, publicly, when he preached to the Germantown congregation, relying upon texts from the Letter to the Hebrews. It is a wholly characteristic recourse for Christians, since, in the Bible, they find a holy history that is human history transfigured and since, in turn, they realize that human history is holy history and since, thus, they dwell in the continuity of the biblical word and the present moment.

Through the late spring and the summer, I had been engaged with the Babylon passages in the book of Revelation, and that effort had influenced my participation in the conversations that were taking place with Daniel and Anthony. With the abrupt interruption of our talk on August 11th, I put aside — though not out of ready reach — the Babylon texts to return to the Acts of the Apostles and to some of the letters that are thought to be chronologically proximate to Acts, specifically James and 1 Peter.

These testimonies, of course, deal with the issues of the apostolic church struggling to distinguish itself from the sects of Judaism, while at the same time confronting the political claims and challenges of the zealots, on the one hand, and the manifest blasphemy and idolatry of the civic religion of Rome, on the other. All these subjects are so familiar in contemporary American reference that it is a temptation to treat them fatalistically (pursuing trite queries, such as, *Is Nixon our Nero?*).

The immediate trauma of the aggression against our household, in which Dan had been taken, spared me from speculations of that sort, however, and I realized while reading Acts that more rudimentary and more fundamental problems had to be faced. I remembered vividly, moreover, how the same matters had plagued and confounded me, years earlier, for all my precocity, and how, in a sense, the situation of August 11th, 1970, had been long since foreshadowed. The episode of the arrest of Peter and John, as told in Acts, following upon the healing of the lame beggar at the temple gate, sums up the issues:

> And as they were speaking to the people, the priests and the captain of the temple and the Sadducees came upon them, annoyed because they were teaching the people and proclaiming in Jesus the resurrection from the dead. And they arrested them and put them in custody. . . . Acts 4:1–3*a*

I read this and read it and read it; the most difficult questions of my initiation in Bible study returned: *What does "the resurrection from the dead" mean if proclaiming it is cause for arrest? Why is healing a cripple so threatening and provocative to the public authorities? Why should this apparent good work count as a crime?*

This arrest of Peter and John, associated publicly with the healing of the lame man and the open preaching of the resurrection, portended a wider persecution of Christians and an official repression of the gospel, but it also relates back to the reasons for the condemnation and execution of Jesus, in which, it must not be overlooked, Jesus' own ministry of healing was interpreted by the incumbent authorities as if it were political agitation and was deemed by them to be a threat to their political authority. Where healing or, more broadly, where the witness to the resurrection is involved, the comprehension and response of Caesar and his surrogates to Christ as well as to the apostles is, significantly, consistent. Such a witness is judged as a crime against the state.

There is a sentimentalistic (and unbiblical) tradition of "Bible stories" in American Christendom that, when coupled with the thriving naivety of Americans toward their own nation, renders it difficult for many citizens, particularly churchfolk, to assimilate the fact that the Christian witness is treated as a criminal offense, even though this is so bluntly and repeatedly reported in New Testament texts. Within the American churchly ethos, biblical references to healing, however they may be interpreted medically, as metaphors or magic or miracles, are generally supposed to be highly private, individual, and personal happenings, having nothing categorically to do with politics. Meanwhile, when it comes to the resurrection as an event and the meaning of the resurrection as the gist of the gospel, the sentimentalization of Scripture has reached a quintessence of distortion, so that to regard the resurrection in a political context, as the New Testament does, seems a most radical incongruity: an unthinkable thought.

At the same time, the simplistic Constantinianism that informs American attitudes toward Christianity and the nation allows Americans to view Rome and the ancillary ecclesiastical-political establishment allowed in the empire at the time of the Crucifixion and during the apostolic era as an aberrant version of the state rather than as an archetypical symbol of all political institutions and authorities in any time or place. There are no doubt some serious distinctions to be kept between Rome and America or between the Nazi state and the United States or between Sweden and the USA or, for that matter, between revolutionary America and contemporary America, but such issues must not obscure the truth that every nation, every political regime, every civil power shares a singular characteristic that outweighs whatever may be said to distinguish one from another. And it is *that* common attribute of the state as such to which the New Testament points where the texts deal with the witness in Christ being condemned as criminal.

The sanction — though it takes different forms, it is, in principle, the *only* sanction — upon which the state relies is death. In the healing episodes, as in other works within the ministry in Christ, as in the proclamation of the resurrection from the dead, the authority of Christ over the moral power of death is verified as well as asserted. It is this claim of the gospel that the state beholds as threatening; it is the audacity to verify this claim in living — in thought and word and action — that the state condemns as crime. The preaching of the resurrection, far from being politically innocuous, and the healing incidents, instead of being merely private, are profound, even cosmic, political acts.

This is how, on August 11th, in the hours soon after Father Berrigan's capture and incarceration, I thought of Dan's ministry and the various ways in which he has exercised his vocation through the years that Anthony and I have known him: as prisoner, as guest, as fugitive, as convicted felon, as Catonsville defendant, as exile, as citizen in protest, as poet, as priest — as a man. Confronted with what I was reading in Acts, I marveled at the patience of Berrigan's witness; I sensed the humor of what he has said and done being construed, especially in the churches, as so radical. It seemed utterly obvious that Berrigan had taken his stand in the mainstream of the apostolic tradition and that his course had been not at all unusual but simply normative.

I do not imply that Berrigan is engaged in some self-conscious imitation of Peter of John or any other of the earlier Christians; I simply mean that to proclaim the resurrection in word and act is an affront that the state cannot tolerate because the resurrection exposes the subservience of the state to death as the moral purpose of the society that the state purports to rule. As has been intimated, the clarity or literalness with which the moral dependence upon death of the state can be discerned may vary much, from time to time and from place to place, but, nonetheless, the American circumstances today represent an instance in which death is pervasive, aggressive, and undisguised in its moral domination of the nation's existence. Theologically speaking, the war in Vietnam is not just an improvident, wicked, or stupid venture, but it epitomizes the militancy and insatiability of death as a moral power reigning in the nation — as that morality in relation to which everything and everyone is supposedly judged and justified. Thus to oppose the war becomes much more than a difference over policy. From the viewpoint of the state, protest against the war undermines the *only* moral purpose that the state has — the work of death — and risks the only punishment of which the state is capable: consignment to death or to some status that embodies the same meaning as death — though it be short of execution — like imprisonment, prosecution, persecution, loss of reputation or property or employment, intimidation to beget silence and conformity.

To those who may think this a grotesque doctrine of the state in America in the present day, I cite, amid a growing accumulation of other evidence, what happened in the case of the Catonsville Nine to the Berrigan brothers and their fellow defendants. Verbal protests against the war, and all it symbolizes, had been of little or no avail, and these citizens had dramatized the issue by destroying draft records with napalm, taking effective precautions against their action causing violence or any harm to human beings, since that would vitiate their witness against the violence of the state. Let it be conceded that the state could not overlook the incident (although, in fact, the state frequently does exactly that in circumstances where its dignity is as much embarrassed). One option for the state would have been to prosecute the defendants on nominal or minimal charges. There exists ample precedent for that and, if that had been done, the authority of the state would have been asserted in a way that recognized the political and, indeed, theatrical, character of the action — as distinguished from one implementing criminal intent — and, it can be argued, the state might then have succeeded in stopping similar protests by minimizing their notoriety. Instead, the state reacted to what the Catonsville Nine had done as if it were a crime of magnitude. Precedent was put aside, along with common sense, and legal process was usurped for a political objective, namely, the quashing of dissent. The manner in which the state undertook the prosecution of the Catonsville Nine betrays a purpose not only to punish the defendants harshly but also to admonish all citizens, emphatically, to be quiet, to behave, to acquiesce, for fear that otherwise they risk a similar retribution.

The intimidating message of the Catonsville prosecution, furthermore, does not stand out alone but is just one of very many other recent pathetic aggressions of the state against citizens, the most urgent of which the Black Panthers have suffered.

In the days that followed upon Dan's capture, many Block Island neighbors, many other friends, and many strangers have told Anthony and myself of their outrage and their apprehension — whatever they might think of what the Catonsville Nine did or of Father Berrigan's fugitive interlude — that the state seemed so anxious and overreactive and was in such hot pursuit of, as one person put it, "a harmless man." In this tentative, uneasy perception, I believe, a host of citizens, otherwise passive, grasp the desperate issue in what is taking place in America now: the power of death incarnate in the state violating, enslaving, perverting, imprisoning, destroying human life in society. To fail or refuse to act against this amounts to an abdication of one's humanness, a renunciation of the gift of one's own life, as well as a rejection of the lives of other human beings, a very ignominious idolatry of death. In the face of that the only way no matter how the state judges or what the state does — is to live in the authority over death that the resurrection is. A person cannot be human and be silent about that, as Acts attests:

> So they called them and charged them not to speak or teach at all in the name of Jesus. But Peter and John answered them, "Whether it is right in the sight of God to listen to you rather that to God, you must judge; for we cannot but speak of what we have seen and heard." Acts 4:18–20

Improvising Church

ONE of the ironies of our present situation is that everyone — those who are against us as much as those who are for us — assumes that we did something for Daniel Berrigan. We did, gladly, give our hospitality to him, of course, as we have on many other occasions. Still, in this visit, the more significant fact is that Dan did something for us.

Those who followed his interviews and articles and other messages during the months he remained at liberty as a fugitive know that Father Berrigan put increasing emphasis upon the necessity of extemporizing new modes of living as community in America even as the inherited social order — including the churchly institutions — is being exposed as antihuman and becomes manifestly desperate.

Berrigan's witness, though fixed upon Vietnam as the gruesome epitome of death, as a moral power, ruling the nation and literally demoralizing its citizens, transcends the war. While being hunted as if he were a criminal, Berrigan has been expounding, exemplifying, nurturing life: Berrigan has been showing us, and all of us, a more excellent way, as it has previously been named, in which life is constantly being emancipated from death, in which human beings are not awed or cowered by the state, in which there is a hope for a society worthy of human life.

"A Common Jeopardy: A Common Hope," *Suspect Tenderness,* 1971, pp. 112–13

We have no doubt that Dan perseveres in this same task from within the federal penitentiary at Danbury. Indeed, we intuit that his fugitive status during the past four months and his fate now as a captive, if not essential to such a ministry today in America, at the least is a seal of its authenticity and of its authority.

And of its appeal. Daniel Berrigan has not been engaged in a solitary or eccentric witness, but one with which *so* many other persons have identified — from the virtually anonymous ranks of those who have, like Dan and like his brother Philip, suffered prosecution and imprisonments for political reasons, to those who have been driven by conscience into exile from their birthright, to still more, like ourselves — that, in truth, an astonishing ecumenical community has been called into being. It is, we suppose, too much to expect official comprehension of this reality by the authorities of the state, or by others imbued with a conspiratorial mentality, or, for that matter, by any Pharisees, or by very many of the hierarchs. Nevertheless, there it is — Father Berrigan has been, and remains, in our midst improvising the church.

All of this is related, obviously, to the specific jeopardy that Berrigan has borne as a defendant, as a convicted felon, as a fugitive, and that he now bears, in solidarity with so many others, as a prisoner. Yet the jeopardy does not attach to him alone, as he knows, and he has not been and is not alone in bearing it. His particular jeopardy symbolizes and represents — it, practically speaking, sacramentalizes — a common jeopardy threatening all citizens who do not conform, who will not lapse into silence, who refuse to acquiesce to the totalitarianization of the nation, and who, thus, decline to resign as human beings.

"A community of resistance" it has been called. Father Berrigan baptized it "a community of risk." Some speak of it as an emergent "confessing movement," in that way invoking a previous experience of Christians and others in the days of the Nazi totalitarianism. We are ready to testify that there is, in America, now, a community of resurrection, sharing a common jeopardy — death — in order to live in a common hope as human beings.

Living Humanly in the
Midst of Death

ONE [of the matters that has particular pertinence to the present American malaise] is that the resistance, undertaken and sustained through the long years of the Nazi ascendancy in which most of Western Europe was conquered and occupied, consisted, day after day, of small efforts. Each one of these, if regarded in itself, seems far too weak, too temporary, too symbolic, too haphazard, too meek, too trivial to be efficacious against the oppressive, monolithic, pervasive presence that Nazism was, both physically and psychically, in the nations that had been defeated and seized. Realistically speaking, those who resisted Nazism did so in an atmosphere in which hope, in its ordinary connotations, had been annihilated. To calculate their actions — abetting escapes, circulating mimeographed news, hiding fugitives, obtaining money or needed documents, engaging in various forms of noncooperation with the occupying authorities or the quisling bureaucrats, wearing armbands, disrupting official communications — in terms of odds against the Nazi efficiency and power and violence and vindictiveness would seem to render their witness ridiculous. The risks for them of persecution, arrest, torture, confinement, death were so disproportionate to any concrete results that could practically be

---

An Ethic for Christians and Other Aliens in a Strange Land, 1973, pp. 118–22

344

expected that most human beings would have despaired — and, one recalls, most did. Yet these persons persevered in their audacious, extemporaneous, fragile, puny, foolish resistance.

Hindsight, of course, has romanticized the resistance to the Nazi occupations to a glorious episode. The testimonies I heard from some of those who survived are contrary; they were engaged in exceedingly hard and hapless and apparently hopeless tasks.

Why would human beings take such risks? It is not, I think, because they were heroes or because they besought martyrdom; they were, at the outset, like the apostles, quite ordinary men and women of various and usual stations and occupations in life. How is their tenacity explained? It is not just because of faith. Some were — all that I have known are — Christians, but many of their peers were not. Perhaps more tellingly, most professed Christians, as well as the established churches, did not resist Nazism in ways that truly endangered them. Most significantly, perchance, some only became Christians out of their involvement in the resistance. Why did these human beings have such uncommon hope?

The answer to such questions is, I believe, that the act of resistance to the power of death incarnate in Nazism was the only means of retaining sanity and conscience. In the circumstances of the Nazi tyranny, *resistance became the only human way to live.*

To exist, under Nazism, in silence, conformity, fear, acquiescence, obeisance, collaboration — to covet "safety" or "security" on the conditions prescribed by the state — caused moral insanity, meant suicide, was fatally dehumanizing, constituted a form of death. Resistance was the only stance worthy of a human being, as much in responsibility to oneself as to all other humans, as the famous commandment mentions. And if that posture involved grave and constant peril of persecution, imprisonment, or execution, at least one would have lived humanly while taking these risks. Not to resist, on the other hand, involved the certitude of death — of moral death, of the death to one's humanity, of death to sanity and conscience, of the death that possesses humans profoundly ungrateful for their own lives and for the lives of others. . . .

These same two insights — the integrity of resistance to the power of death as the only way to live humanly and, what is really a particular version of the same truth, the relevance and resilience of the biblical style of life — I have since encountered elsewhere: upon visits to Eastern Europe during the so-called cold war and the most ruthless phase of the Soviet oppression there; in the Harlem ghetto as the American black revolt matured; in profound illness; in the actions of such friends and fellow Christians as Daniel and Philip Berrigan.

One wishes, in this connection, to mention affirmatively the American churches. But, alas, that is inhibited because the inherited churches in this society have not been bastions of resistance to demonic power, as embodied in churchly and ecclesiastical forms, in the state, or in other American principalities. Indeed, the churchly denominations and sects have notoriously been among the most benighted institutions in America, remarkably undiscerning so far as the reality of the demonic in history is concerned. And, in the apparent hierarchy of principalities, the American churches have more often than not been among the most menial, manipulated, and degraded vassals of the power of death.

There are multiple reasons for this, some of which have previously been mentioned, notably among them the pagan origins of so many of the churches and sects in this culture. It is no great surprise, then, that so many churches on the contemporary scene are not communities in which the Bible has been esteemed or in which the biblical life-style has been much practiced or in which the Jerusalem vocation is deeply comprehended and loved. Still, if when looking at the churches the marks of Jerusalem are not readily beheld, that does not imply the departure of the Holy Spirit from America or the indifference of God to the militancy of death in the nation or the absence of the biblical witness amid the American babel and chaos. It means only that human beings must be open to the marks of Jerusalem where they appear — if only, as it were, momentarily — wherever that may be; that one is called to be truly discerning of the Holy Spirit and of all spirits and to be courageous in naming the same. It means further that a Christian freely affirms the biblical life and acknowledges *that* as the church however, wherever, or whenever that happens and regardless of whether the event of the church occurs in distance from traditional churchly existence.

Among the conventional ecclesiastical principalities, there are, mercifully, as have been cited earlier, occasional congregations and paracongregations, and there are laity and clergy and some few ecclesiastics, that stand — together with more ad hoc communities and happenings and people — within the continuity of the biblical witness. Taken together, I believe, these constitute an emergent confessing movement in the United States: spontaneous, episodic, radically ecumenical, irregular in polity, zealous in living, extemporaneous in action, new and renewed, conscientious, meek, poor. It is to these phenomena, far more profound and much more widespread than is commonly recognized, that a person must look to sight the exemplary church of Jesus Christ acting as harbinger of the holy nation. It is in this confessing movement that the Jerusalem parable is verified, now, in America, right in the midst of the ruin of Babylon's churches and miscellaneous death shrines.

Homily on the Defeat
of the Saints

Bless those who persecute you; bless and do not curse them.

ROMANS 12:14

Also (the beast) was allowed to make war on the saints and to conquer them.

REVELATION 13:7

A most obstinate misconception associated with the gospel of Jesus Christ is that the gospel is welcome in this world. The conviction — endemic among churchfolk — persists that, if problems of misapprehension and misrepresentation are overcome and the gospel can be heard in its own integrity, the gospel will be found attractive by people, become popular, and, even, be a success of some sort.

This idea is both curious and ironical because it is bluntly contradicted in Scripture and in the experience of the continuing biblical witness in history from the event of Pentecost unto the present moment. There is no necessity to cite King Herod or Judas Iscariot

Conscience and Obedience, 1977, pp. 109–12

or any notorious enemies of the gospel in this connection; after all, while Christ was with them, no one in his family and not a single one of the disciples accepted him, believed his vocation, or loved his gospel.

After Pentecost, where the Acts of the Apostles evinces an understanding and the confession of the gospel, resistance and strife concerning the gospel are equally in evidence among the pioneer Christians, while the consternation and hostility of the world for the gospel was very agitated and quickly aggressive. Furthermore, the letters of the New Testament betell congregations nurtured in the faith amid relentless temptations of apostasy and confusion and conformity.

Subsequent events in the life of the church, especially since the inception of Christendom in the Constantinian Arrangement, and with the institutional sophistication of the churches, only modify this situation by complicating it.

There is, simply, no reason to presuppose that *anyone* will find the gospel, as such, likable.

The categories of popularity or progress or effectiveness or success are impertinent to the gospel. That has been implicit, here, in the effort throughout this book to deal simultaneously (rather than separately) and confessionally (instead of academically) with the passages about political authority in Romans and Revelation. The matter is signified forcefully in the introit to Romans 13 by the text, "Bless those who persecute you, bless and do not curse them" (Rom. 12:14). As has been mentioned, this is no adage prompted by sentimentality. It is a statement of the extraordinary relationship between Christians and the ruling principalities radically constituted in the discernment of the imminence of the judgment of the Word of God in history by which Christians are authorized to recall political authority to the vocation of worship and reclaim dominion over creation for humanity. It is a statement about the implication of the lordship of Jesus Christ for the rulers of this age. To bless the powers that be, in the midst of persecution, exposes and confounds their blasphemous status more cogently and more fearlessly than a curse.

In the book of Revelation, the issue is expressed more severely and more straightforwardly than perhaps anywhere in the Bible. "Also [the beast] was allowed to make war on the saints and to conquer them" (Rev. 13:7). On the face of it, this is not an appealing or popular text. That may in itself be an explanation of why it has been so often ignored or even suppressed by commentators or why it has seldom been mentioned, much less commended, by preachers. I have read it, it seems, a thousand times, and I admit that I am tempted to wish it were not there or to locate some pretext to dismiss it or gainsay it. I find no way to rationalize the verse away. Unlike some other passages in Revelation, it does not afford evasion or oversight because it is esoteric or enigmatic. It is a most unambiguous and matter-of-fact statement. It says what it says: during the present age, the Word of God allows predacious ruling authority to wage war on the Christians and to defeat them.

For the time being, in the era of the Fall, until the consummation of this history in the judgment of the Word of God, the beast knows success and indulges victory; the saints suffer aggression and know defeat. Surely the text mocks every effort, undertaken in the name of the Christian witness in this world, that is informed by calculations about effectiveness, progress, approval, acclaim — or any of the varieties of success. And that not only in circumstances where the church openly imitates or emulates the way of the beast but also where the calculation prior to action or program is more guileful or pretentious and claims foreknowledge of how the matter will be judged by the Word of God. The churches and, within them, both social activist and private pietists, are virtually incorrigible — despite the admonition of Revelation 13:7 — in practicing some such deliberation before risking any putative witness. Where that be the situation, the professed saints succumb to the power of death by their profound doubt in the efficacy of the resurrection and by their direct dispute of the activity of judgment in the Word of God. So they — attempting vainly to forestall or obviate defeat — are defeated anyway, ignominiously.

Revelation 13:7 contains no melancholy message. It authorizes hope for the saints — and, through their vocation of advocacy, hope for the whole of creation — which is grounded in realistic expectations concerning this present age, enabling the church — as the first beneficiary of the resurrection — to confront the full and awesome militancy of the power of death incarnate in the ruling principalities, and otherwise, in this world, nourishing patience for the judgment of the Word of God and, meanwhile, trusting nothing else at all. This seemingly troublesome text about the defeat of the saints by the beast is, preeminently, a reference to the accessibility of the grace of the Word of God for living now. To mention the defeat of the saints means to know the abundance of grace. And that prompts no rejection of or withdrawal from the world as it is but, on the contrary, the most fearless and resilient involvement in this world.

Since the rubrics of success or power or similar gain are impertinent to the gospel, the witness of the saints looks foolish where it is most exemplary. One American political prisoner — Philip Berrigan — addressed that characterization of the defeat of the saints when he was sentenced upon conviction for attempting to dig a grave on the lawn of the White House in rebuke of the rule of the beast:

> In pondering a few words for this occasion, I happened on Paul's First Letter to the Church at Corinth. . . . "We are fools on Christ's account" (1 Cor. 4:10). In a modest fashion, I have sought membership in this company of fools. . . . Through over 39 months in prison, through long fasts and bouts of solitary confinement, through two indictments while in jail, I have been reckoned a fool, by pharaohs and friends alike. . . .
>
> Let no one find our foolishness puzzling. It is as simple as honoring the 5th commandment, and rejecting official legitimations of murder. It is obedience to the truth and compassion of Christ; or recognizing no enemy in the world. . . . It is as simple as respecting the planet as common property, as common gift and heritage. That is the idiot vision — that is the summons and task. For that, as Paul promised, one risks becoming the world's refuse, the scum of all (1 Cor. 4:13). . . . [T]he fools will never abandon hope, nor cease to live it.

This foolishness of the saints, this witness in the midst of defeat, is wrought in the relationship of justification and judgment, in which one who knows justification to be a gift of the Word of God is spared no aggression of the power of death but concedes no tribute to the power of death while awaiting the vindication of the Word of God in the coming of Jesus Christ in judgment.

The Circus

IT IS only since putting aside childish things that it has come to my mind so forcefully — and so gladly — that the circus is among the few coherent images of the eschatological realm to which people still have ready access and that the circus thereby affords some elementary insights into the idea of society as a consummate event.

This principality, this art, this veritable liturgy, this common enterprise of multifarious creatures called the circus, enacts a hope, in an immediate and historic sense, and simultaneously embodies an ecumenical foresight of radical and wondrous splendor, encompassing, as it does both empirically and symbolically, the scope and diversity of creation.

I suppose some — ecclesiastics or academics or technocrats or magistrates or potentates — may deem the association of the circus and the Kingdom scandalous or facetious or bizarre and scoff quickly at the thought that the circus is relevant to the ethics of society. Meanwhile, some of the friends of the circus may consider it curious that during intervals when Anthony and I have been their guests and, on occasion, confidants, that I have had theological second thoughts about them and about what the corporate existence of the circus tells and anticipates in an ultimate sense. To either I only respond that the connection seems to me to be at once suggested when one recalls that biblical people, like

Simplicity of Faith, 1982, pp. 87–91

circus folk, live typically as sojourners, interrupting time, with few possessions, and in tents, in this world. The church would likely be more faithful if the church were similarly nomadic.

In America, during the earliest part of this century, the circus enjoyed a "golden age." It was the era of P. T. Barnum, Adam Fourpaugh, and the Ringling Brothers, to name but a few of the showmen who assembled extraordinary aggregations of performers, animals, and oddities. It was then that the circus was most lucidly an image of the Kingdom in its magnitude, versatility, and logistics. There were, for example, few permanent zoological collections in those days, and the circus menagerie was the opportunity for people to see rare birds and reptiles, exotic animals and mammals, wild beasts and other marvelous creatures. Indeed, when the Ringling Brothers advertised their "mammoth millionaire menagerie" as the "greatest gathering since the deluge" it was not a much exaggerated boast. It was similar with the "sideshows" or "museums" traditionally associated with the American circus. A separate feature from the main circus performance, the sideshow originated with Barnum. It assembled and exhibited human "oddities" and "curiosities" — giants, midgets, and the exceptionally obese; Siamese twins, albinos, and bearded ladies; those who had rendered themselves unusual like fire eaters, sword swallowers, or tattooed people. If the sideshow seems macabre because "freaks" were sometimes exploited, it must also be mentioned that in those days little medical help and few other means of livelihood were available to such persons and that the premise of these exhibits was educational. In any case, so long as they continued they symbolized the circus as an eschatological company in which all sorts and conditions of life are congregated.

It is in the performance that the circus is most obviously a parable of the eschaton. It is there that human beings confront the beasts of the earth and reclaim their lost dominion over other creatures. The symbol is magnified, of course, when one recollects that, biblically, the beasts generally designate the principalities: the nations, dominions, thrones, authorities, institutions, and regimes (see Dan. 6).

There, too, in the circus, humans are represented as freed from consignment to death. There one person walks a wire fifty feet above the ground, another stands upside down on a forefinger, another juggles a dozen incongruous objects simultaneously, another hangs in the air by the heels, one upholds twelve in a human pyramid, another is shot from a cannon. The circus performer is the image of the eschatological person — emancipated from frailty and inhibition, exhilarant, militant, transcendent over death — neither confined nor conformed by the fear of death any more.

The eschatological parable is, at the same time, a parody of conventional society in the world as it is. In a multitude of ways in circus life the risk of death is bluntly confronted and the power of death exposed and, as the ringmaster heralds, defied. Clyde Beatty, at the height of his career, actually had *forty* tigers and lions performing in one arena. The Wallendas, not content to walk the high wire one by one, have crossed it in a pyramid of seven people. John O'Brien managed sixty-one horses in the same ring, in what a press agent called "one bewildering act." Mlle. La Belle Roche accomplished a double somersault at great speed and height in an automobile at the time when autos were still novelties.

Moreover, the circus performance happens in the midst of a fierce and constant struggle of the people of the circus, especially the roustabouts, against the hazards of storm, fire, accident, or other disaster, and it emphasizes the theological mystique of the circus as a community in which calamity seems to be always impending. After all, the Apocalypse coincides with the Eschaton.

Meanwhile, the clown makes the parody more poignant and pointed in costume and pantomime; commenting, by presence and performance, on the absurdities inherent in what ordinary people take so seriously — themselves, their profits and losses, their successes and failures, their adjustments and compromises — their conformity to the world.

So the circus, in its open ridicule of death in these and other ways — unwittingly, I suppose — shows the rest of us that the only enemy in life is death and that this enemy confronts everyone, whatever the circumstances, all the time. If people of other arts and occupations do not discern that, they are, as St. Paul said, idiots (cf. Rom. 1:20–25; Eph. 4:17–18). The service the circus does — more so, I regret to say, than the churches do — is to portray openly, dramatically, and humanly that death in the midst of life. The circus is eschatological parable and social parody: it signals a transcendence of the power of death, which exposes this world as it truly is while it pioneers the Kingdom.

FRIENDSHIP

Lou Marsh

HOW then, in this time and in this crisis, is such reconciliation wrought? What signs are to be seen of the cruciform nature of reconciliation?

At the center of the drama of the Crucifixion of Christ is God, bearing the burden of the hostility of both Israel and Rome — in fact, of all human beings and nations. That hostility is dissipated and absolved by God's own assumption of the estrangement between God and humanity. The church, called to be the Body of Christ in this world, and the people of the church, called to be the members of his Body in this world, share in that self-same ministry and service in the world.

The central witness of the church in the racial crisis is to bear the rejection of white people by Negroes, provoked by three centuries of exclusion and exploitation of Negroes by whites, and to bear this terrible, compounding hostility between the races without protest or complaint, without concern for innocence or guilt (that is for God's judgment and forgiveness to reveal), in other words, in the love of Christ for the whole world.

One witness of God's power in reconciling human beings is known now in the death of Lou Marsh.

Lou Marsh died in New York City at ten minutes after nine on the evening of January 9th, 1963.

"The Way to Live," *My People Is the Enemy,* 1964 ed., pp. 142–47

At first his death was not much noticed, although it would have been, had not the metropolitan newspapers been struck at the time. Not that Marsh was famous in a way the world would necessarily remember him, but his death was one of the more shocking homicides in memory, even in New York City. If there had been newspapers, at least the tabloids, in their own way, would have celebrated Lou's death.

Lou worked for the New York City Youth Board, assigned to one of East Harlem's juvenile gangs — the self-styled Untouchables. I remember suggesting that he apply for such a job and later writing to the Youth Board authorities to recommend him for it. When he decided to take the job, he called to tell me of what he hoped to accomplish.

Lou was beaten to death by four guys. He had somehow persuaded the gang — the Untouchables — not to go ahead with a rumble to which they had committed themselves against the Playboys, another gang in the neighborhood. Some of the older boys — alumni, so to speak, of one of the gangs in question — wanted the issue between the two gangs to be settled in the traditional way, according to the canons of gang society, by a rumble. They resented the fact that Lou mediated the dispute or at least accomplished an armistice. Evidently they were humiliated that the younger boys in the gangs followed Lou's counsel rather than their own. So they ambushed Lou and beat him savagely. He lived for two days in the hospital, unconscious. Then he died. One doctor told me that the damage to his brain was so severe and gruesome that if, by some chance, he had survived, he would probably not have been able to function in any ordinary way as a human being. He most likely would have been grotesquely invalided, living on as a vegetable.

Lou died, it seems, an awful death, but a death that was apparently somehow better for him and for those who loved him than mere survival would have been.

Among those who knew of Lou's death, but did not know Lou, there were easy, stereotyped reactions. Mayor Wagner observed that this was the first time in fifteen years that a Youth Board worker had been slain in the line of duty and said that he was outraged. I am afraid that Lou would have been more amused than anything else at the mayor's vague promises to do something about the situation. In his own way, Lou was often quite cynical, but he certainly believed that the mayor was far more so.

And, of course, there were cries for violence to answer the violence of Lou's death. One neighborhood newspaper carried the news of the killing and then editorialized that what was needed was more police, perhaps some extra squads specially trained in guerrilla warfare, to rout and destroy the gangs.

No one realized better than Lou how shrilly inadequate such responses were. He knew that the violence of gang society erupts from the deep frustration of kids who have gone through their whole conscious lives without homes, without fathers, without love, without much of anything. They could hardly have told themselves how much they had suffered, for they had endured by themselves, outside society, without the care of another human being except for the other guys in their gang. And except for Lou, or someone like him, who happened to come along once in a while.

Lou, who had been involved earlier in some of the sit-ins, knew that violence cannot absolve violence, and he knew that the peril to everyone — not just to the gangs — of the police becoming an occupation army in the slum neighborhoods is greater than the danger to him or others in gang warfare.

Besides, Lou knew what it means not to be loved by anybody and what it means not to be loved by everybody.

Lou was a Negro.

He was from a fairly poor family living in the North. He had to save on sleep and work incredibly hard — usually in menial jobs — but because he was intelligent and sensitive, he managed to get a very good education. When I first met him, about five years ago, he was a seminarian at Yale, one of the handful of Negroes who have made it that far. But he grew restless with his studies at Yale; perhaps he felt somehow guilty about being in such a place as Yale Divinity School at all, while his folks were still where they were and while his people were still where they were in this country. For a time, after he left seminary, Lou, in a terrible way, hated the fact that he was a Negro. It was more than feeling sorry for himself; it was as if he complained about his own creation, as if he was rejecting his own birth.

It seemed to him, for a while, better not to live than to be a Negro in America.

After leaving New Haven, he moved to New York City. To act

out his resentment, he virtually disassociated himself from bourgeois white society, drifting about the city, unable to look for a job, living on borrowed money, and, it seemed, borrowed time, staying sometimes in flophouses or on the streets.

As he would say himself, he went through the whole bit.

But then, at last, he understood that all this was some variety of pride, that he was indulging in his own self, accusing and condemning himself, punishing and rejecting himself especially for being a Negro; expecting and even, in a way, wanting to be confirmed in this by the rejection of others. Then he realized that he was engaged in suicide.

That was the moment — when Lou was in hell — in which he knew, I think for the first time, that he was loved by God. That was the event in which, by the power of God in the face of the fullness of death, Lou was emancipated — set free to love himself, to love others, and to welcome and receive the love of others. That was the time of Lou's salvation, the time of his reconciliation with himself and with the rest of the world.

What followed was more or less predictable. Having been so intimate with the presence of death in his own life, but having beheld the reality and vitality of the resurrection in his own life in the same event, Lou was free to live for others.

So that is what he did.

He took this job with the Youth Board and soon was so preoccupied in caring for the kids in his gang that he forgot himself, so fulfilled in his love for others that he lost his self-interest, so confident that he was now secure in God's Word that he was not afraid of death.

He was no longer afraid to die the way he died. He knew about the real risks of his job, especially the way *he* was now free to do his job. The way he died was surely no surprise to Lou. Not that he sought such a death, or any sort of death, any longer, but he was ready to die and was without fear of death. He no longer was in bondage to the alienation of human beings from each other. He was no longer a pathetic, partisan, professional Negro; he had become a full human being. Nor was he any longer an imitation white person, a Negro received nominally into white society, as at Yale Lou had been, but never welcomed as himself; he had become a person. Lou himself had been reconciled, and so his own existence and life could be, for the first time, not just a symbol of grievance and protest — as valid and needed in American society as they may be — but more than that, a ministry of reconciliation. He had become so free that he could give away his own life freely — and surely that is the secret of reconciliation in Christ.

Lou Marsh, when he died, was ready; that is, he had already died in Christ and so was without fear of death. That is the freedom the resurrection bestows upon human beings.

That is the only way to die, which at the same time means that this is the only way to live.

Jacques Ellul

IT IS difficult for me to comment upon the work of Jacques Ellul and its significance for Americans because of a sense I have that any remarks of mine about Ellul will be superfluous, if not self-serving.

Ellul and I have been friends for about twenty years and during that time have had a dialogue, mainly through our correspondence. We enjoy an affinity and have found much in common. In the church, we are both laymen, if somewhat disaffected from the ecclesiastical establishment. Professionally, we are both lawyers, though often uneasy about such an identification. Politically, we are both committed to representative and participatory government, consider political issues without heavy ideological passion or any similar encumbrance, and we both have some direct practical experience in public office or roughly comparable status — Ellul, formerly, as Deputy Mayor of Bordeaux; myself, lately, as Second Warden of Block Island.

Analytically, our views are quite similar, though variously influenced by our differences of nationality and citizenship, on basic social issues like war, consumption, race, technology. We are both nonacademic theologians, and in our respective books in the realm of theological ethics there appears a very strong topical parallelism — e.g., skepticism toward natural law, the importance of the dispossessed and the oppressed, a concern for understanding the principalities and

---

"Kindred Mind and Brother," *Sojourners,* June 1977, p. 12

powers, attempts to elucidate the political reality of the demonic, an effort to comprehend the relationship of the apocalyptic to the eschatological, and the impact upon ethics of that relationship. I attribute this correlation in our writing to the prompting of the Holy Spirit, though some may think it mere coincidence, since Ellul and I have never had prior consultations about what each has been thinking and publishing.

Yet if I thus recognize Ellul as a kindred mind, and more than that, as a brother in Christ, that does not hinder me from appreciating and affirming the contribution of Ellul to Americans who profess or seek a biblical life-style and witness. That is, of course, to be found in Ellul's exemplary use of the Bible. Ellul beholds the biblical testament in a way that confesses the viability and vitality of the Word of God in common history and not only "once upon a time" but here and now. Ellul has entered into a confessional relationship with the Word of God in his study of the Bible that illuminates the characteristic and historic activity of the Word of God in our contemporary setting. Ellul represents the recovery of the most elementary attribute of biblical faith: the discernment of the life of the Word of God in common history, at once verified in the Bible as such and in each and every event subsequent to the biblical era.

In that discernment all things are transfigured. That is why, as it seems to me, Ellul's words are so threatening and so appealing.

Daniel Berrigan

So shall we all at last attain to the unity inherent in our faith and our knowledge of the Son of God — to mature manhood, measured by nothing less than the full stature of Christ. We are no longer to be children, tossed by the waves and whirled about by every fresh gust of teaching, dupes of crafty rogues and their deceitful schemes. No, let us speak the truth in love; so shall we fully grow up into Christ.

EPHESIANS 4:13–15

This passionate one, this meek poet, this exemplary human being, this priest of Christ now gives us a wise, lucid, compelling, and edifying testament affirming the sacramental integrity of human life in this world.

It goes without saying that this is *not* a religious book, though, I suspect, it is likely to be cataloged as such. If the librarians and book editors classify it in that way, it will be a grotesque mistake. Few, if any, religious books are about Jesus Christ since few religious books are about what it means to be a mature human being in this world. I can recollect no religious book that is concerned, truthfully, with that style of life in Christ in this world that authorizes and constitutes

---

Introduction to Daniel Berrigan, *They Call Us Dead Men*, 1968, pp. xi–xii

the most profoundly human life. If this is considered a religious book, that will be misfortune, because those who might be emancipated by it and many who would simply rejoice in it will not find it.

The book is not religious in the conventional sense of that term: it does not expound dogma; it does not resort to jargon; it upholds no ritualistic vanities; it is not argumentative about religious ideas; it advocates no pietism of any sort; it does not cater to the lust for indulgences; it does not assault the conscience, nor does it insult intelligence.

The book is about life, not religion. It is about life in its mundane aspects, here and now, in common history — art and work and leisure and technology and marriage and the traumas of social conflict. It is not about religion that, as St. Paul so often admonished Christian people, always ends in idolatry, superstition, hallucination, or some similar discursion from life in this world.

This is a book about the sacramental integrity of human existence. It discerns that the drama of all time — which is the saga of death and resurrection, not, as the religious suppose, a conflict of evil and good — is impregnant in every and each event in this history: the trivial and the momentous, in the present day as much as long ago, for all human beings, not merely for an exclusive few, and, indeed, for all principalities and powers as well.

To become and be a mature human being, to be alive, in the midst of such a drama in which all people (whether they realize it or not) do in truth live, describes a radical participation. To be alive means, as Father Berrigan puts it, enduring "the crisis of grace." The fruit of the gift of Christ to this world is an unequivocal and utterly vulnerable immersion in the world as it is. It means an involvement innocent of either guile or prudence. It means confronting the withering, ingenious, redundant, bewildering, and apparently inexhaustible assaults of death upon one's very being and upon the existence of everyone and everything else. It means living in such a way that life is welcomed as the extraordinary gift that life is and, then, honoring that gift by extravagance: by giving one's own life away. It means that sanctification — a life that is holy (that is, whole and fulfilled, not good or pure) — is the life expended in freedom from anxiety of death. Or, as St. Paul once more reminds, it means living in this world by dying in Christ in this world.

It means that by the virtue of Christ the mature person in this world is a surrogate of all humankind.

Precisely this triumph of mature humanity in Jesus Christ gives veracity to the gospel.

Father Berrigan now gives us a book that is a eucharist for that gospel.

Saint Matthew's Day, 1965
New York City

Bengt Nordberg

BENGT Nordberg is to blame for this book. It was he, in the months of convalescence on Block Island, after the hospital, who became a persistent and persuasive advocate for those concerns that eventually outbalanced my qualms.

Bengt is the proprietor of a restaurant on Block Island called Smuggler's Cove, a name derived from the uses to which the premises were put during Prohibition. The Cove is a favorite and justly famous place among the summer people from New York and New England who come to the island, but Bengt is no seasonal person and there is hospitality at Smuggler's for island inhabitants through the winter. Bengt is not an indigenous islander, but he is the next to that, having married a direct descendant of one of the settling families; he is a native of Sweden, spent his youth at sea, and moved years ago to Block Island because it is the place in which, as he says, he wants to die. He is a man of imposing physique, of wit worthy of a seaman, and of terrific intellectual vitality; he is expansive, gentle, generous to a fault; he is familiar with all the island lore and a fierce partisan of the island style of life.

Bengt is an inspired raconteur and we would often dine with him and talk long into the nights. The conversations were versatile and far-ranging, though in my recollection they had a theological coherence relating quite diverse topics like politics and food and Block Island history and urban existence and corruption of the churches and racial conflict and inflation and medical ethics and poetry and Sweden and war and work and weather. I take for granted that readers of mine realize that theology is dissimilar from both philosophy and religion: theology is not speculative, on the one hand; theology is not self-justifying, on the other; and theology is not so eminent as to be aloof from life as it is, as are those two exercises. Theology is concerned with the implication of the Word of God in the world's common life. In this context, it must be recognized and affirmed that every person, *if* he or she reflects upon the event of his or her own life in this world, is a theologian. It is only in this sense that I tolerate being sometimes called a theologian myself, though I am aware that I am frequently referred to as a "lay theologian" in an accusatory tone by ecclesiastics and by academic theologians who mean it as a put down and as a way of disavowing my public views. Anyway, Bengt is a theologian in the sense mentioned — though it may surprise him to learn that — and because his reflections are not casual but really rather rigorous, I believe he is a good theologian.

Thus it was that months and months later — after that strenuous and somber winter, after the trip to Roosevelt Hospital, after the failure of every therapy, after surgery, after returning to Block Island, in the midst of recuperation — when Bengt talked of writing about the whole experience, he spoke with an authority, which I could not ignore and which my various qualms did not dismiss.

Karl Barth

BECAUSE of his pointed remarks to me during the public dialogue with Karl Barth, at the University of Chicago, during Barth's American visit in 1962, and his generous reference in *Evangelical Theology,**
I know that many suppose that most of the theological books I have read are books of Karl Barth. The truth is only three are, although, as one might expect, I entertain an intention eventually to read all of Barth. (Also, all of Augustine, all of Luther, all of Bonhoeffer — I am not so sure I will read any more than I have of Aquinas, Calvin, and Tillich.) I am, hence, usually amused when I hear myself being accused (it always sounds like an accusation) of being a "Barthian."

More seriously, I raised with Karl Barth during his visit the matter that is basic here. Again and again in both the public dialogue and in our private conversations, it had been my experience that as Barth began to make some point, I would at once know what he was going to say. It was not some intuitive thing, it differed from that, it was a recognition, in my mind, of something familiar that Barth was

---

* "I was with . . . the conscientious and thoughtful New York attorney William Stringfellow who caught my attention more than any other person." Karl Barth, *Evangelical Theology* (Grand Rapids: Eerdmans Publishing Company, 1963), pp. vii–ix.

---

articulating. When this had happened a great many times while I listened to him, I described my experience to him and asked why this would happen. His response was instantaneous: "How could it be otherwise? We read the same Bible, don't we?"

Jim Pike

But we have this treasure in earthen vessels, to show that the transcendent power belongs to God and not to us. We are afflicted in every way, but not crushed; perplexed, but not driven to despair; persecuted, but not forsaken; struck down, but not destroyed; always carrying in the body the death of Jesus, . . . so that the life of Jesus may be manifested in our mortal flesh. So death is at work in us, but life in you.

2 CORINTHIANS 4:7–12

Three days before James Pike was found dead in Judea, the vicar of St. Clement's told me that this congregation desired that the service this morning be a thanksgiving for the life and for the witness of Bishop Pike. The intention, he said, was that this Eucharist happen whatever the outcome of the search in the desert: whether by this morning Pike remained missing or if discovered he be dead or living.

The subsequent events make this a requiem: Jim Pike is buried in the ground and we pray for his repose. Yet the original intent for

---

"*Expectans expectavi:* A Homily Commending James A. Pike," St. Clement's Church, New York City, September 14, 1969, from Stringfellow and Towne, *The Death and Life of Bishop Pike,* pp. 427–35

this service was different from a dirge, and that intent — which is the only thing that persuaded me to participate — remains sound. Whatever the particulars of his fate, there is good reason in the church today, as there was ten years ago and as there was a year ago and, for that matter, as there will be ten years from now, to pause in gratitude to God for Bishop Pike.

Events make this a requiem, but it is not merely a requiem; if my homily, on the fortieth psalm, is also a eulogy, it is incidentally so.

> I waited patiently for the Lord, and he inclined unto me, and heard my calling,
>
> He brought me also out of the horrible pit, out of the mire and clay, and set my feet upon the rock, and ordered my going.
>
> And he hath put a new song in my mouth, even a thanksgiving unto our God.
>
> Many shall see it, and fear, and shall put their trust in the Lord. (Ps. 40:1–4, *Book of Common Prayer*)

None of us here can overlook the fact of Bishop Pike's death or the way he died or where he died.

We can say nothing of his private death, save to affirm God's mercy, though there are many who knew him or who knew of him who have spent a week titillating themselves with gruesome guesses and cruel speculation about that.

Yet beyond his solitary crisis, there has been the public death of Bishop Pike, which the whole world, more or less, has beheld and by which, it cannot be gainsaid, many have been fearfully edified. Discontent with the fables and fairy tales about Jesus that churchly tradition has hallowed, and unsatisfied, if nonetheless respectful, about mere scholarship, Pike wanted to know the truth about Jesus — or, at the least, he had to have all of the truth that *he* could know of Jesus. He had, in the last years, become excited by glimpses of the splendid humanity of Jesus, and he had to see more. How unusual — how threatening to some of his peers; how efficacious for other folk — to have a bishop with such a passion for Jesus that he forsook ecclesiology!

That passion would require return to the historic sources of the gospel. So Pike would go, again and again, to the habitat of Jesus, to the places where Jesus prayed and preached and healed and walked and even to where he had been tempted by the power of death in the wilderness. Most of us stay satisfied with Sunday school hearsay about Jesus and, thus, we fancy that his forty days in the desert were an ascetic exercise — contemplation, uplift, fasting, perhaps a turn at yoga. The biblical version is contrary. The wilderness episode for Jesus means suffering transcendently the versatility of death's aggression against human life. Perhaps it is this reality of the wilderness experience that explains why the biblical accounts speak of Jesus being "directed" or "driven by the Spirit" or "led" into the desert. Sooner or later, for everyone, there is a confrontation with death in desolate circumstances. We have recently heard that this very thing has happened to James A. Pike in a remarkable way. It is the ministry of Jesus — "driven by the Spirit," as the book says — to be there, in the wilderness, before anyone enters it.

That Bishop Pike's wilderness experience should be so literal is not, I think, to be taken as a macabre coincidence but with matter-of-factness. Although *Time* magazine regarded Pike as impetuous and erratic, in truth the man was possessed by an extraordinary patience. All of his life and then, for some time, as he died in the desert, Pike was waiting patiently for the Lord.

> Blessed is the one that hath set his hope in the Lord, and turned not unto the proud, and to such as go about with lies.
>
> O Lord my God, great are the wondrous works which thou hast done, like as be also thy thoughts, which are to us-ward; and yet there is no one that ordereth them unto thee.
>
> If I should declare them, and speak of them, they should be more than I am able to express. (Ps. 40:5–7, *Book of Common Prayer*)

The conflict between the churches and Jim Pike, since the period of his collegiate agnosticism, was elemental and redundant. The issue was not heresy on the part of Pike but blasphemy on the part of the church as such. It was the very curse of Israel: the church insinuating herself in the place of God; the church boasting God's prerogatives; the church depriving and exploiting human beings by playing God.

One of the other translations of this psalm reads: "Blessed is the one who makes the Lord his trust, who does not turn to the proud, to those who go astray after false gods!" Well, that expresses what was the matter between the church, as all of us know her, and Bishop Pike. Even when controversy between the two became ensnared in the mechanics of the Trinity, what was at stake was the church as a false god. Sometimes it became narrowed to "the tradition of the church," or "the good name of the church," or "the prosperity of the church," or sometimes it was defined as just the Episcopal denomination or as the fraternity of bishops, and when it did become so limited, in ways like these, the vanity of the proud would become vindictive. Still, the issue contested remained consistent: the church, in one sense or another, as idol.

Remembering the admonition of St. Paul — that the infidelity of the church does not dilute or vitiate God's witness in history — I argued mildly against Bishop Pike quitting the organized church on the ground that the gesture lent too much dignity to the church's apostasy. Bishop Pike must have loved the church, but terribly, to hope for so long that within his lifetime she would become and be again merely herself, a servant of humanity in Christ's name instead of a preposterous phony deity importuning humanity.

Pike had the grace, while exposing the church as false god, not to be proud of his own thinking, and speaking, and writing. "If I could create a perfect image of God," he said repeatedly, "it would be blasphemous . . . another idolatry." That did not impress pedantic theologians and was unappealing to ecclesiastical pride, but it *is* the spirit of the psalmist: O Lord my God, great are the wondrous works which thou hast done. . . . If I should declare them . . . they should be more that I am able to express.

> Sacrifice and offering thou wouldest not, but mine ears hast thou opened.
>
> Burnt-offering and sacrifice for sin has thou not required: then said I, Lo, I come;
>
> In the volume of the book it is written of me, that I should fulfil thy will, O my God: I am content to do it; yea, thy law is within my heart. (Ps. 40:8–10, *Book of Common Prayer*)

All religion is based upon a false presupposition that an acceptable sacrifice can be offered to God that at once proves and guarantees the moral worthiness of the supplicant. Both biblical faiths differ from the religions is this respect, and this represents such an elementary distinction that neither Judaism nor Christianity can properly be called religions. In fact it is when the biblical faiths become religious with this foolish notion about sacrifice and justification that they are exposed as corrupt.

The biblical insight is that God has no need of our offerings and is disinterested in our attempts to please or to appease him. In other words, God's love for human beings is unconditional. Analogically, anybody who has ever suffered the love of another knows that: love is undeserved; love cannot be purchased; love cannot be earned; love is a gift. It is curious that something that is such common knowledge — the unconditional character of love — should incite so much resistance and disbelief on the part of the beloved, particularly when the one who loves is God. Yet in some fashion all of us have this struggle because wrapped up in it is the tender, terrible mystery of what it means to be a human being. The event of becoming a Christian — I am not discussing the sacrament of baptism or joining some church or taking a trip down Billy Graham's aisle — concerns the very same thing. To become a Christian means to abandon opposition to God's affirmation of one's humanity. St. Paul, echoing the psalmist, testifies that to be a Christian involves this death to self and this rising as a new person in Christ every day.

James Pike struggled incessantly, fiercely, often beautifully, sometimes elegantly, openly and honestly with this issue of burnt offerings and justification. As such things are measured, he had much to sacrifice. That was verified when he was ordained a priest, leaving a brilliant start as a New Deal attorney that would surely have led him to appointment to the federal bench or into elective politics or could have brought him certain wealth. It was demonstrated again in the fifties at the height of the religious revival when Sheen and Peale and Graham and Pike became national celebrities, Pike as the apologist for what later — when he had outgrown it — he called "smooth orthodoxy." Pike even survived as a man his astonishing success — judged by ecclesiastical, which is to say, worldly, ethics — as bishop of California. In his incumbency, despite a plethora of other endeavors, he attracted more converts, performed more baptisms, confirmed more communicants, deployed more clergy, raised more pledges, started more missions, oversaw more church construction than any other Episcopal bishop, and, as a bonus, he finished building Grace Cathedral. As resigned bishop he joined Robert Hutchins on Olympus, but he was not spoiled there. He possessed, at one time or another, all those things with which people, vainly, make self-justifying claims: professional achievement, wealth within grasp, the envy of his peers, applause, influence, fame, status. He lost them all discovering over and over that God requires no such things, and thereby the gift of his life was constantly renewed. In that, he was content.

> I have declared thy righteousness in the great congregation: lo, I will not refrain my lips, O Lord, and that thou knowest.
> I have not hid thy righteousness within my heart; my talk hath been of thy truth, and of thy salvation.
> I have not kept back thy loving mercy and truth from the great congregation. (Ps. 40:11–13, *Book of Common Prayer*)

When Pike was dean of New York, this city became a great congregation. The cathedral where he presided and preached was, for those years, a living place, not a museum, not just a stop for the tourist buses. His administration as dean was regarded at the time, and is so remembered, as radical and novel. Actually, the truth is the other way around: Dean Pike restored St. John the Divine to the original vocation of cathedrals, and its consignment, both before his office there and ever since, to the rank of museum is a novelty. People, not especially churchpeople, but the people of the city, sense their loss when the cathedral is silent and aloof. A Harlem friend, who telephoned me the day news arrived of Pike's death, said: "When he was dean, we all had a voice."

It was as Dean Pike that Jim Pike became notorious and that detractors began their complaints that he was a publicity seeker. The answer to that, of course, is that he was. If the calling of the cathedral is as a voice for humanity in the city, then the cathedral's dean is called to be vocal. The sheer volume of publicity that attended Pike while dean and then as bishop causes some to overlook the fact that very little of that news had to do with Pike as a personality; most of it that he generated, in contrast to the publicity his enemies instigated, was about issues and not about personality. Indeed, as Anthony Towne

374

and I were to discover in writing *The Bishop Pike Affair* in the midst
of the heresy tempest, Pike was incredibly naive so far as personal
publicity was concerned. He persisted in dealing with issues, while
others were trying to discredit him as a person. But if that be so, be
consoled because it is a prophet's lot to be opposed and abused as a
person while publicizing the Word of God. It is no virtue for a prophet
to be quiet in the great congregation.

> Withdraw not thou thy mercy from me, O Lord; let thy loving-
> kindness and thy truth always preserve me.
>
> For innumerable troubles are come about me; my sins have taken
> such hold upon me, that I am not able to look up; yea, they are
> more in number than the hairs of my head, and my heart hath
> failed me.
>
> O Lord, let it be thy pleasure to deliver me; make haste, O Lord,
> to help me. (Ps. 40:14–16, *Book of Common Prayer*)

One of the incidental indignities that the dead must suffer is the
condescension of their survivors. Especially at wakes and burials and
requiems, the living assume a superiority toward the dead. It is not
just that they pontificate; the survivors tend to talk as if they are
immortal and have *that* eminent perspective upon life that, obviously,
the dead never attained, as is proved by their very deadness. Everett
Dirksen endured, ruefully, no doubt, just such indignity the other day
during Mr. Nixon's eulogy. It is an odd circumstance, since the dead
manifestly have the certain wisdom that there is no immortality.

In this condescending vein, many who survive Bishop Pike
remark how marred by tragedy his life was. One marriage ended in
annulment, another in divorce, a third was criticized ecclesiastically
as a scandal. A son committed suicide. A close working associate died
in a bizarre incident. He was an alcoholic and even joined AA. You
know as well as I do how this conversation goes.

I refute none of these facts, but I deny that Jim Pike's life was
a chronicle of tragedy; I see it as triumphant.

There is, as the dead know, no immortality, but there is resurrection. These are different things, though they be carelessly confused,
especially in church. Immortality postulates an idyllic afterlife in
another world; resurrection concerns the expectancy of the final and

consummate transcendence of death for this world because humans have seen and experienced the imminent transcendence of death here, in this world, and now, in this history, and, already, as it were.

The gospel of Christ bespeaks resurrection. The ministry of Jesus verifies resurrection, not only upon Easter but in all the days earlier — in his victory over death in the wilderness, in his power over death in healing, in his authority over death when confronting Caesar's claims, in his intercession that humans be delivered from death in the Lord's Prayer. The credibility of the resurrection as an ultimate promise for humanity rests upon specific triumphs over the power of death that occur in common life. Death, in many guises, pursued Bishop Pike relentlessly, and in many instances did Pike live in the resurrection, transcending death's power. The most obvious example is Pike's witness against racism, symbolized early in his public career by his refusal of the Sewanee honorary doctorate in "white divinity." Racism is a work of death in this world and the effectual undoing of racism is an instance of resurrection.

This is how I think of Bishop Pike's concern in situations, like his son's suicide, which others call tragedies. I see them as among death's assaults, not to be borne as devastation or defeat but to be transcended in the power of the resurrection to which human beings have access now. That Bishop Pike took an interest in parapsychology does not carry the connotation of playing games at Ouija boards or indicate hallucination. In the context of his life it refers to the possibility of transcendence of death in yet another guise, quite consistent with, for example, that earlier encounter with death in the Sewanee episode.

> Let them be ashamed, and confounded together, that seek after my soul to destroy it; let them be driven backward, and put to rebuke, that wish me evil.
>
> Let them be desolate, and rewarded with shame, that say unto me, Fie upon thee: fie upon thee! (Ps. 40:17–18, *Book of Common Prayer*)

After Bishop Pike was censured in 1966 by the Episcopal House of Bishops, he received a letter from an elderly woman, who wrote: "This is about the way I prayed for you — 'Now look, Jesus and

Moses, you have to help Bishop Pike. The wolves are after him.'" It was an apt intercession for Bishop Pike, not only at the time of the censure and the subsequent heresy ruckus but at most any juncture in his life, including during those last days in the desert, that one was moved to pray for him.

The wolves seemed always to be after him. Death pursued him relentlessly, as has been said. Most poignant, perhaps, was the lust of that pursuit of him within the church. The plain truth is that some bishops, and some others of the church, were determined to kill Bishop Pike. He, somehow, in his existence incarnated so much that threatened and frightened them as men that they conspired to murder him. I am speaking now theologically — their malice amounted to murder, as the Sermon on the Mount puts it — but I am equally speaking empirically — murder took possession of them. Some bishops, not all bishops; there were others: there were a few whose side was the same as Pike's on the issues, personalities aside; there were a lot of temporizers in between. What do you say of people who temporize when life is at stake? The *Book of Common Prayer* counts temporizers as accomplices. So does St. Paul. So did Bishop Daniel Corrigan, during the censure debate, when he described what he saw happening:

> I speak here against this statement, not as a bishop, not even as a Christian, just as — just as a man. The substance I would not wish to argue. The whole process by which a man is publicly tried, excoriated really, and condemned — condemned in some deep sense to death — by God! — heresy is nothing . . . to what we say about this man!

Only Bishop Pike would satisfy them. Now he is dead, but they are confounded and in shame because their malice is not what killed him. He died in the wilderness in Judea, but the wolves had not hurt him.

> Let all those that seek thee, be joyful and glad in thee; and let such as love thy salvation, say always, The Lord be praised.
>   As for me, I am poor and needy; but the Lord careth for me.
>   Thou art my helper and redeemer; make no long tarrying, O my God. (Ps. 40:19–21, *Book of Common Prayer*)

In a day when heroes are not heroic we turn to antiheroes to refresh our recollection of what heroes really are. By the same token, James Pike was an antibishop, embodying what other bishops are not to remind both the church and the world of what bishops truly are.

It could not be expected, after so much tumult and controversy, that the church in any official way would recognize that, not that it matters for Pike, though it matters profoundly for the church. The days when Bishop Pike was missing in the Holy Land coincided with a general convention of the Episcopal Church held at Notre Dame University. A newspaperman tells me that he noted no prayer was said at the convention when the report of Pike being lost first reached South Bend. The journalist asked a dignitary — "Can't you guys even pray for Pike?" "We haven't had a chance to consult about it," was the reply. At the next session, my informant reports, there was a prayer — a "composite" prayer, he called it, mentioning in the same breath Bishop Pike and Ho Chi Minh. As the reporter concluded: "They prayed for all their enemies, all together."

The incident would have been a delight to Jim Pike. And surely the prayer was appropriate, for, wherever they can be said now to be, it is a moral certainty that Bishop Pike and Ho Chi Minh are in the same place.

In the *Book of Common Prayer,* the heading for the fortieth psalm is *Expectans expectavi,* which is translated, variously, "I waited and waited," "I waited patiently," "I waited eagerly." I take that as a rubric for these remarks.

I commend to you James Albert Pike: he waited and waited, patiently, eagerly, for the Lord. The Lord did not tarry too long.

Katherine and Frederick Breydert

FOR instance, we both knew people who, having the freedom of those who die in Christ, can be said to have actually decided when to die. Our neighbor on Block Island, Katharine Breydert, seemed to us to be such a person. She died only three months before Anthony died, and it was not happenstance that they had become great friends through the years that they had been contemporaries on the island. Katharine and her husband, Frederick, had come to America as refugees from the Nazis. Frederick is a gifted composer, his career in music disrupted and curtailed by his concentration camp experience. Katharine, somewhat his senior, had been a pioneer woman physician in Austria. She was born a Jew and was converted to the Christian faith and had become a truly devout Roman Catholic. After arriving in this country, Katharine had been able to resume her medical practice and had worked at that for some years in Greenwich Village before moving to Block Island to retire as a doctor. Soon after meeting the Breyderts, Anthony and I discovered that we shared with them many mutual New York friends. Katharine, as one example, had for years been the personal physician of Dorothy Day — until she withdrew because Dorothy was such an obstinate patient: thus they could remain steadfast friends. The bond between the Breyderts and our household deepened especially during the time of our hospitality to

---

Simplicity of Faith, 1982, pp. 40–41

Daniel Berrigan, S.J., and in the aftermath of his seizure at *Eschaton* by a crowd of federal agents. Dan's most recent island visit, prior to Anthony's death, had been to celebrate the requiem at Katharine's death in the chapel of St. Andrew's parish.

Katharine Breydert was a resolute Christian: pious, but not pietistic; zealous, but patient; fragile, but formidable; long-suffering, but steadfast. She had received abundant gifts, the most remarkable among them being her gift as a liturgical artist. She had honored this gift during the Nazi experience, when she was exiled and separated from Frederick, by making collages of biblical themes from bits of paper. All of these had been carefully kept until, on the island, she and "good Frederick," as she often called him, painstakingly executed them in mosaic or stained glass. In the latter years of her life, Katharine contracted various ailments and, episodically, seemed so frail that one expected her to expire momentarily. Medically, her death was indicated long before it happened. Finally, when she knew that the translation of her program of collages into glass and stone would be completed, she decided to die, and did. It seemed to both Anthony and myself that dying had become for Katharine a matter of protocol between Almighty God and Katharine, and, whatever the attitude of God about it, Katharine would allow no interference with it until her work, her offertory, really, was done. As nurse Mary Donnelly put it once, "Katharine had made a bargain with the Lord, and she kept it." So did the Lord.

That view of Katharine's death was exemplified the night before she died. A few friends had been summoned to the house, since Katharine was thought to be dying. Frederick had been playing his own music for her for some hours. Katharine, lying there, seemed virtually dead. Suddenly, aware of the cluster of people nearby, Katharine opened her eyes, looked at us, and said, quite firmly, "You can all go home. I will listen to Frederick's music!" Katharine died, peaceably, the following evening, ready, at last, to meet the Lord.

Anthony Towne

IT CAME to pass that a rare relationship happened to the Block Island Writers Workshop and Anthony Towne between the time of its beginning and the day of his death.

Members of the workshop have mentioned him as their mentor — the one among them who was already a published author and respected poet, whose critique of their efforts was gentle and truthful and seasoned by humility about his own creative writing. And they recall him as their mediator — the one whose discernment and wit would offer a word to the rest apt for the circumstances whether they were of controversy or discouragement or, most fearful of all, success.

What has not been mentioned, and what perchance I alone have known, was the significance of the workshop to Anthony. It became for him — at the prime of his talent — a way to share who he was and what he knew as a human being with the rest of the world, or at least with some people who valued their own humanity enough to aspire to be civil.

I consider that Anthony regarded the use of the language as the distinguishing feature between that which is civil and human and that which is brutal and dehumanized. The culture, he had noticed long

---

"The Felicity of Anthony Towne," *Simplicity of Faith,* 1982, pp. 50–52. This was originally written as an introduction to an issue of *Works in Progress* (vol. III, 1981), publication of the Block Island Writers Workshop.

since, had gone the latter way and its debasement of language, indeed, its promotion of jargon, verbosity, redundancy, deceit, doublespeak, and similar babel is evidence of a profound decadence. So he was grateful whenever he encountered some civility in people and in society. These are signs of life, he realized, and even of resurrection: indications that the Word of God had not abandoned humanity despite provocations most dreadful.

Anthony Towne struggled poignantly and tenaciously to devote his life and his charismatic gifts to writing. More often than not, the effort was solitary. He was little encouraged in school or family. Poetry is not generally acknowledged as work, though I observed, through Anthony, that it *is* an exacting occupation. At the same time, he considered that there was compromise involved in writing to publish for money. He never sought that, and such of his work that has been published so far was so at the behest of others. He kept no objection to being published posthumously.

Immigrating to Block Island became a turning point in his story as a human being. Creatively, the city had been both stimulant and affront; the ethos and environment of the island offered nurture and husbandry for his gifts. I do not mean that Anthony romanticized the place, as some do, but that the pace and sounds, the style and sights, the austerity and beauty of the island consoled him and suited his vocation.

His vocation — as that may be distinguished from his occupation — was, in principle, monastic, as is my own. (That is the explanation of our relationship.) That is, he and I have understood that we had been called to a life of prayer and that the practice of prayer is *essentially* political — a matter of attention to events and of intercession and advocacy for the needs of human life and of the life of the whole of creation. Prayer, in this sense, is *not* pietistic but, on the contrary, radical involvement in the world as it is prompted in the Word of God. So coming to the island to live and work had no connotation of withdrawal or escapism or default for the two of us or either one of us but, rather, a paradoxical meaning.

Anyway, Anthony came to the island and his vocation matured and his occupation flourished. He had gratitude for his gifts and he honored them as gifts, despite various obstacles to doing that, and, after awhile, he was free to share his gifts with others as he did, notably, in the Writers Workshop.

Anthony Towne

I think it premature to tell about my own grief in Anthony's death, except to mention here that I have not found his death, shocking though it be, depressing, or the mourning of his death, maudlin. That is because I know his life to have been fulfilled.

Advent as a Penitential Season

The Word of God came to John the son of Zechariah in the wilderness; and he went into all the region about the Jordan, preaching a baptism of repentance for the forgiveness of sin. As it is written in the book of the words of Isaiah the prophet.

> "The voice of one crying in the wilderness:
> Prepare the way of the Lord,
> Every valley shall be filled,
> and every mountain and hill shall be brought low,
> and the crooked shall be made straight,
> and the rough ways shall be made smooth;
> and all flesh shall see the salvation of God."

He said therefore to the multitudes that came out to be baptized by him, "You brood of vipers! Who warned you to flee from the wrath to come? Bear fruits that befit repentance. . . ."

And the multitudes asked him, "What then shall we do?" And he answered them, "He who has two coats, let him share with him who has none; and he who has food, let him do likewise."

The Witness, December 1981, pp. 10–12

So, with many other exhortations, he preached good news to the people. But Herod the tetrarch, who had been reproved by him for Herodias, his brother's wife, and for all the evil things that Herod had done, added this to them all, that he shut up John in prison.

LUKE 3:2b–8a, 10–11, 18–20

We live now, in the United States, in a culture so profoundly pagan that Advent is no longer really noticed, much less observed. The commercial acceleration of seasons, whereby the promotion of Christmas begins even before there is opportunity to enjoy Halloween, is, superficially, a reason for the vanishment of Advent. But a more significant cause is that the churches have become so utterly secularized that they no longer remember the topic of Advent. This situation cannot be blamed merely upon the so-called Moral Majority, or the electronic preachers and talkers, or the other assorted peddlers of religion that so clutter the ethos of this society, any more than it can be said, simplistically, to be mainly the fault of American merchandising and consumerism.

Thus, if I remark about the disappearance of Advent I am not particularly complaining about the vulgarities of the marketplace prior to Christmas and I am certainly not talking about getting "back to God" or "putting Christ back into Christmas" (phrases that betray skepticism toward the Incarnation). Instead I am concerned with a single, straightforward question in biblical context, What is the subject of Advent?

Tradition has rendered John the Baptist an Advent figure and, if that be an appropriate connection (I reserve some queries about that), then clues to the meaning of the first coming of Christ may be found in the Baptist's preaching. Listen to John the Baptist.

"Repent, for the kingdom of heaven is at hand" (Matt. 3:2). In the Gospel according to Mark, the report is, "John the baptizer appeared in the wilderness, preaching a baptism of repentance for the forgiveness of sins" (Mark 1:4). Luke contains a parallel reference (Luke 3:3). It should not be overlooked, furthermore, that when John the Baptist is imprisoned, Matthew states, "From that time Jesus began to preach, saying, 'Repent, for the kingdom of heaven is at hand'"

385

(Matt. 4:17). And later, when Jesus charges his disciples, he tells them, "And preach as you go, saying, 'The kingdom of heaven is at hand'" (Matt. 10:7).

For all the greeting card and sermonic rhetoric, I do not think that much rejoicing happens around Christmastime, least of all about the coming of the Lord. There is, I notice, a lot of holiday frolicking, but that is not the same as rejoicing. In any case, maybe outbursts of either frolicking or rejoicing are premature, if John the Baptist has credibility. He identifies *repentance* as the message and the sentiment of Advent. And, in the texts just cited, that seems to be ratified by Jesus himself.

In context, in the biblical accounts, the repentance of which John the Baptist preaches is no private or individualistic effort, but the disposition of a person is related to the reconciliation of the whole of creation. "Repent, for the kingdom of heaven is at hand."

The eschatological reference is quite concrete. John the Baptist is warning the rulers of this world, and the principalities and powers as well as common people, of the impending judgment of the world in the Word of God signaled in the coming of Christ.

There seems to be evidence in the Luke account about John the Baptist that indicates that some of the people and, notably, the ecclesiastical officials did not comprehend his preaching or, if they did, they did not heed it, or they did not heed it promptly. Yet it is equally edifying that the political authorities, represented as Herod the tetrarch, do understand the political scope of John's admonition of the judgment enough to imprison John and, subsequently, subject him to terrible interrogation, torture, and decapitation (a typical fate for political prisoners now, as then). That, in such circumstances, Jesus makes John's preaching his own and instructs his disciples accordingly foreshadows his own arrest, trial, humiliation, and crucifixion, and for that matter, the Acts of the Apostles.

The depletion of a contemporary recognition of the radically political character of Advent is in large measure occasioned by the illiteracy of churchfolk about the Second Advent and, in the mainline churches, the persistent quietism of pastors, preachers, and teachers about the Second Coming. That topic has been allowed to be pre-empted and usurped by astrologers, sectarian quacks, and multifarious hucksters. Yet it is impossible to apprehend either Advent except through the relationship of both Advents. The pioneer Christians, beleaguered as they were because of their insight, knew that the message of both Advents *is* political. That message is that in the coming of Jesus Christ, the nations and the principalities and the rulers of the world are judged in the Word of God. In the lordship of Christ they are rendered accountable to human life and, indeed, to all created life. Hence, the response of John the Baptist when he is pressed to show the meaning of the repentance he preaches is, "Bear fruits that befit repentance."

In another part of the biblical literature traditionally invoked during Advent, the politics of both Advents is emphasized in attributing the recitation of the Magnificat to Mary:

> "He has put down the mighty from their thrones,
> and has exalted those of low degree;
> He has filled the hungry with good things,
> and the rich he has sent empty away." (Luke 1:52–54)

In the First Advent, Christ the Lord comes into the world; in the next Advent, Christ the Lord comes as Judge of the world and of all the world's thrones and pretenders, sovereignties and dominions, principalities and authorities, presidencies and regimes, in vindication of his lordship and the reign of the Word of God in history. This is the truth, which the world hates, which biblical people (repentant people) bear and by which they live as the church in the world in the time between the two Advents.

Christmas as a Parody
of the Gospel

In those days a decree went out from Caesar Augustus that all the world should be enrolled. This was the first enrollment, when Quirinius was governor of Syria. And all went to be enrolled, each to his own city. And Joseph also went up from Galilee, from the city of Nazareth, to Judea, to the city of David, which is called Bethlehem, because he was of the house and lineage of David, to be enrolled with Mary, his betrothed, who was with child. And while they were there, the time came for her to be delivered. And she gave birth to her first-born son and wrapped him in swaddling clothes, and laid him in a manger, because there was no place for them in the inn.

And in the region there were shepherds out in the field, keeping watch over their flock by night. And an angel of the Lord appeared to them, and the glory of the Lord shone around them, and they were filled with fear. And the angel said to them, "Be not afraid; for behold, I bring you good news of a great joy which will come to all the people; for to you is born this day in the city of David a Savior, who

The Witness, December 1982, pp. 10–12

is Christ the Lord. And this will be a sign for you: you will find a babe wrapped in swaddling clothes and lying in a manger." And suddenly there was with the angel a multitude of the heavenly host praising God and saying,

"Glory to God in the highest,
and on earth peace among those with whom
    he is pleased!"

LUKE 2:1–14

In many and various ways God spoke of old to our fathers by the prophets; but in these last days God has spoken to us by a Son, appointed the heir of all things, through whom also God created the world. He reflects the glory of God and bears the very stamp of God's nature, upholding the universe by his word of power. When he had made purification for sins, he sat down at the right hand of the Majesty on High, having become as much superior to angels as the name he has obtained is more excellent than theirs.

For to what angel did God ever say,

"Thou art my Son,
today I have begotten thee"?

Or again,

"I will be to him a father,
and he shall be to me a son"?

And again, when he brings the first-born into the world, he says,

"Let all God's angels worship him."

Of the angels he says,

"Who makes his angels winds,
and his servants flames of fire."

But of the Son he says,

"Thy throne, O God, is for ever and ever,
the righteous scepter is the scepter of thy kingdom.
Thou hast loved righteousness and hated lawlessness;
therefore God, thy God, has anointed thee
with the oil of gladness beyond thy comrades."

And,

"Thou, Lord, didst found the earth in the beginning
and the heavens are the work of thy hands;
they will perish, but thou remainest;
they will all grow old like a garment
like a mantle thou wilt roll them up,
and they will be changed.
But thou art the same,
and thy years will never end."

But to what angel has he ever said,

"Sit at my right hand,
till I make thy enemies
a stool for thy feet"?

HEBREWS 1:1–13

Among the Scriptural passages traditionally in liturgical use during the Christmas season are certain excerpts so variegated in style or syntax that it presses the imagination to affirm that they concern the same event — the birth of Jesus Christ.

It is not that one account or commentary refutes others, but rather that one variation amounts to satire of another. This circumstance is, manifestly, further complicated by the assortment of pagan and secular versions of Christmas that abound under commercial, political, and cultural auspices. Thus the bewilderment of church people — to mention no one else — about the significance of Christmas is immeasurably multiplied.

This parody of Christmas that emerges from the contrasts among the various Christmas texts is illustrated by the two citations set forth above — the story of the manger scene and the visit of the shepherds from the Gospel according to Luke, on the one hand, compared with the discourse on cosmic aspects of the birth of Jesus Christ that opens the Letter to the Hebrews. Other passages might as readily be mentioned in the same connection (cf. Matt. 1:18–25, 2:1–12, and John 1:1–14). Superficially, the dissimilarities between the Luke story and the Hebrews sermon are pronounced; Luke is quaint, Hebrews is majestic; the former pastoral, the latter esoteric; the one homely, the other awesome. I think these distinctions between the two passages are superficial. That is, they represent literary differences rather than those of substantive content. Yet, at the same time, they signify the very incongruity of the Incarnation. They partake of the mystery of the Word of God beheld in human life. In that purview the formulations of Hebrews are as appropriate as the narrative of Luke, while the concrete report of Luke is as essential as the expansive apologetic of Hebrews. In short, these passages seem in parody because the Christmas event itself is a parody both apt and good of how the Word of God elects to redeem fallen creation. Or, as the Luke text reminds, the manger is a sign in the midst of what Hebrews names as the final age (see Luke 2:12; Heb. 1:2).

When I say that the substantive message of Christmas in both Luke and Hebrews is similar, despite noticeable literary contrasts between the two passages, I refer to the political character of the Christmas event itself, as each text bespeaks that, albeit each in its own manner. The politics of Christmas does not have narrow, self-serving, mean connotations like those associated with common politics as the politics of Quirinius the governor, or Herod the king, or, for what it matters, Reagan the president. Moreover, the politics of Christmas categorically has nothing to do either with ecclesiastical politics or with the politics of the churches as a faction in society. Instead, the politics of the birth of Jesus Christ concern the comprehensive, versatile, ecumenical, and resilient governance of this universe and the totality and diversity of created life within this universe, in the Word of God imminently as well as consummately. In short, the politics of the Christmas event has to do with the *active* sovereignty of the Word of God in common history in this world here and now.

I realize that the association of politics with Christmas seems curious, perchance offensive, to some who have supposed all along that Christmas is, in spite of the biblical reports, somehow nonpolitical or even antipolitical. So I beg you not to heed me in this issue but to be open to the witness of the passages themselves.

Consider, for example, that the most poignant part of the Luke account — *"And she gave birth to her first-born son and wrapped him in swaddling clothes, and laid him in a manger, because there was no place for them in the inn"* (Luke 2:7) — constitutes, within itself, a political statement identifying Jesus with those who have no shelter or who are homeless, vagrant, destitute, or otherwise deprived. That, and more audacious identifications with human need, become redundant during the historic ministry of Jesus.

Then notice that this simple aspect of the birth of Jesus — he was laid in a manger — political statement as it is on its face — is exposed by the angel of the Lord as a sign to the shepherds of the coming of the Savior or Messiah (Luke 2:10–12).

Meanwhile, in the context of Hebrews, it becomes clear that the realm of Christ's authority politically is not merely that of a liberator, as one who delivers Israel from Rome's oppression, or some kindred secular revolutionary capacity. The political status of Jesus Christ is far more radical and durable than that. He is named the Son of God; he is elected heir to the universe; he is the one through whom God created the world; he reveals the very glory of God (Heb. 1:2–3). The political claim, according to Hebrews, for Jesus, at Christmas, is that he is *Lord,* that he exercises the sovereignty of the Word of God in this world.

That same extraordinary political claim that Christ is Son of God or Lord of history, exercising dominion over the whole of creation is further attested in Luke when the angel, which has brought this good news to the shepherds, is suddenly attended by *"a multitude of the heavenly host praising God"* (Luke 2:13). The heavenly host signifies all created life in assembly before the throne of God in adoration. What the shepherds behold in that scene, which prompts them to journey to Bethlehem to find the child in the manger, is a preview of the court of the Kingdom of God. The parallel reference in Hebrews is the sixth verse of the first chapter: *"when he brings the first-born into the world, he says, 'Let all God's angels worship him.'"*

It is part of the integrity of the worship of God in the Kingdom, on the part of the whole of created life, that every confusion concerning worship and idolatry is undone and finally ended. It is to the dispelling of just such confusion that much of the issue of the superiority of Christ to the angelic powers, in the Hebrews discourse, is addressed. Biblically, angels have many associations and the name is attributed to a diversity of created life. In the book of Daniel, for instance, the connection of angels as guardians or patrons of nations, and of the ethos of nations, is mentioned (Dan. 4:13–23, 10:10–21). At the same time, there are New Testament references to fallen angels or rebellious angels (2 Pet. 2:4; Jude 6) and a remark about *"the devil and his angels"* is attributed directly to Jesus in Matthew (Matt. 25:41). Thus the concern in Hebrews about the status of angels in relation to the office of Christ is not esoteric or poetic but concretely political, having to do with upholding the authenticity of the worship of God and with that not being corrupted by or confused with the idolatry of rebellious angels, including any associated with nations or other principalities.

In both Luke and Hebrews, the political character of the birth of Jesus Christ becomes most explicit in anticipation of judgment. If, in a manger, the office and authority of Christ is, to some, obscure, in the Kingdom his identity and vocation as judge of all life is eschatologically notorious. Thus, the peace on earth — so famous as a Christmas slogan — is, according to Luke, bestowed in the judgment *"among those with whom he is pleased"* (Luke 2:14*b*). In Hebrews, in much the same vein, the question is posed: *"But to what angel has he ever said, 'Sit at my right hand, till I make thy enemies a stool for thy feet?'"* (Heb. 1:13).

I do not suppose that it is tenable to observe Christmas without taking seriously the truth, verified in Luke and Hebrews and elsewhere, that the message of Christmas *is* political — that it concerns the incumbency of the Word of God sovereign over the life of the whole fallen creation. If that message is heard as good news, as it was by the shepherds, it is also to be heeded as an admonition since the Lord who reigns now comes, in the end, as judge.

Holy Week

And they all forsook him and fled.

MARK 14:50

Christians are, nowadays, so accustomed to esteeming the disciples as exemplary in the faith that it seems a surprise to notice that the New Testament Gospel accounts do not report any of the disciples as believers.

Attention has focused, of course, upon Judas' betrayal and Peter's denial, amid the tumult of Holy Week, and then upon Thomas' doubting, in the aftermath of the resurrection. This has tended to minimize or suppress the fact that none of the disciples — nor, for that matter, any one of Jesus' family — can be said on the basis of the texts as these have been received to have understood Jesus or to have either comprehended or liked his teaching or to have recognized his works or to have acknowledged his authority or to have welcomed his vocation or to have believed Jesus Christ to be the Lord of creation.

The truth, poignant as it may be, is that the disciples were profoundly skeptical about Jesus. In their experience of his ministry they were variously enthralled, mystified, bemused, apprehensive, con-

---

"Exemplary Disbelief: A Meditation on Holy Week," *Sojourners,* March 1980, pp. 13–14

founded, disillusioned. During Holy Week, their elation on Palm Sunday very quickly turns into consternation; by Good Friday they have become fearful and hysterical; by Easter they are both embittered and bereft. And through all of it they remain steadfast in their disbelief.

If, for us, the disciples can be said to exemplify anything, then they must be said to exemplify not faith but incredulity. This represents, I suggest, the most significant identification of the disciples with contemporary Christians. If any of us are to claim a biblical attitude of faith in Christ, it is necessary first of all to cope with the exemplary disbelief of the disciples.

With respect to that, the events now commemorated as Holy Week culminate and consummate what has previously transpired in the disciples' sojourn with Jesus, even as these same events foreshadow or anticipate all that is yet to come after Holy Week.

The Gospels are redundant in verifying the reality — one might also say, the versatility — of the skepticism of the disciples about Jesus Christ as Lord. When, for instance, Jesus asks them, "Who do you say that I am?" the true response of Peter is found not in his impulsive reply, "You are the Christ, the Son of the living God," but in his retraction of that confession, after Jesus began to show his disciples that he must suffer many things, be killed, and on the third day be raised (Matt. 16:13–21). Confronted with this version of the vocation of the Christ, Peter exclaims, "God forbid, Lord! This shall never happen to you" (Matt. 16:22–23). Thus Peter rehearses himself for Good Friday (Mark 14:66–72).

The disciples show a similar misunderstanding of Christ's Kingdom when the assorted claims and disputes among them concerning honor and status surface, as when they argue which of them is the greatest (Luke 9:46–48); or as when the sons of Zebedee, James and John, seek the places beside Jesus in his glory (Mark 10:35–45); or as when Peter, not knowing what he said, proposes that the three tabernacles be built (Luke 9:33*b*). On Maundy Thursday, at the table of the Last Supper, the disciples are still indulging the same matters (Luke 22:24–27; John 13:1–11).

The disciples find themselves impotent to exercise the authority Jesus offers them (Matt. 17:14–21) for the same reason — their lack of faith — that they suspect his authority when he stills the tempest (Matt. 8:23–27) or when he walks the water (Matt. 14:22–33), and they remain no less bewildered about the nature of such authority when the fig tree withers one morning during Holy Week as Jesus and the disciples return to the city and the temple (Matt. 21:18–22).

Until the parade on Palm Sunday and the ensuing events of Holy Week, there is a cryptic, even enigmatic, aspect to the public ministry of Jesus. Until then, characteristically, he would in his teaching tell a parable and conclude the recital with the remark, "He who has ears, let him hear" (Matt. 13:9). And, typically, the disciples are reported to be astonished by the parables; at times they protest that he teaches in parables, and sometimes they seek from Jesus private explanations of parables (Matt. 13:36–51, 13:10–17). Yet their hearing does not seem to be clarified during Holy Week, though Jesus' utterances are then no longer so guarded. And when Jesus speaks directly to the disciples, very bluntly, plainly, and without parable, of his imminent passion, for example, Luke observes: "They understood none of these things: this saying was hid from them and they did not grasp what was said" (Luke 18:34; Mark 9:32).

In Jesus' ministry prior to the days of Holy Week, when his authority is recognized (when he is named Christ the Lord) or when his authority is exercised and thereby exposed (as in a healing or exorcism), Jesus commonly admonishes those privy to the happening to keep silent about it (Matt. 8:29–30; Mark 5:43; Luke 4:41, 8:56). But as the events of Holy Week unfold, Jesus omits this caution and, indeed, appears more and more intent upon showing his authority by word and action, from cleansing the temple to washing the feet of the disciples (Luke 19:45–46; John 13:1–20). Throughout their whole experience with Jesus, in Holy Week as well as earlier, the disciples are found misconstruing his authority, or doubting it, or, sometimes, opposing it.

Indeed, if one were to single out an episode in the entire relationship of Jesus and the disciples to typify the attitude of the disciples so far as faith in Christ is concerned, it would be Gethsemane (Mark 14:32–42).

And if one goes no further than this, there is a warning for people now in these New Testament reports of the skepticism or incredulity of the disciples (and of Jesus' family) despite their intimacy with Jesus. This should be enough to render people wary of huckster preachers or celebrity evangelists who assert that mere intimacy with

Jesus of an intense, private, or exclusive nature is faith. This is a fascinating, tempting, simplistic, but unbiblical doctrine, and multitudes are seduced by it into fancying that to be, somehow, in the presence of Jesus is so compelling and so positive an experience that doubt of all sorts is dispelled quickly, conclusively, as if magically. Yet there is no basis in the New Testament for any such supposition or delusion; on the contrary for all of their unique experience in the company of Jesus, the disciples did not believe him or believe in him. What seems most surprising and crucial, furthermore, is that the disbelief of the disciples persisted even after the resurrection.

One would have thought, after all that they had been through with him, all that they had heard and beheld, and, consummately, all that took place in Holy Week and after the resurrection, that all doubt would have been resolved and that the enigma that Jesus had been for the disciples during his ministry would, at last, have been transcended by their insight. But, according to the New Testament, the disbelief lingers, admixed with hurt and bewilderment, in the immediate aftermath of the resurrection. Luke's accounts of the postresurrection episodes are both emphatic and caustic about this. Confronted with the risen Christ, the disciples still do not know who he is and only lament, "We had hoped that he was the one to redeem Israel" (Luke 24:21; Acts 1:6).

However obtuse or apprehensive or hysterical or skeptical the disciples may have been about Jesus, there was nothing of the sort among either the ecclesiastical or the political authorities. In Holy Week, as they confront Jesus, over and over again, they do perceive who Jesus is and they do recognize the dimensions of Christ's lordship (Matt. 21:45). Earlier, some of the people of Jerusalem had wondered: "Can it be that the authorities really know that this is the Christ?" (John 7:26*b*). In Holy Week, in their interrogations and testings of Jesus, and then again when Jesus is arraigned and brought to trial, and indeed when he is mocked and crowned with thorns, Jesus allows them to confess that he is the Christ: "And the high priest said to him, 'I adjure you by the living God, tell us if you are the Christ, the Son of God?' Jesus said to him, 'You have said so'" (Matt. 26:63–64*a*). "Now Jesus stood before the governor; and the governor asked him, 'Are you the King of the Jews?' Jesus said to him, 'You have said so'" (Matt. 27:11). The authorities thus confess who Jesus truly is, even in the midst of their intent to crucify him, just as earlier in his ministry Jesus had been recognized and acknowledged by the demons (Luke 4:41) and in the wilderness by the power of death incarnate as the devil (Luke 4:1–13). And one recalls how similarly the authorities regarded Jesus at the time of his coming into the world when Herod sought frantically to assassinate the child (Matt. 2:13–16).

In the drama of the redemption of the world in the Word of God, Holy Week is heavy parody. If in such events the disciples exemplify not faith in Christ as Lord but doubt, and if meanwhile the public authorities, in spite of themselves, confess Christ as Lord, what are we, nowadays, to make of this?

If the authorities of this world — including the whole diverse array of principalities and powers, ecclesiastical, political, military, commercial — recognize Jesus as Christ the Lord, it is because his reign is active now and constantly disrupts and confounds their rule and exposes their power, which is no more than the sanction of death, as transient and fraudulent. If the disciples are ambivalent, recalcitrant, incredulous toward Jesus as the Christ and toward the reality of his reign in the world, it is because they anticipate some other kingdom — one associated merely with the emancipation of Israel or one that appears immediately or miraculously: another worldly regime or an otherworldly realm — and thence they are hindered in seeing the ridicule of such fragile and false hopes as these when Jesus processes into the city mounted on an ass, and their Palm Sunday expectations turn into demoralization and fear.

The Kingdom of which Christ is Lord is not worldly but it is not otherworldly; for it is a Kingdom in this world, a historical and political reality, which both devastates and consummates the apparently prevailing order and all of its regimes and putative regimes or revolutionary causes. The life to which those in Christ are called consists of living as a society, now under the reign of the Word of God, beholden to Christ as Lord of all of life within the whole of creation, until that day when his reign is vindicated and the fullness of the power of death is exhausted, and all persons, principalities, and powers are rendered accountable, and this history ends.

So I have not offered any of these remarks with intent to be harsh on the disciples, for I remember that on Maundy Thursday Jesus promises the disciples that they will be made sufficient in the Word of God to be the witnesses to Christ's reign throughout the world (John 14). That same promise is ratified when Jesus, risen, appears to the disciples (Luke 24:44–49). On the day of Pentecost that promise is fulfilled and it is attested in Acts that the disciples become worthy of the promise.

Good Friday and Easter:
A Song of Hope

THE issue of abandonment is no esoteric theological matter. It is preeminently an existential question that commonly plagues persons at the time of death and was uttered by Jesus himself from the cross.

When I was an adolescent, precocious as I then may have been, the mystery of the Incarnation much exercised my mind. At the time in life when (I suppose) I should have been obsessed with football, sex, or pop music, as my peers seemed to be, I was very bothered about the identity of Jesus — preoccupied by issues of who he was and who he is — particularly by the matter of the relationship *in* Jesus Christ of humanity and deity.

I do not know — yet — how to account for this preemptive and passionate curiosity that disrupted my youth. I had not been treated in my upbringing, in either family or church, to sectarian stereotypes of Jesus as chum or sentimental intimate. Indeed, I regarded these as vulgar, possibly perverse, and certainly pretentious familiarities, denigrating to Jesus, even though they often induced for the indulgent ecstasies equivalent to a high attained through alcohol or drugs. I had suffered, instead, prosaic indoctrinations that asserted the "humanity of Jesus," while simultaneously alleging the "divinity of Christ." Such instructions

Simplicity of Faith, 1982, pp. 105–13

had left me with a strong impression that Jesus was an extraordinary schizophrenic. Meanwhile, adoptionist notions that I heard rumored I rejected as probable sophistry since they seemed impotent to dispel the essential incoherence of dogma. In the congregation I received comfort from the introit of the Gospel according to John, which was recited at the end of every Eucharist, because it seemed to affirm the integrity — and indivisibility — of the life of the Word of God in this world, and to do so in appropriate syntax (see John 1:1–14).

Perennially this concern of mine would find focus in the reports in the Gospels of the Crucifixion of Jesus, especially the reference to his cry: "My God, my God, why hast thou forsaken me?" (Mark 15:34; cf. Matt. 27:46). Oh, dreadful words! Ghastly question! Pathetic lament! Ultimate despair! Exquisite agony! This is *Jesus* crying out. *Why would Jesus speak this way?* How *could* Jesus do so?

Then, one Good Friday while I was still in high school, I heard a preacher, more edifying for the laity than others had been, remark that these words of Jesus from the cross were the opening verse of Psalm 22.

> My God, my God, why hast thou forsaken me
>   and art so far from saving me, from heeding my groans?
> O my God, I cry in the day-time but thou dost not answer,
> in the night I cry but get no respite.
>
> (Ps. 22:1–2)

Later that same day I read the twenty-second psalm — perhaps a hundred times — but it did not quiet my agitation. I still had all my questions, although I recall that the effort distilled them: Why had not Jesus begun the recital of the twenty-*third* psalm, rather than the twenty-second (like, I thought to myself, more or less everybody else does at the moment of death)?

> And yet thou art enthroned in holiness,
>   thou art he whose praises Israel sings.
> In thee our fathers put their trust;
>   they trusted, and thou didst rescue them.
> Unto thee they cried and were delivered;
>   in thee they trusted and were not put to shame.
>
> (Ps. 22:3–5)

It was some time after I had exhausted my adolescence when I began to hear the twenty-second psalm as a hymn of eschatological hope rather than a dirge of ultimate despair. If it is concluded that the outcry of Jesus from the cross attributes the whole of Psalm 22 to Jesus, then one evidence that hope is the topic, rather than despair, is the radical identification of Jesus with Israel. And this is not simply a matter of inheritance, of Jesus indicating that he shares in Israel's heritage and custom — as had frequently happened in earlier episodes in his life, going back to the time of his circumcision. But in the midst of the Crucifixion, much more is involved; the identification relates to Israel's vocation as the holy nation called in history to recognize the reign of the Word of God in the world and to pioneer the praise and worship of God as Lord of creation on behalf of all nations, tribes, peoples, and principalities. And, even more than that, the connection between Jesus and Israel signified in the psalm concerns the disposition of Israel's vocation. Thus, condemned by the Roman rulers, defamed by the ecclesiastical authorities, disfavored by the multitudes, betrayed, denied, abandoned by disciples, friends, and family; reviled, rejected, humiliated, utterly beset, crucified: Jesus, crying aloud from the cross, speaks *as* Israel. In that moment, there is nothing, there is no one left who is Israel except Jesus. He is, then, "King of the Jews," as the indictment affixed to the cross states; but he is, at the same time, within himself, the embodiment of the whole people of God, and he alone, then and there, assumes and exemplifies the generic vocation of Israel to trust and celebrate the redemptive work of the Word of God in history. In the drama of the Crucifixion, Jesus' invoking the twenty-second psalm signifies that the cross is the historic event in which Jesus Christ *becomes* Israel.

> But I am a worm, not a man,
>   abused by all men, scorned by the people.
> All who see me jeer at me,
>   make mouths at me and wag their heads:
> "He threw himself on the Lord for rescue;
> let the Lord deliver him, for he holds him dear!"
>
> (Ps. 22:6–8)

Another way to behold the peculiar and intense identification of Jesus with Israel's vocation is in terms of the historic fulfillment of that which is written. Jesus was conscientious about this throughout his public ministry, from the time of his first appearance in the synagogue — and his reading from Scripture there (Luke 4:16–30; cf. Matt. 13:54–58; Mark 6:1–6). What is involved in this, so far as I understand, is not some simplistic or mechanistic process but faithfulness in the performance of the witness to which one is called. So, here, the words from the cross foreshadow the scenario of the psalm, while the psalm portends the event of the Crucifixion, so that the narrative of the Crucifixion in the Gospel accounts becomes a virtual recital of the psalm.

> But thou art he who drew me from the womb,
> who laid me at my mother's breast.
> Upon thee was I cast at birth;
> from my mother's womb thou hast been my God.
> Be not far from me,
> for trouble is near, and I have no helper.
> A herd of bulls surrounds me,
> great bulls of Bashan beset me.
> Ravening and roaring lions
> open their mouths wide against me.
> My strength drains away like water
> and all my bones are loose.
> My heart has turned to wax and melts within me.
> My mouth is dry as a potsherd,
> and my tongue sticks to my jaw;
> I am laid low in the dust of death,
> The huntsmen are all about me;
> a band of ruffians rings me round,
> and they have hacked off my hands and feet.
> I tell my tale of misery,
> while they look on and gloat.
> They share out my garments among them
> and cast lots for my clothes.
> But do not remain so far away, O Lord;
> O my help, hasten to my aid.
> Deliver my very self from the sword,
> my precious life from the axe.

Save me from the lion's mouth,
　　my poor body from the horns of the wild ox.

(Ps. 22:9–21)

The psalm bespeaks one utterly assailed by the power of death: beset by the pervasiveness, militance, and versatility of death; bereft of any ability to cope with death. The psalm bemoans the agony of death by crucifixion: the psalm bespeaks the helplessness of humanity against the relentlessness of the great array of death. *I am laid low in the dust of death.*

That is the human destiny; more than that, that is the destiny of the whole of creation, apart from the event of the Word of God in history. And it is that radical confession of helplessness that is at once the preface of faith and the invocation of the grace of the Word of God. Sin is, actually, the idolatry of death. The last temptation (in truth, the *only* one) is to suppose that we can help ourselves by worshiping death, after the manner of the principalities and powers. That final arrogance must be confessed. Jesus confessed that in our behalf when he cried aloud from the cross. When that confession is made, we are freed to die and to know the resurrection from death.

The recital in the Apostles' Creed, *He descended into hell,* has a similar significance: hell is the realm of death; hell is when and where the power of death is complete, unconditional, maximum, undisguised, most awesome and awful, unbridled, most terrible, *perfected.* That Jesus Christ descends into hell means that as we die (in any sense of the term *die*) our expectation in death is encounter with the Word of God, which is, so to speak, already there in the midst of death.

I will declare thy fame to my brethren;
　　I will praise thee in the midst of the assembly.
Praise him, you who fear the Lord;
　　all you sons of Jacob, do him honor;
　　stand in awe of him, all sons of Israel.
For he has not scorned the downtrodden,
　　nor shrunk in loathing from his plight
nor hidden his face from him,
　　but gave heed to him when he cried out.
Thou dost inspire my praise in the full assembly;

and I will pay my vows before all who fear thee.
Let the humble eat and be satisfied.
    Let those who seek the Lord praise him
    and be in good heart forever.
Let all the ends of the earth remember
    and turn again to the Lord;
let all the families of the nations
    bow down before him.
For kingly power belongs to the Lord,
    and dominion over the nations is his.

(Ps. 22:22–28)

The outcry from the cross is no pathetic lament, but a song for Easter. And the hope it expresses is not vague, illusory, or fantasized, but concrete, definitive, and empirical. The twenty-second psalm (hence, Jesus on the cross) manifests that hope in political terms. The influence of the psalm on the Crucifixion accounts underscores the political character of the Crucifixion. The psalm elaborates the politics of the cross.

Any public execution is, obviously, a political event in a straightforward and literal sense, but the public execution of Jesus Christ has political connotations of immense, complex, and, indeed, cosmic scope. This becomes apparent, for example, when the images of the psalm portray the powerless victim threatened by predatory beasts, a familiar biblical way of denominating political principalities and powers. It is, after all, in the name of Caesar, the overruling principality, that the sovereignty of the Word of God over creation is disputed and mocked (cf. Luke 23:1–2; Matt. 22:15–22; Mark 12:13–17; Luke 20:19–26; Matt. 27:27–31; Mark 15:16–20; John 19:1–3).

The political reality of the Crucifixion is accentuated in the psalm where it is announced that the cry of the forlorn is heard and heeded (Ps. 22:24*b*). Notice the circumstances: the scene is the judgment, with the whole of creation in assemblage, and with all who fear the Lord of history praising God. Let it be mentioned here that the attribute that chiefly distinguishes Christians is, simply, that they fear the Lord *now*, or already — before the day of judgment. That means specifically that they acknowledge that they live and act in the constant reality of being judged by God. Thus, nowadays, when people assemble as congregations in praise and worship of the Lord, this is an anticipation or preview of the judgment. Where, instead, the regime is glorified, superstition prevails, or religiosity is practiced, then the congregation indulges in scandalous parody of the judgment.

Notice as well that in the context of the psalm, the event of the judgment is, so to say, the *first* day that the downtrodden are no longer scorned (Ps. 22:24*a*). For the poor, the diseased, the oppressed, the dispossessed, the captive, the outcast of this world, the day of judgment in the Word of God means not only the day of justice but also the day of justification, when their suffering is exposed as grace.

The politics of the cross delivers a message to the nations, to all regimes and powers, and even unto the ends of the earth, marked by the cry of Jesus that invokes the psalm: *kingly power belongs to the Lord, and dominion over the nations is his* (Ps. 22:28). *That* is truly what the Incarnation is all about.

> How can those buried in the earth
>   do him homage,
> how can those who go down to the grave
>   bow before him?
> But I shall live for his sake,
>   my posterity shall serve him.
> This shall be told of the Lord to future generations;
>   and they shall justify him,
> declaring to a people yet unborn
>   that this was his doing.
>
> (Ps. 22:29–31)

In the psalm, the last word in the cry of Jesus from the cross is an assurance of the efficacy of the resurrection. To become and be a beneficiary of the resurrection of Jesus Christ means to live here and now in a way that upholds and honors the sovereignty of the Word of God in this life in this world, and that trusts the judgment of the Word of God in history. That means freedom *now* from all conformities to death, freedom *now* from fear of the power of death, freedom *now* from the bondage of idolatry to death, freedom *now* to live in hope while awaiting the judgment.

The Second Advent of the Lord

THE biblical treatment of both Advents, the narratives attending Christ's birth and the testimonies about the Second Coming of Christ, is manifestly political. Yet, curiously, people have come to hear the story of the birth as apolitical and even as antipolitical, while, I venture, most listen to news of Christ coming again triumphantly with vague uneasiness or even outright embarrassment. What with the star and the sheep and the stable, it has been possible to acculturate the birth, to render it some sort of pastoral idyll. But the scenic wonders, the astonishing visions, the spectacular imagery associated with the next Advent have confounded the ordinary processes of secularization and thus the subject of the Second Coming has been either omitted or skimmed in the more conventional churches or else exploited variously by sectarians, charlatans, fanatics, or huckster evangelists.

Insofar as these allegations are sound, the mystery of both Advents has been dissipated, whereas it is an affirmation of the mystery of both events that is most needed in order to be lucid, at all, about either Advent.

So I begin by affirming the mystery of these happenings and, furthermore, by noticing that what can be known of the two Advents is no more than that evident in their biblical connection. It is the coherence of one Advent in the other Advent, the first in the second and, simultaneously the second in the first, that is crucial.

Conscience and Obedience, 1977, pp. 76–85

Or, in other words, I do not know if, when Jesus was born, there appeared a special star over Bethlehem, any more than I know whether, when Jesus comes as Judge and King, he will be seen mid-air, descending amid the clouds. Nor do I have need to know such things; they by no means control my salvation, much less the world's redemption. Yet, since both Advents are mysteries, these styles bespeak those mysteries aptly, or so it seems to me.

There is a secret in the First Advent, a hidden message in the coming of Jesus Christ into the world, a cryptic aspect in the unfolding of Christmas. Indeed, the biblical accounts of the birth of the child in Bethlehem, in such quaint circumstances, represents virtually a parody of the Advent promise.

A similar discreetness — at times of such degree as to be ironical — marked the entire public life of Jesus Christ, according to the Bible. He taught in parables, finishing his stories enigmatically with the remark — *if you have ears that can hear, then hear* (cf. Matt. 1:1–23). When he healed a person or freed a demoniac, he admonished witnesses to *see that no one hears about this* (as in Mark 7:31–37). When he was accused by the religious and political authorities and confronted by Pontius Pilate, *he refused to answer one word, to the governor's great astonishment* (Mark 15:5).

The first chapter of the Gospel of St. John tells this mystery in the coming of Jesus Christ: "He was in the world; but the world, though it owed its life to him, did not recognize him. He entered his own realm, and his own would not receive him."

For primitive Christians, so much defamed and so often harassed and sometimes savaged in first-century Rome, the secret of the First Advent was thought to be in the consolation of the next Advent. The pathos and profound absurdity of the birth of Jesus Christ was understood to be transfigured in the Second Coming of Jesus Christ. The significance of Advent could only be realized in the hope of the return of Jesus Christ.

It is the book of Revelation that most eagerly anticipates the Second Coming, and in Revelation one hears a recurring theme, summed up, for instance, in the eleventh chapter at verse 15: "The sovereignty of the world has passed to our Lord and his Christ, and he shall reign for ever and ever!"

The same is repeated, again and again and again in Revelation, in the names and titles ascribed to Christ. He is the *ruler of the kings of the earth*. He is *the sovereign Lord of all*. He is *the King of kings*. He is the *judge* of the nations. He is the One *worthy to receive all power and wealth, wisdom and might, honor and glory and praise!*

All of these are political designations and point to the truth, from the vantage of the next Advent, that the First Advent's secret is political. And that truth becomes evident in the traditional stories recalled and recited in observance of the First Advent.

Thus, the journey of Joseph and the pregnant Mary took place in order that they be enrolled for a special tax that was not simply a source of revenue for the Roman occupying regime but, as all taxes are, also a means of political surveillance of potentially dissident people.

And the profound threat that the coming of Christ poses for mundane rulers is to be seen in Herod's co-option of the Magi to locate the child so that Herod could slay him. When the attempt fails, Herod's anxiety becomes so vehement that he slaughters a whole generation of children in seeking to destroy Christ.

Later, John the Baptist, whose calling as a messenger and herald is especially remembered in the season of Advent, suffers terrible interrogation and torture, imprisonment and decapitation because his preparation for the ministry of the Christ who has come is perceived by the rulers as a most awesome warning.

Or, again, the manger scene itself is a political portrait of the whole of creation restored in the dominion of Jesus Christ in which every creature, every tongue and tribe, every rule and authority, every nation and principality is reconciled in homage to the Word of God incarnate.

Amid portents and events such as these, commemorated customarily in the church, the watchword of Christmas — "peace on earth" — is not a sentimental adage but a political utterance and an eschatological proclamation, indeed, a preview and precursor of the Second Coming of Christ the Lord, which exposes the sham and spoils the power of the rulers of the age.

Those first-century Christians, pursued and persecuted, scorned and beleaguered, as they were because of their insight, were right: the secret of the First Advent is the consolation of the Second Advent. The message in both Advents *is* political. It celebrates the assurance that in the coming of Jesus Christ the nations and the rulers of the nations are judged in the Word of God, which is, at the same time, to announce that in the lordship of Christ they are rendered accountable to human life and to that of the whole of creation.

Each Advent of Christ is attended by mystery, what is now known of either event is not all that is to be known, but what is confessed by Christians as to both Advents is known to them through the conjunction of the two.

That which is known and affirmed now because of the First Advent and in the expectancy of the Second Advent is, however, enough to be politically decisive, that is to say, enough to edify choice and action in issues of conscience and obedience with respect to the rulers of the world. In the First Advent, Christ comes as Lord; in the next Advent, Christ the Lord comes as judge of the world and the world's principalities and thrones, in vindication of his reign and of the sovereignty of the Word of God in history. This is the wisdom, which the world deems folly, which biblical people bear and by which they live as the church in the world for the time being.

The message that the life and witness of the church conveys to political authority, hence, always, basically, concerns the political vigilance of the Word of God in judgment. That news is, at once, an admonishment to all earthly rulers that Christ the Lord reigns already, as the First Advent signifies, and an anticipation of the destruction of all worldly political authority at the Second Coming.

Judgment — biblically — *does* mean the destruction of the ruling powers and principalities of this age. I am aware that this is, for professed Christians in America and in many other nations, an unthinkable thought even though it be biblical (1 Cor. 15:24–28; cf. Acts 2:34–36).

The Constantinian mentality that afflicts the church equivocates contemplation of the judgment of the Word of God. Within the Constantinian ethos, the church even seeks, in the name of the Word of God, to broker compromises of that judgment with princes and presidents, regimes and systems. The capacity of God for anger is gainsaid, though it be in the face of the chaos — the war and hunger and famine and disease and tyranny and injustice — over which the rulers of this age in truth preside. Nevertheless, the biblical emphasis upon the judgment cannot be omitted or denied, including those references, most disconcerting to emperors and their like, which render judgment vehemently, as the *wrath* of God or as his vengeance or retribution.

More than that, the biblical witness expects that the devastation of political authority is coincident in the judgment with the fulfillment of political authority. All that political authority signifies in fallen creation, in consignment to the power of death, has its consummation and perfection in the vindication of the reign of Christ. The rule of the powers of this age, which incarnates death and which is futile, is undone and ended in judgment that substantiates Christ's dominion over the whole of creation. The judgment of the Word of God means that ending of time and history that constitutes the restoration of creation and, within that, the return of political authority to its own vocation as God's servant for the benefit of human life.

Christians rejoice, on behalf of all humanity and, indeed, all creation, at the prospect of the judgment because in that Last Day the destruction of political authority at once signals its consummation in the Kingdom of God.

The rejoicing is constant, the anticipation is eager, the eschatological expectation is imminent. While — as has been said — the apocalyptic reality impends in any moment in any event in the diffusion of this age, so, simultaneously, the eschatological truth is represented in any moment in any event in this world, to those whose eyes see and whose ears hear.

I believe that the gifts of discernment are undiminished today as compared to the day of the apostles; indeed, I regard discernment as still definitive of faith as well as witness. Yet I am aware that the discerning gifts are much scorned and often neglected in the contemporary church. That is significantly evident in the absence now of the sense of eschatological imminence, which, the New Testament reports, so agitated the apostolic Christians. In turn, insofar as that imminent expectancy of the Second Coming of the Lord has been lost, the Christian witness vis-à-vis the powers that be has been disconcerted, and the rejoicing has been greatly inhibited. But I consider that the Second Advent *is* imminent and that Christians in the twentieth century may, and should, regard it with as much passion and excitement as did those of the first century.

While saying this, I know that the prevailing view, chiefly sponsored by church historians, is different. The usual construction nowadays is that the first Christians expected the coming of Christ, in glory, promptly, and that this expectation lapsed as time continued, necessitating, eventually, drastic revisions in eschatology, if not its suppression altogether.

In just this connection, the Constantinian comity is, once again, pertinent because the loss of the conviction about the imminence of the Eschaton so readily abets the dependency of the church upon the political powers and other institutions of the status quo, in place of a raison d'être of the church as the historic pioneer of the Kingdom of God. From there the descent is quick and facile into the sophistries about "Christian nations" and into pagan idealism that distorts the biblical precedent of the church. At the same time, in counterpoint, there have come and gone in Christendom assorted sects assembled by fundamentalist or sorcerous calculations purporting to fix the hour of Christ's return.

I conclude that both forecasters and scholastic revisionist misconstrue the meaning of eschatological imminence.

Because time inheres in the reality of death and because the Kingdom destroys death's reign and abolishes time, to think and speak, at all, of the coming of the Kingdom must comprehend the significance of the ending of time. At the outset, it must be realized, thought and speech are taxed because both remain confined in time. The entire vocabulary in human usage is temporal. To employ any of it to attempt to elucidate the finale of time is an extraordinary and incongruous effort in which words can never mean simply what they say.

Recognizing that much cautions against any simplistic literalism or any merely historically conditioned interpretations and prays for a more mature and profound communication in which the words, uttered in time, are sacramentalized or transfigured, and that fittingly, since the topic is the Eschaton.

Characteristically, the biblical witness, in Scripture as such and in the life of the church, speaks in marvelously versatile and appropriately diverse ways of the Second Advent: prophetically, metaphorically, parabolically, ecstatically, sacramentally, dogmatically, poetically, narratively — in every tongue or style or syntax or idiom available. The biblical witness speaks, thus, multifariously of the coming of the King and his Kingdom to show that the subject is inexhaustible and one that truly exceeds the capabilities of human speech.

This is an aspect of the sense of imminence biblical people have concerning the Kingdom. More than that, imminence expresses eternal reality in time, a way of representing how the eschatological is freed from time, or of bespeaking the ending of time before time has ended. The relationship, in other words, between the Word of God and creation, even in time, transcends time and is, from a human point of view, imminent at any time. In the Word of God a thousand years are not more than a moment.

If some have put aside the expectation, it is not because Christ is tardy and not because God has postponed the next Advent but because the consciousness of imminence has been confused or lost. I regard the situation of contemporary Christians as much the same as that of our early predecessors in the faith so far as anticipation of the Second Coming matters. We expect the event at any moment. We hope for it in every moment. We live in the imminence of the Eschaton. That is the only way, for the time being, to live humanly.

The conviction of eschatological imminence that informs the witness of biblical people during this passing age is grounded in the insight they bear, on behalf of the life of the world, into the political secret of the First Advent, which also inheres in creation itself in spite of the Fall, that is, the lordship of Christ. Knowledge of the truth hidden in the First Advent, confession of Christ as Lord, means recognition of the sovereignty of the Word of God acting in history to restore dominion to humanity in creation. The anticipation of the Second Advent is for the consummation of Christ's reign as Lord so that what is secret becomes notorious, what is revealed is transfigured triumphantly, what is witnessed biblically is publicly vindicated.

In the dispensation between (as it were) the two Advents, which is no more than a moment for the Word of God or in the expectation of the people of God, the task of Christians is shaped by the imminent, constantly impinging, eschatological hope. And, as I was saying, it is this that becomes crucial in decisions and actions of conscience and obedience in nation and in church, rather than, as is so vainly and persistently supposed, the operation of some great principle. The ethics of biblical people concerns events not moral propositions. And if to the world, to fellow citizens of some nation or to the ruling powers, the way of the biblical witness seems enigmatic, inconsistent, sometimes apparently contradictory, suspect, foolish, then so be it. Christians do not covet anyone's approval or applause, least of all do they seek or envy the sanction of governments. The Christian life has its only — and its only possible — explication in the judgment of the Word of God.

So biblical people live patiently, awaiting the coming of the Lord, in the midst of death's feigned rule over fallen creation, discerning pervasive portents of the impending devastation while beholding profuse signs of the redemption of fallen creation. To live, thus, in hope, or to live by grace, or to confess the vitality of the judgment of the Word of God in history: all these mean the same thing.

Evidently, many of the people of the churches do not participate in this hope that trusts the judgment but are enticed by futile hopes or entrapped in false hopes that betray a witness that is conformed and doomed. These are plethora, and I make no effort to enumerate or refute them here, except to notice that they commonly signify a particular misapprehension of the gospel, a specific confusion express-ing bewilderment about the promise of Christ's Second Advent and skepticism about the veracity of Christ's resurrection. It is, typically, a witness that acts as if the triumph of the Word of God over the power of death in this world had not been enacted and verified in the resurrection of Christ but remains, somehow, incomplete or incon-clusive so that the task assigned to Christians is to finish or achieve that victory. What issues, in consequence, is an expectancy that the Kingdom marks such a success. In this manner *the perfection of the resurrection is actually substituted for the coming of Christ as Judge and King!* If there be subtlety in this transposition, there is nothing subtle about its implications: it ignores the political secret of the First Advent while it radically diminishes the office of God in judgment of the world; it denies the efficacy of the resurrection in demonstrating the accessi-bility, here and now, of the Word of God enabling human life to transcend the fear and thrall of death, while it distorts and inflates the calling of Christians and the mission of the church in this age. It may occasion, variously, the cooption of popular ideology or of transient revolutionary causes or of programs for political and social reform or idealism but is just as adapted to stupid allegiance to the powers that be. And these, or any of these, are then misnamed for the gospel. Curiously, though it vainly aspires to conquer death, being reluctant to believe the resurrection of Christ, it actually, fatally, underestimates the wiles of the power of death. It succumbs to exactly the temptations that Jesus refuted in the wilderness.

If there is no resurrection from death, Christians are to be pitied (cf. 1 Cor. 15:14). If Christ is not raised, the faith is in vain. If, by virtue of Christ's resurrection, human beings are not offered freedom now from bondage to death in this world, then there is no hope worthy of human belief at all. "But in fact Christ has been raised from the dead" (1 Cor. 15:20a). Christians are those human beings who live now within the efficacy of his resurrection. And in their peculiar witness to the power of the resurrection, Christians eagerly expect and patiently await the Second Coming of Jesus Christ, with a glad and trustworthy knowledge that what is vindicated in the judgment is the Lordship of Christ, *not* the Christians since they are also judged by the Word of God.

Bibliography: The Works of
William Stringfellow

Prepared by Paul D. West

Bibliographers note: There are also a number of minor articles that Stringfellow wrote for high school and college newspapers that may be found as part of his scrapbooks, 1940–1956, along with other personal papers and unpublished materials. All are located in the Cornell University Library.

1947   Stringfellow, William, "Does the World Hate America: What an Innocent Learned Abroad" in *The Churchman,* October 15, 1947, pp. 10–11.

1948   "Political Emphasis Week" in *Motive,* January 1948, p. 18.

        "USCC Means Unity, Cooperation — Your Help is Need for Success" in *Collegiate Forth,* December 1948, pp. v, viii.

        "The Election . . . Norman Thomas" in *Motive,* October 1948, p. 28.

1949   "Will USCC Ever Be SCM?" in *The Intercollegian,* May–June 1949, vol. 66, no. 9, pp. 17–18.

        "Statements of Faith by Students" in *Motive,* October 1949, p. 17.

        "Politics is Evangelism" in *Motive,* December 1953, pp. 14–15.

1955   *The Life of Worship and the Legal Profession,* The National Council of the Episcopal Church, 1955, 22 pages.

        "Christianity and Law: The Fifth Amendment Controversy

and the Vindication of the Law" in *Christianity and Society,* Spring 1955, vol. 20, no. 2, pp. 13–17, 30.

1957   "The Christian Lawyer as a Churchman" in *Christian Scholar,* 1957, vol. 40, pp. 211–37. Reprinted in the *Vanderbilt Law Review,* August 1957, vol. 10, no. 5.

"Christian Faith and the American Lawyer" in *Federation News,* May–August 1957, pp. 79–81.

Untitled book review of *The Moral Decision* by Edmond Cahn in *The Christian Scholar,* September 1957, vol. 40, no. 3, pp. 251–52.

1958   "Christian Vocation and the Legal Profession" in *The Church Review,* April 1958, vol. 16, no. 5, pp. 3–4, 8–10.

1959   "Christianity, Poverty and the Practice of Law" in the *Harvard Law School Bulletin,* June 1959, vol. 10, no. 6. Also in the *Capital University Law Review,* 1979, vol. 8, no. 3. Translated as "La Misère, Le Christianisme et Le Droit" in *Foi et Vie,* Paris, March–April 1960, pp. 83–96.

"Law, Polity, and the Reunion of the Churches" in the *Ohio State Law Journal,* Summer 1959, vol. 20, no. 3, pp. 412–36. Also in "Law, Polity and the Reunion of the Church; the Emerging Conflict between Law and Theology in America" in *The Ecumenical Review,* April 1961, vol. 13, pp. 287–312.

"Work As Mission, Secular Work and Christian Vocation," The World's Student Christian Federation, Geneva, July 1959, 7 pages.

1961   "Poverty, Piety, Charity and Mission" in *Christian Century,* May 10, 1961, vol. 78, pp. 584–86.

"Comments by a North American Lawyer" in *Laity,* World Council of Churches, #11, August 1961, pp 20–21.

"Secret of Christian Unity" in *Christian Century,* September 13, 1961, vol. 78, pp. 1073–76.

1962   *A Private and Public Faith,* Eerdmans Publishing Co., 1962, 93 pages.

"Race, Religion, and Revenge" in *Christian Century,* February 14, 1962, vol. 79, pp. 192–94.

"Loneliness, Dread and Holiness" in *Christian Century,* October 10, 1962, vol. 79, pp. 1220–22.

"Race, the Church, and the Law" in *The Episcopalian,* November 1962, pp. 31–34.

"The Mission of the Church in the Decadent Society" in the *Episcopal Theological School Journal,* Winter 1962, vol. 8, no. 1, pp. 3–8. Reprinted as "The Church in the City" in *Theology Today,* July 1963, vol. 20, pp. 145–51.

1963　*Instead of Death,* Seabury Press, 1963, 72 pages, revised edition 1976, 112 pages.

"The Way to Life: Comments on the Murder of Lou Marsh" in *The Witness,* February 7, 1963, pp. 10–11.

"Care Enough to Weep" in *The Witness,* February 21, 1963, p. 13.

"Just So They Be There" in *Christian Century,* April 3, 1963, vol. 80, pp. 431–32.

"The Ministry of the Church" in *The Pulpit,* May 1963, vol. 34, no. 5, pp. 4–5.

"The Freedom of God" in *The Witness,* August 8, 1963, pp. 8–10.

Summary Presentation, National E.Y.C. Study Conference, Sewanee, Tenn., August 27, 1963, 12 pages.

"Corny If Not Profane" in *Christian Century,* September 18, 1963, vol. 80, pp. 1135–36.

"The Witness of Presence" in the *Christian Herald,* October 1963, pp. 44, 81–83.

"Protestants on the Spot" in *The Episcopalian,* October 1963, vol. 128, no. 10, pp. 39–41.

"Evangelism and Conversion" in *International Journal of Religious Education,* November 1963, pp. 6–7, 22.

"The Word and West Side Story" in *One,* November 1963, pp. 6–7.

1964　*My People Is the Enemy: An Autobiographical Polemic,* Holt, Rinehart and Winston, 1964, 149 pages.

Free in Obedience: The Radical Christian Life, Seabury Press, 1964, 128 pages.

"That Which Must Never Be Lost Sight of Is Baptism" in *Behold,* February–April 1964, pp. 10–11.

"Of Poverty, Injustice, and the Gospel" in *Presbyterian Life,* June 1, 1964, vol. 17, no. 11, pp. 22–27.

"My People Is the Enemy" in *Negro Digest,* June 1964, vol. 13, no. 8, pp. 71–90.

"God, Guilt, and Goldwater" in *Christian Century,* September 2, 1964, vol. 81, pp. 1079–83.

"The Unity of the Church as the Witness of the Church" in *Anglican Theological Review,* October 1964, vol. 46, no. 4, pp. 394–400.

"Ecumenicity and Entomology: New Church Problem" in *Christian Century,* October 7, 1964, vol. 81, pp. 1239–41.

"The Loneliest Time of the Year" in the *Presbyterian Survey,* December 1964, vol. 54, no. 12, pp. 8–9.

"The Political Witness of the Church of Christ" in *The Witness,* December 3, 1964, pp. 8–11.

1965 "Through Dooms of Love" in *New Theology No. 2,* edited by Martin E. Marty and Dean G. Peerman, The Macmillan Company, 1965, pp. 288–96.

"The Violence of Despair" in *Notre Dame Lawyer,* Symposium 1965, vol. 40, no. 5, pp. 527–33.

"What is Poverty?" in *Pageant,* February 1965, vol. 20, no. 8, pp. 106–8.

"Poverty, Law and the Ethics of Society" in the *North Dakota Law Review,* March 1965, vol. 41, no. 3, pp. vi–x. Reprinted in *The Baptist Student,* December 1965, pp. 18–21.

"Involvement in the World is the Sign of the Authentic Christian" in *Faith at Work,* March 1965, pp. 25–27.

"Sin, Morality and Poverty" in *Christian Century,* June 2, 1965, vol. 82, pp. 703–6. Also in *New Wine,* Spring 1965, vol. 3, no. 3, pp. 29–35.

"A Protestant's Disenchantment" part of "Pessimist's Guide to the Vatican Council" in *Ramparts,* October 1965, vol. 4, no. 6, p. 34.

"Liturgy As Political Event" in *Christian Century,* December 22, 1965, vol. 82, pp. 1573–75.

1966 *Dissenter in a Great Society: A Christian View of America in Crisis,* Holt, Rinehart and Winston, 1966, 164 pages.

"The Case against Christendom and the Case against Pierre Berton" in *The Restless Church: A Response to the Com-*

fortable Pew, edited by William Killbourn, J. B. Lippincott Co., 1966, pp. 11–25.

"The Crisis Accepted" in *Youth in Crisis: The Responsibility of the Schools,* edited by Peter C. Moore, Seabury Press, 1966, pp. 35–42.

"L'Anatomie de la Pavreté" in two parts in *La Revue Notre-Dame du Sacré-Coeur,* Quebec, January 1966, vol. 64, nos. 1 & 2, pp. 36–38, and February 1966, pp. 62–69.

"Money and What It Means" in the *Presbyterian Survey,* January 1966, vol. 56, no. 1, pp. 20–22. Reprinted in *The Lutheran Standard,* November 1, 1966, vol. 6, no. 22, pp. 5–6; *Southern California Presbyterian,* November 1966, pp. 4–7; *Findings,* November 1966, vol. 14, no. 9; *Saints' Herald,* January 15, 1967, pp. 6–8, and *Church and Home,* May 1, 1967, vol. 4, no. 9.

"The Ethic of Violence" in *Crossbeat,* Wayside Chapel, Potts Point, Australia, March 1966, vol. 2, no. 1, pp. 3–6.

"Stringfellow Speaks out about the Church" in *The Witness,* March 17, 1966, p. 7.

"The Celebration of God's Presence" in *The Mennonite,* June 14, 1966, pp. 396–97. Reprinted as "The Incarnation and Social Action" in *The Presbyterian Record,* July–August 1966, vol. 91, no. 7–8, p. 21. Reprinted in *Saints' Herald,* December 15, 1966, p. 11. Reprinted as "The Incarnation and Social Responsibility" in *Christian Living,* November 1966, pp. 24–25, 27.

"A Style of Witness" in *The Mennonite,* July 19, 1966, p. 463. Reprinted as "Marks of Christian Involvement" in *World Call,* October 1966, vol. 48, no. 9, p. 25, and in *The Covenant Companion,* February 10, 1967, vol. 56, no. 3, pp. 14–15.

"Difference between Gospel and Religion" in *The Mennonite,* August 30, 1966, p. 517. Reprinted as "Our Obsolete Religion," in *Christian Living,* February 1967, p. 36.

"The Beatles and the Unpopularity of Jesus" in *Presbyterian Life,* September 15, 1966, vol. 19, no. 18, p. 36. Reprinted as "The Unpopularity of Jesus" in *Southern California Presbyterian,* October 1966, vol. 31, no. 8, p. 3; in *Mes-*

senger, November 24, 1966, pp. 9–10, in *Presbyterian Survey,* November 1966, and in *Classmate,* April 1967, vol. 74, no. 8, pp. 30–31.

"The Great Society as a Myth" in *Dialog,* Autumn 1966, vol. 5, pp. 252–57. Reprinted in *Lutheran Social Welfare Quarterly,* December 1966, vol. 6, no. 4, pp. 3–12, and in *Catholic World,* May 1967, vol. 205, pp. 83–89. Excerpts reprinted as "News and Views: The Great Society Myth," in *Commonweal,* November 18, 1966, vol. 85, p. 188.

"Viet Nam and the Churches" in *The Christian Herald,* November 4, 1966. Reprinted in *Southern California Presbyterian,* February 1967. Reprinted as "An American Tragedy" in *Christian Living,* January 1967, p. 32.

"Negro Anti-Semitism" in *The Covenant Companion,* November 1966, vol. 40, no. 22, pp. 7, 26. Reprinted in *World Call,* January 1967, vol. 49, no. 1, p. 29. Reprinted as "The Irony of Negro Anti-Semitism" in *Christian Living,* April 1967, p. 40, slightly revised.

"What's Right with Christmas" in *McCalls,* December 1966, vol. 94, p. 149.

"The Representation of the Poor in American Society: A Subjective Estimate of the Prospects of Democracy" in *Law and Contemporary Problems,* Duke University School of Law, Winter 1966, vol. 31, no. 1, pp. 142–51.

1967   and Anthony Towne, *The Bishop Pike Affair, Scandals of Conscience and Heresy, Relevance and Solemnity in the Contemporary Church,* Harper & Row, 1967, 266 pages.

Count It All Joy: Reflections on Faith, Doubt, and Temptation, Eerdmans Publishing Co., 1967, 93 pages.

Untitled Article in *Negro and Jew: An Encounter in America,* A symposium compiled by *Midstream* Magazine, edited by Shlomo Katz, Macmillan Co., 1967, pp. 114–17.

1969   *Impostors of God: Inquiries into Favorite Idols,* Witness Books, Geo. A. Pflaum, 1969, 127 pages.

"Reparations: Repentance as a Necessity to Reconciliation" in *Black Manifesto: Religion, Racism, and Reparations,* edited by Robert S. Lecky and H. Elliott Wright, Sheed and Ward Inc. 1969, pp. 52–64.

"The Shadow of Judas" in "The Steeple in Perspective: Four Views" in *Christianity and Crisis,* March 3, 1969, vol. 29, pp. 40–41.

"The Demonic in American Society" in *Christianity and Crisis,* September 29, 1969, vol. 29, pp. 244–48.

1970 *A Second Birthday: A Personal Confrontation with Illness, Pain, and Death,* Doubleday and Co., 1970, 203 pages.

"American Importance of Jacques Ellul" in *Katallagete,* Winter–Spring 1970, vol. 2, pp. 47–48.

"Jesus the Criminal" in *Christianity and Crisis,* June 8, 1970, vol. 30, pp. 119–22.

"An Authority over Death" in *Christianity and Crisis,* September 21, 1970, vol. 30, pp. 181–83.

"Why is Novak So Uptight" in *Christianity and Crisis,* November 30, 1970, vol. 30, p. 259.

"Harlem, Rebellion and Resurrection" in *Christian Century,* December 11, 1970, vol. 87, pp. 1345–48.

1971 and Anthony Towne, *Suspect Tenderness: The Ethics of the Berrigan Witness,* Holt, Rinehart and Winston, 1971, 177 pages.

"The Relevance of the Revelation" in *The Cresset,* Valparaiso Univ. Press, January 1971, pp. 6–8. Reprinted as "The Relevance of Babylon" in *The Post-American,* January–February 1973, vol. 2, no. 1, pp. 8–9.

"Christmas Card from the FBI" in *Commonweal,* January 15, 1971, vol. 93, p. 364.

"Why Are There No Bishops in Jail?" in *The Fourth Quadrant,* St. Clement's Church, New York, Spring 1971, pp. 1–3.

1972 "Must the Stones Cry Out" in *Christianity and Crisis,* October 30, 1972, vol. 32, no. 18, pp. 233–38. Reprinted as "The Vassal of Death" in *Event,* April 1973, vol. 13, no. 4, pp. 9–15.

"Impeach Nixon Now" in *Commonweal,* May 26, 1972, vol. 96, pp. 280–81.

"Election Reflections" in *Christianity and Crisis,* November 27, 1972, vol. 32, p. 258.

"Failure of Conscience" in *Thesis Theological Cassettes,* August 1972, vol. 3, no. 7.

1973   *An Ethic for Christians and Other Aliens in a Strange Land,* Word Books, 1973, 156 pages.

"Watergate and Romans 13" in *Christianity and Crisis,* June 11, 1973, vol. 33, pp. 110–12.

"Do We Need a New Barmen Declaration" in *Christianity and Crisis,* December 24, 1973, vol. 33. Reprinted in *The Post-American,* April 1974, vol. 3, no. 3, pp. 12–14.

1974   "The Bishops at O'Hare; Mischief and a Mighty Curse" in *Christianity and Crisis,* September 16, 1974, vol. 34, pp. 195–96.

"The Secret of the Holy Spirit" in *The Witness,* October 13, 1974, vol. 58, no. 1, p. 4.

"Bishop Wilmer's 'Schismatical Consecration' " in *The Witness,* October 27, 1974, vol. 58, no. 2, pp. 10–11.

"Response to 'The Occult: Demonology' " in *The Christian Ministry,* November 1974, vol. 5, no. 6, p. 27.

"Gerald Ford's Eccentric Conscience" in *The Witness,* December 8, 1974, vol. 58, no. 4, pp. 10–11.

1975   "The Church in Exile, the Church's Untold Story" in *The Witness,* March 9, 1975, vol. 58, no. 8, pp. 6–7.

"On Being Haunted by the Angel of the Church at Sardis" in *The Witness,* September 1975, pp. 4–6.

"The Politics of Advent" in *The Witness* December 1975, pp. 9–10.

1976   and Anthony Towne, *The Death and Life of Bishop Pike,* Doubleday, 1976, 443 pages.

Instead of Death, Seabury Press, revised edition 1976, 112 pages.

Untitled Column, *Sojourners,* January 1976, vol. 5, no. 1, p. 19.

Untitled column, *Sojourners,* February 1976, vol. 5, no. 2, pp 6–7.

Untitled column, *Sojourners,* March 1976, vol. 5, no. 3, p. 6.

William Stringfellow: Prophet to America; Digest of Days with William Stringfellow, February 15–17, 1976, First United Methodist Church, Seattle, Wash., 36 pages.

"On the Sentencing of Good Father Wendt" in *The Witness,* March 1976, pp. 6–7.

"Justification, the Consumption Ethic and Vocational

Poverty" in *Christianity and Crisis,* April 12, 1976, vol. 36, pp. 74–79.

Untitled column, *Sojourners,* April 1976, vol. 5, no. 4, p. 10.

"From *The Death and Life of Bishop Pike*" in *The Witness,* April 1976, pp. 4–13.

"Unlikeable Gospel" in *Sojourners,* May–June 1976, vol. 5, no. 5, p. 6. Reprinted as "Living with Defeat" in *The Witness,* May 1977, pp. 13–14, with one paragraph added at the end concerning Philip Berrigan.

"The Nation's Destiny and the Problem of Hope" in *The Witness,* June 1976, pp. 4–8.

"The Bible and Ideology" in *Sojourners,* September 1976, vol. 5, no. 7, pp. 6–7.

"On Living Biblically Now" in *The Witness,* September 1976, pp. 4–6, 14.

and Anthony Towne, "What's At Stake in '76" in *Christianity and Crisis,* October 18, 1976, vol. 36, pp. 234–36.

"Open Letter to Jimmy Carter" in *Sojourners,* October 1976, vol. 5, no. 8, pp. 7–8.

"Technocracy and the Human Witness" in *Sojourners,* November 1976, vol. 5, no. 9, pp. 14–18.

1977   *Conscience and Obedience: The Politics of Romans 13 and Revelations 13 in Light of the Second Coming,* Word Books, 1977, 112 pages.

"Kindred Mind and Brother" in *Sojourners,* June 1977, vol. 6, no. 6, p. 12.

"Myths, Endless Genealogies, the Promotion of Speculations and the Vain Discussion Thereof" in *Sojourners,* August 1977, vol. 6, no. 8, pp. 12–13.

Untitled Response to "Professional Responsibility: Who is Responsible for What?" by James P. Shannon in *The NICM Journal,* Summer 1977, vol. 2, no. 3, pp. 69–71.

1978   "A Fragile Place Worth Preserving: Politics on Block Island" in *Sojourners,* January 1978, vol. 7, no. 1, pp. 16–18.

"The Embarrassment of Being Episcopalian" in *The Witness,* February 1978, pp. 12–13.

"Authority as Parable" in *The Witness,* July 1978, vol. 61, no. 7, pp. 8–9.

1979 "The Crisis of Confidence and Ethics in the Legal Profession" in *Capital University Law Review,* 1979, vol. 9, no. 1, pp. 1–6.

"A Matter of Conscience: The State of the Church, Part I" in *The Witness,* May 1979, vol. 62, no. 5, pp. 4–6.

"Let the Dead Bury the Dead: The State of the Church, Part II" in *The Witness,* June 1979, vol. 62, no. 6, pp. 8–9, 19.

"Sexuality and Priesthood: The State of the Church, Part III" in *The Witness,* July 1979, vol. 62, no. 7, pp. 7–9.

"Has God Abandoned the Episcopal Church? The State of the Church, Part IV" in *The Witness,* August 1979, vol. 62, no. 8, pp. 8–9.

1980 "An Open Letter to the Presiding Bishop" in *The Witness,* January 1980, vol. 63, no. 1, pp. 10–11.

"A Matter of Repentance" in *Christianity and Crisis,* January 21, 1980, vol. 39, pp. 341–42.

"Exemplary Disbelief: A Meditation on Holy Week" in *Sojourners,* March 1980, vol. 9, no. 3, pp. 12–14.

"Living Biblically" in *Journal of Religious Thought,* Fall–Winter 1980–81, vol. 37, pp. 59–62.

1981 "The Acts of the Apostles (continued)" in *Christian Century,* April 1, 1981, vol. 98, pp. 341–42.

"A Lamentation for Easter" in *The Witness,* April 1981, vol. 64, no. 4, pp. 4–6.

"Trickle-Down Violence" in *Christianity and Crisis,* April 27, 1981, vol. 41, pp. 115, 126.

"Biography as Theology" in *Katallagete,* Winter 1981, vol. 7, no. 4, pp. 36–39.

"Advent as a Penitential Season" in *The Witness,* December 1981, vol. 64, no. 12, pp. 10–12.

1982 *A Simplicity of Faith: My Experience in Mourning,* Abingdon, 1982, 143 pages.

"Abandonment and Hope: Thoughts on the Church and Psalm 22" in *Sojourners,* March 1982, vol. 11, no. 3, pp. 12–15.

"The Joy of Mourning: On Grief and the Meaning of Resurrection" in *Sojourners,* April 1982, vol. 11, no. 4, pp. 29.

"Revelation Amidst Pain," *Thesis Theological Cassettes,*
August 1982, vol. 13, no. 7.

"Christmas as Parody of the Gospel" in *The Witness,*
December 1982, vol. 65, no. 12, pp. 10–12.

1984   *The Politics of Spirituality,* Westminster Press, 1984, 90 pages.

"High Crimes and Misdemeanors: The Macabre Era of
Kissinger and Nixon" in *Sojourners,* January 1984, vol.
13, no. 1, pp. 33–34.

"The Politics of Pastoral Care" in *The Witness,* February
1984, vol. 67, no. 2, pp. 12–14.

"Stringfellow Responds" in *The Witness,* June 1984, vol. 67,
no. 6.

"An Assault upon Conscience: Violence in the Technocratic
Society," in *Sojourners,* October 1984, vol. 13, no. 9, pp.
22–25.

1985   "Quotations from Bill Stringfellow" in *The Witness,* May
1985, vol. 68, no. 8, pp. 6–9.

Index